SECRET WEAPONS
AND WORLD WAR II

MODERN WAR STUDIES

Theodore A. Wilson
General Editor

Raymond A. Callahan
J. Garry Clifford
Jacob W. Kipp
Jay Luvaas
Allan R. Millett
Carol Reardon
Dennis Showalter
David R. Stone
Series Editors

SECRET WEAPONS AND WORLD WAR II
JAPAN IN THE SHADOW OF BIG SCIENCE

WALTER E. GRUNDEN

UNIVERSITY PRESS OF KANSAS

© 2005 by the University Press of Kansas

All rights reserved

Published by the University Press of Kansas (Lawrence, Kansas 66049), which was organized by the Kansas Board of Regents and is operated and funded by Emporia State University, Fort Hays State University, Kansas State University, Pittsburg State University, the University of Kansas, and Wichita State University

Library of Congress Cataloging-in-Publication Data

Grunden, Walter E.
  Secret weapons and World War II : Japan in the shadow of big science / Walter E. Grunden.
     p.   cm.—(Modern war studies)
  Includes bibliographical references and index.
  ISBN 0-7006-1383-8 (cloth : alk. paper)
  1. Weapons systems—Japan—History—20th century. 2. Weapons systems—History—20th century. 3. World War, 1939–1945—Equipment and supplies. I. Title. II. Series.
  UF505.J3G78 2005
  355.8′0952′09044—dc22
                                                                        2004026485

British Library Cataloguing-in-Publication Data is available.

Printed in the United States of America

10 9 8 7 6 5 4 3 2 1

The paper used in this publication meets the minimum requirements of the American National Standard for Permanence of Paper for Printed Library Materials Z39.48–1984.

In memory of
Robert Ray Grunden
(1926–1995)
Veteran of the Pacific War

CONTENTS

(Photo insert follows p. 164)

Acknowledgments	ix
Introduction	1
1 Mobilizing Science and Technology for War	13
2 Nuclear Energy and the Atomic Bomb	48
3 Electric Weapons: Radar and the "Death Ray"	83
4 Aeronautical Weapons: Rockets, Guided Missiles, and Jet Aircraft	124
5 Chemical and Biological Warfare	165
Epilogue: The Impact of World War II on Science in Japan	197
Appendix	205
Notes	241
Bibliography	297
Index	317

ACKNOWLEDGMENTS

Many people contributed to the completion of this book. I would especially like to thank James R. Bartholomew of the Ohio State University, who instilled in me a fascination for Japanese science history during my early graduate school days and who has continued to be an inspiration in the years since. I would also like to acknowledge intellectual debts to OSU Professors Mansel Blackford and Allan R. Millett for their generous support and encouragement during those years. At the University of California, Santa Barbara, I was fortunate to have had the opportunity to work with such excellent scholars as Luke Roberts, Lawrence Badash, Joshua Fogel, and Michael Osborne, who were great mentors and good friends. I would also like to thank my colleagues at Bowling Green State University, especially Donald Nieman, Peter Way, Gary Hess, Liette Gidlow, and Robert Buffington, all of whom either offered critical advice, read parts of the manuscript, or otherwise contributed to its completion in some significant way.

Among the greatest debts incurred along the way has been to Yamazaki Masakatsu at the Tokyo Institute of Technology. Professor Yamazaki was instrumental in arranging my stay in Tokyo during the 2001–2002 academic year, and he graciously shared documents, resources, and a great deal of time assisting my work in numerous ways. Similarly, I am indebted to Professors Kawamura Yutaka and Nakajima Hideto for sharing documents and publications, as well as indulging me in many conversations. Professor Waragai Toshiharu kindly allowed me to occupy his office for the year, and Okada Daisuke provided essential technical support. I am grateful to Fukuda Yukari for helping to take care of the numerous administrative details and for her other countless acts of kindness. I am indebted to Yagi Eri for introducing me to Professor Yamazaki, and for many favors to facilitate my stay in Japan. I am also grateful to Professor Ichikawa Hiroshi of Hiroshima University for many interesting discussions as well as for taking me on a grand tour of Okunoshima Island and the Hiroshima area. The participants in the weekly Tuesday seminars (*kazemi*) at Tokyo Tech in the Graduate School of Decision Science and Technology kindly welcomed me into their group and allowed me to work out some of the ideas that are a part of this book.

Many more colleagues, both in the United States and abroad, contributed in important ways. Professor Mark Walker at Union College invited me to participate in several fruitful conferences and panels where I was able to discuss some of the ideas contained in the book at length with distinguished scholars from around the world, including Helmut Maier and Morris F. Low. Nishiyama Takashi, Otsubo Sumiko, Mizuno Hiromi, Ito Kenji, Keiko Nagase-Reimer, William Tsutsui, Ed Fields, Zuoyue Wang, and Clark Hultquist provided documents, suggestions, ideas, and a lot of support along the way. At BGSU, the administrative staff in the Department of History, Tina Amos, Jan Finn, and Dee Dee Wentland, were invaluable in completing the requisite paperwork and helping me to meet deadlines. James Rose, Peter Kuebeck, Brent Fisher, and Hu Chenhui provided research assistance.

I am grateful to the staffs of all the many archives and libraries that kindly allowed access and use of their collections. In the United States, I am particularly grateful to the research staff at the U.S. National Archives in College Park, Maryland. John Taylor, the venerable doyen of archivists, and Richard Boylan were tremendously helpful. I am also indebted to the research staffs of the Smithsonian Institution National Air and Space Museum Library, United States Air Force Wright-Patterson Museum Library in Dayton, Ohio, the Maxwell Air Force Base Library in Huntsville, Alabama, and to Maurice Toler at North Carolina State University, where Henry Kelly permitted me access to the Harry C. Kelly collection. The staff at the National Defense Agency Research Institute, Military History Library, in Meguro-ku, Tokyo, was very helpful during my many visits.

This book could not have been completed without the generous financial support of the Japan Society for the Promotion of Science, which, in conjunction with the Social Science Research Council, provided a full year of funding to complete research in Japan. The Association for Asian Studies Northeast Asia Council provided two grants, one domestic and one international, for research. The foundation for this study was laid during the completion of the Ph.D. dissertation, so acknowledgment is due also to the United States Department of Education, which provided Title VI grants for language development, and both the Ohio State University and the University of California, which provided several fellowships, grants, and assistantships for which I am very grateful. Thanks are also due to Bowling Green State University for allowing me the year off in Japan to complete the research. I would also like to thank the many people of the University Press of Kansas involved in the production of this book, especially Michael Briggs, Larisa Martin, Susan Schott, and Karen Hellekson, for their ongoing support and patience. I wish also to thank reviewers Mark R. Peattie and Edward J. Drea, who offered excellent insights and suggestions for improving the manuscript. Finally, I would like to thank my parents and family for their support throughout the many years it took to complete the manuscript, and my daughter Hannah, who kept me grounded through some trying moments and helped me to laugh and smile when I most needed to remember what is really important.

A note on style is probably in order. Throughout the book, Japanese names appear according to the Japanese convention of stating family name first and given name second. This practice is also followed when citing Japanese publications. When citing English-language publications by Japanese authors, however, names are sometimes provided according to the western convention of listing given name first, depending upon how they are listed for that particular publication. Translations of Japanese titles have been provided in the bibliography and occasionally in the endnotes. Titles of journals have not been translated. Some English renditions are cited as provided by the authors and may not be exact translations. Any significant omissions are unintentional. Any errors pertaining to scholarship are my own.

INTRODUCTION

By the late 1930s, the very thought of some fantastic new weapon of incredible destructive power being created and unleashed upon the world by an eccentric scientist in a secret laboratory—once only the stuff of science fiction—no longer appeared to be so far-fetched. An entire generation had already lived to see some of the wild contraptions sprung from the imagination of the nineteenth-century French novelist Jules Verne become reality.[1] In 1914, the British author H. G. Wells described the destruction of the world's major cities by "atomic bombs" in his novel *The World Set Free*. In a subsequent book, *The Shape of Things to Come,* published in 1933, Wells presented another horrific vision of the world devastated by weapons of mass destruction.[2] In Germany, director Fritz Lang was turning out the world's first science fiction films. His *Frau im Mond (Woman in the Moon),* released in 1929, depicted space travel and inspired young rocket enthusiasts around the world. Some of them would go on to develop the V-2 missile for the Third Reich.[3] In the United States, comic book serials such as *Amazing Stories* and Saturday afternoon matinee cliffhangers like *Buck Rogers* and *Flash Gordon* also made "death rays" and biological scourges, such as the "Purple Death," part of the popular imagination.[4] Perhaps to a generation that had come of age witnessing the horrendous effects of poison gas on fathers, uncles, and older brothers in the Great War, the possibility of some chemical or biological weapon threatening the very existence of all humanity may have seemed much more like science fact than science fiction. And with the discovery of nuclear fission in 1938, even Wells's ominous predictions of nuclear devastation now seemed plausible.

But such ideas were not a monopoly of the West. In Japan, too, science fiction had also become infused with similar themes, especially as the nation became increasingly militarized. Popular magazines, such as *New Youth* and *Boys' Club,* began to appear on news store racks along with imported copies of *Amazing Stories*. Serials written for young male readers glorified the military and depicted Japanese soldiers going off to war in such mechanized marvels as flying submarines and invisible airplanes.[5] All around the world, wherever science had begun to intersect with popular culture, such ideas began to grow. The era of wonder weapons had arrived.

World War I spurred this interest in new weapons and science. During that conflict, the horse gave way to the tank, the airplane evolved from a novelty machine to formidable aerial fighters and multiengine bombers, and the clunky submarines of the late nineteenth century became the much feared swift U-boats of the German navy. Poison gases and other chemical weapons concocted in prestigious laboratories throughout Europe also emerged and were used in combat with devastating results. Yet for all these innovations, the Great War remained largely an industrial war and, at best, a chemist's war. Although it may be considered the first total war in which resources were mobilized on a national scale, science, on the whole, still played a relatively minor role in the outcome.[6]

Science and scientists were to become far more important in World War II. As the military forces demanded more devastating and efficient weapons, scientists were called upon to deliver them. But their ability to do so depended on a few essential factors, which varied considerably from nation to nation. To produce technologically advanced weaponry required more than just sufficient numbers of trained personnel with high levels of education in the sciences and engineering; it also needed a developed economy with access to various natural resources, modern industry (including the most advanced scientific equipment), and efficient organization. Among the principal belligerents of World War II, there were considerable differences in the competitive advantages enjoyed by each nation where these basic elements were concerned.[7]

Just how important science was in determining the outcome of World War II, however, is still a contested issue. Some scholars have argued that new weapons were not at all decisive, that "the war was won with tanks, aircraft, artillery and submarines, the weapons with which it was begun."[8] Others contend that without the new weapons produced by science, especially radar, the Allies would have lost.[9] Whatever the case may be, the question of *what impact science had on the war* has been relatively neglected in the historiography of World War II.[10] Where the Pacific War is concerned, the answer to this question might seem apparent and, on the surface, even deceptively simple. Nevertheless, the details of this story have yet to be told in any single study. But perhaps the more significant and interesting question here is, rather, *what impact did the war have on science in Japan?* These issues are the subject of the study that follows.

By one estimate, over 70,000 books have already been written on World War II.[11] Monographs focusing exclusively on science and technology in the war, however, are comparatively few. Although some excellent studies of science under Nazi Germany and the Allied nations have recently been published, the story of Japan has yet received only marginal attention, especially in the West. According to one historian, where Japan is concerned, "a satisfactory work that discusses how science and technology affected the whole of the war has yet to be produced."[12] Why should this still be the case more than fifty years after the war?

One explanation may be that military historians traditionally have not had much interest in science, whereas science historians have generally been averse to studying "things military."[13] Moreover, the two subfields of military and science history have rarely converged. In the words of technology historian Alex Roland, "The bad news is that military history has been studied often but not well; the history of science has been studied well but not often."[14] But this situation has begun to change somewhat for the better in recent years, at least where histories of the United States and Europe are concerned. Military historians have broadened their scope beyond the conventional subjects of operations and biography, and there are now more monographs in science history being published on a wider range of military-related topics. Some recent books on specific weapons projects, excellent in their scholarship, have begun to fill this gap.[15] Yet where some other important topics are concerned, such as science policy and mobilization, for example, there is still only a handful of notable works.[16]

In the case of Japan, the news is much worse. Studies of the Pacific War have tended to focus overwhelmingly on the strategic, political, and economic factors that led to Japan's defeat. Comparatively speaking, science and technology have largely been ignored. Here too, books dedicated to specific weapons projects tend to dominate.[17] Only a few works examine wartime science policy and mobilization in any detail.[18] Where Japan is concerned, Roland's axiom seems particularly applicable. With very few exceptions, historians of science have tended to shy away from the Pacific War. And it may be significant to note here as well that military historians studying the European theater still greatly outnumber those specializing in Japan and the Pacific.

Likewise, in the history of science field, those studying the West still greatly outnumber those studying the East. Science historian Nakayama Shigeru has argued that Japan, and East Asia in general, have been relegated to the periphery of the history of science field by scholars in the West, and he correctly identifies linguistic barriers as a primary factor in this state of affairs.[19] This observation may also be true of military history in general. There have been too few western scholars possessing both the interest in wartime science and technology and the language skills necessary to conduct research in Japanese.

Indeed, it has been a sparsely populated area of specialization.[20] Nor have many Japanese scholars necessarily been willing to step into the breach. Although the Pacific War remains a popular topic for publication in Japan, especially among amateurs, there are comparatively few professional historians engaging the subject, and far fewer still with specific interests in science and technology.[21] This situation has resulted in a dearth of publications that can be considered of much scholarly value, despite the popular appeal they might otherwise enjoy.

There may yet be another, fundamental historiographical reason that science in World War II Japan has been relatively neglected. It is tempting to argue that Japanese scientists produced nothing significant for the war effort, and so it is a story of no consequence, unworthy of examination. But such reasoning leads us immediately too far down the path of positivist historiography. It would also lead us to ignore a complex and rich chapter in the history of Japan's modern development, particularly where science is concerned. After all, it was during the war years that the physicist Yukawa Hideki further refined the meson theory, which he first proposed in 1934, and for which he was awarded the Nobel Prize in 1949.[22] Like many other industrialized nations in the 1930s, Japan stood at a critical juncture in its scientific and technological evolution. While other nations, such as the United States, Great Britain, National Socialist Germany, and the Soviet Union were able to make a complete transition from a "modernized traditional technology"–based society to a "science-technology"–based one, Japan was not. Why this was so merits closer consideration.

Science historian Nakajima Hideto has argued that there are four categories of technology, and by implication four stages of technological development.[23] The first stage, traditional technology, began before the Christian era, with guilds serving as the organizational basis, and silk, cotton fibers, rudimentary arms, and infrastructure being examples of technological artifacts from this category. Second, the modernized traditional technology stage began with the Industrial Revolution (the Second Scientific Revolution) and saw the beginning of the professionalization of science and engineering. Technology was wed to modern industry, producing the steam engine and other artifacts common to heavy industries. Japan lagged behind the West in these, but by the end of the Meiji Period (1868–1912), it was able to achieve general parity in most areas of industrialization. In the third stage, science-technology, with its origins in the mid-nineteenth century, science and technology became inextricably linked, science and engineering education became institutionalized and further professionalized, university and industrial research laboratories were established, and new technological artifacts were produced from basic research, including synthetic dyes and electronics. Extensive funding became necessary, and monopoly capital entered the picture. The fourth stage, high technology, emerged in the 1970s and need not concern us much for now. Suffice it to say that this stage saw the development of semiconductors, superconductivity, and biotechnology.

Nakajima argues that Japan had reached a level "nearly equal" to that of the most industrialized nations of the West in stages two and three before the outbreak of World War II. Indeed, he notes, by the 1930s, Japan was even capable of manufacturing sophisticated products such as vacuum tubes. Nakajima states, "Japan occupied the rear position in the group of the advanced countries. This is illustrated by the fact that Japan joined World War II, a war among advanced nations, as one of its main actors . . . Japan was not underdeveloped before World War II. She had a considerable level of technology."[24] Yet during the war, scientists in Great Britain invented the resonant cavity magnetron, which led to an advanced form of microwave radar, engineers in National Socialist Germany developed the V-2, a long-range ballistic missile, and scientists and engineers in the United States produced nuclear weapons. Scientists and engineers in the Soviet Union could also boast of important innovations. But Japan, as a nation, fell short of such major accomplishments. It was not enough simply to be one of the main actors of the war, for Italy was too, and although it was a modern, industrialized nation, it was arguably not on par with Germany, Britain, or the United States. With the specific exception of the field of biological warfare research, Japan began the war behind the nations of the West and finished the war even further back. Unlike its more developed western counterparts, Japan was unable to progress to the advanced stages of a level three science-technology society by the end of the war. What accounts for this disparity? Nakajima does not say.

The present study argues that Japan's failure to organize large-scale research and development projects for the war effort stalled its progress toward the fourth stage of high-technology development. Although Japan also engaged in efforts to produce nuclear weapons, radar, and technologically sophisticated missiles, it did not effectively mobilize its pool of scientific and engineering talent en masse toward this end. State funding for such projects remained comparatively sparse, and often it was too meager even on its own terms. In most cases, Japanese academic and industrial laboratories had too few technologically advanced apparatuses for basic research, or did not have them at all. Moreover, Japan lacked even the administrative organization to plan and coordinate such efforts toward concrete goals on a national scale. In short, there was no Big Science revolution in Japan as occurred elsewhere in the West during World War II.

Some may argue that the use of the term *Big Science* here is anachronistic, and this point merits further discussion. The idea of Big Science probably emerged in the 1930s with the construction of the large cyclotrons (nuclear particle accelerators) at the laboratories under the supervision of Ernest O. Lawrence at the University of California in Berkeley. Most scholars would agree that the era of Big Science really began with the formation of the Manhattan Project, the multifaceted effort of the United States to develop nuclear weapons during World War II. But it was not until after the war that the term *Big Science* came into use. Beginning in 1949, Lew Kowarski, technical director of the French Atomic Energy Commission (Commissariat à l'Energie Atomique, CEA), was among the first to identify specific elements of what was to become known as Big Science in an article published in *Bulletin of the Atomic Scientists*. Physicist Hans Bethe may have been the first to actually use the term in a book review of Roberg Jungk's *Brighter than a Thousand Suns*, which he wrote for the *Bulletin* in 1958, but it is Alvin Weinberg, a physicist and then director of the Oak Ridge National Laboratory, who is most often credited with having coined the phrase in an article published in the journal *Science* in 1961. Science historian Derek J. de Solla Price subsequently brought the term into wider circulation with his book *Little Science, Big Science*, published in 1963, and further defined the phrase for social scientists. By 1982, the term had even become part of popular culture in the West, as evidenced by the title of a record album of the same name by avant-garde musician and performance artist Laurie Anderson.[25]

But what does Big Science mean, and what is its significance to the present study? The term implies a type of science that is necessarily large in scale and scope, but size alone is not the most distinguishing characteristic. Big Science requires the intersection of three essential elements: science, economy, and the state. The element of science entails technologically advanced (and usually large) equipment and modern laboratories, the concentration of human resources with advanced education and training in a variety of scientific and technological fields, and the collaboration of these experts across the boundaries of discipline and often language. The element of economy requires various natural and industrial resources, which may be scattered over a wide geographical range, and may require monopoly capital for their acquisition and processing. Finally, the element of the state entails the contribution of huge amounts of financial capital, and often mobilization and administration of human and natural resources on a national, and perhaps even international, scale. These roles can be assumed by a civilian government or military hierarchy, or can be shared by both. Certainly, these elements were present in the Manhattan Project, and arguably so in other secret weapons projects elsewhere during World War II, so it does not seem inappropriate or necessarily anachronistic to use the term *Big Science* in the context of the present study.[26]

Although many types of "secret weapons" were researched in Japan during World War II, this study is concerned primarily with those whose development depended largely on the successful intersection of science, economy, and the state. It is in the area of advanced weaponry—such as the atomic bomb, radar, guided missiles, and to a lesser degree, chemical and biological warfare—that the interaction among these three constituents is most visible. These Big Science weapons necessitated the expansion of scientific knowledge beyond what was commonly understood at the outset of the war in the 1930s. For example, atomic bomb research pushed nuclear physics, physical chemistry, and to some extent metallurgy to new experimental limits; radar development led to advances in electronics and new microwave technologies; and guided missile development led to attempts to combine aeronautics with newly emerging technologies, such as infrared, radar, and television.

In the present study, priority is given to the examination of new, higher technology weapons, as opposed to discussion of technical improvements on more conventional weapons, such as artillery, machine guns, tanks, torpedoes, and submarines, which were available before the war and did not require the extensive interplay of science, economy, and the state at that time. Although chemical weapons certainly existed before the outbreak of World War II, a discussion of their development is included in this study because of the historically close relationship to biological weapons development in the case of Japan, and because Japan was a relative latecomer to this type of warfare. Unlike the western powers involved in World War I, Japan did not develop chemical weapons until after that conflict and did not use them until war erupted in China in the 1930s. Unfortunately, other potential Big Science projects having more civilian applications that were undertaken during the war, such as those involving the chemical and medical industries, for example, must remain beyond the scope of this study.

In all areas but chemical and biological warfare, the various research and development programs initiated in World War II Japan were generally unsuccessful in producing advanced new weapons for the war effort. This failure can be attributed to three primary factors: a paucity of resources, limited industrial capacity, and the ineffective mobilization of the nation's science and technology infrastructure. To some extent, these disadvantages might have been less debilitating had the government established a more efficient administrative system for science and technology mobilization, which some technocrats attempted to do in the late 1930s just before the outbreak of war with the United States, but failed. As one military historian has written, "victory in

World War II did not go to the side whose soldiers fought the hardest, or that came up with the most brilliant operational schemes. Rather, those belligerents gained the upper hand whose administrators, scientists, and managers developed the means by which to set up gigantic technological systems and run them as efficiently as possible."[27]

The manner in which science and scientists were mobilized for the war varied significantly from nation to nation. The United States emerged from World War II with the most centralized and highly integrated administrative system for science mobilization the world had yet seen. Arguably, a partial explanation for the success of the Manhattan Project was its efficient organization and management. In contrast, Japan's science infrastructure remained decentralized throughout most of the war, and its mobilization effort proved to be one of the least effective of all the belligerents. In the evolution of Big Science in Japan, this was to become as debilitating a factor as the lack of natural resources and the nation's comparatively diminutive industrial capacity.

The story of science mobilization in wartime Japan is one of rivalries: not just the well-known rivalry between the army and navy, but among the various civilian agencies and bureaucrats, between the civilian bureaucrats and the military, between the bureaucrats and the scientists, and between the scientists and the military. The oft touted spirit of Japanese harmony, or *wa*, alleged by some to be a unique and inherent cultural trait of the Japanese, and often cited in the literature of the 1980s as one of the keys to understanding Japanese economic and industrial success in the postwar period, in many cases seems to have gone all but missing during the war. Although the wartime rivalry between the military services has been examined with some frequency, the rivalries in the civilian sector, particularly where scientists were involved, and its impact on the war, has scarcely been considered and will be one of the prominent themes of the present study.

Chapter 1, "Mobilizing Science and Technology for War," examines the trajectory of science and technology mobilization policy from its formative stage in World War I to the end of the Pacific War in 1945. The chapter begins with a comparison of how the principal belligerents mobilized science and technology for the war effort to underscore how Japan's decentralized system became a significant impediment to research in advanced weapons. In particular, this chapter focuses on the "New Order of Science and Technology" policy initiative, which led to the formation of the Technology Agency. The Technology Agency was intended to serve as a centralized government office with supreme oversight of science and technology mobilization, but as a result of sectionalism within the government and the variant policy agenda of the army, this organization was reduced to little more than a supervisory agency for army aviation research. The New Order of Science and Technology ultimately had little impact. No single unifying agency emerged that was capable of coordinating resource allocation, the rationalization of industry, and collaborative research efforts, which were all important components of science mobilization and advanced weapons development, as well as being critical to the evolution of Big Science in Japan.

Chapter 2, "Nuclear Energy and the Atomic Bomb," examines wartime nuclear research in Japan and is the first of several case studies presented to demonstrate how the three factors of poor resources, limited industrial capacity, and ineffectual mobilization hindered the development of advanced weapons in Japan. The chapter begins with an overview of the impact of the discovery of nuclear fission and how the principal belligerents responded in policy initiatives and mobilization, particularly as World War II began in Europe in 1939. The focus of the chapter is Japan's two attempts to exploit nuclear energy for military use. The navy's B-Research and the F-gō projects pursued development of an atomic bomb and considered development of a nuclear reactor to power ships and submarines. The army's NI-gō was larger in scale and focused primarily on development of a nuclear weapon. This chapter examines how the deficiency in resources, particularly uranium, inadequate research equipment and industrial capacity, and the lack of coordination of research efforts across institutional boundaries, all contributed to the failure of these projects.

Chapter 3, "Electric Weapons: Radar and the 'Death Ray,'" briefly examines the development of radar in Europe and the United States, then focuses on the case of Japan. It examines Japanese navy and army efforts to develop radar as well as the "death ray," a weapon that was intended to focus a beam of microwave energy on an enemy target, which remained under development during the last days of the war. A short discussion of the invention of the magnetron is also included because it became integral to the development of more advanced types of microwave radar sets and was to become an essential component of the death ray.

Chapter 4, "Aeronautical Weapons: Rockets, Guided Missiles, and Jet Aircraft," compares research and development in these weapons among the principal belligerents with a focus on Japan. The chapter examines specific Japanese projects, such as the navy's *Funryū*, or "Raging Dragon," guided missile, among others. Technology transfers from Germany helped to accelerate development of two experimental aircraft, the rocket-propelled *Shūsui* and the twin jet engine *Kikka*, modeled on the Messerschmitt 163 and 262, respectively. But these came too late to contribute to the defense of Japan. Compartmentalization within the services and a general reluctance to fully mobilize university scientists and engineers for particular projects also slowed research and development of advanced aeronautical weapons. Here again, ineffective mobilization stymied development—in some cases, arguably as much as the paucity of resources and industrial production.

Chapter 5, "Chemical and Biological Warfare," demonstrates how the biological weapons development program was able to succeed by averting the problems of resource deficiencies, weak industrial capacity, and limited mobilization as encountered in the other projects dealing with weapons of mass destruction. The chapter begins with a brief overview of chemical and biological warfare in modern history, then examines the history of chemical and biological weapons development in Japan to illustrate the close connection in the evolution of the two programs. This chapter argues that biological weapons development suited Japan's situational imperatives in that it offered cheap and plentiful weapons of mass destruction without requiring the same level of resources, investment, technological progress, and coordination that was necessary for other advanced weapons programs. The biological warfare program also enjoyed a high level of support from the army. Coupled with the complete lack of moral restraint of the Unit 731 researchers in using human subjects for experimentation, Japan's biological warfare program emerged as one of the most formidable among all of the belligerents by the end of the war. It may also be the weapons program that came closest to emerging as a Big Science project during the war.

In the end, one cannot convincingly argue that a more thorough exploitation of science resources would have radically changed the outcome of the war for Japan. Even by the most optimistic estimate, one could only have expected, for example, a more advanced form of radar, and possibly a more effective deployment of a British-style Chain Home network. Another possibility might have been the development of some type of advanced guided missile or jet-propelled intercept aircraft. If used together, such weapons might have increased Japan's self-defense capabilities and thus potentially prolonged the war in some way. This is, of course, all conjecture and need not concern us much for the present. The study of science in wartime Japan is important for other reasons. The more tangible and fruitful line of investigation should instead lead us to discover what impact science in Japan had on the Pacific War in general, and what impact the war had on science in Japan in particular. In this context, the following study hopes also to shed light on other, more specific issues of importance, such as the role of the government and military in promoting science, the role of the scientist in wartime, and different patterns of science mobilization, to name a few.

It is particularly important to understand how the war affected science in Japan, for without knowing what occurred during the war, we are less able to assess the significance of historical developments in science and technology in the postwar period. This point may be especially true where the formation of Big Science in Japan is concerned. Although Japan did not quite make the transition to Big Science during the war, the foundations for that evolutionary phase were being laid all the while. Consequently, Japan was able to make that transition rather quickly in the more peaceful and favorable economic environment of the postwar era. There are yet many related continuities between wartime scientific research and the postwar economic "miracle" that remain to be discovered, and this is a subject that has only recently begun to be examined in any depth.[28] When viewed in this light, World War II was indeed a "useful" war, as well as an important phase in Japan's modern development.[29] This study hopes to begin to shed more light on the critical role of science in that particular stage of this complex process.

Finally, a word on sources. Numerous documents were destroyed in Japan at the end of the war, and much has been lost to history. After the war, the United States dispatched various intelligence missions to investigate Japan's wartime scientific research, and to some degree, these were successful in reconstructing that period of activity.[30] But there are important caveats. We now know, for example, that a conspiracy existed to mislead the initial U.S. investigations into biological weapons research, and such documents on this subject must be used with considerable skepticism and care. In recent years, some Japanese scientists and doctors have also come forward to offer testimony about their experiences during the war, thus bringing more information to light. But memories fade, and such accounts can also be misleading and unreliable for many other reasons. Thus, it is not uncommon for two sources to present conflicting information. Not only do significant gaps remain, as with most historical subjects, but contradictory evidence abounds. In such cases, I have attempted to verify information by cross-referencing the Japanese- and English-language sources and referring to both in the citations where possible.

What follows is an attempt to explore the intersection of science and the state in World War II Japan and to understand the consequences of that interaction. By examining the efforts to develop advanced weapons, we can begin to reveal the conditions under which scientists worked at the highest levels to reach the cutting edge of technology, and we can begin to understand the limitations and frustrations they experienced. Through a transnational comparison, we can begin to properly situate Japan's efforts along various spectrums of organization, funding, and levels of research. This book does not aspire to be a comprehensive study of science in wartime Japan or of Japanese weapons. On these subjects, there is plenty more research waiting to be done—and more books to be written. It is hoped that this study will stimulate further interest in the history of Big Science in modern Japan, and that it will serve to introduce some lesser-known but important publications in Japanese to a broader, western audience.

1
MOBILIZING SCIENCE AND TECHNOLOGY FOR WAR

Historians generally agree that World War II was the first "scientific" war. During World War I, basic research remained narrow in scope. Far more attention was given to applied sciences, especially in chemistry, mass production technologies, and mechanization, which resulted in the production of better machine guns and artillery, as well as new weapons such as the tank and the airplane. World War I is often also called the "chemist's war" because of the integral role of the chemist in the production of armaments and in the development of poison gases. But it was not until World War II that scientists from nearly every field were mobilized for a total war effort. Although the Great War had revealed the importance of supporting basic research to meet military and industrial needs in wartime, by the start of World War II, few nations had an adequate science infrastructure in place for such a purpose.

Mobilization of the economy, rearmament, and military mobilization preceded science mobilization, and the principal combatants of the war approached these in a variety of ways. In Germany, where the Versailles Treaty of 1919 imposed severe limitations on weapons production, rearmament began in the 1920s under a veil of secrecy, and the nation's science and technology infrastructure continued to operate throughout the interwar period as an amalgam of independent public and private research institutions. A movement was afoot in 1937 to centralize Germany's science institutions under the Reich Research Council, but the nation's science and technology infrastructure remained decentralized throughout the war. In Japan, technocrats began to lobby for science and technology mobilization in the 1930s, largely in response to the need to secure resources and to rationalize industry for the war in China as well as for the general preservation of the empire. In Japan, too, there was a call for greater centralization and control of science resources, but no direct action was taken until the early 1940s. The military leaders of Germany and Japan appear not to have felt any immediate sense of urgency

13

concerning science mobilization at the outset of the war. By far the bigger challenge to both nations was to be the total mobilization of economic resources, which was arguably of greater concern to Japan than Germany at the time. As for Italy, its industrial base was comparatively small, and its science and technology infrastructure was even smaller.

Great Britain took an early defensive posture in response to German rearmament and brought its scientific and industrial resources to bear on the problem of national defense, ultimately resulting in the development of radar and the Chain Home system. But on the whole, there was no significant movement toward centralization beyond the general supervisory role taken on by the Department of Scientific and Industrial Research. The United States was woefully underprepared for war as a result of military demobilization after World War I, severe cuts in the military budget in the interwar period, and the prevalent mood of isolationism, which continued to influence American foreign policy even as Germany invaded Poland in September 1939. The situation began to change in the summer of 1940, in large part, as a result of the efforts of a few influential scientists, such as Vannevar Bush, who saw the United States as vulnerable under the growing threat of war. With the help of a cooperative administration, Bush created the National Defense Research Committee and later the Office of Scientific Research and Development, which became the central agency for the oversight of science and technology in the United States during World War II. At the other end of the political spectrum, the Soviet Union also moved toward a more centralized system. Ideology thus appeared to have little to do with a nation's approach to the problem of mobilization.[1]

To gain a better perspective of Japan's experience in mobilizing science and technology for the war effort, it may be useful to first briefly compare how the other principal belligerents in the war responded to the demands of the first "scientific" war. To what extent were the government, military, and scientists involved in mobilizing science and technology for the war effort? What imperatives drove wartime science and technology policy? What impact did the various approaches to mobilization have on the ultimate shape of the nation's science and technology infrastructure? And how much did this matter? Through a transnational comparison of mobilization efforts, a spectrum of responses emerges, with the United States appearing to have the most centralized—and arguably most efficient—system on the one end, and Japan with the most decentralized and arguably least efficient wartime mobilization system on the other end. In Japan, where the lack of natural resources and limited industrial capacity remained critical weaknesses during the war, one might expect to find greater efforts being made toward rationalizing the nation's science and technology infrastructure. Some measures were taken, but these were generally unsuccessful. Understanding why these efforts failed sheds light on why so many of the Big Science weapons projects undertaken during the war also resulted in failure.

THE BELLIGERENTS PREPARE FOR WAR

World War I was a wake-up call. The Great War strained the economies, industries, and science institutions of the nations involved in that conflict and exposed their inherent weaknesses. Nations responded as they could during the war, and even in the postwar era of pacifist movements and military demobilization, reform of national research institutes remained a priority throughout Europe, the United States, and Japan. Great Britain was among the first nations to respond by creating the Department of Scientific and Industrial Research (DSIR) in December 1916. The mission of the DSIR was to address basic research deficiencies in such areas as dyestuffs, optical glass, and pharmaceuticals, as well as other industries severely affected by the termination of trade with Germany. The DSIR was provided an independent laboratory and helped to fund research cooperatives in private industry. In 1920, the DSIR became the principal agency for the coordination of defense-related research among the nation's three military services, including the British army, the Admiralty, and the Royal Air Force. Sir Henry Tizard, a chemist by training, was appointed assistant secretary to the boards of each service. His responsibilities included coordinating the research of the military services in the fields of physics, chemistry, and engineering. In 1927, Tizard was appointed the permanent secretary of the DSIR, making him the leading science administrator in the British government.[2]

The pattern of reform in Britain during the interwar period was to establish additional research institutions as extensions of existing organizations. The government adopted this strategy as a stopgap measure to address weaknesses in the nation's science infrastructure, particularly where the military was concerned. For example, in 1920, the Admiralty Research Laboratory was established as the primary institute for basic research in the navy, as there was at that time no other agency dedicated to that purpose. In this manner, Britain's science infrastructure grew in an ad hoc fashion, with no central agency to coordinate or organize research for the nation as a whole. The DSIR came close to fulfilling this function, but it operated mainly to coordinate research among the *military* services and not civilian agencies more broadly. As Britain began to rearm in the 1930s, no fewer than twenty new research facilities were established for weapons development.[3]

Throughout the period of rearmament in the 1930s and into World War II, the government and military agencies dedicated to weapons research and development functioned as a loose confederation bound by personal ties and academic affiliations. Control over these agencies remained in the hands of a few directors who were personally well acquainted and met with one another frequently, whether formally or informally. They maintained close liaison with one another when establishing their respective programs, and through semi-official exchange of information, they largely managed to avoid duplicating research efforts. This seemingly casual research system continued to operate throughout the war without significant change and with much apparent success, considering the wide range of technologically advanced weaponry produced by Great Britain during the war. It was a unique arrangement that likely could not have functioned as well in most other nations at that time.[4]

The Soviet Union was still suffering from the disruptions of the 1917 revolution when the Great War came to an end, and it was several years before institutions of science gained a solid footing under the new socialist regime. Few state research institutes had been established under the czars before World War I, and like many other nations, the Soviet Union suffered severe dislocations in its economy and science infrastructure after being cut off from Germany, which it had heavily relied on for imports of raw materials and technology. The fledgling government attempted to redress these problems, and by the end of 1919, had helped to form thirty-three new research institutes. Expenditures for scientific research increased fourfold under the first Five Year Plan initiated in 1924. Industrial research institutes also experienced a period of high growth between 1928 and 1933, rising from 24 to 238 with an estimated tenfold increase in manpower. By the early 1930s, the USSR had undergone such a proliferation of new research institutes that it began to experience diminishing returns in the form of an overabundance of understaffed and poorly equipped facilities. A program of rationalization measures soon followed.[5] In 1932, a commission on the mobilization of scientific research for defense was convened to address this problem as it related to national defense. In December, a leading member of the committee, Mikhail Tukhachevskii, then serving as chief of staff of the Red Army, proposed the formation of an agency to centralize and coordinate all scientific research from the factory level to the Soviet Academy of Sciences for defense-related research. The new agency was to operate under the aegis of the Defense Commission as the Special Scientific-Technical Committee (Osobyi Nauchno-Tekhnicheskii Komitet pri Komissii Oborony).[6]

Throughout the 1930s, the Soviet science infrastructure was mainly composed of three distinct hierarchies. First among them was the academy system, at the apex of which was the Soviet Academy of Sciences. Second were the university and technical schools. The third hierarchy consisted of research institutes under the various government ministries. The State Planning Commission of the Council of Ministers held authority over these organizations and controlled their budgets. In turn, the State Planning Commission was accountable to the Communist Party, which acted through the Politburo, or Central Committee. With rare exceptions, these high-level government agencies generally did not interfere with research conducted in the academies, universities, or industry.[7]

The Soviet Academy of Sciences came under the direction of the government by decree of the Politburo on 25 November 1933, and the academy was moved to Moscow the following year. The directors of the various institutes involved in the development of military technologies, weapons, and materials for the defense industry were among the most distinguished of the academy's membership. In 1935, the Division of Technical Sciences was established under the academy to further assist in the coordination of research for national defense. By 1940, it was responsible for overseeing some of the nation's leading science institutions and their branch laboratories, including the Physical-Technical Institute, the Institute of Chemical Physics, and the Radium Institute. A board of military representatives from the People's Defense Committee was formed to serve as liaison to the Presidium of the Academy of Sciences and to help coordinate research and development of new weapons and military technology.[8]

At the outbreak of World War II in 1939, however, the science infrastructure of the Soviet Union was something less than the sum of its parts. Despite repeated calls for centralization by Tukhachevskii and others, the Soviet Union still lacked a single government agency responsible for science policy formation and mobilization. Moreover, Stalin's purges in the "Great Terror" (1936–1938) had a deep and wide-ranging impact on scientists and science institutions in the Soviet Union and all but paralyzed the Soviet Academy of Sciences. Some of the nation's most capable scientists and engineers, such as physicist Lev D. Landau and aeronautical engineer Andrei N. Tupolev were arrested. Many brilliant scientists languished in prison or were executed.[9] Tukhachevskii himself was executed as a traitor in 1937.[10]

The precarious situation of Soviet science began to change only after the German invasion of the USSR in June 1941 and the subsequent adoption of the "everything for victory" policy. The invasion prompted an immediate reformation of the national bureaucracy. The State Defense Committee (Gosudarstvennyi Komitet Oborony, GKO), established on 30 June 1941, assumed responsibility for strategic command of the war effort under the aegis of the

General Headquarters of the Supreme High Command (Stavka Verkhovnogo Glavnokomandovaniya), over which Stalin presided as supreme commander in chief. The State Defense Committee then subsumed the powers of the People's Defense Committee, which was dissolved under the new system.[11] A Scientific-Technical Council was formed under the purview of the State Defense Committee to coordinate defense-related research and development. The Scientific-Technical Council became the central agency for policy formation and science mobilization for the war effort, and it served as the primary government liaison to the numerous science institutions under the Soviet Academy of Sciences.[12] Yet despite these efforts, as a result of limitations of resources, skilled labor, and a challenged industrial infrastructure, Soviet policy favored development of weapons that were simple and rugged in design, as well as inexpensive to mass produce, thus precluding much development of technologically advanced weaponry throughout the war.[13]

Although the United States had entered World War I comparatively late, it also began to reform its science infrastructure around that time. In 1915, the government formed the National Advisory Committee for Aeronautics (NACA) to supervise and direct scientific studies in aviation. The Council of National Defense was created in 1916 to coordinate industrial production and natural resources for the war effort, and the National Research Council was established by executive order in May 1918 to "stimulate research in the mathematical, physical and biological sciences, and in the application of the sciences" in times of war and peace.[14] By the spring of 1940, however, it had become apparent to a few influential and well-positioned scientists in the United States that the nation was about to be drawn into a war for which it was ill prepared. Four of the nation's leading scientists, including Vannevar Bush, then president of the Carnegie Institution and chair of the NACA, Karl T. Compton, president of the Massachusetts Institute of Technology (MIT), James B. Conant, president of Harvard University, and Frank B. Jewett, president of the National Academy of Sciences and the Bell Telephone Laboratories, met to discuss the mobilization of the scientific community for the development of new weapons and national defense. Bush envisioned a new organization to direct science and technology mobilization, and on 27 June 1940, he presented his plan for the agency to President Franklin D. Roosevelt.[15]

Bush was most concerned with reforming the nation's science and technology infrastructure in preparation for war. His experience as an electrical engineer working on submarine detection equipment in World War I had revealed to him the extent of "administrative confusion" and the "lack of organization" that characterized the American system at the time. Bush understood that modern science had progressed to the point where military leaders no longer knew what they might reasonably demand of scientists for weapons development, and he sought to remedy this problem by providing an official means for bringing scientists to the military. President Roosevelt approved Bush's proposal "on the spot" and the National Defense Research Committee (NDRC) was born.[16] The NDRC was to "coordinate, supervise, and conduct scientific research on the problems underlying the development, production, and use of mechanisms and devices of warfare."[17] The committee included Compton, Conant, Jewett, the commissioner of patents, and two representatives each from the War and Navy Departments. The president appointed Bush chair.[18]

Although the NDRC provided an official venue for bringing together civilian scientists and the military, there remained significant gaps in the system, especially where research and development (R&D) in new weapons technology were concerned. Better coordination among the military services and NACA was needed, and a few heads of other governmental agencies were beginning to challenge the jurisdiction of the NDRC.[19] The president also wished to form a committee based on the model of the NDRC to oversee research in military medicine. To address these needs and issues, Bush proposed the formation of a larger, more dominant agency. Roosevelt approved the plan on 28 June 1941, and the Office of Scientific Research and Development (OSRD) became the nation's new center for science and technology mobilization. The OSRD assumed the responsibilities of the NDRC and subsumed the NDRC itself, which remained as an advisory board, and a new Committee on Medical Research was established. Bush was appointed the first director of the OSRD, and Conant replaced him as chair of the NDRC. The formation of the OSRD further concentrated authority over new weapons development in the hands of Bush, who became a kind of "czar of research" in the U.S. government.[20] With the formation of these agencies, particularly the OSRD, the U.S. government created what was to be the most centralized, highly structured, and well-coordinated organization for science and technology mobilization the world had yet seen. Throughout World War II, these agencies, staffed with brilliant and forward-looking men of science, played a critical role in science and technology policy and directed the development of such revolutionary new weapons as the atomic bomb.

Germany dominated most fields of science in the early twentieth century. Much of this hegemony was due to superior research facilities in the nation's university system, as well as such world-renowned institutions as the Imperial Institute for Physics (Physicalisch-Technische Reichsanstalt, PTR), established in 1887, and the Kaiser Wilhelm Society for the Advancement of the Sciences (Kaiser Wilhelm Gesellschaft zur Förderung der Wissenschaften,

KWG), founded in 1911. The Kaiser Wilhelm Society, with its many institutes for physics and chemistry, played an important role in World War I. The Kaiser Wilhelm Institute for Physical Chemistry, for example, became the center for chemical warfare research in Germany under the direction of Fritz Haber, who won the Nobel Prize in 1919 for his work in nitrogen fixation. The Kaiser Wilhelm Foundation for Military Technical Science (Kaiser Wilhelm Stiftung für kriegstechnische Wissenschaft), considered the German analog to the British DSIR, was formed in 1916 and brought together committees of experts led by accomplished scientists from the universities.[21] After World War I, the science infrastructure of the nation was reformed in accordance with the demands of the Versailles Treaty and the more democratic agenda of the Weimar Republic. Some institutions, particularly those that had supported armaments production, were closed, but others, such as those of the prestigious KWG, not only survived but thrived in the new atmosphere of freedom.[22]

This brief period came to an abrupt end with the rise of the National Socialist regime in 1933. With the enactment of the Civil Service Law in that year, universities were brought under the Nazi heel, and faculties were purged of Jews.[23] In the spring of 1934, plans were enacted for the reorganization of science under a more centralized and federalized system. By 1937, a new Reich Ministry of Education (Reichserziehungsministerium, REM) had assumed control over the various public institutions concerned with science under the previous Prussian and Reich ministries, and policy came to focus on controlling science, particularly through ideological education at the higher schools and universities. A plan was in the works to merge the PTR and KWG, and a new military-style hierarchy was proposed for the organization of science institutions. But resistance from representatives of the various government agencies and science institutions over such matters as jurisdiction defeated the move toward greater centralization. This fruitless effort was not only symptomatic of the polycratic nature of the German political system, but it also reflected the regime's failure to appreciate the significance of the potential role of science in the service of the state, especially for the military, which was not fully comprehended until well into World War II. Instead, science was to serve the economic and political agendas of Hitler's Four Year Plan for German autarky.[24]

A second attempt at centralization came in March 1937, with the formation of the Reich Research Council (Reichsforschungsrat) under the Ministry of Education. The Reich Research Council (RRC) consisted of eighteen scientists and engineers who were responsible for different areas of research ranging from chemistry to metals. Among them were the directors of the various laboratories of the Kaiser Wilhelm Society, as well as high-ranking members of the National Socialist Party, including REM Minister Dr. Bernhard Rust, and Reichsministers Professor Rudolf Mentzel and Dr. Erich Schumann, to name a few. General Karl Becker, head of the Army Weapons Office (Heereswaffenamt), and dean and professor in the Faculty of Defense Technology at the Technische Hochscule in Berlin, was named its first director.[25]

After the war began in 1939, the RRC and other government science agencies, such as the German Research Association (Deutsche Forschungsgemeinschaft), were brought under Rust's authority at the Reich Education Ministry. Becker proved to be an ineffective director of the RRC, and when he died in 1940, Rust assumed his post. But Rust also proved ineffective. Like his predecessor, Rust could do little to advance the agenda of the council. Poor leadership was only part of the problem. Many German military leaders believed that new weapons development required at least four years from concept to production, leaving no time for the introduction of innovative weapons in what they presumed would be a short war. The swift victory over France in 1940 especially convinced the generals of their ability to win the war quickly, and they saw no great necessity to mobilize scientific personnel on a larger scale at that time. By 1942, however, the situation had changed. The military increasingly turned to the scientists to provide new weapons with which to attack the Allies. Under increasing pressure from the military for quick results, in June 1942, the Reich Research Council underwent a major reorganization.[26]

First, authority over the council was transferred from the Ministry of Education under Rust to the Ministry of Armaments and War Production under Albert Speer, who was to prove to be a superior administrator. The restructured RRC became responsible for mobilizing scientists and for coordinating all R&D undertaken for the war effort. It was to serve as a central repository for information on research being conducted throughout the nation, by whom, and under what contracts. A Planning Office was established to assist in this mission and to take a more aggressive role in promoting scientific research. Rudolph Mentzel was appointed the new administrative director of the council, and in June 1943, Werner Osenberg, a member of the SS, an engineer, and director of a branch institute of the Technische Hochschule in Hannover, was named director of the Planning Office. Osenberg's primary objective was to bring greater organizational efficiency to the RRC. In August 1944, he established the War Research Association, which was intended to coordinate R&D in ongoing projects, advise on the possible applications of fundamental research, and assign scientists to appropriate projects in their specific fields of expertise.[27] But Osenberg came on board just as the SS began to expand its influence over such projects as the V-1 and V-2 rockets, which, among other weapons programs, diverted disproportionate amounts of resources and funds with arguably less strategic returns than more conventional weapons.[28] Consequently, despite early efforts at reorganization, Germany's science institutions continued to operate throughout the war under a comparatively decentralized and highly polycratic administrative system. Even so, Germany managed to produce an astonishing array of advanced weaponry.

Italy hardly merits mentioning here, but as one of the primary Axis belligerents, it should not escape our attention. Science mobilization was not attempted on a national scale, and there was little or no collaboration among the military services and civilian scientists at the universities.[29] Furthermore, with the rise of state-supported anti-Semitism in the 1930s, Italy suffered a significant brain drain as many of the nation's leading scientists, such as Enrico Fermi, Emilio Segré, and Bruno Pontecorvo, fled the country to escape persecution and oppression under the fascist regime of dictator Benito Mussolini.[30] But most significantly, Italy lacked the raw materials and industrial infrastructure necessary to sustain a modern armaments industry of the level that was to emerge in the more developed nations of World War II. Italy's military expenditures as a proportion of gross domestic product were the lowest of all the principal belligerents, and its war economy was dependent on foreign support, of which there was little to none. Although the number of new engineers increased, Italy's science infrastructure was too underdeveloped to support any significant advanced weapons projects during the war.[31]

SCIENCE POLICY AND MOBILIZATION IN JAPAN

Science and technology policy in Japan can be said to have evolved in three distinct phases. The years from World War I to 1937 were a formative period in which policies were formulated to strengthen science institutions and to exploit natural resources found throughout Japan's colonial empire in East Asia. During the second phase, 1937 to 1942, policy focused on securing resources, strengthening industrial capacity, and mobilizing institutions of science and technology for the war effort, particularly with the introduction of the New Order of Science and Technology in 1940. Mobilization policy at this time, however, amounted to little more than promotion of research by specific government offices. The third phase, 1942 to 1945, may be considered a crisis stage, wherein the military joined the government in taking more proactive measures to mobilize and coordinate scientific research toward a more efficient exploitation of resources and development of new weapons.[32]

The establishment of the Technology Agency (Gijutsu-in) in January 1942 was the culmination of efforts by a determined cadre of technocrats and a select few government officials to reform the nation's system of science mobilization. As originally conceived, the Technology Agency was to serve as the central administrative office in the national mobilization of science and technology and in matters concerning science and technology policy. The Technology Agency, as it emerged in 1942, however, was something quite different. Hard-liners in the army thwarted the technocratic agenda and representatives of various government ministries squabbled over jurisdiction, ultimately leaving the Technology Agency little more than an oversight board for army aeronautical development.[33]

THE FORMATIVE YEARS, WORLD WAR I TO 1937

Like many nations of Europe and the United States, Japan also learned from the experience of World War I. With the termination of trade relations with Germany during the war, Japan soon found its own industries and institutions of science incapable of replacing German manufacturers in such key areas as artificial dyes, chemicals, and optical glass. As in Europe, the USSR, and the United States, the war had revealed the weaknesses of the nation's science and technology infrastructure. By the end of the war, a movement emerged in government and industrial circles to build up institutions of science and technology in order to strengthen domestic industrial capacity and to reduce dependence on foreign nations. The establishment of the Institute for Physical and Chemical Research (Rikagaku Kenkyūjo, commonly known by its Japanese acronym, Riken) on 20 March 1917, in particular, was a watershed event in the history of science and technology in Japan.[34] Numerous research institutions were established soon thereafter. Among private enterprises, Mitsubishi, Asahi Glass, and Tokyo Shibaura Electric (later Toshiba) all formed industrial research laboratories in 1917, and the large industrial combines (*zaibatsu*), such as Sumitomo and Furukawa, soon followed. In 1918, the Aeronautical Research Institute (Kōkū Kenkyūjo) was established at Tokyo Imperial University. The military services also established research centers, including the Army Technical Department (Rikugun Gijutsu Honbu), the Army Institute of Scientific Research (Rikugun Kagaku Kenkyūjo) in 1919, and the Navy Technical Research Institute (Kaigun Gijutsu Kenkyūjo) in 1923[35] (Appendix, Table A1).

Another important step taken toward national independence in science and technology was the formation of the Japan National Research Council (Nippon Gakujutsu Kenkyū Kaigi) in 1920. This organization was established to serve as a chapter of the International Science Council, founded in 1918 by the United States and the various nations of Europe, ostensibly to promote the exchange of scientists and scientific knowledge across national borders. (In fact, the International Science Council served more the purpose of isolating German scientists from the global community as a reprimand for having contributed to the war effort.) The mission of the Japan National Research Council was to help coordinate scientific research domestically and abroad, to promote scientific research by acting as a liaison to the West, and to facilitate interaction with similar organizations overseas. For Japan, the Japan National Research Council presented an opportunity to break free from dependence on Germany by joining a broader international scientific community.[36]

The recession that hit Japan after World War I resulted in a wave of business failures, industrial rationalization, and retrenchment among some of the new research institutes. The Riken, for example, received less than half the donations pledged beforehand by private enterprises and was consequently forced to incorporate and venture into manufacturing for itself. The Riken established several small factories and used profits from manufacturing liquor and vitamins to continue funding research. The Great Kantō Earthquake of 1923, followed by the Great Depression of 1929, delivered another series of shocks to the economy. Research institutions were forced either to reduce their staff members drastically or to close altogether. By 1930, even the Mitsubishi Shipbuilding Company opted to shut down its laboratory and transfer its research operations to the Riken.[37]

In the late 1920s and into the 1930s, the imperatives of industrial policy, namely the strengthening of heavy industries through better resource management and rationalization, to some degree eclipsed the other developmental priorities of science and technology policy. New links were forged between the government, academia, and industry for the purpose of strengthening industrial capacity. For example, the Cabinet Resources Bureau (Shigenkyoku) was created in 1927 in order to assess the availability of natural resources within the empire and to create a framework for their allocation and control in times of national emergency.[38] The government also enacted a series of industrial rationalization laws in order to strengthen domestic enterprises and to reduce dependence on foreign capital, especially in areas of immediate concern to the military.[39] In recognition of the critical link between a sound industrial base and basic research, several new industrial laboratories and university research facilities were also established. Many of these had an obvious potential benefit to the military.[40]

The formation of the Japan Society for the Promotion of Science (Nihon gakujutsu shinkōkai, JSPS) in 1932 was yet another important link forged between industry, academia, and government in the strengthening of industrial capacity and science at this time. The JSPS, established under the aegis of the

Ministry of Education, was to support research by awarding grants and private endowments for selected programs. It was also charged with the responsibility of coordinating research efforts between various academic institutions and for reforming the system of research funding at the universities.[41] In 1933, the Ministry of Education allotted the JSPS an initial budget of ¥1 million (approximately $250,000 in 1933 dollars), about half of which was parceled out as research subsidies for the year. By 1941 the JSPS was providing nearly half the ¥5 million ($1.25 million) in public funds apportioned annually for research to scientists at government, university, and industrial laboratories.[42] (About 75 percent of JSPS funding for scientific research came from the Ministry of Education with the balance obtained from private industry.[43]) Not only did the JSPS provide necessary funding for scientific research at a critical time, it also continued to help coordinate academic research with industrial and military needs throughout the 1930s and 1940s.[44]

Other important measures undertaken around this time included the formation of the Provisional Bureau of Industrial Rationalization (Rinji sangyō gōrikyoku) in 1930, and the enactment of the Industrial Control Law in 1931. Established under the aegis of the Ministry of Commerce and Industry, the Provisional Bureau of Industrial Rationalization was charged with coordinating the demands of industry with research being conducted in public laboratories. By the end of the year, over three hundred public laboratories had an affiliation with a private enterprise. The national government directly controlled twenty of these laboratories, and another seventy became associated either with a local government or one of the imperial universities.[45] The Industrial Control Law further rationalized priority industries according to the needs of the military and provided for their protection against foreign competition. In the era of the Great Depression, Japanese firms proved even less capable of competing with western companies in international markets. As a consequence, they increasingly turned toward the army and navy for production contracts, thereby further militarizing the national economy.[46]

The military services had begun to take a more proactive role in the affairs of the nation's economy after the outbreak of World War I. Ranking officials in the Army Ministry (Ministry of War), in particular, became increasingly concerned over Japan's ability to mobilize its national resources for a modern, total war. In previous conflicts, the policy was to rapidly mobilize the essentials of warfare—manpower, arms, and finances—with an eye toward a quick and decisive victory. World War I revealed that it may become necessary in the future to harness the full potential of the nation's economy in order to wage a prolonged and all-inclusive war, a type of warfare for which Japan was ill prepared and poorly suited. As Japanese staff officers observing the war in Europe began to realize, those belligerents who were not self-sufficient "were lost."[47] For some of the more prescient army brass, autarky had become a paramount objective.

Investigations conducted by the Army Ministry in 1917 revealed that neither the home islands of Japan nor the territories of its empire held sufficient natural resources to support a total war. Japan proper was lacking in the materials of modern industry, as were the colonies of Formosa, Korea, and south Sakhalin—the latter having been acquired along with additional Russian territorial rights in northeast China as a result of Japan's victory in the Russo-Japanese War of 1904–1905. China's northeast provinces, however, appeared more promising.

Yet army brass also recognized that even the acquisition of sufficient natural resources abroad would be of no use without a comprehensive plan for the mobilization of the domestic economy. After conducting a study of European models of economic mobilization for the war effort, the Army Ministry drafted a bill proposing the formation of a central agency responsible for mobilizing and controlling industries essential to a total war. In March 1918, the Diet passed the bill, enacted as the Munitions Mobilization Law, but restricted its application to full-scale wars only. The law provided for a modest Munitions Bureau (Gunjukyoku), to be staffed by representatives of the army and navy under the aegis of the prime minister, and was made responsible for investigating Japan's economic capacity and outlining plans for its mobilization in case of war. These efforts soon came to naught, however, as the Munitions Bureau was disbanded in November 1922 for its apparent meddling in affairs under the jurisdiction of other government ministries. In 1924, the recently appointed Minister of the Army, Major General Ugaki Kazunari (aka Kazushige), who had helped champion the concept of a centralized agency for mobilization, revived the bureau as the Equipment Bureau (Seibikyoku) under the aegis of the Army Ministry. Ugaki assigned the duty of resource mobilization to capable young officers under his direction and appointed the "brilliant" Lieutenant Colonel Nagata Tetsuzan, who had served as a military attaché in Europe during World War I and was a staunch supporter of Ugaki's agenda, as head of the ministry's Mobilization Section. By 1927, Ugaki's efforts toward creating a centralized mobilization agency had contributed a great deal to the establishment of the aforementioned Cabinet Resources Bureau.[48]

As Army Minister, Ugaki was not only responsible for the maintenance of the military service under his direction, but was also concerned with its preparation for meeting the demands of total war. From Ugaki's perspective, the army was in dire need of modernization. Not having been directly involved in the conflict in Europe during World War I, the Imperial Japanese Army had not been forced to modernize at the same pace as the military forces of the

West. As a result, the Japanese army had missed the technological revolution in warfare brought about by the introduction of such innovations as mechanized transport, the tank, improved artillery and machine guns, the airplane, and poison gas. Despite a nearly threefold increase in the army's budget between 1914 and 1921, the Imperial Japanese Army lagged behind in these key technologies and by the mid-1920s was a comparatively second-rate military force. With the further economic dislocations caused by the Great Kantō Earthquake of 1923, neither the army, nor the government more broadly, could afford the expenditures necessary to bring the Japanese army on par with the military forces of the West at this time. Moreover, in the early 1920s, opposition parties within the Diet, prompted largely by growing public criticism over the military budget, began to call for a reduction in military spending.[49] The problem now facing the army was how to modernize under such serious economic and political constraints.

In May 1925, Army Minister Ugaki introduced a novel plan to modernize the army. His idea, which came to be known as the "arms reduction" (*gunshuku*) plan, called for serious consolidation and rationalization of the army's forces. Ugaki's proposal entailed reducing the army by four full divisions and diverting the funds saved through the decrease in personnel to pay for upgrades in technology. But the Ugaki plan quickly met with serious opposition. A faction of old guard traditionalists, led by the likes of General Araki Sadao and supported by junior-grade officers imbued with the ethics of *bushidō*—the feudal samurai warrior code—fought Ugaki's agenda for modernization, which they perceived would be achieved mostly at the expense of the common soldier. Largely as a result of this opposition, Ugaki's initial reform effort had only a minimal impact on the modernization of the army and ultimately was little more than a first step toward this end.[50]

Later, in March 1928, Lieutenant Colonel Nagata Tetsuzan, who was himself emerging as a leading advocate for army reform, introduced a general mobilization plan to restructure the Army Ministry as well as to better coordinate resource exploitation between the military and civilian sectors. But this too met with opposition from traditionalist hard-liners. The ideological schism between the two groups widened further. On the one hand were the total war reformers, led by Ugaki and Nagata, who saw the necessity of preparing for national mobilization and modernizing the army by equipping it with technologically advanced, science-based weaponry. On the other hand were the traditionalists, led by Araki, who clung tenaciously to the belief in a modern variant of *bushidō* known as *seishin*, the ideology of the superior "fighting spirit" of the Japanese soldier, which was widely believed to have been a determining factor in Japan's victory over Russia in the Russo-Japanese War.

Although the latter faction may be described as having been decidedly antiscience, for a comparatively poor nation like Japan at the time, their emphasis on morale and training over material improvements in the army had a certain logic and enjoyed no small amount of sympathy and support in the military and among the public.[51]

The extent to which this factional strife ultimately affected technological modernization and the effectiveness of the Japanese army later in the Pacific War is difficult to assess. Although improved radio equipment, machine guns, artillery, tanks, and chemical weapons were eventually introduced throughout the following decade, it is clear that the traditionalists considerably impeded the modernization agenda of the reformers and significantly delayed the introduction of new technologies to the Japanese army. Consequently, the Imperial Japanese Army never closed the technological gap with the West during this critical period. Throughout World War II, its standard weapons and equipment were to remain imitative and inferior to those of the Allies.[52]

Moreover, this ideological schism in the army gave rise in the early 1930s to an extreme form of factionalism, with the traditionalists evolving into the Imperial Way faction (Kōdōha) and the reformers emerging as the rival Control faction (Tōseiha). This factionalism had a profoundly negative impact on the Japanese army throughout the interwar years.[53] The Imperial Japanese Navy, for its part, did not suffer the same ideological split over scientific and technological modernization and fared much better. (Its internal divisions were caused by other issues, such as disagreements over the ratification of the London Naval Treaty of 1930.[54]) By the outbreak of the Pacific War in 1941, the Japanese navy's conventional ship-based weaponry and aircraft were arguably first-rate for the time, whereas the army largely retained the policy of "depending on inexpensive men, rather than expensive weapons."[55]

Despite these ideological splits, however, most army brass agreed that securing the resource-rich province of Manchuria in China's northeast was essential to the nation's economic survival should Japan become embroiled in a total war. Manchuria, they felt, must be defended against Japan's greatest potential enemy on the Asian continent, the Soviet Union. With its rich mineral deposits and possibilities for industrial development, Manchuria became central to Japan's plans for economic mobilization and national defense, and to some, Japan's drive toward autarky. Since winning territorial concessions there in 1905, Japan had expanded its presence and enjoyed considerable political, economic, and military control in the region. The port of Dairen on the Liaotung Peninsula and the South Manchuria Railway (SMR), both within Japan's sphere of influence, were particularly vital to Japan's economic and national defense interests. The South Manchuria Railway Company, a national policy company of Japan, controlled the network of railroads that formed the backbone of Japan's transportation and mining industries throughout China's northeast.[56]

Manchuria had to be made secure, and leading officers in Japan's Kwantung Army conspired to make it so. From 1905, Japanese military forces had been posted in Manchuria to protect the SMR and the Liaotung Peninsula. In 1919, the government in Tokyo conferred upon the Kwantung Army independent status, and its prestige became such that young soldiers coveted assignments to this elite branch of the Japanese army.[57] Tensions in the area began to mount in the late 1920s as Chiang Kai-shek emerged as the leader of the Chinese Nationalist (Kuomintang) Army and began a campaign to unify China by ousting the regional warlords. In 1928, when the local warlord, Chang Tso-lin, proved to be an unreliable and recalcitrant ally for the Japanese against the encroaching Kuomintang forces, staff officers in the Kwantung Army had him assassinated. The Kwantung Army conspirators had hoped his son and successor, Chang Hsueh-liang, would prove more compliant. But when it became clear he was attempting to ally himself with the Chinese Nationalists, officers in the Kwantung Army, led by Lieutenant Colonel Ishiwara Kanji, Colonel Itagaki Seishirō, and Colonel Doihara Kenji, plotted the overthrow of Chang and the complete occupation of Manchuria by the Kwantung Army.

To begin, on 18 September 1931, the officers contrived an act of sabotage, setting off an explosion on the tracks of the SMR near the city of Mukden (Shenyang), and blamed Chinese Nationalists for the attack. Claiming self-defense, the Kwantung Army used the incident as a pretext to call on reinforcements from Korea, and within days it had completely invaded and occupied Manchuria. In the following year, the region became a nominally "independent" state—Manchukuo—but it was, in fact, little more than a puppet regime established by the Japanese under the titular rule of "Henry" Pu Yi, the so-called Last Emperor of China. The Manchurian Incident, as these events collectively came to be called, not only cinched Japan's control over Manchuria, and subsequently additional provinces in China's northeast, but also launched the nation inexorably on a trajectory toward total war.[58] Ironically, by Japan's own actions, the comprehensive mobilization of the empire's resources was becoming ever more necessary and urgent.

Japan's science and technology infrastructure would also soon be caught up in this sweep of historical events, and research institutes in the colonies would be among the first to be mobilized for the coming total war effort. By the time of the Manchurian Incident, not only had Japanese industries established a strong presence in China, but so too had institutions of science. Science had spread with Japanese imperialism, and the era of "Colonial Science" began soon after Japan gained a foothold in China's northeast following the Russo-Japanese War. The Central Chemical Laboratory (Chuo Shikensho), for example, was established in 1907 in Dairen under the auspices of the SMR, and the Shanghai Science Institute was opened in 1925.[59] The Continental Science Institute (Tairiku Kagakuin), also known as the Continental Science Academy, was established in Changchun in 1935. Hoping to surpass even the prestige and capacity of the Riken, its director, Ōkōchi Masatoshi (aka Seibin), built the Continental Science Institute based on the examples of the world-famous Kaiser Wilhelm Institutes in Germany and the Soviet Academy of Sciences in the USSR. The Continental Science Institute was created with the objective of unifying scientific research facilities in the areas of chemistry, metallurgy, mechanical engineering, and geology under a single, centralized administration, and Ōkōchi hoped the institute would serve as a model of science mobilization for the homeland. This dream was never realized, however, because of the ubiquitous sectionalism among bureaucrats in Tokyo.[60]

More than sectionalism, however, it was army factionalism that was to have dire consequences for the total war advocates in the 1930s. In 1935, the total war coalition, led by Nagata Tetsuzan, who had been promoted to the rank of major general in 1932 and appointed chief of the Military Affairs Bureau in 1934, succeeded in bringing about the establishment of two new Cabinet agencies, the Cabinet Policy Council (Naikaku Shingikai) and the Cabinet Research Bureau (Naikaku Chōsakyoku). The Cabinet Policy Council was to serve as a forum for members of the Diet, leading party politicians, and businessmen to present policy recommendations to the Cabinet, whereas the Cabinet Research Bureau, composed of technocrats from the various ministries and representatives of the military, provided a "new channel" for military participation in civil administration and was to have oversight of the most important national policies. (In May 1937 the Cabinet Research Bureau would be upgraded to the Cabinet Planning Office [Kikaku-chō] as part of a broader five-year plan for industrial mobilization; the Cabinet Policy Council disbanded with the end of the Okada Cabinet in March 1936.) Nagata's reform efforts toward national mobilization, and his lobbying with like-minded "revisionist" bureaucrats in the civil service who favored a planned economy, further alienated radical elements in the Imperial Way faction, many of whom considered such policies as inherently socialist. On 12 August 1935, Colonel Aizawa Saburō murdered Nagata over the forced resignation of a general belonging to the Imperial Way faction, the result of policies carried out under Nagata's reforms.[61]

Nagata's assassination impacted the subsequent direction of total war mobilization efforts. During Aizawa's trial, on 26 February 1936, junior-grade officers in the military, many of them influenced by the Imperial Way faction, attacked several government offices and assassinated prominent officials in an attempted coup d'état. The coup failed, however, and Aizawa was executed along with several collaborators. In the aftermath, senior officers of the Imperial Way faction were purged from the army, and Nagata's successors became increasingly influential within the civilian government. Chief among them was Ishiwara Kanji, who had played a leading role in the Manchurian Incident and was actively involved in suppressing the 26 February coup. By 1936, Ishiwara had been promoted to section chief in the Operations Division of the Army General Staff, where he continued to advocate mobilization for a national defense state. Ishiwara's goals included rationalizing every major industry, creating a central government agency for mobilization, reforming the existing cabinet system, and focusing on preparations for total war against the Soviet Union, while calming tensions in China and maintaining peaceful relations with the United States. Among these proposed measures was a call for a Science Research Bureau "to correct deficiencies of natural resources" by coordinating public and private research.[62] Ishiwara's agenda met opposition in the Army Ministry and the Diet where these measures were considered far too radical. There were few immediate results of his efforts, but among the more significant for national mobilization was the expansion of the Cabinet Research Bureau into the greater Cabinet Planning Office on 14 May 1937.[63]

As the Cabinet Planning Office set out to formulate national policy toward the goal of autarky, which was to begin with a five-year plan to expand industrial production, events in China would soon doom plans that Ishiwara and the total war advocates had only just begun to put in order. On 7 July 1937, soldiers of Japan's China Army garrison engaged Chinese Nationalist forces in a skirmish near the Marco Polo Bridge (Lukouchiao) outside Beijing.[64] The Marco Polo Bridge Incident, as it came to be known, marked the beginning of full-scale war in China and derailed Japan's drive toward autarky, which would have required at least five more years of peace to achieve.[65] After the incident, the army began to pressure the government for greater control over the domestic economy and stated its objectives as follows:

> In order to meet the needs of the defense services in wartime and to enable them to devote the whole national strength to war operations, while at the same time keeping the national life untouched, it is of paramount importance to adapt all national activities to war conditions, to place manpower, material, and all other visible and invisible resources at the disposal of the government, and thereby, to utilize them rationally and economically for war purposes. This is general mobilization . . . The

scope of general mobilization is far reaching. It includes guidance of national morale in time of war, supplementation of insufficient resources, realignment of financial organs, control and allocation of war materials, and other appertaining measures. In time of war, industries should be brought under national control with a view, first to supplying war materials, and then, to meeting the needs of the people at large. Unless industries are readily integrated into the wartime structure, it is inevitable that the nation's economy will be overwhelmed, the supply of materials will become uneven and scarce, and, as a result, the determination to fight out the war will be seriously impaired.[66]

Representatives of the army continued to press the government for a total mobilization office, and as a result, in October 1937, the Cabinet merged its Planning Office with the national Resources Bureau to form the Planning Agency (Kikaku-in). Under the authority of the prime minister, the Planning Agency became responsible for drafting and implementing policy concerning national mobilization.[67] The first order of business for the nascent Planning Agency was to push through the National General Mobilization Law. This decree, enacted on 1 April 1938, essentially gave the government absolute control over the nation's economic, industrial, scientific, and technological resources for "the realization of national defense."[68] Although the National General Mobilization Law provided monolithic powers of control over the nation, sectionalism in the government and factionalism in the military did not suddenly cease to exist, and the various branches of the government continued to find it difficult to act with uniformity of purpose. Policies concerning science and technology were no exception—a fundamental schism existed in the system where these were concerned. Specifically, the Ministry of Education traditionally had taken responsibility for matters concerning science policy, while the Ministry of Commerce and Industry dealt with affairs concerning technology policy.[69] There was at that time no single agency responsible for oversight of both science and technology policy together, which was to become a point of serious contention in the years that followed.

THE ERA OF THE NEW ORDER OF SCIENCE AND TECHNOLOGY, 1937–1942

In the 1930s, the Cabinet's Planning Agency and the Ministry of Education emerged as the two most powerful government offices involved with science policy. These organizations developed two separate and competing lines of administration, and there were frequent conflicts between them. The Cabinet established several offices under the aegis of the Planning Agency to manage science policy related affairs. In February 1938, the Science Mobilization Council (Kagaku Dōin Kyōgikai) was formed to coordinate mobilization policy among the various government ministries. Important academic and industrial leaders, such as Ōkōchi Masatoshi, director of the Riken, Honda Kotarō, president of Tohoku University and Japan's leading metallurgist, Wada Koroku, director of the Aeronautical Research Institute at Tokyo Imperial University, and Shibusawa Genji, industrialist, were named to the committee. On 15 April 1938, the Cabinet's Science Council (Kagaku Shingikai) was formed to address the problems of resource deficiencies and material shortages in industry, as securing natural resources and developing industrial capacity remained the primary focus of national mobilization policy at this time.[70]

As the war in China expanded, the Japanese also found themselves involved in border conflicts with the Soviet Union that threatened to escalate into full-scale war.[71] The demands on industry grew, and various fundamental industrial technologies were found to be lacking. In order to address this problem, among others, in May 1939, the modest Science Office operating under the Planning Agency's Industrial Bureau was upgraded to a new Science Section (Kikaku-in Kagakubu).[72] Although the Planning Agency itself retained responsibility for the general mobilization of raw materials, electric power, shipping, industrial personnel, and communications, the new Science Section was given oversight of research activities for developing the war economy.[73] In an effort to provide greater latitude to the new Science Section, on 12 December 1940, the Planning Agency established the Science Mobilization Association (Kagaku Dōin Kyōkai) as an adjunct executive body. With the prime minister as director, and the chair of the Planning Agency as vice director, the Science Mobilization Association was to assist the Science Section in affairs concerning science mobilization, the allocation of funding for research, and in the general promotion of research in various fields of science.[74] In April 1941, the Science Section was further promoted to the level of the Planning Agency's other six departments and designated "Division Seven."[75]

The Ministry of Education also established a hierarchy of agencies under its own jurisdiction to attend to science policy. Because of its general responsibility for the oversight of national education, including the universities, the Ministry of Education had actively participated in the administration of science policy related issues since its establishment in 1871. As previously noted, the Ministry of Education established the Japan National Research Council in 1920 and the JSPS in 1932 to implement various science policy agendas under its jurisdiction. On 15 August 1938, the Ministry of Education also formed the Association for the Advancement and Investigation of Science (Kagaku Shinkō Chōsakai), which was to serve as the ministry's advisory board for science policy, act as a liaison to other government offices, and deliberate on reform of the university system. The association's membership was to include representatives from various government agencies, including the Ministries of Education, Agriculture and Forestry, Commerce and Industry, Communications, and Finance, as well as the army and navy, and the vice director of the Planning Agency. It was to be chaired by the Minister of Education, who at that time was Araki Sadao, the Imperial Way hard-liner and former army general who had been forced into retirement in 1936 for having tacitly supported the failed 26 February coup d'état.[76]

In 1940, the Ministry of Education established a Science Division (Kagakubu) of its own, which was to operate under the direction of the Association for the Advancement and Investigation of Science. The Ministry of Education's Science Division was appointed oversight of university research projects as well as responsibility for managing the finances of the various research institutes under the ministry's jurisdiction. Later that year, the Ministry of Education formed the All Japan Federation of Scientists and Technicians Association (Zen-Nihon Kagaku Gijutsu Dantai Rengō), which was assigned principal responsibility for the mobilization of scientists for the war effort and was to operate under the aegis of the Ministry of Education's Science Division.[77]

With the formation of these various agencies, the Japanese government began to mobilize its science infrastructure on a nationwide scale for the very first time. The focus of science and technology mobilization at this point still remained on addressing the two problems of resource deficiency and inadequate industrial capacity, but because of the competing agendas of the Planning Agency and the Ministry of Education, mobilization efforts remained limited in scope and efficacy. Numerous agencies emerged under the aegis of these offices, resulting in a decentralized, polycratic bureaucracy. Including military research institutions, by late 1941, the organization, direction, and funding of scientific research in Japan was being carried out independently by no fewer than four separate entities—the Cabinet's Planning Agency, the Ministry of Education, and the Imperial Japanese Army and Navy. There was as yet little or no coordination of science policy or collaborative research among them.[78] As long as Japan remained at war with a technologically inferior nation like China, this fragmented science infrastructure would not necessarily become a significant factor. But when Japan attacked the United States in December 1941, it began a war with a nation already mobilizing its ample natural resources, immense industrial capacity, and powerful science and technology infrastructure. Within less than a year of war against the United States,

Japan entered into a period of crisis from which it could not emerge without a more efficient mobilization and exploitation of the empire's resources and its own science and technology infrastructure.

A few prescient technocrats had foreseen this situation and sought to avert it. Chief among them was Miyamoto Takenosuke, an engineer by training who had participated in drawing up economic development plans for northern China. In 1937, Miyamoto and a coalition of scientists, industrialists, government officials, and fellow bureaucrat-engineers spearheaded a movement to create a new science and technology system.[79] The technology produced by this new system was to be an integral component in what they envisioned as a defense-oriented state. First on their agenda was the efficient exploitation of the natural resources found in China, Manchuria, and Korea for strengthening the nation's economy and industrial base. By combining the raw materials of Japan's Asian colonies with Japanese know-how, a Greater East Asian Co-Prosperity Sphere would be created in which Japan would emerge as the leading nation in science and technology. The Asian Development Board (Kō-A-in) was established in 1938 to fulfill the purpose of resource allocation and technical mobilization within the Japanese empire.[80] In order to realize the goal of complete technical mobilization of the state, Miyamoto began to lobby for reform of the nation's science and technology infrastructure. In May 1940, he submitted the first of several petitions to the Cabinet proposing the creation of a new agency to oversee and coordinate scientific research in Japan. With the close cooperation of the triumvirate of the Planning Agency, the Asian Development Board, of which Miyamoto served as director, and the National Defense Technology Committee (Kokuho Gijutsu I-in), the movement for a New Order of Science and Technology began to gain momentum.[81]

Miyamoto's agenda paralleled in part a similar initiative by members of the Cabinet to improve the system of national science mobilization. In August 1939, the Cabinet invoked Article 25 of the National General Mobilization Law to enact the General Order for the Mobilization of Experiments and Research, which empowered the Cabinet to direct research at various agencies and institutions toward the war effort. In a Cabinet meeting on 12 April 1940, an outline proposal for wartime mobilization policy was introduced including the following objectives: improve coordination of research, exploit scientific resources and materials more efficiently, promote and direct applied research for national mobilization needs, and promote research toward self-sufficiency in selected resources, especially in chemical products and precious metals.[82] In this environment, many in the government appeared to be receptive to Miyamoto's argument for reform. But the means toward that end were another matter.

Numerous drafts and amendments to Miyamoto's proposal for the establishment of a New Order of Science and Technology were submitted to the Cabinet for review.[83] The second Cabinet of Prime Minister Konoe Fumimaro, formed in July 1940, appeared to be firmly behind the effort and in August introduced "The Prospectus on Fundamental National Policy," which included an optimistic proviso in one article proclaiming an era of "epochal promotion of science and rationalization of industry."[84] It was certainly a premature declaration, for the movement for systemic reform was about to encounter its first wave of resistance. In September 1940, the "Outline for the Establishment of a New Order of Science and Technology" was formally submitted to the Cabinet. Among the proposals listed in the document, the most controversial was the plan to establish a Technology Agency, a national, centralized administrative board that would concentrate authority over science and technology policy in a single office. When the contents of the proposal were made public, bureaucrats in the various government ministries, reluctant to relinquish jurisdiction over their own organizations, strongly opposed the agenda of consolidation and centralized control over the nation's research institutions. Many university scientists also opposed the plan, fearing the potential loss of academic freedom of research. Industrialists were also suspicious and complained that such a powerful agency might deny private enterprise any voice in technology policy matters and refuse them certain protections under existing patent laws.[85]

The greatest opposition came, perhaps predictably, from bureaucrats in the Ministry of Education and the Ministry of Commerce and Industry, who were territorial and refused to relinquish power over their own institutions to the proposed Technology Agency. There was simply no precedent for a single, central authority to manage science and technology policy together. But advocates of the Technology Agency fired back, leveling particularly harsh comments at scientists in academia by labeling their "freedom of research" defense as "feudalistic" thinking and their resistance to greater supervision as nothing less than an excuse for personal sloth.[86] The agenda to create a higher-defense nation through a New Order of Science and Technology had thus precipitated a "crisis" of science policy.[87]

In the meantime, the Technology Agency's parent organization, the Planning Agency, experienced a crisis of its own. Members of the business community and the Japan Economic Federation became increasingly frustrated with the Planning Agency over economic policies concerning industrial control associations, price controls, and conflicting regulations. They were joined in their dislike of the Planning Agency by the military, whose leaders grew angry over what they perceived as poor management of resources by the agency as well as its plans for materials allocation in the 1941 fiscal year budget, which projected shortfalls of critical materials, such as steel, for both services. It also did not help that Minister of Commerce and Industry, Kobayashi Ichizō, harbored considerable ill will toward the president of the Planning Agency, Hoshino Naoki. In what became known as the Planning Board Incident, on 17 April 1941, members of the Planning Agency were arrested on charges of "communist activity." Hoshino remained free but resigned his position under duress. His nemesis, Kobayashi, who likely had a hand in orchestrating the incident, also resigned. Their vacated positions were subsequently filled by military men, thus further deepening military control over key civilian, government institutions.[88]

In the wake of the Planning Board Incident, after having considered the comprehensive international survey of science and technology policies conducted by the Planning Agency's Science Division, and after significant revision of the earlier proposals, on 27 May 1941, the Cabinet finally ratified the "Outline for the Establishment of a New Order of Science and Technology."[89] The original agenda for the New Order was considerably altered. Although the "Outline" provided for the creation of the Technology Agency (Gijutsu-in), it was to be a significantly less powerful administrative agency for science and technology policy than originally proposed. The broader agenda for the Technology Agency, specifically endowing it with wide-ranging authority over the nation's science and technology research institutions, was scrapped because of continued resistance from the various government ministries, corporations, and scientists in academia. The "Outline" established a Science and Technology Council (Kagaku Gijutsu Shingikai) to serve as an advisory board for the new Technology Agency.[90] The Science and Technology Council was to act as a standing committee responsible for advising the representatives of various government ministries and the military on matters of science policy, a role not unlike that which the NDRC assumed upon the creation of the OSRD in the United States. The council consisted of experts from various "deliberative societies" (*shingikai*), including the Cabinet's Science Deliberative Society, the Ministry of Education's Aeronautical Deliberative Society, and the Invention Promotion Committee, all essentially government-sponsored science-policy committees working separately under the Cabinet, the Ministry of Education, and the government Patent Office.[91]

The Outline for the Establishment of a New Order of Science and Technology was officially enacted from 1 September 1941, but debate over the range of the Technology Agency's authority continued over the next several months. Adding to the difficulty was the army's stubborn demand that the Technology Agency focus primarily on promoting development of aeronautical technology. With this agenda firmly in mind, the army strong-armed the inauguration of the Technology Agency without gaining the consensus of bureaucrats in the Ministry of Education and the Ministry of Industry and Commerce.[92] After a few more months of debate, the office of the Technology Agency finally opened on 31 January 1942, with Inoue Tadashirō, former director of the Industry Management Committee (Kōseikai) named as president. The Technology Agency subsumed the Science Divisions of both the Planning Agency and the Ministry of Education. It operated on an annual budget of about ¥1 million (approximately $250,000), which was to be used to support research at public and private institutions.[93] Ideally, the Technology Agency was to coordinate and support research from conception through development, whereupon the Ministry of Munitions would take over responsibility for production.[94] But even before the Technology Agency officially opened, it was relegated to being little more than an oversight board for army aeronautical development, and it could expect little in the way of cooperation from government ministries, industry, or academia.[95] In the meantime, Miyamoto Takenosuke, Japan's leading technocrat and former director of the Asian Development Board, died in 1941 without ever seeing his vision of mobilization under the Technology Agency come to fruition.[96]

THE CRISIS YEARS, 1942–1945

The defeat of the Imperial Japanese Navy in the Battle of Midway in June 1942 signaled that the tide of war had begun to turn against Japan, and the military services grew anxious for new "decisive" weapons to stop the advance of Allied forces in the Pacific. Science and technology mobilization had entered a crisis phase. As one indication of the sense of urgency, representatives of the army and navy met on 13 June 1942 to discuss plans for the formation of a joint committee on technology, resulting in the creation of the Army-Navy Technology Committee (Riku-Kaigun Gijutsu Iinkai).[97] At the first plenary session of the joint committee, held on 22 July 1942, it was determined that the committee would meet biannually to deliberate on reports provided by the committee's seven subcommittees, each charged with the responsibility for conducting research on various weapons ranging from artillery, ammunition, explosives, chemical weapons, observation technology, communications and electronics, and metals.[98] Research in aeronautics was not included because this field remained under the purview of two previously existing organizations, the Cooperative Committee of the Army-Navy Aeronautics Department (Riku-Kaigun Kōkū Honbu Kyōchō Iinkai), established in September 1936 to facilitate interservice cooperation in resource allocation and manufacturing in the military aviation industry, and its affiliated council, the Army-Navy Aeronautics Committee (Riku-Kaigun Kōkū Iinkai), which had been formed in January 1941 to facilitate interservice deliberations on policy concerning the strengthening of the aviation industry for the war effort.[99]

Meanwhile, the military also pressured the government to help mobilize science and technology resources more efficiently. As a result, in August and October of 1943, the Cabinet issued two new directives, the "Outline of Urgent Measures for Scientific Research" and the "Comprehensive Policy for the Mobilization of Science and Technology." These were to promote research for the war effort at the national universities and encourage greater coordination of science-technology research nationwide.[100] In November 1943, the Cabinet formed the Research Mobilization Committee (Kenkyū Dōin Kaigi) under the aegis of the Technology Agency's Science and Technology Council to ensure that these measures would be carried out. The prime minister, who at this time was none other than General Tōjō Hideki, was to serve as chair of the committee with the president of the Technology Agency serving as vice chair.[101] Under such leadership, this committee, in theory, should have wielded considerable influence over science and technology mobilization. But by the autumn of 1944, however, it was becoming increasingly apparent that neither the Technology Agency nor the Research Mobilization Committee was proving particularly effective.

Nor were the army and navy efforts at collaboration bearing much fruit. Where the military aviation industry was concerned, there was too much overlap between the functions of the Cooperative Committee of the Army-Navy Aeronautics Department and its affiliated policy oversight agency, the Army-Navy Aeronautics Committee. To rationalize their functions and to strengthen collaboration in weapons research in particular, on 9 August 1943, the Army-Navy Aeronautical Technology Committee (Riku-Kaigun Kōkū Gijutsu Iinkai) was established, and the Cooperative Committee of the Army-Navy Aeronautics Department was disbanded.[102] In addition, in order to facilitate interservice collaboration in other key areas of research, in August 1943, the Army-Navy Radio Wave Technology Committee (Riku-Kaigun Denpa Gijutsu Iinkai) was established to accelerate development of electronic weapons that used radio-wave technologies, and the Army-Navy Fuel Technology Committee (Riku-Kaigun Nenryō Gijutsu Iinkai) was created for the cooperative development of new and alternative fuels.[103]

In the months that followed, however, such interservice consultative committees proved insufficient for the task at hand. In what was to become a last-ditch effort to better enforce collaboration between the military services in scientific research more broadly, on 5 September 1944, the ministers of the army and navy agreed to form yet another joint working group, the Army-Navy Technology Enforcement Committee (Riku-Kaigun Gijutsu Unyō Iinkai).[104] This committee superseded the aforementioned committees and was intended to be more comprehensive in scope than its predecessors. It was not only supposed to facilitate cooperation between the military services, but also to serve as a liaison between the military and civilian research institutions, and to oversee collaborative research projects among the military services, universities, and industry. The committee included four representatives from the Ministry of the Army and the Ministry of the Navy each, as well as seven representatives from academia.[105]

At the first meeting of the committee, held in December 1944, the military services together submitted nearly a hundred proposals for research projects. Yagi Hidetsugu, who had replaced Inoue Tadashirō as president of the Technology Agency in November 1944, and who was then also serving as a founding member of the new committee, thought this to be far too many requests to consider in the first meeting. Yagi asked the military services to submit a revised list the following month. There were few cuts in the amended list, however, and the committee was forced to accept them, even though, according to Yagi, many of the proposals were "trivial."[106] Coordination of research was proving difficult.

The organizational crisis came to a head in the spring of 1945. During a session of the Diet in March 1945, members of Japan's Parliament severely criticized Yagi as head of the Technology Agency for failing to produce the "decisive" weapons desired by the military. The navy had resorted to suicide tactics to defend its positions throughout the Pacific, and Yagi boldly expressed his opinion that such measures could not win the war. He argued that precious resources should not be wasted on the production of suicide weapons but should be dedicated to the development of innovative technologies, such as the German V-1 and V-2 rockets, instead. Under severe pressure from members of the Diet and the military, by May 1945, Yagi was forced to resign as president of the Technology Agency.[107]

Lieutenant General Tada Reikichi, former director of the Army Institute of Scientific Research, succeeded Yagi as president and immediately went on the offensive against the critics of the Technology Agency. He argued that the primary reason no new decisive weapons had been developed was because of the friction that existed between the Technology Agency and other government agencies charged with the oversight of scientific research. Tada also stated that "the agency had tended to fritter away its energies looking after a multitude of small demands made upon it by the army and navy authorities, instead of concentrating on the one task of thinking up a powerful new weapon."[108] The Technology Agency was also beset with many other difficulties. Because it was forced to compete with the military and various civilian agencies for resources, it constantly suffered from material shortages. Researchers funded by the Technology Agency often had to improvise with substitute materials.[109] Because the Technology Agency had been stripped of its general powers of oversight for national science policy and mobilization from the beginning, as a mere tool of the army, it was ultimately unable to impose cooperation on any of the military or civilian organizations.

THE FAILURE OF WARTIME MOBILIZATION

Although numerous attempts were made to reform the system and to facilitate greater cooperation among the various government, military, and academic institutions, these were largely unsuccessful. How can this failure be explained? In a statement given to U.S. intelligence officers after the war, Watanabe Satoshi, a prominent Japanese scientist, provided several explanations why Japan had lost the scientific war. Beyond the problem of resource deficiencies, Watanabe cited the government's failure to establish a comprehensive and effective science policy, which he attributed largely to the inability to overcome deeply entrenched institutional rivalries, the ambivalent relationship between the military and civilian scientists, and the continuation of "feudalistic" attitudes among scientists at the universities.[110]

According to Watanabe, a principal reason the government was unable to implement a comprehensive science and technology mobilization policy was the persistent lack of cooperation at all levels of the civilian bureaucracy as well as the obstinate attitude of the military services.[111] Sectionalism often poisoned relations among the various government ministries, and between the military and civilian institutions, wherein instances of competition for resources and battles over jurisdiction in the bureaucracy ranged from the trivial to the essential. Factionalism within the army itself obstructed early plans for modernization, and interservice rivalry between the army and navy continued throughout the war, despite some modest efforts to collaborate. Yagi Hidetsugu, former director of the Technology Agency, stated after the war, "a general and an admiral would rather lose the war than shake hands."[112]

Each service sought self-sufficiency in research and development capabilities and established several institutions of its own. The army ran no less than twenty-one institutes, including ten ground forces facilities, eight air force institutes, a separate facility for radar development (the Tama Army Technical

Institute), a fuels laboratory, and the Army Weapons Administrative Department (Appendix, Tables A2 and A3). The navy also had several facilities for research and development, the most important of which was the Navy Technical Research Institute in Meguro, Tokyo, which fell under the administrative purview of the Navy Department of Ships (Kaigun Kansei Honbu)[113] (Appendix, Table A4). But there was ultimately little significant collaboration between the laboratories of the army and navy, despite even such initiatives as the formation of the Army-Navy Technology Enforcement Committee in September 1944. A general policy of the military services throughout the war was to jealously guard the technology developed in their own laboratories.

Not only was there minimal collaboration between the two services, but cooperation within each service was also frequently lacking. It was not uncommon for researchers in one laboratory to be assigned development of a component for equipment being produced in another laboratory without complete knowledge of the design of the end product or its purpose.[114] Compartmentalization was a prominent feature of the Manhattan Project in the United States, where security was a primary concern; however, it made little sense for less ambitious research projects in wartime Japan, where there were fewer scientists and far fewer resources. To a lesser degree, the same situation existed when the military arranged R&D contracts with private enterprises. Scientists and technicians in uniform were isolated from their corporate counterparts, and in many instances were even prohibited from exchanging ideas and information with them. Manufacturers often were denied feedback regarding even the technical performance of their products in the field. Moreover, if a manufacturer happened to be assigned a development project by both military services, no matter how similar the production design, in many cases, the two projects were kept entirely secret from one other.[115]

Less commonly known than the interservice rivalry, but perhaps equally debilitating to science mobilization, was sectionalism in the public sphere.[116] The rivalry between the Cabinet's Planning Agency and the Ministry of Education in particular had a seriously deleterious impact on science and technology policy, especially where mobilization was concerned. Although the Technology Agency was originally intended to help overcome such obstacles by serving as a supreme administrative body for science policy and mobilization, in the end, it had no ability to enforce policy or to mandate research.[117] The failure to establish an agency with such influence may be explained, in part, by considering the hierarchy of government offices and their relationship to the military and the national research system during the war. In the case of the Technology Agency, the army asserted its authority from the agency's inception, and it was never able to act independently of the army's agenda. In its charter, the president of the Technology Agency was made accountable to the Cabinet and the prime minister, who, during much of the war, was Tōjō Hideki, himself a high-ranking army officer. The president of the Technology Agency had no authority over the military services and no real influence on the prime minister.[118] Moreover, some of the top brass in the military resented the agency and considered it a meddler in their "private affairs." As a result, the Technology Agency was not taken fully into the confidence of the military in new weapons research, which rendered the office ineffective in coordinating any such programs.[119] No matter how well intended the Technology Agency might have been as originally conceived by Miyamoto and other technocrats, it was effectively thwarted by the prejudices and agendas of the military services.[120]

Moreover, the Technology Agency also proved weak vis-à-vis other government offices. Before the formation of the Technology Agency, two separate and competing lines of authority over science policy existed in the public sector—one under the Cabinet's Planning Agency, and the other under the Ministry of Education. By 1944, there were several competing agencies within these two hierarchies. On the one hand were the organizations under the aegis of the Cabinet's Planning Agency, including the Science Council, the Science Mobilization Council, the Science Mobilization Association, and, until 1942, the Science Division, as well as the Technology Agency, the Technology Agency's Science and Technology Council, and the Research Mobilization Committee. On the other hand were the institutions operating under the authority of the Ministry of Education, including the Japan National Research Council, Japan Society for the Promotion of Science, the Association for the Advancement and Investigation of Science, the All Japan Federation of Scientists and Technicians Association, and, until 1942, the Ministry of Education's Science Division[121] (Appendix, Table A5).

This plethora of committees, divisions, societies, and associations reflected the polycratic nature of Japan's civil administration where interest groups vied for influence in a highly decentralized bureaucracy. Although this system may have suited Japan well enough in peacetime, during the war it proved to be a significant impediment to science mobilization. The conflict that emerged between the Technology Agency and the Ministry of Education is a prime example. Although the Technology Agency supported research at both public and private institutions, the Ministry of Education, as a matter of policy and precedent, considered all of the imperial universities to fall within its own jurisdiction. Significant tension developed between the two agencies over where the lines of authority were to be drawn, making cooperation and unity of action between them in science policy matters quite difficult to achieve.[122] And then there was the Ministry of Commerce and Industry, which traditionally had managed affairs of technology policy and proved unwilling to give up that role.

The nation's top science policy administrators proved unable to overcome such sectionalism. During an interview conducted with U.S. army intelligence officers after the war, Nagaoka Hantarō, the doyen of the Japanese physics community and then chair of the JSPS Advisory Council, revealed the predominant state of mind among the bureaucrats. When asked whether he thought it would have been more efficient for the funding of research undertaken separately by the Technology Agency, the Japan National Research Council, and the JSPS to have been combined and managed under a single administration, Nagaoka replied that it would not. Such an agency, he argued, would have been too large for any single group to manage effectively.[123]

Other factors explaining the ineffectual mobilization of science in wartime Japan include the general weapons development policy of the military services and their condescending attitude toward civilian scientists. In most cases, the military determined what they needed and attempted to develop technologies in their own laboratories without civilian participation, if possible. If their own technicians proved insufficient for the task, the military services would turn to the civilian sector and present their demands to scientists in industry or at the universities.[124] Japan had no analog to the NDRC/OSRD by which scientists could be formally introduced to military brass and offer assistance. Also, instead of offering contracts for research to universities and research institutes as a whole, as a general practice, the military largely delegated research projects to individual scientists. This policy stood in stark contrast to that of the United States, where the OSRD contracted with numerous universities, such as MIT, the University of California, and Columbia.[125] For the most part, the military assigned civilian scientists narrowly defined research problems, and it was not uncommon for such assignments to be poorly matched to the particular talents or training of a given scientist.[126] Civilian scientists were also given research topics with little or no immediate military value, such as "ions in the air" and "fog in Hokkaido." Occasionally they were assigned more important work, such as improving the food supply or designing superlarge aircraft, but as often as not, such work was equally suitable for military technical officers or technicians in private industry.[127] Relatively few university scientists and engineers actually joined the staffs of military laboratories as full-time employees, and of those tapped for military research, most served only as occasional consultants. The majority of civilian scientists continued their normal teaching and research duties throughout the war.[128]

Why did the military not make better use of civilian scientists? One explanation is that many university scientists had lived abroad in the United States and Europe, and therefore, their loyalty to the emperor and nation was suspect in the minds of some of the more xenophobic military leaders.[129] According to Yagi Hidetsugu, the military even treated civilian scientists "as if they were foreigners."[130] Some of the scientists stated after the war that they felt they were viewed "almost as enemies" by the military.[131] But many military leaders, such as Admiral Isoroku Yamamoto, had also studied abroad, and so this explanation alone is insufficient to explain the attitude of distrust the military had toward civilian scientists. To an extent, however, the cause of this suspicion was political. Some university professors were known to espouse liberal—even socialist—political views, which were antithetical to the ideology of State Shinto and the emperor system. One of the more famous of the ideologically left scientists was Taketani Mitsuo. Taketani advocated a Marxist approach to theoretical physics and was involved in the publication of *Sekai bunka* (World Culture), a journal critical of Japanese imperialism in Asia. For this reason, Taketani was imprisoned from September 1937 to April 1939.[132]

Another explanation may be that the scientists in uniform were resentful of their civilian counterparts. The military, in general, did not attract the best and brightest of the university graduates and had relatively few scientists with graduate-level training of their own. Students of exceptional ability tended to remain in higher education when possible and pursued academic careers. For the most part, military laboratories were staffed with what might be considered second-class scientists throughout the war. (There were notable exceptions, such as navy Captain Itō Yōji, as will be seen in subsequent chapters.) Another idiosyncrasy of the military's science infrastructure was the common custom of promoting senior researchers to administrative positions after only a few years, thus leaving the direction of the actual technical work of the laboratories to less experienced men.[133] This policy explains why junior-grade officers were sometimes left in charge of advanced research projects—a task for which they were usually not well qualified. In such cases, military technical officers may have been reluctant to enlist the aid of better-trained, and hence more qualified, civilian scientists.

Whatever the case may be, there was no across-the-board mobilization of civilian scientists for the war effort in Japan, and comparatively few university professors and researchers ever became directly involved in scientific research for the military. By one estimate, only about 10 percent of university professors and academics in Japan were mobilized for war research.[134] Furthermore, unlike their counterparts in the United States, Japanese scientists largely remained at the periphery of science policy formation, which predominantly remained the purview of bureaucrats in the government. What was perhaps the most important sector of Japan's pool of scientific talent—university scientists—thus went largely untapped throughout the entire war.

But according to Watanabe, the universities also were not without fault. After the war, some scientists strongly criticized the university research system, noting the "feudal" pattern of behavior in the university laboratories. Department chairs were described as having disproportionate discretion in determining funding for research projects, and a system of award based on merit alone was absent in all but a few institutions. Favoritism based on familial ties and political connections was still prevalent. In many university laboratories, staff meetings proved to be little more than an exercise in building group consensus with minimal argumentation over methodology or research results. Some scientists considered such practices to be stifling to the scientific process, wherein the dynamic of argumentation is a central component.[135]

CONCLUSION

Thus, a picture emerges wherein conflict plagued the Japanese system from the macro level of government organization to the micro level of the individual scientist in the laboratory, whether military or civilian. Japan was unable to mobilize its science and technology infrastructure to its full capacity during World War II largely as a result of the polycratic nature of the national government and the ubiquitous interservice rivalry. The government proved ineffective in implementing policies to coordinate scientific research across institutional boundaries, including those of the military, government, and academia, and was powerless to overcome the sectionalism in these sectors. Not only were governmental institutions such as the Technology Agency and the Ministry of Education unable to coordinate policy objectives, but they remained in direct competition with one another for resources and squabbled over matters of jurisdiction throughout much of the war. The problem of science mobilization was evident to policy makers. As stated in the summary report of the U.S. scientific intelligence survey conducted under Karl Compton after the war, "The number of these organizations and the frequency with which they were changed bears some evidence of hysteria as well as of comprehension that the efforts of the scientists were not being well directed."[136]

Sectionalism obstructed coordination of policy objectives, while interservice rivalry prevented significant technical cooperation between the army and navy until late in the war. Although a previous effort was made to coordinate research in aeronautics, it was not until the autumn of 1944 with the formation of the Army-Navy Technology Enforcement Committee that any significant attempt was made to pool the scientific and technological resources of the military services more broadly. Although joint research was initiated on a few projects, such as nuclear weapons and the rocket-propelled intercept aircraft Shūsui, such efforts were plagued by trivial conflicts instigated by both services. In the end, army-navy cooperation in scientific research contributed nothing to the war effort as it proved to be far too little, and came much too late.[137]

Although comparatively far fewer than in the United States and Germany, there were in Japan numerous scientists who potentially could have made significant contributions to the war effort if properly employed. The U.S. intelligence officers who investigated wartime scientific research in Japan were clearly impressed with the nation's leading scientists, stating that "the top men, particularly in university scientific circles and in industry, are really first-class."[138] But the military did not generally trust civilian scientists and did not often take them into confidence on weapons development projects unless their own technicians first proved unqualified for the task at hand. In sum, Japan failed to fully mobilize its science and technology resources for the war effort because the government proved unable to unite the various competing agencies under a central administrative structure, and the collective resources of these agencies could not be brought to bear on critical science policy objectives. Sectionalism in the civil bureaucracy, and interservice rivalry in the military, contributed to the defeat of the technocratic vision of a unified administrative system under the central authority of the Technology Agency. The impact of this policy failure on the development of advanced weaponry, including the atomic bomb, radar, guided missiles and jet aircraft, and chemical and biological weapons, is the subject of the chapters that follow.

2
NUCLEAR ENERGY AND THE ATOMIC BOMB

The discovery of nuclear fission in 1938 stirred great hopes and fears in the world scientific community. Although many scientists looked optimistically toward a new age powered by nuclear energy, others voiced serious concern about unleashing the destructive potential of the atom. As the shadow of war spread across Europe in 1939, scientists in the United States grew anxious, fearing that their counterparts in Nazi Germany were already hard at work creating a new atomic superweapon. Alarmed by the potential threat of Hitler acquiring such a device, the United States and Great Britain combined their research efforts to form the Manhattan Project, an enormous $2 billion program to develop the world's first nuclear weapons.

No one had such fears about Japan. In his memoir, *Now It Can Be Told*, General Leslie Groves, the military director of the Manhattan Project, stated that the Allies did not make any appreciable effort to gather information on Japanese nuclear research during the war. According to Groves, scientists at the University of California at Berkeley who had helped train some of Japan's younger physicists and knew them personally, concluded that Japan did not possess the resources, the industrial capacity, or the large number of qualified scientists needed to succeed in such an endeavor.[1] They proved to be right. U.S. Army Intelligence (G-2) investigations conducted after the war confirmed that the Japanese government had not created a Manhattan Project of its own. G-2 discovered that although both the Japanese army and navy had undertaken nuclear research, they did so independently and on a comparatively small scale. There was no extensive organization created to support nuclear research, and no single government agency was established for the oversight of nuclear weapons development such as there had been in the United States with the Manhattan Project under the Office of Scientific Research and Development.[2]

Among the principal belligerents, only the United States committed fully to the development of nuclear weapons, securing the necessary resources and the cooperation of the private, public, and military sectors to achieve its objective. In stark contrast, Japan's efforts failed not only because of the inability to procure enough uranium and insufficient industrial capacity, but also because the government did not commit itself to creating the infrastructure necessary for such a massive enterprise. How, then, did the Japanese mobilize for nuclear weapons development, how far did they get in the research, and how did national science policy affect the outcome?

INTERNATIONAL REACTION TO THE DISCOVERY OF NUCLEAR FISSION

In 1933, Ernest Rutherford, director of the Cavendish Laboratory at Cambridge University, proclaimed at the annual meeting of the British Association for the Advancement of Science, "Any one who says that with the means at present at our disposal and with our present knowledge we can utilize atomic energy is talking moonshine."[3] Rutherford was annoyed by what he considered wild speculation in the press over recent developments in nuclear physics. Ironically, Rutherford himself was partly to blame: he had been the first to demonstrate nuclear disintegration, when in 1919 he bombarded nitrogen atoms with alpha particles. Subsequent experiments by Rutherford and James Chadwick at the Cavendish led to the discovery of the neutron in 1932. The neutron was the long-sought magic bullet, which held the potential for splitting atomic nuclei. (Having no electrical charge of its own, the neutron could strike electrically charged atomic nuclei without being repelled.) Together with the development of the Cockcroft-Walton particle accelerator, named for its inventors John Cockcroft and Ernest T. S. Walton, unleashing the power of the atom seemed ever closer.[4]

Despite Rutherford's pessimism, significant advances toward unleashing the power of the atom were soon to come. After the discovery of artificial radioactivity by Frédéric and Irène Joliot-Curie in Paris in 1934, Enrico Fermi, Italy's foremost physicist, began a series of experiments using neutrons to bombard elements in the periodic table. Beginning with the lightest elements, Fermi irradiated water to test hydrogen and oxygen simultaneously. Then came lithium, beryllium, boron, carbon, iron, copper, silver, barium, magnesium, and lanthanum, among others, until at last he came to uranium. Through these experiments, Fermi discovered that bombarding uranium with neutrons appeared to produce a new, transuranic element. But definitive proof was still needed. Scientists in the United States and Europe attempted to reproduce Fermi's results by bombarding uranium with neutrons. Two of Fermi's Italian colleagues, Emilio Segrè and Edoardo Amaldi, traveled to the Cavendish Laboratory to collaborate with physicists under Rutherford. Irène Curie and Paul Savitch led experiments in France, while radiochemists Otto Hahn and Fritz Strassmann, in collaboration with Lise Meitner, led the research in Germany. In the United States, physicists flooded the fledgling scientific periodical, *Physical Review,* with reports of their own research.[5]

In Japan, physicists stayed abreast of these developments in nuclear research by reading western periodicals and maintaining correspondence with colleagues abroad. Technical officers in the Japanese navy also took a keen interest in the matter. Curious as to whether Fermi's research might lead to the development of a new type of superweapon, in 1934, the navy sponsored a modest investigation to find out. Although the conclusion of the study was negative, the concerned technical officers attempted to stay informed of any major developments in the field. To help them do so, in 1937, they invited Osaka Imperial University's Professor of Physics, Asada Tsunesaburō, to give a series of lectures on physics and various scientific subjects. Asada lectured bimonthly at the Navy Technical Research Institute (Kaigun Gijutsu Kenkyūjo) in Tokyo and at the Navy Aeronautics Laboratory (Kaigun Kōkūki Shikensho) in Yokosuka until the outbreak of the war. His lectures focused on the most recent research published in foreign scientific periodicals, including the new phenomenon discovered by Hahn and Strassmann involving the release of energy from uranium bombarded with neutrons.[6]

In December 1938, Otto Hahn and Fritz Strassmann, working together at the Kaiser Wilhelm Institute for Chemistry in Dahlem, Germany, observed an intriguing result after bombarding uranium with slow neutrons. With some degree of uncertainty, they concluded they had produced barium. Puzzled by the results of the experiments, Hahn wrote his longtime friend and scientific collaborator of nearly thirty years, Lise Meitner, for confirmation. The Nazi persecution of Jews in Germany and Austria had forced Meitner into exile earlier in the year. Now in Sweden, she corresponded with Hahn over the Christmas holiday and took up the subject of Hahn's experiment with her nephew, Otto Frisch.[7]

A very capable physicist himself, Frisch held a position at the Institute of Theoretical Physics in Denmark, where he worked under the eminent Danish physicist, Niels Bohr. Meitner and Frisch interpreted the hazy Hahn-Strassmann conclusion as a real splitting of uranium nuclei and roughly calculated the energy released. After the Christmas holiday, Frisch returned to Denmark and explained the situation to Bohr. Meitner, Frisch, and Bohr all agreed that Hahn and Strassmann had accomplished fission of a uranium atom, and Frisch sought to confirm by physical tests the chemical results from Germany. On 6 January 1939, Hahn and Strassmann published the results of their research, but they refrained from declaring that they had discovered fission. But Meitner, Frisch, and Bohr were more certain. In January 1939, Bohr arrived in the United States to take up temporary residence at the Institute for Advanced Study in Princeton. At the Washington Conference on Theoretical Physics held in late January 1939, Bohr announced the successful fission of the uranium nucleus by Hahn and Strassmann. Bohr's announcement had a profound and immediate impact. Physicists and chemists the world over set out to replicate Hahn and Strassmann's experiment. By the end of 1939, there were nearly one hundred papers published on the subject.[8]

Harnessing the power of the atom no longer seemed so much moonshine, as Rutherford had once proclaimed. With the discovery of a new phenomenon of nature, Rutherford's statement "with the means at present at our disposal" had been superseded. Although the media were quick to sensationalize the discovery, there were also a few physicists who recognized the darker potential of nuclear fission. Among them was Leo Szilard, a Jewish émigré who had fled Germany in 1933. Szilard conceived of the possibility of a chain reaction while in England in the early 1930s. He took out several patents on the subject, and to keep them secret, he turned them over to the British Admiralty.[9] In December 1937, with rumors of war stirring on the Continent, Szilard left England for the United States. Two years later, in January 1939, he met up with Enrico Fermi, who had just arrived in New York after fleeing Italy. Fermi, who had been awarded the Nobel Prize in physics the previous year, used the award money to escape persecution with his Jewish wife and took a temporary teaching appointment at Columbia University.[10]

When Fermi and Szilard discussed the recently announced news of Hahn and Strassmann's results, they disagreed over the implications. Szilard worried that the Nazis would try to exploit the discovery to develop a new weapon, but Fermi argued that any such weapon based on nuclear fission must be at least twenty-five to fifty years in the future. Szilard eventually managed to convince Fermi otherwise.[11] With a newfound sense of urgency, Fermi arranged to meet with representatives of the U.S. Department of the Navy and the Naval Research Laboratory (NRL) on 17 March 1939 to discuss military applications of a controlled nuclear chain reaction. The NRL scientists recognized the potential for developing new submarine engines, while the navy representatives expressed interest in creating a new explosive device. Three days after meeting with Fermi, the NRL provided the modest sum of $1,500 to begin research.[12]

In April 1939, an article in the British scientific journal *Nature* announced that Frédéric Joliot, Hans von Halban, and Lew Kowarski, working in France, had observed 3.5 neutrons released per fission.[13] Scientists in Germany, as elsewhere, were quick to react to this news. On 24 April 1939, Professor Paul Harteck, a physical chemist, and his assistant, Wilhelm Groth, penned a letter to the German War Office outlining recent research in nuclear physics and emphasizing the potential of uranium fission for use in a weapon. But Harteck's letter proceeded slowly through the German bureaucracy, until August 1939, when it reached the desk of Kurt Diebner in the German army's Ordnance Department. A nuclear physicist himself, Diebner clearly understood Harteck's letter, but he lacked sufficient influence to act on his own. Diebner passed the letter on to Professor Hans Geiger, coinventor of the Geiger-Müller counter, who then encouraged the War Office to proceed with research in nuclear fission. As a result of Geiger's prodding, a laboratory was established at Gottow within a section of the army's rocket-projectiles and explosives research division at Kummersdorf outside Berlin. The Army Ordnance Department subsequently established an independent nuclear research office, of which Diebner was put in charge.[14]

Harteck was not the only German scientist who recognized the military potential of nuclear fission. Nikolaus Riehl, an industrial physicist and head of a research department at the Auer Company, also brought the idea of nuclear power to the attention of the army. Riehl even offered the services of the Auer Company for uranium production, but the army was apparently not interested in his offer at the time. Meanwhile, physicists Wilhelm Hanle and his superior at Göttingen University, Georg Joos, were busy considering the employment of uranium fission in an energy-producing reactor, which they referred to as a "uranium burner," and together informed the Reich Ministry of Culture of their research. The Ministry of Culture forwarded their letter to the Ministry of Education, which promptly assigned Professor Abraham Esau, then president of the Reich Bureau of Standards and head of the physics section of the Education Ministry's Reich Research Council, to organize a conference on the subject. The organizational meeting of this "uranium club" was held in Berlin on 29 April 1939, just days after Harteck had written his letter to the War Office.[15] The meeting led to a consensus on a few key issues. First, radium was to be supplied from the Joachimsthal mines in Czechoslovakia to facilitate further research. Second, a ban on the export of uranium from Germany was to be put into effect. And finally, a formal atomic research program was to be established.[16]

Scientists in the Soviet Union had learned of the discovery of nuclear fission through journals imported from the West and reacted to the news with the same excitement and interest as their peers throughout the world. The Soviets were well positioned to pursue this line of research at the time. In the early 1930s, physicists Georgi Gamov, Piotr S. Kapitsa, and Kirill Sinelnikov, all of whom had studied at the Cavendish, began to establish research centers in the Soviet Union, including the Ukranian Physico-Technical Institute in Kharkov. The Leningrad Physico-Technical Institute, under the direction of Abram F. Ioffe, and its Department of Nuclear Physics, led by Igor Kurchatov, in particular, emerged as a major center for physics research in the Soviet Union. By the time the Joliot team published their results in April 1939, physicists Georgii Flerov and Lev Rusinov had independently reached a similar conclusion as their counterparts in France concerning the number of neutrons emitted per fission. Soviet scientists were keeping pace with their peers in Europe and the United States, but most took a long-term view toward fission research and did not see the exploitation of atomic energy as a possibility in the near future.[17]

Back in the United States, Leo Szilard continued to work behind the scenes to gain further government support of nuclear fission research. On 16 July 1939, Szilard met with world-famous physicist, Albert Einstein, and informed him of the possibility of a chain reaction from nuclear fission. Szilard's immediate objective was to get Einstein to warn the Belgians, particularly the queen of Belgium, to whom he had access, of the possible danger posed by Nazi Germany acquiring uranium from the Belgian Congo. Einstein agreed to contact the Belgian Cabinet. On the advice of fellow physicist, Eugene Wigner, however, Szilard and Einstein determined that it would be prudent to inform the U.S. State Department of their intentions first. Szilard drafted a letter to President Roosevelt, which he persuaded Alexander Sachs, an economic consultant to the president, to deliver.[18] But the letter did not immediately reach the president, as Sachs had to wait for a lull in Roosevelt's schedule to present it. The outbreak of the war in September 1939 delayed the presentation of the letter even further. And so it was that by the start of World War II in Europe, of all the principal belligerents, only Germany had an office devoted exclusively to research on the military applications of nuclear energy.[19]

Although Germany had taken the lead, other nations were not far behind. In the United States, Szilard's letter was soon to reach the president, which would be the first tangible step toward forming the Manhattan Project. In England, research in nuclear fission was underway at the Cavendish Laboratory, as well as in Birmingham under Mark Oliphant, Rudolf Peierls, and Otto Frisch. In France, Frédéric Joliot led his nation in nuclear research. And in the Soviet Union, Igor Kurchatov had begun to investigate neutron-uranium reactions.[20] For its part, the Japanese military kept informed of international developments in nuclear fission research through reading foreign science journals, the responsibility for which was delegated mostly to lower-ranking technical officers.[21]

ORGANIZATION OF NUCLEAR WEAPONS R&D IN WORLD WAR II

On 11 October 1939, Alexander Sachs delivered the Szilard-Einstein letter to President Roosevelt. The letter strongly urged a liaison between the government and the nation's scientists to study the potential of nuclear fission, and to this Sachs added a memorandum of his own emphasizing the potential threat of German research, the danger of the German seizure of Belgian uranium, and the need for the United States to gain access to the uranium ore of the Belgian Congo. The next day, Roosevelt established the President's Advisory Committee on Uranium. He appointed physicist Lyman J. Briggs, director of the National Bureau of Standards, to serve as its chair. The Briggs Committee convened for the first time on 21 October 1939. In attendance were representatives from the U.S. army and navy, the National Bureau of Standards, and the Carnegie Institution. At the meeting, Szilard and two fellow Hungarian émigré physicists, Edward Teller and Eugene Wigner, outlined what they believed were the necessary steps to achieve a chain reaction. On 1 November 1939, the Briggs Committee submitted a report to the president on the potential application of a controlled, nuclear chain reaction as a source of motive power for submarines. The report also briefly mentioned the possibility of exploiting the chain reaction in a weapon. Although the committee recommended funding nuclear fission research, the army allocated only $6,000 for Fermi and Szilard's experiments, and no official government program resulted at that time.[22]

In a paper published in the summer of 1939, Niels Bohr argued that the isotope responsible for the slow-neutron fission that Fermi had observed was uranium-235 (U-235). By March 1940, scientists at Columbia University confirmed Bohr's theory and proceeded to demonstrate that the uranium-238 (U-238) isotope could fission when bombarded with fast neutrons, although it seemed less likely to sustain a chain reaction this way. With these discoveries, atomic energy as a source of motive power appeared more possible than ever before. A nuclear weapon, however, would require concentrations of U-235 separated in mass quantity from U-238. The Columbia scientists, including Fermi, Harold C. Urey, and John R. Dunning, thus set out to determine the best method of isotope separation.[23]

In England, Otto Frisch and Rudolph Peierls demonstrated that, in theory, it would be possible to develop a nuclear weapon of sufficiently moderate size, and that it could even be built within a reasonable length of time, possibly in time for the war. According to their study, an atomic bomb might be feasible if the right amounts of U-235 could be slammed together quickly enough to cause an explosion from a fast chain reaction. They shared the conclusions of the study with fellow physicist, Mark Oliphant, who subsequently informed Sir Henry Tizard, the chair of the Committee for the Scientific Survey of Air Defense. Tizard ordered the formation of a special committee to consider the Frisch-Peierls report. Subsequently designated the MAUD Committee, it included among its members physicists George P. Thomson, James Chadwick, Philip B. Moon, John D. Cockcroft, and Mark Oliphant.[24]

In the summer of 1940, the United States took additional steps to further its own nuclear research program. In June, the recently formed National Defense Research Committee (NDRC) subsumed the Briggs Committee. This action effectively assured greater direct support from the government while reducing dependence upon the military, and it facilitated closer cooperation with civilian scientists. The American program also received a significant boost in August with the arrival of the Tizard Mission, the delegation of British scientists led by Sir Henry Tizard. With the NDRC now in control of the program, and with the additional technical information supplied by the British, which possibly saved the American program several months of additional research, the United States took a significant leap forward.[25]

German scientists were also busy with nuclear research, just as Leo Szilard suspected. Werner Heisenberg worked on calculations to determine whether a chain reaction in uranium were possible, Erich Bagge measured the capture cross section of the heavy-hydrogen nucleus, and Paul Harteck experimented with a Clusius tube to separate U-235 by the thermal diffusion process. In January 1940, the German War Office took over the Kaiser-Wilhelm Institute of Physics in Dahlem, and that winter, scientists at the institute began to construct an atomic reactor. For a moderator, they opted at an early stage to use deuterium oxide, or heavy water, because using graphite appeared then to be too expensive and time-consuming. Germany secured a steady supply of heavy water in April 1940, when, during the invasion of Norway, the German army captured the production facilities of the Norwegian Hydroelectric Company (Norsk Hydro), the largest producer of heavy water in the world.[26] During the summer of that year, a new facility for nuclear research was established in Berlin near the Kaiser Wilhelm Institute of Physics. As a security measure, it was built on the grounds of the Institute of Biology and Virus Research and given the foreboding name of Virus House, ostensibly to frighten away anyone who might get too curious about the new building. By the end of the summer, Germany had acquired thousands of tons of high-grade uranium ore for its nuclear research program, and by the end of the year, construction of the first uranium pile at the Virus House had begun. Like the United States, Germany also appeared to be making important strides toward developing nuclear energy for military use.[27]

Scientists in Japan followed the research in nuclear fission with great interest, learning what they could from imported science journals. They too were keenly aware of the explosive potential of the fast nuclear chain reaction. But unlike their counterparts in the United States, scientists in Japan did not feel any sense of urgency to develop an atomic bomb, nor were they likely to have thought themselves to be in a nuclear arms race at the time.[28] As a point of contrast, the impetus for nuclear weapons research in Japan came not from the civilian scientists, as was the case in the United States and Germany; rather, the initiative was to come from both military services.[29]

Although Japan was a relative latecomer to the modern sciences, the Japanese had caught up to the level of most western nations in nuclear physics by the 1930s.[30] In 1934, Arakatsu Bunsaku, a physicist who had studied under Einstein and Rutherford, constructed a particle accelerator based on the Cockcroft-Walton model. By 1936, Arakatsu was using the accelerator to disintegrate atomic nuclei.[31] In October 1939, ten months after Hahn and Strassmann's announcement of nuclear fission, Arakatsu, together with Hagiwara Tokutarō, a professor of physics at Kyoto Imperial University, published an article determining that approximately 2.6 neutrons were released with each fission of an atomic nucleus. The article also suggested that a chain reaction was possible.[32] Such results demonstrated that civilian scientists in Japan were indeed keeping pace with their western counterparts in nuclear physics research.

Technical officers in the Japanese army also tried to keep up by monitoring international developments in nuclear physics. In the late 1930s, Lieutenant General Yasuda Takeo, an electrical engineer and director of the Army Aeronautical Technology Research Institute (Rikugun Kōkū Gijutsu Kenkyūjo), closely studied the international scientific literature imported into Japan. After reading about the discovery of nuclear fission, in the spring of 1940, Yasuda ordered Lieutenant Colonel Suzuki Tatsusaburō of the Army Aeronautics Department (Rikugun Kōkū Honbu) to "explore the possibility of an atomic bomb."[33] Suzuki was no physicist, but he had more than a superficial knowledge of physics. In 1937, he had attended Tokyo Imperial University as a commissioned student and attended lectures by some of Japan's leading scientists. He studied under physics professors such as Nishikawa Seiji, Japan's leading expert on X-rays, and Sagane Ryōkichi. Suzuki read what he could find in western journals on nuclear fission. But for more insight, he readily consulted with Professor Sagane, with whom he completed several calculations on the matter. After some months of study, in October 1940, Suzuki submitted a twenty-page report to Yasuda concluding that Japan might have sufficient deposits of uranium ore at home and abroad to produce a weapon.[34] The report was no secret—it was distributed widely among the military and industry, including airplane and steel manufacturers, and was allegedly even available to the public.[35]

But the report did not elicit immediate action. It was not until April 1941 that Lieutenant General Yasuda ordered Suzuki to contact the director of the Institute for Physical and Chemical Research (Riken), Ōkōchi Masatoshi, and request him to conduct a feasibility study on a weapon exploiting nuclear fission. Ōkōchi turned the problem over to Nishina Yoshio, head of the newly formed nuclear physics laboratory at the Riken.[36] With over 110 scientists on the research staff, and claiming some of the best and brightest nuclear physicists in the nation, Nishina's laboratory was the mecca of Japanese nuclear physics research. It was here under the Atomic Nucleus Research Project that the nation's most advanced research on the atomic nucleus, cosmic rays, and radiation was taking place.[37]

But when Nishina received the assignment for the army's feasibility study in the spring of 1941, he was hardly enthusiastic about it. He was more concerned about completing the assembly of the laboratory's 60-inch cyclotron and getting it to work, and he expressed little interest in Yasuda's project.[38] At the time, Arakatsu and Hagiwara at Kyoto Imperial University were further along on the specific issue of nuclear fission. In May 1941, Hagiwara presented a lecture entitled, "Super-explosive U-235," which provided an overview of existing knowledge on the subject. From his work with Arakatsu, Hagiwara concluded that a chain reaction depended specifically on the U-235 isotope, and that massive quantities of U-235 isolated from U-238 would be necessary to achieve a chain reaction.[39] Isolation, or "separation," of the U-235 isotope had become a priority among scientists in the United States and England since the summer of 1940. Because isotopes of the same atomic number possess identical chemical properties, chemical separation methods were of no use. New methods of separation exploiting differences in mass were needed. As the U-235 isotope comprises only 0.7 percent of uranium, the problem of separation was exceedingly tedious and difficult.

There were four potential methods of U-235 separation. The first was by way of a high-speed centrifuge, which utilized centrifugal force to separate the isotopes of uranium. Uranium hexafluoride, the only gaseous form of uranium, was first to be pumped into the centrifuge. In theory, the heavier U-238 isotope would spin to the outer edge, while the lighter U-235 isotope collected within the inner part of the centrifuge. The second method was gaseous barrier diffusion. In this method, uranium hexafluoride gas was to be pumped through a series of barriers riddled with microscopic pores. The lighter isotope would pass through the filter leaving the heavier U-238 behind, whereupon U-235 isotopes could be collected at the end of the series of barriers.

The third method, thermal diffusion, used an apparatus known as a Clusius tube, developed in 1938 and named for its inventor, Klaus Clusius, a German physical chemist.[40] In this method, uranium hexafluoride was to be pumped through a chamber of concentric tubes having extreme temperature differences. In theory, the cooler of the tubes would attract the heavier isotope, and the lighter isotope would gravitate toward the warmer tube. Ernest O. Lawrence at the University of California at Berkeley developed the fourth method, electromagnetic separation. This method entailed shooting the isotopes through a magnetic field on a concentrated ion beam. The lighter U-235 isotope was to be pulled by the magnetic force in one direction, where it was collected at the end of an arc-shaped track, while U-238 was pulled in yet another direction. All of these methods of isotope separation were still experimental at the end of 1940.[41]

Adapting these separation methods to large-scale, mass-production levels would require advanced engineering and vast technological and industrial resources. By the summer of 1941, only the United States, Germany, and possibly Great Britain possessed such capacities. Japan did not. And the German invasion of the Soviet Union in June 1941 effectively removed the Soviets as possible contenders. Although nuclear fission research continued on a limited scale under Igor Kurchatov, any hope the Soviets had for a nuclear weapons project of their own came to an abrupt end with the Nazi invasion. Thereafter, most scientific research was directed toward meeting the immediate demands of the war, and physicists concentrated on the development of radar, armor, and the demagnetizing of ships.[42] Of all these nations, only the United States considered itself potentially to be in a nuclear arms race.

The United States was soon to take important and unprecedented organizational steps that would propel its nuclear weapons research program far ahead of the other belligerents. In June 1941, with the formation of the Office of Scientific Research and Development (OSRD), responsibility for nuclear weapons research was transferred from the NDRC to a specially designated department under the OSRD, the Uranium Section, also known by its code name, S-1.[43] Research kept pace with organizational changes. In September, Enrico Fermi began conducting experiments on the chain reaction using a uranium pile, a rudimentary nuclear reactor made of graphite and uranium oxide. Nuclear reactions within the pile appeared to produce an intriguing by-product—plutonium—a man-made transuranic element discovered in the previous year.[44] Building on such success, on 6 December 1941, the U.S. government further expanded its nuclear weapons program by allocating over $1 million for reactor construction and research in isotope separation. Nuclear weapons research had become a government priority.

Early in 1942, a new department was established within the Army Corps of Engineers. Designated the Manhattan Engineering District, its primary objective was to construct large-scale industrial sites for the separation and enrichment of U-235, all intended for the production of an atomic bomb. Administrative delays from the Corps of Engineers prompted Vannevar Bush, chair of the OSRD, to form the Military Policy Committee to oversee coordination between the civilian and military sectors. Bush then sought out a dynamic military leader to take charge of the Manhattan Engineering District program. He chose Colonel Leslie Groves. As deputy chief of construction for the United States Army, Groves had supervised the building of the Pentagon, and he appeared well suited for the new assignment. On 23 September 1942, Groves was appointed Brigadier General and officially put in charge of the Manhattan Engineering District. He worked quickly and decisively. By the end of 1942, he had chosen the principal sites for erecting the vast industrial complexes and laboratories that would be needed to develop the atomic bomb, including Oak Ridge, Tennessee; Hanford, Washington; and Los Alamos, New Mexico. The Manhattan Engineering District had become the military headquarters of the Manhattan Project.[45]

Ironically, just as the nuclear weapons program in the United States was gaining momentum, research in Germany suffered a number of setbacks, especially in the spring and summer of 1942. The Clusius tube Harteck constructed failed to work, and the first prototype of the isotope-separating ultracentrifuge blew apart. Heisenberg's L-IV uranium pile in Leipzig overheated and exploded, destroying the laboratory and wasting the precious uranium metal and heavy water in the reactor.[46] Organizational difficulties also hindered progress. When Reichsminister Albert Speer met with Hitler on 23 June 1942, Hitler showed little interest in nuclear weapons research, which he considered dabbling in "Jewish physics," and he offered no additional support.[47] Although the Reich Research Council took over supervision of nuclear fission research earlier in the year, by the end of June 1942, there was still no extensive government commitment or large-scale funding of nuclear research efforts in Germany. Of all the belligerents, only the United States had such a program.

NUCLEAR WEAPONS RESEARCH IN WORLD WAR II JAPAN

Navy Projects: B-Research and F-gō

Sometime in 1939, a rumor began to spread among the top brass in the Japanese navy that scientists in California had succeeded in the experimental application of nuclear energy by powering a small turbine. Coupled with reports of the U.S. embargo placed on uranium exports in the previous year, the story was enough to set the wheels in motion in the Japanese navy, though only slowly. Before the outbreak of the war with the United States, navy brass was keenly interested in finding not only a new source of motive power, but in developing a powerful new weapon as well. Nuclear energy, some thought, might hold such potential.[48]

One of the first naval technical officers to take up this line of research was Captain Itō Yōji, chief of the First Section of the Electronics Division of the Navy Technical Research Institute (NTRI). Itō was among the brightest of the scientists in uniform and perhaps the most important technical officer in the Japanese navy. He had an impressive résumé. After graduating from Tokyo Imperial University's Department of Electrical Engineering in 1924, the navy sent him to Germany in 1926 to study electronics under the direction of Professor Heinrich Barkhausen at Dresden Technical University. Within three years, Itō had earned his doctorate. At the beginning of 1941, the navy sent him back to Germany for several months, along with a technical inspection mission, to learn about radar.[49] As a ranking technical officer for the navy, Itō had been monitoring international developments in science and regularly attended the physics lectures given by Professor Asada Tsunesaburō. Aware of the reports that the United States had stopped exports of uranium ore in 1939, Itō considered the possibility of developing an atomic bomb. In November 1941, not long after his return to Japan, he raised the subject at a meeting at the NTRI. Those in attendance were reportedly excited by the prospect of a nuclear weapon and wondered whether this might be something to emerge in the "next" war.[50]

Itō kept the inquiry moving. After the November meeting, Itō took up the issue with two of his associates, Hino Juichi, a professor at Tokyo Imperial University Medical College, and Sagane Ryōkichi, the very same physics professor that army Lieutenant Colonel Suzuki had already consulted on nuclear fission. Both professors agreed that scientists in the United States were likely conducting research in nuclear energy for the military, and suggested the Japanese navy ought to look into it as well. At the end of the month, Itō submitted a report on his findings to his superiors at the NTRI. Lieutenant Commander Sasaki Kiyoyasu, head of the Electronics Division, listened to the opinions of Hino and Sagane in earnest, and after discussing their conclusions with the relevant personnel, the decision was made to take up research on nuclear fission at the NTRI.[51]

The outbreak of war with the United States in December 1941 does not appear to have had any immediate impact on nuclear research at the NTRI, but the defeat of the Japanese navy in the Battle of Midway in June 1942 apparently did. Between January and March 1942, Itō began a preliminary study and drafted plans for nuclear research to be undertaken at the NTRI. In March, Itō submitted a report recommending research focusing on the exploitation of atomic power for nuclear engines, artificial radium, luminous paint, and metals research, among others. A nuclear weapon was not specifically mentioned, but according to Itō, it was understood to be their primary interest. Itō recommended the formation of a special committee to oversee research in nuclear fission. The navy consented, and in the spring of 1942, the Committee for Research on the Application of Nuclear Physics was formed.[52]

After the defeat at Midway on 5 June 1942, Admiral Yamamoto Isoroku, commander in chief of the Combined Fleet of the Imperial Japanese Navy, specifically ordered the NTRI to produce "epoch making" weapons for the war effort.[53] Itō responded with plans for the development of radar and electric-wave weapons (A-Research) and weapons exploiting nuclear fission (B-Research). As a result, Itō's fledgling committee was upgraded as the Committee for Research on the Application of Nuclear Physics (B-Research), and the navy provided ¥2,000 (approximately $500) to initiate and support committee meetings for discussions on nuclear research. Nishina Yoshio of the Riken was consulted and was soon brought in as chair of the new committee.[54]

This assignment put Nishina in an awkward position. Since April 1941, he had been responsible for the army's feasibility study on nuclear weapons, and now he found himself leader of a similar navy project. Both services had ordered secrecy. Nishina must have been aware of the intense rivalry between the military services, but around this time—the exact date is unclear—he asked his army contacts to unite the military efforts and to have the Army Aeronautics Department serve as the sole window to the Riken.[55] Doing so would have required the navy, which had just begun nuclear weapons research, to transfer its autonomy over to the army, an unlikely scenario at that time. The war situation would grow much worse before such measures could be taken. As a result, nuclear fission research for the military services proceeded for months along separate lines of authority, with no practical efforts taken to facilitate collaboration between them.

The navy's "Physics Committee," as Nishina called it, included some of the most prominent scientists in Japan.[56] From the prestigious Riken were Nagaoka Hantarō, the doyen of Japanese physicists, and Nishina. Professors Nishikawa Seiji, Sagane Ryōkichi, Hino Juichi, and Mizushima Sanichirō represented Tokyo Imperial University. Asada Tsunesaburō and Kikuchi Seishi from Osaka Imperial University, Watanabe Satoshi and Nishina Tamotsu of Tōhoku Imperial University, and Tanaka Masamichi of the Tokyo Shibaura

Electric Company comprised the rest of the civilian brain trust. The chief technical officers of each division of the NTRI were also included in the committee, with Captain Itō serving as the navy's coordinating director. Between July 1942 and March 1943, the committee met on ten or so separate occasions, usually gathering at the Suikosha naval officers' club near Shiba Park in Tokyo.[57]

At the first meeting on 8 July 1942, Itō stated that the navy wanted to know if it were possible for the United States and Great Britain to produce a nuclear weapon during the war. If so, he asked, would Japan be able to produce such a weapon first?[58] He probed the scientists for a response. Professor Kikuchi replied that the American embargo on exports of uranium, thorium, and radium suggested that the United States was already working on the problem. To this, Asada added, "If America were to develop such a weapon, it would be extremely dangerous for Japan. Therefore . . . I feel we must, for our self-defense, if for no other reason, find out if we can develop it."[59] Others pointed out that one of the main problems would be acquiring sufficient amounts of uranium. Almost all of them knew from reading science journals imported from Germany that it was the U-235 isotope that fissioned with slow-neutron bombardment, that U-235 comprises only 0.7 percent of uranium, and consequently, that enormous amounts of uranium ore would be required to make even a few bombs.[60] Asada pointed out that no one in Japan knew the exact amount of U-235 necessary to create a chain reaction at that time, and as yet, there was no known mechanism available to induce it even if they did. Moreover, no one in Japan had ever successfully separated uranium isotopes.[61]

The first priority appeared to be finding enough uranium for research. Nishina stated that there were several tons of uranium-bearing ores at the Riken, but that the amount of actual uranium contained in them was minimal.[62] But the lack of uranium was only one of many problems facing the committee. The scientists were unable to state with any certainty whether they could produce a nuclear weapon. Nor could they even predict how soon they might know. Itō encouraged the scientists to intensify their efforts, and with this, they brought the first meeting of the Physics Committee to a close. The scientists adjourned with the understanding that the committee was to convene once a month thereafter, until more definitive conclusions could be offered.[63]

At the second meeting of the Physics Committee on 8 August 1942, the scientists reported on the progress of their research. Sagane discussed the results of the calculations he had made over the last month and concluded by stating he believed it would take years for Japan to build a nuclear weapon. Nishina introduced his concept of a "heat engine," a kind of crude nuclear reactor utilizing a mixture of enriched uranium and water as a moderator. Scientists at the Riken had determined back in the summer of 1940 that a combination of plain uranium and water would not result in fission. A reactor utilizing enriched uranium, they theorized, might work.[64] Another significant obstacle, then, would be separating the uranium isotopes for enrichment. Asada stated that even in the United States, scientists had only succeeded in separating a small amount of the U-235 isotope. Itō allegedly chastised the scientists for being too conservative and ended the meeting by urging them to press on with their research.[65]

Meanwhile, technical officers elsewhere in the navy were also looking into potential military applications of nuclear fission. Sometime in late 1940, Lieutenant Commander Murata Tsutomu, a staff officer at the Explosives Arsenal of the Navy Department of Ships, came across an intriguing article entitled "America's Super-bomb" while perusing the German journal of science *Nitrocellulose*. The article, originally published in November 1940, discussed explosives research in the United States and claimed that scientists there had determined that a tremendous explosion would result from the nuclear fission caused by bombarding a single gram of U-235 with slow neutrons. Thinking the article would be of interest to others, Murata translated it and distributed fifty copies to executive officers in the Department of Ships and various navy arsenals. The article was especially well received among technicians involved in explosives research, who had begun to feel they could make no further progress in their field.[66]

Captains Iso Megumu and Mitsui Matao of the First Division of the Navy Department of Ships had found the article on "America's Super-bomb" intriguing, and both agreed the subject should be investigated further. As they attempted to learn more about nuclear fission, they soon realized that the Department of Ships' technical personnel lacked the requisite expertise and equipment to conduct a feasibility study on military applications of nuclear fission. They decided to entrust the matter to a scientist at their alma mater, Kyoto Imperial University, and sometime in mid-1942, they paid a visit to Professor Arakatsu Bunsaku in the Physics Department. After discussing the subject, Arakatsu agreed to assist them with their research. Iso and Mitsui subsequently provided him ¥3,000 (about $750) to begin.[67]

Arakatsu submitted his report, "Research on the Feasibility of a Chain Reaction Due to Uranium Fission," to Captains Iso and Mitsui at the Department of Ships sometime around September 1942. While he cautioned that further research was necessary, the report stated that it may be possible to achieve a nuclear chain reaction. However, there would be numerous problems to solve, and Arakatsu informed them that the research would be expensive. The scope of such a project was well beyond the means of his laboratory, and he insisted the Department of Ships would have to take primary responsibility for support.[68] Iso and Mitsui accepted and allocated Arakatsu an additional ¥5,000 ($1,250) to continue his research.[69] Such a paltry sum was only enough to keep Arakatsu working for awhile, and it was certainly not enough to launch a viable nuclear weapons program.

In the meantime, Itō's Physics Committee met for what would be the last time on 6 March 1943. The scientists concurred that development of a nuclear weapon was theoretically possible, but they expressed doubt that Japan could produce one in time for the war. Not even the United States, they thought, would be able to do it.[70] Itō dissolved the Physics Committee, bringing the B-Research project and committee to an abrupt end. From that point forward, Itō dedicated himself to research on other advanced weapons projects in the field of electronics, including radar, which appeared to be the more practical and more immediately necessary technology to pursue, as well as the proximity fuse, and the "Death Ray," which remained at the theoretical stage of development but still appeared more possible than a nuclear weapon. Research on these projects was already underway at the NTRI under the collective designation of A-Research.[71]

Given the comparatively slow and moderate manner in which both services approached nuclear fission research, it seems apparent that atomic bomb development was not a high military priority at this time. After the war, Itō claimed that the purpose of the Physics Committee had been to determine whether it would be possible to produce a nuclear weapon during the war, not to actually initiate such a project.[72] He also stated that the navy knew of the army's involvement in nuclear research. On the matter of cooperation between the services, Itō stated that the navy simply wanted to conduct an investigation of its own first, and then it would consider collaborating with the army on the basis of the results. He further stated that the navy had no intention of initiating a rival project.[73] It is difficult to determine the veracity of such remarks; they evoke the type of revisionist controversies surrounding Werner Heisenberg and other German scientists involved in nuclear research since the end of the war.[74]

By the spring of 1943, the navy high command was growing anxious for new weapons to stop the advance of Allied forces in the Pacific. With the Physics Committee now disbanded, only the small team of physicists under Arakatsu Bunsaku at Kyoto Imperial University remained involved in nuclear weapons research for the navy. In May 1943, the Department of Ships upgraded the project, bestowed it with an official designation, F-gō, and allocated an additional ¥300,000 ($75,000) for research.[75] When Arakatsu expressed doubt about the success of the project, a navy officer allegedly replied, "Even if it can't be done in time for this war, it would be good to have it in time for the next."[76]

Although Arakatsu had serious misgivings about the success of the F-gō project, he continued to accept support from the Department of Ships. He was in the process of constructing a cyclotron in his laboratory at the university, and he reasoned that the additional funds and material support promised by the navy would help him complete it.[77] Moreover, the Department of Ships had permitted him to request additional technical assistants and junior scientists, because there was hardly anyone left to do even menial tasks. The project thus provided Arakatsu a way to protect some of the younger scientists from military conscription and saved them from being sent to the front lines. In Japan, as elsewhere during the war, it was not uncommon for senior scientists to attempt to save their younger colleagues in this manner in order to preserve the next generation of scientists.[78]

The fate of the F-gō project was squarely in the hands of Arakatsu, six senior scientists, and a few research assistants at Kyoto Imperial University[79] (Appendix, Table A6). Arakatsu served as director of the project and conducted general research. Kobayashi Minoru attempted to calculate the amount, or critical mass, of U-235 needed to create a chain reaction, as well as other theoretical problems. Yukawa Hideki, the future Nobel Prize winner, was available to him for consultation. Associate Professors Kimura Kiichi and Shimizu Sakae worked on the design of a centrifuge to be used in isotope separation. Sasaki Shinji conducted research on the chemical properties of gases, and Okada Shinzō from the Department of Engineering led the effort to produce uranium metal.[80]

Sometime around late 1943 or early 1944, Arakatsu paid a visit to Nishina at the Riken.[81] He found Nishina was already pursuing isotope separation through the thermal diffusion method, so Arakatsu chose to work on the centrifugal process instead.[82] On the basis of data found in imported science journals, Arakatsu understood that he would need to build an ultracentrifuge, an apparatus capable of achieving between 100,000 to 150,000 revolutions per minute (rpm).[83] Given the technology and resources available to him at that time, however, the best Arakatsu could hope to do was build a centrifuge capable of reaching 40,000 rpm.[84]

The lack of uranium still remained one of the greatest obstacles for the project. On the basis of critical mass calculations conducted by physicists Francis Perrin and Siegfried Flügge in 1939, Arakatsu determined that approximately one ton or more of uranium oxide mixed with water might result in a critical mass. He further estimated that about 44 pounds (20 kilograms) of uranium oxide, enriched to 10 percent of U-235, might also yield a critical mass. In any case, over a ton of uranium oxide would be needed in order to concentrate even this amount of the U-235 isotope.[85] The use of deuterium oxide, or heavy water, instead of regular water would further reduce the amount of uranium needed, but as Nishina had found for himself, only very limited quantities of the precious liquid were available. Arakatsu could only obtain about 20 grams of heavy water per month for himself.[86] Given such conditions, he completely ruled out trying to construct a nuclear reactor.

With both army and navy nuclear projects progressing only slowly, by the summer of 1944, military representatives from each service began to discuss collaborating in research. Across the board, the military services were experiencing difficulty in producing advanced weapons, and this crisis eventually resulted in the formation of the Army-Navy Technology Enforcement Committee in September 1944. But interservice rivalry was not so easily overcome. It took nearly a year of additional negotiations before a tentative agreement could be reached concerning nuclear weapons research. In June 1945, officers in the Navy Ministry agreed to take a supporting role in the effort after determining that the army project had already progressed well beyond their own. Perhaps as a concession, Captain Mitsui Matao of the Navy Department of Ships, who had previously initiated the F-gō project with Arakatsu, was made chief of general planning for the combined program.[87]

The Department of Ships allocated Arakatsu an additional ¥300,000, which he received at some point just before the end of the war.[88] It was, of course, of little use by then, as Japan was already all but defeated. Sasaki had made minimal progress in the production of uranium hexafluoride, and Okada had only succeeded in creating a piece of uranium metal about the size of a postage stamp. The design of the ultracentrifuge was finished in early July 1945, but construction had only just begun. The F-gō project team remained mired in the experimental stage of isotope separation, and production of a nuclear weapon was still years away, even if it were at all possible for Japan.[89]

The scientists of the F-gō project had their last formal meeting with their navy sponsors on 21 July 1945. Arakatsu gave a general presentation on the status of the project, and they discussed the design of the centrifuge. Kobayashi gave a report on the critical mass investigations, and Yukawa presented a lecture entitled "World Atomic Energy," which discussed theoretical aspects of nuclear research. Yukawa offered his opinion that production of an atomic bomb was theoretically possible, but it was not likely to be produced in time for the war effort. Discouraged, the navy officers accepted the news and terminated the F-gō project, leaving only the NI-gō team to carry on for the army.[90] No one at the meeting was aware that the United States had already successfully tested a nuclear device in Alamagordo, New Mexico, just days before.

The Army's NI-gō Project

After consulting with Nishina in 1941, Lieutenant General Yasuda Takeo realized that the Army Aeronautical Technology Research Institute, of which he was the director, lacked the necessary personnel and equipment to undertake a nuclear weapons development project on its own.[91] But Yasuda did not give up. After some time, he was able to convince his superior officers at the Army Aeronautics Department that nuclear weapons research should go forward. In August 1942, the army approached Nishina and requested that he assume responsibility for the project at the Riken.[92] They gave him a year to conduct fundamental research, and after two years, Nishina was to report on the feasibility of building a nuclear weapon. The Army Aeronautics Department agreed to fund the research and to supply what materials it could. For his cooperation, Nishina was permitted to select ten young scientists of special aptitude, to whom the army would grant draft deferrals so they could work on the project.[93]

One of the ten was Kigoshi Kunihiko. Kigoshi was no stranger to the Riken. As a student, in October 1941, he had used the smaller cyclotron at Nishina's laboratory to conduct research on nuclear fission for his thesis. Upon graduating from Tokyo Imperial University in September 1942, he was immediately conscripted into the Japanese army and assigned to the air service. On 1 October 1942, however, as a result of Nishina's agreement with the army, Kigoshi was appointed as a staff member at the Riken. Nishina assigned Kigoshi the difficult task of helping to produce enriched uranium by distilling the highly toxic gas, uranium hexafluoride.[94] Another of Nishina's recruits was Takeuchi Masa. In December 1942, when Nishina summoned him to the Riken, Takeuchi was conducting research on cosmic rays as a member of the Cosmic Ray Group at the Army Aeronautical Technology Research Institute.[95] Takeuchi was initially taken aback by the idea of working on an atomic bomb, but like many of his fellow physicists throughout the world, he was drawn by the challenge of nuclear fission research and agreed to assist Nishina in the project.[96] None of them knew that earlier that month, Enrico Fermi had achieved the first sustained chain reaction in a uranium pile assembled beneath the stands of an abandoned squash court at the University of Chicago.

On 15 January 1943, Nishina's nuclear research group held its first formal meeting. It was understood that the general purpose of the research effort was to determine how best to exploit nuclear fission according to the needs of the army. But before any type of weapon could be made, or before fission could even be achieved, the research group needed sufficient amounts of enriched uranium. Discussion soon turned to the various methods of U-235 separation then known to the group and then to deciding which method under the circumstances was most practical for them to pursue. After careful consideration of the paucity of materials, the state of current technology at hand, and the severe time constraints involved, the scientists concluded that the thermal diffusion method was the least problematic.[97] The electromagnetic method would require the construction of a mass spectrometer with a very large magnet, for which they had neither the time nor the materials. An ultracentrifuge would take them at least a year, perhaps two, to construct, if the necessary materials were available. Manufacturing a filter for the gaseous barrier diffusion method posed several difficult engineering problems beyond their capability. Even determining whether or not the thermal diffusion method was possible required more research.[98]

Around this time, Nishina began to seriously contemplate which to try to build first, a nuclear reactor or an atomic bomb. From before the meeting of the navy's Physics Committee in August 1942, he had mulled over the idea of a heat engine. Since then, Tamaki Hidehiko, a theoretical physicist working under Nishina at the Riken, had calculated the critical mass of a type of slow reactor using pure U-235 and light (natural) water with various reflectors.[99] To improve the constants needed for Tamaki's calculations, physicists at the Riken measured the thermal capture cross section of U-238 and the number of neutrons emitted per absorbed neutron in the "normal" uranium-water mixture. On the basis of such results, Nishina speculated that under a kilogram of U-235 might suffice for a bomb, and even nonenriched material might produce fission if properly moderated.[100] As a result, he began to envision a type of bomb that was more or less an uncontrolled slow-neutron-activated nuclear reactor utilizing enriched uranium and light water.[101] But producing enriched uranium would have to be the first obstacle to overcome.

The Nishina team met again on 27 February 1943. Takeuchi presented a report summarizing various calculations on the critical mass needed for fission.[102] Takeuchi and Tamaki had also begun drawing up plans for a Clusius tube, and they discussed the types of materials that might be used in its construction.[103] On the basis of Takeuchi's research, on 19 March 1943, Nishina announced the decision to proceed with the thermal diffusion method using the Clusius tube and uranium hexafluoride.[104] For his part, Takeuchi had little experience with a Clusius tube, and he knew less about how to build one. He heard that Professor Kikuchi Seishi and his research assistant, Takeda Eiichi, at Osaka Imperial University had recently built one and had succeeded in separating chlorine isotopes. Toward the end of March 1943, Takeuchi visited Kikuchi's laboratory in Osaka. He noted that Kikuchi and Takeda had used glass for the separation tubes, but he knew that he would be unable to do so because of the extremely corrosive nature of uranium hexafluoride. Takeuchi decided gold plating was best for the tubing, but there was none to be found. Instead, he would have to improvise with copper.[105]

When Takeuchi returned to the Riken from Osaka, he suggested to Nishina that Takeda be brought into their research team. Nishina ignored the idea, just as he had disregarded a similar request made previously by another member of the group, Kimura Kiichi.[106] Although he would likely have welcomed the additional help, asking Professor Kikuchi to give up his own assistant in such a manner would have been a serious breach of etiquette. Under the circumstances, Nishina had no appropriate means by which to make such a request. His research for the army was supposed to remain secret, and even had he gone through official military channels, he must have understood that it would have put Takeda in the uncomfortable position of abandoning his mentor and research group, something not easily done at the time.

Meanwhile, rumors of American and German efforts in nuclear weapons development reached the top brass in the army. At a Cabinet meeting held at the Army Ministry sometime in early spring 1943, Tōjō Hideki, then serving as both Prime Minister and Minister of the Army, called for the acceleration of nuclear research efforts under the army. Major Generals Kawashima Toranosuke and Taniguchi Hatsuzō subsequently met with Yasuda on the status of the army's project underway at the Riken.[107] After meeting with Kawashima and Taniguchi, Yasuda appointed Kawashima the army's chief liaison to Nishina. Soon thereafter, Kawashima and Taniguchi visited Nishina to see what measures could be taken to quicken the research.[108] They knew nothing of the technical aspects of developing nuclear weapons, and Nishina had to explain even the most basic principles involved. They reiterated to Nishina that the army wanted a bomb, but they also stated that the army air service needed a new source of power for its aircraft. Supplies of petroleum were diminishing quickly, and they were desperate for a substitute. According to Kawashima, they could only humbly bow their heads and ask "please." They promised to provide Nishina with as much money and materials as he needed to perform the research.[109]

In May 1943, Yasuda upgraded Nishina's nuclear fission research at the Riken to the status of an official army program, called NI-gō.[110] Having recently been promoted to chief of the Army Aeronautics Department, and as the general director of NI-gō, Yasuda pledged greater support and allocated Nishina some ¥700,000 ($175,000) and a new building in which to conduct research. Over thirty principal researchers were now involved in the NI-gō project, with an additional 110 scientists at the Riken available for consultation and assistance. Major Koyama Kenji was assigned responsibility for planning and oversight of research at the Riken (Appendix, Table A7). The NI-gō project was given the highest classification of secrecy within the army, but with the new status of the program, Nishina was also now permitted to seek assistance from the physicists at Osaka Imperial University on an as-needed basis.[111]

The increase in support from the army and the newly granted freedom to consult with scientists outside the Riken may have boosted the morale of the NI-gō team somewhat, but the central problems remained. How was the bomb to be made? How could the critical mass be achieved? How much uranium would be necessary? There was only a minimal supply of uranium available, leaving very little for even basic research. At the conclusion of the first meeting with Kawashima and Taniguchi, Nishina had told them that he would need great supplies of uranium, but neither truly understood its importance to the success of the program. Still, they vowed to find what they could.[112]

A curious thing happened at about this time in the spring of 1943. A retired physicist from Tokyo Imperial University, Tanakadate Aikitsu, serving as a member of the Diet, appeared before the House of Peers proclaiming that "the progress of nuclear physics has made it possible to utilize atomic energy. It is now possible to produce a bomb the size of a matchbox which has the explosive power to sink a battleship!"[113] The House of Peers received Tanakadate's announcement with great skepticism. After all, it was Tanakadate who had advocated replacing the Japanese writing system with the Roman alphabet, and other members of the Diet had come to see him as something of an eccentric. The Japanese press, however, perhaps desperate for encouraging news, printed Tanakadate's announcement, and the story received wide publicity in Japan.[114]

In contrast to Tanakadate's outrageous claim, and despite the recent pledge of increased support from the army, Nishina's NI-gō project remained at a formative stage. The building constructed for NI-gō research, for example, was little more than a modest two-story wooden structure—designated Building 49—with a total floor space of only 3,000 square feet. On the first floor, Takeuchi busied himself designing a Clusius tube and making preparations for its construction, while on the second floor, Kigoshi tried to produce uranium hexafluoride.[115]

In June 1943, Takeuchi presented Nishina with a design for the Clusius tube, which Nishina approved. Copper cylinders for the apparatus arrived about a week later, and Takeuchi immediately began to assemble the components. The copper tubes, measuring roughly 16 feet tall (5 meters), were to fit snugly one inside the other in concentric rings with approximately only 2 millimeters between them.[116] It took Takeuchi only one day to assemble the Clusius tube, and by 26 June, he was ready to start testing the vacuum in the new machine.[117] But securing the vacuum was to prove far more difficult than the basic assembly.

On 2 July 1943, Major General Nobuuji from the Second Army Arsenal visited Nishina at the Riken to inquire about the progress of the NI-gō research.[118] There was some discussion about requests coming in from various branches of the army, such as the General Affairs office of the Army Ordnance Department, for research on the application of nuclear fission to engines, fuel, and explosives. Nishina requested the Army Aeronautics Department to take care of coordinating these in a single commission. Nobuuji told Nishina to report directly to him at the Second Army Arsenal. Then the discussion turned to technical matters. Nishina attempted to explain the thermal diffusion process and stated isotope separation would likely require a huge factory. He discussed the need to use U-235 as the primary material, theoretical methods of initiating fission, and devices used for generating the neutrons necessary.[119]

Meanwhile, on the second floor of Building 49, Kigoshi Kunihiko and his small team were struggling with the difficult task of producing uranium hexaflouride.[120] First, they planned to make the fluorine gas, then uranium metal. Kigoshi's idea was to combine the gas and the metal to initiate a chemical reaction resulting in the uranium hexafluoride. They encountered numerous difficulties in producing the fluorine and the uranium metal, but after nearly a year of effort, Kigoshi's team succeeded in manufacturing sufficient amounts of both to experiment with. By November 1943, they were ready to try to produce uranium hexafluoride.[121] But fluorine and uranium metal powder were too volatile a combination to mix in the air. When combined, the two easily combusted. A vacuum was needed for blending the two, but under the circumstances, developing an apparatus specifically for this purpose was extremely difficult. Kigoshi had to find another way to produce the uranium hexafluoride, and he began to doubt whether he would ever be able to provide any for Takeuchi to use in his Clusius tube.[122]

At this point, Kigoshi and Takeuchi felt certain that Japan could not produce a nuclear weapon in time for the war, but they carried on with the research despite their pessimistic outlook.[123] To circumvent some of the difficulties posed by both the lack of proper equipment and uranium, Kigoshi developed a compound of uranium carbide to substitute for the uranium metal powder. The replacement worked, and by January 1944, he succeeded in producing a small crystal of uranium hexafluoride about the size of a grain of rice.[124] It was a minor breakthrough, but it gave them faint hope.

Major General Nobuuji returned to the Riken for a status report on 2 February 1944. Nishina reported that the Clusius tube was nearly ready, but the uranium hexafluoride was proving extremely difficult to produce. There were other problems as well. The larger of the two cyclotrons, a 210-ton, 60-inch accelerator, which they hoped to use for neutron generation, was finally operational, but it was running at only a low level of energy because they had not been able to obtain the high-frequency-generating vacuum tubes required to operate it. The low operating voltages at which the cyclotron ran limited the number of neutrons that it could produce, which significantly compromised its utility. Nobuuji then asked about uranium. Nishina answered that about 22 pounds (10 kilograms) of U-235 enriched to approximately 50 percent purity might suffice for a bomb, but that further tests were still necessary to be certain. Such experiments, Nishina added, could be performed more quickly if he could get the large cyclotron to work properly. Nishina impressed upon Nobuuji that his team could "accomplish a great deal" then. After the meeting, Nobuuji set out to acquire the necessary parts for Nishina.[125]

Such technical difficulties continued to plague the NI-gō project. By spring 1944, Takeuchi's Clusius tube was finally operational, but Kigoshi had not been able to produce much of the uranium hexafluoride with which to conduct the isotope separation experiments. By the beginning of summer, only about 450 grams were available for basic research. Moreover, preliminary experiments using argon instead of uranium hexaflouride had also failed, indicating that the thermal diffusion apparatus was not working properly.[126]

In November 1944, the army officers returned to the Riken again for a progress report. Nishina did not have encouraging news. Because of the highly corrosive nature of the uranium-hexafluoride gas, the soldering in the copper tubing was breaking down and the Clusius tube was proving ineffective. Separation of the U-235 isotope in sufficient quantity for even basic research was proving too difficult, and Nishina had calculated he would need at least 10 kilograms for a nuclear weapon. When one of the army officers allegedly asked Nishina—out of complete ignorance—why not simply substitute 10 kilograms of a "conventional explosive" for the uranium, Nishina is said to have replied, "That's nonsense."[127]

Even if Takeuchi's Clusius tube had worked efficiently, thousands of such separators would have been needed to manufacture the minimum amount (10 kilograms) of enriched U-235 that Nishina estimated would be necessary to make an atomic bomb. The isotope separation process also required great amounts of electric current for the nichrome heating coils operating within the tubes. By one estimate, the energy that would have been required for the mass separation process alone would have equaled about one-tenth of the total amount of electricity then available in all of Japan. Although they realized the difficulty, if not the impossibility of their endeavor, the NI-gō project scientists worked on, apparently hoping that their research might be of some use after the war.[128]

By February 1945, the Riken team had produced a very small amount of material with the Clusius tube. It was time for a test. Nishina placed the material in the smaller of the two cyclotrons and bombarded it with neutrons to induce fission. A Lauritsen electroscope was on hand to measure radioactivity. But to their disappointment, they found that virtually no U-235 had been distilled from the uranium hexafluoride gas.[129] Then, on the night of 13 April 1945, an Allied bombing raid struck close to the Riken, setting Building 49 ablaze. Scientists rushed to extinguish the fire, but by morning, the building was all but consumed by flames. Takeuchi's Clusius tube was destroyed, but somehow the cyclotrons survived undamaged. Fearing another air raid, the scientists began to evacuate the laboratory equipment out of Tokyo. With its primary research facility for nuclear weapons development lying in ruin, in June 1945, the army's NI-gō project was, for all intents and purposes, at an end.[130]

HEAVY WATER AND THE SEARCH FOR URANIUM

Sometime in the spring of 1943, Nishina committed his group to developing a bomb, and he abandoned the idea of constructing a reactor. The army's strong demand for a new weapon certainly influenced Nishina's choice.[131] But there were other factors as well, the paucity of material resources being perhaps the most critical. In the United States, Fermi had built his first reactor using graphite as a moderator. In 1942, scientists in the United States estimated that approximately 5 tons of heavy water (deuterium oxide) would be needed to build a small reactor, and there was no such quantity available. Given the level of technology at the time, it would have taken at least a year to produce this amount. Such limitations, together with the promising results of Fermi's experiments with graphite, led the United States away from using heavy water as a moderator.[132] In Germany, almost the reverse occurred. Physicists there chose heavy water over graphite as a moderator because heavy water was cheaper and became available to them in abundance from Norwegian Hydroelectric.[133] As for Nishina, graphite, in the quantity necessary for a reactor, was simply not available to him in Japan, and it is just as likely that the industrial capacity needed to purify the graphite was also inadequate. On the basis of calculations conducted with Tamaki, Nishina also opted at about this time to work with light instead of heavy water. But would it have been possible for Nishina, or Arakatsu, to construct a reactor using heavy water if they had wanted to try? Was heavy water available in sufficient quantities during the war?

In 1934, Arakatsu Bunsaku and Kimura Kiichi at Kyoto Imperial University became the first scientists to produce heavy water in Japan.[134] Shortly thereafter, heavy water became available in small amounts. The opportunity to begin production on an industrial scale came two years later. In 1936, Dr. Fritz Hansgirg, then vice president of the Austro-American Magnesium Company, visited the manufacturing site of Japan Nitrogenous Fertilizer Corporation (Nitchitsu), a new *zaibatsu* operating in the heavily industrialized port city of Hungnam in the northern half of the Korean peninsula, a colony of Japan since 1910.[135] Hansgirg tried to sell Nitchitsu executives on the idea of manufacturing heavy water by a new method he had recently developed that used a carbon monoxide conversion catalyzer process. Preliminary plans were drafted for constructing a heavy water production plant, but because of difficulties encountered with the prototype equipment, Nitchitsu dropped the project.[136]

But Nitchitsu was to enter the heavy water manufacturing business soon thereafter, in Japan. In 1940, Kubota Masao, chief of research and head of the newly established Nobeoka laboratory of Noguchi Enterprises, the parent company of Nitchitsu, proposed heavy water production to meet the demand of university scientists, who wished to use heavy water in chemistry and physics experiments.[137] Noguchi Jun, the founder of Noguchi Enterprises, was not one to miss an opportunity for profit, even in a niche market as specialized as heavy water production appeared to be. By September 1941, the Nobeoka laboratory was manufacturing heavy water for commercial sale. Processing equipment at Nobeoka consisted of five 100-liter and five 32-liter electrolytic cells. By using 0.1 percent deuterium oxide as the base material, according to Kubota's method, about 40 liters of approximately 0.4 percent heavy water could be manufactured during one production cycle.[138]

After the outbreak of the war with the United States, plans were made to increase production to 100 milliliters per month of 100 percent heavy water. The demand came from none other than Nishina Yoshio at the Riken, who at that time intended to use the heavy water in experiments involving the cyclotron.[139] By August 1942, the Nobeoka plant was producing 8 liters of 1.2 percent heavy water per month using 0.4 percent heavy water as an electrolyte. By the end of 1942, the Nobeoka plant was able to produce heavy water of more than 90 percent purity, and the productive capacity of the plant reached about 10 milliliters per month, still short of the projected goal.[140] From around the beginning of 1943, about 10 milliliters of 100 percent heavy water per month was realized, and from April 1943, this amount increased to nearly 50 milliliters per month.[141] In January 1944, the manufacturing process was improved with the construction of a three-step, continuous electrolysis apparatus that had been adapted from equipment used in the synthesis of ammonia. By April 1944, a higher concentration of 0.5 percent deuterium oxide was achieved, and by using this material as an electrolyte, it became possible to produce 50 milliliters of 90 percent or purer heavy water per month more efficiently.[142]

But heavy water production remained on a small scale throughout the war, possibly because there was so little demand for it. When Nishina encountered difficulties with the construction of the large cyclotron, it caused delays in his research schedule, and as a result, he had no immediate demand for the heavy water. Without its principal customer, there was no need for Nobeoka to increase production, and so heavy water was produced thereafter only on an as-needed basis. Nishina's experiments with the cyclotron never reached the stage of necessitating large quantities of heavy water, and consequently, heavy water production was never brought to full capacity.[143] By the time he considered using heavy water for a nuclear reactor, there was too little available, and it would have taken far too long to produce the quantity needed. Japan had only minimal amounts of heavy water for experimentation, and tons of it would be required for even a small reactor.[144] But Nobeoka was no Norsk Hydroelectric.[145]

Chitani Toshizō, a professor of chemistry at Osaka Imperial University and a participant in the F-gō project, also purchased heavy water from Nobeoka, which he used as a tracer in various experiments involving chemical reactions. Throughout the war years, Nobeoka supplied Chitani with heavy water in various grades, ranging from 1 percent, 10 percent, and 100 percent, well after the demand from Nishina at the Riken fell off. Thereafter, the majority of the Nobeoka plant's heavy water went to Chitani, and the balance was apportioned to various other university laboratories throughout Japan.[146] For example, Arakatsu Bunsaku received about 10 grams of heavy water from Nobeoka per month. He also received an additional 10 grams per month from another source, which was, according to Arakatsu, an ammonium manufacturer in Korea, undoubtedly Nitchitsu.[147]

Conspiracy theorists attempt to exploit such tidbits of information as evidence that Japan built and tested an atomic bomb in Hungnam, Korea, in the closing days of the war.[148] But as with many such conspiracy theories, there is only a kernel of truth at the heart of the matter. The supplier of Arakatsu's heavy water was indeed most likely Nitchitsu. Before and during the war, Nitchitsu operated several factories in Korea that utilized the electrolytic process in the manufacture of industrial chemicals, such as in the synthesis of ammonia, and heavy water was produced as a by-product. Nitchitsu was also involved in the manufacture of hydrazine hydrate and hydrogen peroxide for the navy, which intended to use these as ingredients in the fuel for experimental jet-engine and rocket-propelled aircraft. The production of these fuels also resulted in heavy water precipitating as a by-product, which Nitchitsu apparently sold to Arakatsu. But as noted above, the company did not build or operate a plant for the specific purpose of manufacturing heavy water. Despite the presence of a large hydroelectric generating plant in the area, which is suggestive of Norsk Hydro, there is no evidence to suggest that Japan had ever built a comparable facility.[149] As for traces of uranium found in Korea, the Korea Synthetic Petroleum Company Ltd. (Chosen Jinseki Kabushiki Kaisha) in northern Korea used uranium compounds as a catlyzer in the manufacture of synthetic methyl alcohol, specifically for fuel in aircraft with injection-type engines.[150] But the presence of such small amounts of uranium and heavy water are insufficient evidence to conclude anything like a full-scale nuclear weapons project was underway in Korea.

Incidental production of heavy water continued at the industrial complex in Hungnam until the last days of the war. But heavy water production in Japan came to an abrupt end on 29 June 1945 when an incendiary bomb destroyed the electrolysis plant at Nobeoka.[151] Heavy water thus never took on the significance to Japan's nuclear weapons research that it had in Germany. Without enriched uranium, light water alone would not do. And without sufficient quantities of either heavy water or graphite, Nishina ultimately had little choice but to rule out trying to build a reactor. Together with pressure from the army to build a bomb, Nishina's options were indeed limited.

The paucity of uranium was another insurmountable handicap for Nishina and the other Japanese scientists involved in nuclear weapons research to overcome. Nishina reportedly had just over 2 pounds (1 kilogram) of uranium oxide with which to experiment in the spring of 1943, but it was barely enough to conduct even basic research.[152] By simply scrounging on his own, Kigoshi Kunihiko, who needed uranium to start producing uranium hexafluoride, had acquired an additional 100 pounds (45 kilograms) or so of various chemical mixtures from ceramics manufacturers in and around Tokyo. Uranium compounds, especially uranium oxide, were often used for coloring in the glazing process, and Kigoshi hoped that what he had gathered would contain enough uranium to begin experimenting.[153]

Responsibility for obtaining the necessary uranium had fallen upon Major General Kawashima Toranosuke, the army's liaison to Nishina at the Riken, who knew as little about uranium as he did about the atomic bomb research itself. Kawashima did not know where to begin to search for uranium, and so he consulted Nishina, who in turn sent him to the Riken's rare elements specialist, Iimori Satoyasu. From 1919 to 1922, Iimori had studied radiochemistry under leading experts in the field in England, including Rutherford at Cambridge and Frederick Soddy at Oxford. Upon his return to Japan, he explored domestic sources of radium-bearing compounds. By the time the Pacific War had begun, Iimori was perhaps Japan's foremost authority on rare elements.[154] Iimori advised Kawashima to begin his search at the Ishikawa mine in Fukushima prefecture. Iimori had found traces of uranium and thorium there before the war. In any case, he thought, it was the only known mine in Japan that might yield large amounts of uranium-bearing ores. The Ishikawa mine, however, yielded only sparse amounts of low-grade monazite, which contained very little uranium.[155] Kawashima had to look elsewhere.

Around this time, Kawashima requested Lieutenant General Tada Reikichi of the Technology Agency, which Tada was later to chair, to acquire uranium for the army's NI-gō project. Tada was already occupied with the search for rare elements to be used in the manufacture of vacuum tubes, but at Kawashima's request, he dispatched a survey team to China and commenced processing tantalum and zirconium ores in Korea.[156] But the search for uranium proved difficult. Iimori directed Kawashima to potential mines in Korea, where the Kikune mine near Seoul, in particular, appeared to be most promising. Kawashima flew to Seoul with three assistants from the Army Aeronautics Department. When he arrived at the military headquarters there, Kawashima encountered a recalcitrant chief of staff, who demanded to know why he wanted access to the mines. Kawashima reluctantly explained that they were searching for materials to be used in producing a nuclear weapon. After conferring with the governor-general of Korea, the mine was opened. The mine was a disappointment, however, as they calculated that with the technology at hand it would take a thousand miners working for an entire year to produce enough ore for about 22 pounds (10 kilograms) of refined (but not enriched) uranium ore.[157]

There were other mines in Korea known to contain rare minerals, such as fergusonite, but the uranium content of these were unknown. Nonetheless, Kawashima gave the order to begin mining.[158] The army issued priority orders to field commanders in Manchuria, China, and in the South Sea Islands to find uranium. Research expeditions were sent as far away as Mongolia and Burma.[159] Three to five tons of previously mined uranium-bearing ores were located in Manchuria, and Kawashima ordered them to be shipped as soon as possible. But as a result of logistic difficulties, they were never sent. Tons of amang ore containing monazite and zircon were discovered in Malaya, and Kawashima had them shipped to Riken refineries. Approximately 4,500 tons of the amang from Malaya arrived before Allied submarines made further shipments all but impossible.[160]

To facilitate the allocation of scarce materials for the F-gō project, the Navy Department of Ships established the Special Materials Division, apparently in order to bypass existing bureaucratic procedures, which had become increasingly more cumbersome and time-consuming as the war dragged on. Lieutenant Commander Takao Tetsuya, head of the Rare Chemicals Section in the Special Materials Division, was made responsible for the requisition, procurement, and delivery of uranium oxide to Arakatsu. The Department of Ships managed to procure about 100 pounds (45 kilograms) of uranium oxide of varying degrees of purity from ceramic shops in and around Kyoto.[161] But it was nowhere near enough for F-gō project demands. At some point in 1944—the date is again uncertain—Arakatsu submitted a request for one ton of uranium ore. Despite the efforts of the Special Materials Division, however, it took the Department of Ships over a year to locate any significant quantity. In the spring of 1945, Arakatsu received a shipment of about 200 pounds (91 kilograms) of uranium oxide, some of which was allegedly obtained through the black market in Shanghai.[162]

In Japan, some thirty-nine plants were reported to have engaged in the treatment or processing of rare metals and ores. Only three of these, however, processed any uranium-bearing ores—at a rate of about one ton per plant per month—and the product was mostly used in the manufacture of pyrophoric alloys.[163] Despite the frantic searches for uranium-bearing ores by the military, they turned up very little, and uranium processing itself during the war appears to have been minimal.[164] Moreover, there is no evidence to suggest that any pilot plant was constructed in Japan specifically for the mass separation of U-235 isotopes from uranium or for the production of any other fissionable material.[165] No significant stores of uranium or separated U-235 were ever found by U.S. intelligence officers in Japan after the war.[166]

Nor had Germany been of much help in providing uranium to Japan. After concluding a Technical Exchange Agreement on 2 March 1944, which resembled to some extent the Lend-Lease agreements between the United States and its allies, Germany was a little more forthcoming in sharing information on its more advanced weapons technologies.[167] Late in 1944, the Japanese Ambassador in Berlin, Oshima Hiroshi, arranged to have 2 tons of pitchblende, an ore high in uranium content, sent to Japan for the army's research program. The ore was to be sent by U-boat in two separate shipments. The U-boat carrying the first load of pitchblende left for Japan early in 1945, but it was sunk en route. The second shipment never arrived either. The latter U-boat, ironically designated *U-234,* was loaded with some 1,200 pounds

(560 kilograms) of uranium oxide, together with numerous technical documents and assorted equipment for radios and aircraft. The *U-234* was dispatched in March 1945, but when Germany surrendered in May, the submarine changed course and surrendered to American authorities in the Atlantic.[168]

CONCLUSION

The atomic bombing of Hiroshima on 6 August 1945 came as a great shock to the Japanese scientists involved in nuclear weapons research. Few of them had believed it possible for any nation to develop nuclear weapons during the war, even the United States. But the United States had several advantages that Japan did not share in common. The United States had access to plentiful supplies of uranium-bearing ores and graphite, and it possessed an expansive industrial infrastructure to process them in massive quantities. As shown above, Japan had neither sufficient resources nor the industrial capacity to succeed in such an endeavor. The lack of coordination in research efforts between the military services was also a critical factor. In the United States, it took the formation of special agencies at the highest levels of government, namely the NDRC and the OSRD, before the Manhattan Project could be established. Under the auspices of these agencies, General Leslie Groves managed research at numerous sites, including Los Alamos, New Mexico; Oak Ridge, Tennessee; and Hanford, Washington. Groves enlisted the aid of such industrial giants as Du Pont and Union Carbide to overcome the many engineering problems involved. Although various aspects of the Manhattan Project were compartmentalized for security, Groves worked closely with the project's civilian director, J. Robert Oppenheimer, to coordinate the disparate elements of the program.

Japan, by contrast, had no such administrative structure. Nuclear research was almost entirely a military affair of the army and navy, each with its own independent projects. The Technology Agency, one of the government's many civilian offices responsible for coordinating scientific research, was only marginally involved as an oversight agency and provided modest funding late in the war. Otherwise, there was no central office created to coordinate all the disparate aspects of such a complex enterprise comparable to the roles of the OSRD and the Manhattan Engineering District in the United States. The overall picture of Japan's mobilization for nuclear weapons development is one of a bottom-up approach, in contrast to the United States' top-down model, and in this regard is more comparable to the German effort. Scientists in the United States had taken their case to the highest level of government, the president himself, who used his executive powers to establish the appropriate offices and to allocate the necessary funding and resources. In Japan, however, beyond the desperate demands of the top brass for a decisive new weapon, it was the technical officers in the military, like Itō and Yasuda, who initiated the projects and sought the assistance of civilian scientists when their own technicians in uniform proved incapable for the task at hand.

Moreover, interservice rivalry between the army and navy prevented collaboration until late in the war. There was no single military leader in charge of the nation's nuclear weapons research effort, as with Groves in the U.S. Manhattan Project. Groves was given an unprecedented degree of responsibility and control over military aspects of the Manhattan Project, and Oppenheimer proved to be a very capable civilian manager. There were no such analogs in Japan. Although navy Captain Mitsui Matao was put in charge of planning for the combined army-navy venture late in the war, he shared responsibility with several other officers, and he was never given authority comparable to that of Groves. Even the authority of Captain Itō Yōji and Lieutenant General Yasuda Takeo combined did not approach that enjoyed by Groves. Nor was there an analog to Oppenheimer. Nishina Yoshio had served as chair for both the army and navy feasibility studies, and he headed the army's NI-gō project, but he was never put in charge of a well-coordinated, combined national effort as was Oppenheimer.

At the laboratory level, there was but minimal collaboration between project scientists. Arakatsu appears to have consulted informally with Nishina only once during the war, and Nishina only provided navy researchers information on the Clusius tube and U-235 separation at some point early in 1945. Beyond the occasional sharing of data, however, there was no formal or direct collaboration between the scientists of the NI-gō and F-gō projects.[169] The cooperative agreement reached between the army and navy in nuclear weapons research in the summer of 1945 accomplished nothing, and the war ended before the formal order for collaboration had even been issued.[170] Moreover, there were far too few scientists in Japan to have assembled a research team on the order of magnitude of the Manhattan Project. Most of the research for the navy's F-gō project was conducted under the supervision of Arakatsu at Kyoto Imperial University. Some scientists from the Imperial Universities of Nagoya, Osaka, and Tōhoku were also involved as consultants in various stages of the project. Technicians from private industry also participated. In all, however, there were no more than nineteen principal scientists and technicians engaged in F-gō research at any one time. As for the NI-gō project, as previously stated, there were over 30 principal researchers involved, and an additional 110 scientists were available for consultation and assistance at the Riken.[171] Combined, the personnel and equipment available are more substantial, and begin to approach the more impressive resources of the Germans (Appendix, Table A8).

Yet as Arakatsu pointed out to an American intelligence officer after the war, the organization of research for the promotion of nuclear physics in Japan might have "looked very well on paper, but [it] really amounted to very little because nuclear physicists in different Japanese laboratories did not work in coordination."[172] As a result, technical resources were never used to their fullest. For example, the equipment at Osaka Imperial University, which by the end of the war included a cyclotron, a mass spectrometer, a Cockcroft-Walton accelerator, and a Van de Graaff generator, were used only peripherally in both the army and navy projects. A Clusius tube had also been built, but no attempt was made to assemble a cascade apparatus by combining the separators at the Riken and Osaka laboratories.[173] In 1937, Japan became the first country in the world outside the United States to build and successfully operate a cyclotron. It is illustrative of Japanese engineering skills and resourcefulness that by the end of the war they had built more.[174] The cyclotrons at the Riken were used to determine whether Takeuchi had succeeded in separating U-235, but otherwise they appear not to have been put to much use in the broader NI-gō project research. The cyclotrons could have been converted into mass spectrographs and then used to concentrate U-235 by the electromagnetic method, which was a process Ernest O. Lawrence had invented at Berkeley in 1941.[175] However, there is no evidence that this idea ever went much beyond the theoretical stage in Japan. Thus, although Japan had advanced apparatuses for conducting research in nuclear physics, the full potential of the machinery was never realized.

By the time Japan surrendered in August 1945, the Japanese army had spent over ¥1.2 million (approximately $300,000) on the effort to develop nuclear weapons.[176] If expenses for the procurement of uranium bearing ores are included, the figure is much higher.[177] The Japanese navy spent over ¥600,000 (approximately $150,000) on Arakatsu's research alone, and given various procurement expenses, it is likely that it expended more than available documents reveal.[178] Sources do not provide precise numbers for the total amount of funds allocated to Japan's nuclear weapons research. Estimates range from ¥2.6 million ($650,000) to over ¥45 million ($11.2 million).[179] But even the highest of these estimates does not approach the $2 billion spent on the Manhattan Project.

Even if sufficient amounts of uranium had been available, it is questionable whether a Manhattan Project–style effort could have been assembled in Japan, given the absence of any government agency to help coordinate all the disparate elements. Given the comparatively low levels of technology and industrial support capacity at the time, it is also doubtful anything less than a national, concentrated effort combining nearly all the available human resources of the imperial universities and industry could have succeeded. Where nuclear weapons development was concerned, the three strikes of resource deficiency, limited industrial capacity, and poor mobilization of science infrastructure and personnel were more than enough to ensure that Japan would not succeed in such a complex technical endeavor during the war.

3
ELECTRIC WEAPONS: RADAR AND THE "DEATH RAY"

The invention of radar cannot be credited to a single person, or even to a particular nation. Like nuclear fission, by the late 1930s, the idea of using radio waves for detecting ships and aircraft was a concept whose time had come. Important discoveries in the fields of electromagnetism, radio, and electronics in the late nineteenth and early twentieth centuries opened the path for the development of radar, and several scientists and engineers throughout the world were hard at work developing the new technology. Japan was no exception. But the pace of radar development depended on several factors, chief among which was support for research. In most cases, support was to come first from the military services. Private corporations did not yet perceive a great market demand for such a device. In the early 1930s, radio detection had yet to demonstrate its reliability as a navigational aid for ships, and commercial air transport was only in its infancy. There was as yet no clear need for radar technology.[1]

By the mid-1930s, however, most of the principal belligerents of World War II had become involved in radar research and development to some degree. But it was Great Britain that emerged as the leader in this technology by the beginning of the war. Britain was the first to deploy radar sets and to establish a functioning defense command. This turn of events was prompted largely by Germany's open rearmament in the mid-1930s and the perceived threat that it posed to the United Kingdom. And so it was that Britain's lead in this technology came about as a result of its preoccupation with developing a practical defense against Nazi Germany. Likewise, radar development in the United States also focused from the early stage on the defensive capabilities of this new technology, with many of the first radar sets being installed along the coastlines of both oceans, near forward bases, such as Pearl Harbor in Hawaii, and on patrol ships. Much of the early emphasis was also placed on developing fire-control radar for antiaircraft systems. But the enemy threat was less immediate in the United States, and so there was less urgency. Thus, it is not surprising that radar development lagged somewhat behind that of Great Britain at this time.

By way of contrast to the Allied situation, radar was not at all an early priority for either National Socialist Germany or Japan. At the outset of the war, both nations were on the offensive and sought to produce weapons more applicable to the blitzkrieg style of warfare. Although radar offered some obvious advantages for offensive use, at the outset of the war, it was still largely considered a defensive weapon. It was to remain so until its utility was demonstrated in the Battle of the Atlantic against Germany's U-boats, as well as in the numerous naval engagements in the Pacific. Consequently, both Nazi Germany and Japan came to realize the importance of radar later than the Allies, and although both stepped up their efforts to develop radar during the war, neither were able to reach parity with Great Britain and the United States in this important new technology by war's end. The following section will examine the many paths toward radar development taken by the various nations of the West through the 1920s and into World War II. By comparison, it will become clear in the subsequent sections that Japan's approach to radar and its experience with it during the war was neither unique nor exceptional, but was in many ways comparable to that of National Socialist Germany.

DEVELOPMENT OF RADAR IN EUROPE AND THE UNITED STATES

The idea of radar can be traced to the late nineteenth century, but its evolution into a useful technology was a gradual process to which several brilliant minds contributed.[2] In Karlsruhe, Germany, in 1887, working from Maxwell's equations, physicist Heinrich Hertz was the first to produce electromagnetic waves and to demonstrate their reflectivity and refraction.[3] Around the turn of the century, inventors such as Nikola Tesla and Christian Hülsmeyer began to experiment with electromagnetism and radio waves, and both hit upon the idea of locating distant objects with them. Hülsmeyer may have been the first to build what could be called a functional radar set in 1904, and Hans Dominik followed not long after in 1916. But they were unable to generate interest in the apparatus from the military. Indeed, at the height of World War I, the German Imperial Navy responded to Dominik that his invention would require at least six months of continued development, and so it would not be useful in the present war! This same attitude was to carry over into World War II as well.[4]

Although some important improvements occurred in radio technology during World War I, there were no significant advances toward the development of radar until about the 1930s. Guglielmo Marconi, the Italian engineer and winner of the Nobel Prize in 1909 for his work in wireless telegraphy, was among the first to anticipate the use of reflected radio waves for the detection of ships. In 1922, at a conference in New York, Marconi presented a paper building on Hülsmeyer's earlier work that clearly outlined the fundamentals of radar. Incredibly, it did not excite much interest even among the military in the United States. It would take nearly another decade before any government became sufficiently interested to support research on a significant level. And so, during the 1920s, scientists and engineers throughout the world continued research on a small scale, focusing on radio wave propagation and the study of the ionosphere. Despite the broader lack of interest, by the early 1930s, rudimentary forms of radar began to appear.[5]

Although research and development of radar began almost simultaneously in the United States, Europe, and Japan, it was Great Britain that first realized the potential application of radar technology to national defense. As Germany began to openly rearm under the National Socialists in the mid-1930s, those responsible for the defense of Britain grew increasingly alarmed. The experience of the Great War was still fresh in the minds of politicians and military leaders, not to mention the average citizens of London and other cities that had suffered destruction during the war. In May 1917, German Gotha bombers, the twin-engine behemoths of the air that replaced the zeppelins for bombing sorties, began to appear over the skies of London. For a year, until May 1918, the great Gotha bombers wreaked havoc on the major cities of England, dropping large payloads of bombs with impunity and killing or wounding nearly 5,000 citizens. Great Britain's Royal Flying Corps lacked fighter planes that could reach the Gotha's 12,000-foot ceiling, nor could the newly designed antiaircraft artillery reach that altitude. Moreover, England had no effective early warning system to alert the air corps and citizenry that the bombers were on the way.[6]

In June 1934, Albert P. Rowe, a civilian scientist and personal assistant to the Air Ministry's Director of Scientific Research, H. E. Wimperis, warned that unless some new method of defense was invented, any war fought in the next ten years would surely be lost. Acting on this counsel, in autumn, Wimperis formed the Committee for the Scientific Survey of Air Defense, with Rowe serving as secretary and Professors P. M. S. Blackett and A. V. Hill serving as independent members. In December, Wimperis appointed Henry Tizard as chair, whereupon it became known simply as the Tizard Committee. Tizard was a logical choice. Education and experience had provided him with the necessary understanding of not only operational needs but also with the scientific capacity to address them. A chemist and lecturer in natural science at Oxford until the outbreak of World War I, he joined the Royal Garrison Artillery after being rejected by the Royal Navy because of poor eyesight, but later he managed to be assigned to the Royal Flying Corps. After World War I, from 1927 to 1929, he served as secretary of the Department of Scientific and Industrial Research, and in 1933 was appointed chair of the Aeronautical Research Committee.[7]

Meanwhile, it fell to Wimperis to investigate any and all claims of inventions and innovations that might be of use for national defense. The recent scientific discoveries of X-rays and radioactivity fed the popular imagination, and fantastic devices such as "ray guns" and "death rays" began to turn up in comic books and Saturday matinee films. Numerous reports were submitted to government and military offices by self-proclaimed inventors declaring that they had produced such weapons. These outrageous claims, of course, proved to be bogus. But was it actually possible to build such a weapon? For example, was it possible to build a device capable of focusing a concentrated beam of electromagnetic waves strong enough to destroy living tissue and airplane engines, or to explode bombs on approaching enemy aircraft? It was incumbent upon Wimperis as the Air Ministry's director of scientific research to find out. In early January 1935, he turned to Robert Watson Watt, superintendent of the Radio Research Station at Slough, and requested him to investigate the feasibility of such a "death ray" weapon. In turn, Watson Watt turned to his assistant, Arnold F. "Skip" Wilkins, for help in answering Wimperis's query.

Wilkins quickly performed the calculations and concluded that the power necessary to operate such a device was well beyond current technology. When Wilkins submitted his calculations to Watson Watt, a discussion ensued as to how electromagnetic wave technology might otherwise be applied to national defense. Wilkins mentioned that he knew of some engineers with the post office who had observed interference in radio reception when airplanes flew nearby, and that this phenomenon might have some application in detecting enemy aircraft, which of course, would be useful for national defense. Watson Watt penned a brief memo to Wimperis informing him of the impossibility of developing a death ray for destruction, but alerting him to the possibility of using radio waves for detection.[8]

When the Tizard Committee convened its first meeting on 28 January 1935, Wimperis, having received Watson Watt's memo within only ten days of his inquiry, was able to report that a death ray would not be feasible, but that radio detection offered some promise. The committee wanted more information on the theory of radio detection, and Wimperis returned to Watson Watt requesting more details. Within two weeks, Watson Watt produced a paper on the subject: "Detection and Location of Aircraft by Radio Methods."[9] Wimperis and Tizard agreed that the matter was worth pursuing further, whereupon Wimperis approached his superior, Air Marshal Sir Hugh Dowding, to request funding. Dowding refused. He would need evidence first to prove that such a device could be made to work before allocating any money for research. Watson Watt and Wilkins quickly assembled a crude apparatus and arranged a demonstration for Dowding, which was subsequently held on 26 February 1935 near Daventry. The device worked beyond their expectations, locating the target aircraft, which by a twist of fate had flown off its predetermined course, leaving even its crew uncertain of its position. Dowding was sufficiently impressed. The next day, he approved £12,300 for research. A modest research facility was established at Orfordness about 65 miles northeast of London on the North Sea, and a small four-man team was assembled to work on the project under the supervision of Wilkins.[10]

By May 1935, Watson Watt and his colleagues had designed a prototype apparatus they deemed sufficient for deployment. In September, the Air Defense Research Committee approved the construction of a network of radar arrays to be built along the southern and eastern coasts of England. The network was to become known as Chain Home. In December 1935, the government provided £100,000 for the construction of five Chain Home stations.[11] By September 1938, the five Chain Home stations had been built, and a year later, when war erupted on the Continent, there were no fewer than eighteen operational stations in the Chain Home system. But there were still significant gaps in the network. Chain Home had difficulty detecting aircraft at lower altitudes because reflections from the ground and other obstacles flooded the cathode-ray screens. The solution was Chain Home Low, a network of radar arrays designed for detection at low altitude. Chain Home Low finally became operational in February 1940.[12] Had the Battle of Britain begun before then, the outcome might have been very different.

Meanwhile, Watson Watt's team had outgrown their rustic facilities at Orfordness, and in March 1936, a new research center was provided for them at Bawdsey Manor. Situated northeast of London on the Suffolk coast, Bawdsey was an isolated and sprawling mansion surrounded by forests, ideal for secrecy, but large enough to host the Air Ministry's expanding radar research and development program. Watson Watt was an excellent leader to his young team. He established at Bawdsey Manor a casual atmosphere where colleagues often discussed research problems as much in the laboratory as at play on the manor's tennis courts. But in May 1938, Watson Watt accepted a promotion to director of Communications Development at the Air Ministry and turned the management of Bawdsey over to A. P. Rowe.

Rowe was more of a stickler for decorum than his predecessor and established a more officious tenor at Bawdsey. Ironically, however, he also instituted a new practice, the Sunday Soviets. These were unofficial meetings that brought together the various scientists, engineers, technicians, and administrators at the manor for informal discussions. These casual meetings were to prove invaluable for the free flow of information among the disparate groups at Bawdsey.[13] Bawdsey Manor was to serve as the center of the British Air Ministry Research Establishment radar development program until 1940, when concerns over its vulnerability to enemy bombing forced relocation and physical decentralization to various sites throughout the United Kingdom, including Dundee University and later St. Athan in South Wales.[14]

From 1935 until the end of the war, the British produced several types of radar and radar related innovations. Among these were sets for airborne interception (AI), night-fighter interception (AI Mark II, AI Mark III, AI Mark IV), aircraft-to-surface-vessel (ASV), long-range ASV, and various units for the Chain Home system, including models for antiaircraft fire control, gun-laying units, and various ground-mobile units.[15] But perhaps the greatest British contribution to radar was the development of the resonant cavity magnetron, invented in February 1940 by John Randall and Henry Boot at the University of Birmingham under the direction of Marc Oliphant.[16] The production of an efficient magnetron represented the successful evolution of the British program to the final stage of radar development.[17] The resonant cavity magnetron, a type of vacuum tube that generated centimetric waves (microwaves) under 10 centimeters, allowed for much greater power output with vastly improved precision over its predecessors. The resonant cavity magnetron produced by the British revolutionized radar and was the technological artifact that enabled the Allies to leap far ahead of the Axis powers in the field of radio detection.

The other great innovation of the British, however, came in October 1938 with the establishment of the operations center at Bentley Priory, to which all the Chain Home stations were linked by telephone trunk lines and where all data were collected. Located in the suburbs of London, Bentley Priory served as the nerve center where incoming enemy positions were plotted and monitored by operations specialists, many of them women, who in turn relayed pertinent information back to the various stations as well as to the pilots of the Royal Air Force. Bentley Priory represented the culmination of all the innovations in technology and operations devised by such visionaries as Watson Watt and Wilkins, who led in the creation of the technical artifacts, and Dowding and Tizard, who combined the technology with the demands of logistics and communications to revolutionize radar systems operations.[18]

The full story of radar development in Great Britain was not so smooth as this brief summary would suggest, however, and it would be misleading to end the discussion here without some mention of the difficulties surrounding the Lindemann-Tizard conflict. In November 1932, in a session of Parliament in which the subjects of the disarmament conferences and appropriate measures for air defense were debated, Lord President Stanley Baldwin proclaimed, "the bomber will always get through." Frederick Lindemann (later Lord Cherwell), professor of experimental philosophy and head of the Clarendon Laboratory from 1919, published a strong rejoinder to this statement in the 8 August 1934 edition of the *Times,* in which he rebuked Baldwin for his defeatist attitude. Lindemann was joined in his stand by his longtime friend, Winston Churchill. Although his party was out of power at that time, Churchill was nonetheless quite vocal about events on the Continent and the rising threat Hitler posed. Churchill was persistent in his view that something must be done concerning air defense. As a result, in 1935, he was appointed a position on the Imperial Defense Committee. On 14 February 1935, Churchill and Lindemann met with Prime Minister Ramsay MacDonald and lobbied him to form a subcommittee on air defense under the Imperial Defense Committee. None of them then knew of the recent formation of the Tizard Committee.

When MacDonald consulted his Air Minister about Churchill's proposal, he was informed that a committee for air defense had already been formed under Tizard. When MacDonald met with Churchill again, Churchill convinced him that the new subcommittee would make the Tizard Committee superfluous and argued for its dissolution. MacDonald agreed, but Sir Maurice Hankey, Secretary of the Cabinet, who favored the Tizard Committee, intervened. When it was suggested that Lindemann serve as a consultant on the Tizard Committee, Churchill and Lindemann were livid. After much wrangling over the issue, a compromise was reached. Instead of disbanding the Tizard Committee, on 30 April 1935, the Committee on Air Defense Research was established under the Imperial Defense Committee with Sir Philip Cunliffe-Lister, Lord Swinton, Secretary of State for the Colonies, as chair. Lord Swinton's appointment gave the committee Cabinet-level access, for which Churchill had lobbied. On paper, the Tizard Committee then became a "technical" subcommittee of the Swinton Committee. But in practice, the Swinton Committee acted more or less as an advisory board. Despite the tension, Lindemann was appointed as a member of the Tizard Committee after all.

The cause of the bad blood between Lindemann and Tizard is still uncertain. They were, at one time, close friends, but had long since become estranged. (Lindemann had favored development of infrared and "aerial mines" and was rather obstinate in his support of these leading to no small amount of friction among his colleagues, who disagreed. But it is doubtful such disputes alone led to the falling out with Tizard.) Lindemann's appointment to the Tizard Committee threatened to disrupt the harmony within the old boys' network enjoyed by the likes of Tizard, Hankey, Lord Swinton, and Baldwin, and throughout the following year, tensions between Tizard and Lindemann continued to mount. Action was needed. Members of the Tizard Committee thereupon devised a scheme to remove Lindemann. In October 1936, they resigned their positions and dissolved the committee, then reformed it under new leadership without Lindemann. The situation remained tense for nearly two years, when in November 1938 Lindemann was appointed to the Swinton Committee. When Churchill became prime minister in 1940, he named Lindemann his science advisor. Although this appointment gave Lindemann greater authority over the nation's science infrastructure, it effectively removed him from the morass involving the Tizard Committee. What had been a potential powder keg of sectional rivalry was thus contained. As for Tizard, he was to play one of the most important roles of the entire Second World War as leader of the scientific exchange mission to the United States in 1940.[19]

For their part, scientists in the United States had also made significant progress in radar development. While experimenting with radio wave propagation and communication between ships on the Potomac River in the autumn of 1922, Dr. A. Hoyt Taylor and Leo C. Young discovered a curious phenomenon, a distortion, which they called the phase shift effect, which suggested that enemy ships passing through an active beam between two vessels could be detected "irrespective of fog, darkness, or smoke screen."[20] Taylor and Young reported their findings to the Navy Department, but no immediate action was taken on their results. In June 1930, while experimenting with radio direction-finding equipment, Young and his colleague Lawrence Hyland, at the Naval Research Laboratory (NRL) in Anacostia, D.C., observed that passing aircraft could also be detected using radio waves. A subsequent report submitted by the director of the NRL in November 1930 led the Bureau of Engineering to request further research on the use of radio waves for the detection of enemy ships and aircraft, and two radio detection programs were established.[21]

Like their contemporaries around the world, in the 1920s, scientists in the United States also were still working with continuous-wave (CW) transmitters. But in 1925, while conducting experiments to determine the height of the ionosphere, Dr. Gregory Breit and Dr. Merle A. Tuve of the Carnegie Institution hit upon the idea of using short bursts of radio waves, or pulses, in their measurements. The idea eventually caught on, and in 1933, Leo Young and Robert Page at the NRL began to develop transmitters and receivers that used pulsed waves. This work resulted in the development of the duplexer, an apparatus that allowed transmission and reception with a single antenna. In 1935, the House of Representatives' Committee on Naval Appropriations provided the NRL with $100,000 for further research and development of radio detection. By April 1937, the navy had installed a primitive radar set on the ship *Leary,* and by the end of 1938 had installed two, more advanced sets on the battleships *New York* and *Texas.* By 1941, the navy had contracted with Bell Telephone Laboratories for the production of fire-control radar sets, the first of which was installed aboard the USS *Wichita* in June 1941.[22]

The U.S. Army Signal Corps during the 1920s was attempting to develop radio and infrared detectors using microwaves but still lacked the technology to generate sufficient power at this wavelength for such devices to be practicable. These lines of research were terminated in favor what had become the standard line of radar development. By November 1938, the Signal Corps was experimenting with antiaircraft detectors for use with searchlight control and gun laying. By June 1939, the Signal Corps had begun to experiment with prototypes that were to develop into the SCR-270 and SCR-271 early warning sets. In May 1940, the SCR-270 long-range detection set was approved for standard issue, and in August, the Signal Corps contracted with Westinghouse for their production. About a year later these sets were being deployed to various U.S. military installations, and it was one of the SCR-270 units that detected the approach of Japanese aircraft at Pearl Harbor in December 1941.[23]

With the formation of the National Defense Research Committee in June 1940, Karl Compton, appointed chief of Division D, soon formed a department to conduct research on the application of microwaves to radar detection. Initially established as Section D-1, the department was eventually promoted to division level and became Division 14 of the NDRC. Alfred L. Loomis, a World War I veteran, lawyer, and amateur scientist who had made a name for himself in microwave research, was named its director. Division 14 quickly expanded to include accomplished scientists and engineers from academia and industry, who collectively came to be known as the Microwave Committee.[24] But progress in this field could not be achieved without first developing a vacuum tube capable of generating microwaves of great intensity. This innovation was to be the resonant cavity magnetron.

The resonant cavity magnetron, called "the most valuable cargo ever brought to our shores," arrived from England with the Tizard Mission in September 1940.[25] It was, to say the least, a great boost to the American effort to develop microwave radar. At the recommendation of the Tizard Mission, on 18 October 1940, the NDRC reached a decision to establish a new laboratory for the exclusive purpose of investigating microwaves at the Massachusetts Institute of Technology. The so-called Radiation Laboratory was established on 10 November 1940. Dr. Lee DuBridge from the University of Rochester was named its first director. Dr. E. G. Bowen of the Tizard Mission stayed on as the British liaison, which helped to assure close collaboration between the allies in this critical area of research.[26] In 1942, the staff of the "Rad Lab" grew from 450 to over 1,700, and by the end of 1943 it employed some 2,700 combined personnel. Throughout the war, Division 14 received around $141 million for radar related research. By July 1945, the U.S. military services were using thousands of radar sets of 150 different designs, all of which had ultimately cost some $3 billion to produce.[27]

At the outset of the war, German radar was arguably more advanced than that of Great Britain and the United States. German scientists and inventors such as Hülsmeyer and Dominik had built primitive radar sets as early as 1904 and 1916, but it was not until the 1920s that the German military became actively interested in the new technology. In 1923, the German navy established the Communications Research Laboratory (Nachrictenmittel-Versuchs-Anstalt, NVA) in Kiel to develop the emerging field of electronic warfare. At the NVA, research focused primarily on applications of "underwater sound" for communications and radiolocation. When this line of research proved unproductive, Dr. Ruloph Kühnhold, physicist and science director at the NVA, looked to exploit radio waves above the surface. Toward this end, in 1934 he consulted with a manager at Telefunken, a leading electronics firm in Germany, for possible assistance.

Although interested in the technology that was to become radar, Telefunken's research director, Dr. Wilhelm Runge, did not share Kühnhold's vision for using microwaves, which he deemed too impractical at that time. Runge was of the opinion that the type of vacuum tubes that would be needed for such a device could not be developed in the near future. Moreover, he flatly told Künhold that he did not have sufficient staff or resources to divert to such work. Runge was only a middle-level manager, but he had severely aggravated Kühnhold, who perhaps mistakenly took his rebuff as a rejection by Telefunken as a whole. Kühnhold then turned for assistance to a smaller, little-known electronics firm, Tonographie, and its two owners, the brilliant young engineers Paul-Günther Erbslöh and Hans-Karl Freiherr von Willisen.[28]

Kühnhold found Erbslöh and von Willisen far more agreeable than Runge, and a partnership soon emerged between the NVA and Tonographie. As their research and plans for future development expanded, the trio agreed to establish a new firm to separate the military line of research from the commercial at Tonographie. The result was the Gesellschaft für Electroakustische und

Mechanische Apparate, an unwieldy appellation (in any language) that came to be better known by the acronym, GEMA. Erbslöh and von Willisen began to hire talented engineers out of the Heinrich-Hertz Institute, including Dr. Theodor Schultes and Dr. Walter Brandt, who were to manage the high-frequency and low-frequency laboratories respectively, as well as Dr. Hans Hollman, who was retained as a consultant. Kühnhold himself did not become a member of the new firm, but remained at the NVA.

As elsewhere, CW experiments at GEMA proved fruitless, and by 1934, Hollman and Schultes had turned to development of a pulsed-wave transmitter, which proved more successful. Later that year, they secured funding for their research from the German navy's Torpedo Research Institute (Torpedoversuchsanstalt), and thereafter their work continued under the strictures of military secrecy. In January 1936, they demonstrated a pulsed-wave set for Kriegsmarine commander Admiral Erich Raeder, who was interested in radar for its potential in detecting torpedoes. Sufficiently impressed, Raeder allocated an additional 160,000 Reichsmarks (approximately $40,000) for GEMA research. Within the year, GEMA developed the DeTe-I surface-search radar and the DeTe-II long-wave air-warning models of the Seetakt series. They proved to be less than ideal for navy use and required improved vacuum tubes, which the team continued to work on throughout the 1930s. But in April 1936, considering the devices adequate, the German navy made the decision to install the DeTe-I Seetakt sets on all its cruisers and battleships. For his part, Kühnhold remained committed to microwave research, which he continued at the NVA into the 1940s. But it was not until February 1943, when the Germans captured a British microwave radar set, that microwave radar was to become part of the German technological arsenal.[29]

In making the decision to equip its capital ships with the DeTe-I model in 1936, the German navy might appear at first glance to have been comparatively progressive in its attitude toward radar. But such a characterization would not be entirely accurate. According to radar historian, Louis Brown, in the case of Germany, "radar had come from below" and had not been ordered from above. Equipping ships with this first of Germany's operational radar was "more the result of the individual initiative that came to all commanders who encountered the powerful new eye, rather than from high-level interest or understanding."[30] Furthermore, there were many problems yet to be solved. Because of the inhospitable environment aboard warships in which the delicate radar sets had to work, there were numerous failures, and GEMA had constantly to redesign accordingly. Initially, the navy's radar operators and maintenance personnel were poorly trained, and as a result of demands for secrecy, did not even carry instruction manuals. It was not until near the end of the war that the Kriegsmarine appointed officers to supervise the operation and maintenance of radar aboard their vessels.[31]

As with many other weapons development projects in National Socialist Germany during the war, interservice rivalry also became an obstacle for radar. In July 1938, commander of the Luftwaffe, Field Marshal Hermann Göring, witnessed a demonstration of the DeTe-II type radar at the navy's Torpedo Research Institute laboratory. He was reportedly infuriated that this technology had not already been shared and had the director of the Luftwaffe's Signals Research Institute, General Wolfgang Martini, order several sets for the air force. These were to be designated by the Luftwaffe as Freya. Martini ordered some 200 sets, but GEMA lacked the capacity to meet the demand and produced only 50 by March 1939.[32]

Meanwhile, Telefunken succeeded in developing a set of its own, the Würzburg, which combined all the key elements typical of World War II radar, including "a well defined beam with high directional accuracy, excellent range accuracy and a common antenna."[33] The firm demonstrated the Würzburg to Wehrmacht officials in July 1939, whereupon it was adopted for use. A third firm, Lorenz, also developed radar sets for early warning, searchlight, gun laying, and tracking, and became an important producer later in the war. By the outbreak of the war, then, Germany had two main manufacturers of radar and a third that gained importance as the war progressed. Together, these firms produced several types of radar, with the Freya and Würzburg series constituting the mainstay of the German models.[34]

Although National Socialist Germany had begun the war with a technological advantage, it eventually fell behind the Allies in radar development and production. There were several reasons for this turn of events. First, radar was not a priority of German offensive military policy during the war, as it had been in the defensive policy of Great Britain. Hitler's well-known decree prohibiting all weapons projects that would not produce usable technologies in mere months also prevented significant support for R&D in microwave radars, thus holding back research toward a cavity magnetron on par with the Allies.[35] Moreover, there was no attempt to coordinate and comprehensively exploit the available scientific resources for a concentrated research and development program. No central office or laboratory was established to supervise research, such as the British had at Bawdsey Manor and the Americans had at the MIT Rad Lab. Interservice rivalry became a factor as engineers attempting to promote radar had to constantly contend with competing interests in the military services. They also had to contend with the two most dominant figures in Nazi Germany, Hitler and Göring, who were notoriously anti-intellectual, scientifically illiterate, and generally opposed to long-term weapons development.

Unlike in Great Britain and the United States, civilian scientists and engineers in Germany also did not set the agenda for development of radar, but were subject to military contracts to conduct research on specifically designated problems.

Furthermore, German scientists on their own proved unable to progress to the third stage of radar development—that is, using microwaves, even though there were efforts to develop microwave radar below the 50-centimeter range throughout the 1930s. Once the Freya and Würzburg types of radar became available, however, the military apparently became complacent with these models, and the prevailing attitude in the German military around 1940 was that there was no immediate need for a more expansive research effort. As a result of all these factors, the Germans failed to develop the resonant cavity magnetron, and by the end of the war, they lagged far behind the Allies in this critical technology. The Germans also failed in the other great British innovation: organization. Although Germany had numerous radar outposts, it failed to incorporate radar into a more comprehensive system of operations for national defense. They never developed a centralized ground control office to make use of data gathered by the numerous sets dispersed across the country, as did the British at Bentley Priory.[36] These were the main factors that inhibited progress in radar research and development, as well as its most effective exploitation, in National Socialist Germany throughout the war.

Great Britain, the United States, and National Socialist Germany were the main contenders in the contest to develop radar during the war, but the story of radar development in the West would not be complete without mentioning the also-rans. The Soviet Union arguably had taken the early lead in radar research at the outset of the 1930s, and by 1934, the Soviet state was providing more funding for radar research than any other nation at the time. Brilliant academicians and engineers, such as Abram F. Ioffe, Pavel Oshchepkov, and Y. K. Korovin, were emerging as potential world-class leaders in this new field. But by 1941, the USSR had fallen behind the other principal belligerents because of a fractious radar feud between research institutions concerning which type of technology to pursue, a lack of coordination between the various organizations involved, and the failure of the military services to take a leading role in determining the course of research and development in partnership with industry.[37]

The Main Artillery Administration (Glavnoe artilkeriiskoe upravlenie, GAU), the engineering branch of the Red Army, sought to develop new technologies for national defense, and in the area of detection, they looked to the fields of acoustics and infrared. With its own technical resources already stretched to the limit, in 1932, the GAU turned the problem over to the All-

Union Electro-Technical Institute (Vsesoy-uznyi Elektro-tekhnicheskii Institut, VEI). Like the British and Americans, the Soviets also first investigated the possibilities of infrared detection technology, but they also found it impractical for the time, and in 1935, they abandoned this line of research. Meanwhile, the GAU had also turned to the Scientific-Research Experimental Institute of the Red Army Signal Corps (Nauchnoissledovatel'skii Ispytatel'nyi Institut Svyazi RKKA, NIIIS KA) to investigate a radio-technical solution to the problem of enemy detection. The NIIIS KA soon replied that such a system was not feasible because of the amount of electrical power that was necessary. But in October 1933, the GAU turned the problem over to the Central Radio Laboratory (Tsentral'naya Radiolaboratoriya, TsRL), which was more sanguine about developing a radio-technical method for aircraft detection. The GAU also initiated a duplicate project with the Leningrad Electro-Physics Institute (Leningradskii Elektrofizicheskii Institut, LEFI).[38]

Unlike many other weapons development programs in the Soviet Union, which were subject to a great deal of centralization and control, especially during the war years, radar research and development proceeded under a comparatively decentralized network that suffered from excessive competition and sectionalism among no fewer than sixteen separate offices. At about the same time that the GAU initiated research at LEFI, Pavel Oshchepkov in the Air Defense command (PVO) had independently hit on the idea of radiodetection on his own. With support from the Defense Commissariat, in January 1934, Oshchepkov assembled several leading academics from the Soviet Academy of Sciences and other prestigious research organizations for a conference on the subject. Disagreements emerged on the course of research concerning wavelengths and other technical matters, but as a result of the conference, experts from the PVO teamed up with LEFI to attempt to build an experimental radar apparatus. By the end of 1934, the LEFI and TsRL had become the principal research institutions concerned with radar development, but in the years that followed, fourteen additional research institutions would also become involved. In 1935, the NIIIS KA argued again that radio detection was not viable and lobbied the GAU to terminate its support for all such research programs. Great rifts emerged between institutions vying for resources and funding as well as scientists and engineers who continued to disagree over the correct path of research.[39]

These tensions came to a head during the political purges of 1936–1938, resulting in a seriously deleterious impact on radar development in the Soviet Union. The NIIIS KA instigated several investigations of rival institutions. Scientists such as Oshchepkov, for example, were imprisoned in the infamous gulags. The purges not only removed great scientific and engineering talent, but also many of the high-ranking military officers who might otherwise have continued to support radar research with generous funding. Despite such setbacks, the USSR was still able to produce a few radar sets during the war, including the RUS-1 Rhubarb, the RUS-2 Redoubt, and the Zenith. But by 1940, the Soviet Union trailed even the Japanese in radar development, and throughout the remainder of the war, it was largely dependent on technology transfers from the British and the United States through the lend-lease program for improvements in this much-needed technology.[40]

France and Italy were also involved in radar research but contributed little to its technological progress during the war. There were notable early developments in France, as well as in the Netherlands, but the outbreak of war and the invasion brought these lines of research to a premature end. By the time war erupted in September 1939, all the major belligerents, save Italy, had made significant progress with radar.[41] Italy's efforts in radar research and development were minimal at best and were certainly not in the same class as the other principal belligerents in the war. Some work was undertaken in 1936, almost single-handedly, by Professor Ugo Tiberio at the Royal Institute for Electro-technics and Communication (Regio Instituto Elettrotecnico e della Communicazioni della Marina, RIEC), and this line of research led to the production of the EC-2 pulsed-wave set, which proved so unsatisfactory that development was discontinued. The Italians did not take a serious interest in radar until well into the war. The turning point in Italian radar policy came with the defeat of Italian naval forces in the Battle of Cape Matapan, 28 March 1941, in which the Italians lost three cruisers and two destroyers during a nighttime naval engagement with the British fleet. British advantage in radar technology was determined to have been a decisive factor. But by the time the Italians realized the importance of radar, there was little that could be done to establish a viable research and development program for the war effort.[42]

RADAR DEVELOPMENT IN PREWAR JAPAN

Before the outbreak of war in Europe in 1939, radar development in Japan had more or less kept pace with that of Great Britain, the United States, and Germany, although Japan certainly trailed them all. But Japan also had its share of pioneers in the field of electronics. It was Yagi Hidetsugu, professor of Electrical Engineering at Tōhoku Imperial University in Sendai and later dean of science at Osaka Imperial University, and his colleague Okabe Kinjirō, also an accomplished electrical engineer, who led the early investigations into radar research in Japan. Yagi became internationally famous for inventing in 1926 the dipole array antenna, known widely as the Yagi antenna, which, after the war, came into common use throughout the world as a television-receiving antenna.[43] The British and Americans both adopted the Yagi antenna for use in their long-wave airborne search systems early in the war, even while its application for such a purpose went largely unrecognized in Japan. It was not until the capture of a British searchlight control apparatus in Singapore in July 1942 that the use of the Yagi antenna in this capacity was recognized by the Japanese army.[44] Okabe gained some measure of international recognition in 1927 for having developed the split-anode magnetron for microwave generation.[45]

But the exact origins of radar in Japan are difficult to determine. After returning from a trip to Germany in 1914, Yagi is said to have theoretically conceived of a rudimentary form of radar. Together with Okabe, Yagi began to study the effects of objects in radio fields. But development of a viable prototype radar apparatus did not begin in Japan until 1936, when Okabe constructed equipment for detecting aircraft using the optical Doppler effect.[46] Meanwhile, in 1927, Professor Kujirai Tsunetarō of Tokyo Imperial University began theoretical studies of radio waves reflected by aircraft in a thesis entitled "Very High Frequency Waves and Aircraft." But this line of investigation did not result in further progress at the time.[47]

Although civilian engineers took the lead in radar-related research in Japan, the military services did not remain idle. Since 1909, the navy had been active in developing radio direction finders. Between 1928 and the outbreak of the Pacific War, navy technicians produced several types of medium- and high-frequency direction finders for use on board ships and aircraft.[48] Sometime in the mid-1930s, an unidentified Japanese engineer visiting the United States had an opportunity to inspect iceberg-detecting equipment installed on the French liner *Normandie* while it was docked in New York City, and he subsequently submitted a report to the navy.[49] The Navy Technical Research Institute was involved in related research at the time, but it did not establish a dedicated program for radar until later. The army was also interested in the technology and was engaged in some preliminary research, but neither service made a serious commitment to a radar development until after the outbreak of the war in Europe.

Captain Itō Yōji, who was the driving force behind the organization of the Physics Committee that conducted the feasibility study on nuclear weapons development for the navy, was also to play a critical role in radar development in Japan. As previously mentioned, Itō traveled to Germany in 1926 to study electronics under Heinrich Barkhausen. While in Germany, Itō met fellow Japanese engineers Kato Nobuyoshi and Watanabe Yasushi, who were also to become involved in radar research for the Japanese navy during the war. During his return to Japan in the summer of 1929, Itō by chance met Commander Kusaka Ryunosuke. The two, traveling by ship, were able to become well acquainted on their long journey home, and Kusaka took an interest in Itō's research. Toward the end of 1929, apparently as a result of his relationship with Kusaka, Itō found himself transferred to the Navy Technical Research Institute's Electrical Research Department. The NTRI was then involved in research on such things as the application of radio to telephones, high-powered transmitters and receivers, wavelength meters, on-board stations for ships and aircraft, underwater sound, and the electrical transmission of photographs (early facsimile, or fax, machine technology). Itō himself was interested in pursuing research on electron tubes and the so-called Kennelly-Heaviside layer, or ionosphere, research for which he would receive the Navy Ministry's Meritorious Award in 1942.[50]

Upon his arrival, Itō found the NTRI in serious need of technically competent personnel, because too few graduates with advanced education in science and engineering seemed willing to join the military. To address this deficit, the NTRI had recently adopted a temporary policy of hiring civilians with the desired education and skills to fill much-needed positions. But Itō went a step further, moving "against the customs of the times" by also contacting the Japan National Research Council and requesting the assistance of additional outside engineers. For research in radio propagation, Itō tapped the council's Radio Propagation Research Committee for its expertise, and likewise consulted colleagues whom he had come to know in Germany, like Watanabe Yasushi, as well as academic scientists, such as Nagai Kenzo, a graduate of Tōhoku Imperial University who was then serving as an assistant professor.[51] This style of recruitment was typical of the bottom-up approach that was to become a characteristic feature of Japan's wartime science mobilization effort.[52]

Radar research in the navy did not make much progress during the early to mid-1930s. One of the first known discussions of radar among navy personnel came in 1935 when an unidentified Japanese American, then employed by the NTRI, claimed that an American engineer was offering to sell a radio detection apparatus capable of sensing aircraft at a distance of 100 kilometers. The navy's Department of Ships convened a meeting to discuss the report, and Itō attended. Nothing came of the meeting, however, because the committee apparently doubted the veracity of the report.[53] Some research was undertaken with FM CW radar in 1937, resulting in successful ranging up to 5 kilometers in Tokyo Bay. However, subsequent experiments proved unsatisfactory, and as with radio direction finding technology in the previous decades, the navy opted to terminate this line of research in favor of purchasing foreign equipment for study before attempting to develop and produce radar sets domestically.[54]

In the spring of 1937, Itō made a second visit to Europe to attend a series of conferences, one held in Bucharest by the International Consultative Committee in Radio Communications, and the other, on microwaves, held in Vienna. During the trip, Itō again met with his old German mentor, Heinrich Barkhausen, who updated him on research being conducted in Germany. Later, the Japanese Naval Attaché in Italy arranged for Itō to visit with famed inventor Guglielmo Marconi in Rome. Through these meetings and discussions, Itō learned that research on a new weapon that could utilize radio waves appeared to be in the works throughout Europe. He dutifully reported this finding to the military attaché in Berlin, who forwarded it back to Tokyo, but again, the Japanese navy took no immediate action.[55]

In 1938, with the assistance and support of Professors Yagi Hidetsugu and Nagaoka Hantarō, Itō arranged for Barkhausen to visit Japan. Barkhausen arrived on 14 September 1938, and Itō, who was fluent in German, served as his guide and interpreter. Barkhausen visited numerous research institutes and industrial sites, including the Riken, the imperial universities of Tokyo and Kyoto, and Tōhoku Imperial University's Communications Research Laboratory and the Metals Research Laboratory. Among private firms, Barkhausen visited Tokyo Shibaura Electric, Fuji Electric, the Kawanishi Machine Manufacturing Company, and the Japan Broadcasting Corporation (Nippon Hōsō Kōkai, NHK), to name a few. Barkhausen was allegedly quite critical of what he saw. Although quite circumspect in public, privately he strongly criticized the Japanese university system for operating too much like a vocational or senior high school with too little academic freedom and overly rigid instruction, and he noted the "handed down from above" pedagogical method so ubiquitous in the Japanese educational system. He was similarly critical of Japanese industry, observing that manufacturers of comparable products tended to use the same materials and production techniques, which, he remarked, made for poor competition. Although impressed with the likes of Nishina Yoshio and the Riken, on the whole, Barkhausen concluded that, academically and scientifically, Japan remained a second-class nation.[56] The observations of his mentor were not lost on Itō, who apparently took the criticisms to heart and became ever more determined to raise the level of science and technology in Japan.

In 1939, the navy finally came around to radar research. Primarily, the navy was determined to improve its maneuvering and combat capabilities at night and sought a system to prevent collisions between ships while in battle formation.[57] In that year, the navy funded research on a 3-centimeter wave transmitter and small radar sets to be used on torpedo boats. But the results were less than satisfactory. The NTRI team was unable to produce equipment with an accurate range of more than 100 meters. The decision was made at that time to switch from research on pulse-type radar to the FM-type system, which also proved difficult as the team continued to have problems producing a working receiver. It was not until sometime in 1941 when information on British and German radar was obtained that the NTRI team went back to researching the pulse-type system. During this time, Itō was in charge of research on VHF communications equipment at the NTRI, which also dovetailed with related work then underway on magnetrons for the production of electric waves.[58] It was a connection that was later to lead to Itō's involvement in the Japanese navy's death ray research.

Although the exact year is in question, the Japanese army appears to have begun radar related research around the mid-1930s. Major General Tada Reikichi, director of the Army Institute of Scientific Research (Rikugun Kagaku Kenkyūjo, AISR), was looking into new applications of radio waves and secured support from the Japan Society for the Promotion of Science for a collaborative effort with scientists in academia and industry.[59] Research on radio-wave detection got underway at the AISR and affiliated laboratories shortly thereafter. Conducted under the general supervision of Colonel Satake Kinji, preliminary research focused on using the CW Doppler-type system, which led to the development of the so-called Kō or Type A radar.[60]

Some of the momentum for army radar research also came from the private sector. In 1938, Kobayashi Masatsugu, head of the Vacuum Tube Section of Nippon Electric Corporation (NEC), returned from a fact-finding tour in the United States and Europe, where he had been sent to learn all he could about television for broadcasting the Olympic Games to be held in Tokyo in 1940. While observing an experimental television broadcast in Britain, he noticed that an airplane passing nearby disrupted the transmission. Intrigued by the phenomenon, on his return to Japan he carried out a series of small-scale experiments involving radio interference. From these tests, he deduced that a radio-wave-detecting apparatus could be built, and he presented his idea to the army. With the cancellation of the Olympics because of the escalation of the war between China and Japan, Kobayashi was free to pursue this new line of research, and he became a leading member of the army's research team in radiolocation. He consulted with experts at Osaka and Tokyo Imperial Universities, including Yagi and Okabe, as well as specialists in private firms such as Tokyo Shibaura and Japan Radio Corporation.[61] Okabe's work on Doppler-type radar, in particular, contributed a great deal to the production of the Type A model.[62]

In February 1939, an experimental apparatus utlizing a 20-centimeter wavelength achieved moderate success in detecting a passing aircraft.[63] In May, another set using a 4-meter wavelength achieved similar results, and this model was put into trial production. In 1939, a 3-watt set was used experimentally in Hangzhou, China, with "good" results, and was ordered into production in March 1940. The latter set was formally designated the "Type A Bistatic Doppler Interference Detector," but was better known informally as the "Bow Wow" type because of the sound made by the detection apparatus. Additional sets in this series were developed with models ranging from 3 to 40 watts' output, and a Type A system for aircraft detection and warning later became operational in 1941. Some 120 sets of this type were erected along the coast on the Sea of Japan for defense against a potential air assault from the Soviet Union.[64] But these sets proved fairly inaccurate at detecting oncoming aircraft at a distance, and basic research on this type was terminated. Further research toward the weaponization of radar was turned over to the Army Technical Department (Rikugun Gijutsu Honbu). Despite the suggestive results in early testing, and the benefit of providing early warning against enemy aircraft and ships, radar still remained a low-priority item.[65]

Motivated by the success of the blitzkrieg in Europe, the Japanese army dispatched a military observation mission to Germany in December 1940. The mission included twenty-one high-ranking officers whose purpose was to investigate weapons technology and materials used in armaments manufacturing, to observe manufacturing facilities and research institutes, and to attend lectures on various topics of interest, including armaments and equipment.[66] When the mission returned in 1941, it brought a report concerning British use and production of VHF pulsed radar, which apparently inspired Japanese research in this area.[67] Army brass subsequently consulted Okabe and Yagi, who was then serving as dean of science at Osaka Imperial University, and requested their assistance in making use of the document. Okabe used the information to help the army develop the Type B pulse radar. The Type B offered significant advantages over the CW Doppler systems, thus resulting in a shift of focus from the Type A to Type B radar sets in the army.[68]

Not to be outdone by the army, the Japanese navy sent an observation mission to Germany in January 1941. The navy mission comprised thirty-six members, including Itō Yōji, then a commander, who joined as a radio specialist. Of primary interest to the navy mission were inspecting German naval facilities, procuring machine tools, examining new weapons, and obtaining information on the South Pacific, specifically the Marshall Islands, which the Germans had held as a colonial territory for over thirty years. Itō himself was most interested in gathering knowledge of technology policy, aviation, and shipbuilding.[69] The information gathered during the mission prompted the Japanese navy also to take a more active interest in radar, and it too turned to Okabe for assistance. Within five months of their return, a 3-meter VHF radar set was produced and installed at an observation post in Katsuura city in Chiba prefecture.[70] Yet although the Japanese navy was quite active in magnetron research, they apparently remained unaware that microwave radar systems were even then being developed by the Allies.[71]

NAVY RADAR R&D IN WORLD WAR II JAPAN

To better understand Japan's comparatively low level of achievement in radar research, development, and production, it is instructive first to consider the administrative structure of the military research organizations and the pattern of mobilization.[72] In the navy, development of electronics and radar was managed under the purview of three primary agencies: the Department of Radio (Denpa Honbu), the Department of Ships (Kaigun Kansei Honbu), and the Navy Aeronautics Department (Kaigun Kōkū Honbu). Operational matters were the concern of the Navy General Staff. The organizational structure was to function as follows.[73] The General Staff would first recognize a need for a specific technology and then consult the Department of Naval Affairs for an assessment of the potential designs and production problems. Naval Affairs would determine whether the designs and production were feasible. If approved, Naval Affairs would then instruct the Navy Ministry to assign the project to the appropriate department. All electronics-related projects for the navy were assigned either to the Navy Technical Research Institute under the Department of Ships, which handled research and development of all shipborne and shore-based equipment, or the Navy Aeronautics Research Department in Yokosuka, which dealt with all airborne electronics.[74] All electronics-related projects assigned to the NTRI were to be reviewed by the institute's Administrative Section, which would then pass down the order to the appropriate technical department. The head of the designated technical department then would assign the research to the engineer deemed most qualified for the project. Design, development, production, testing, and installation were then to be the responsibility of the designated section or division. In collaboration with the section or division head, the project engineer would assign research and development to an appropriate laboratory. A single laboratory rarely produced whole units. Rather, production of components was generally assigned to the individual research groups considered most capable.[75] The principal laboratory for radar research under the NTRI was the Radio Section headquartered in Meguro, Tokyo.[76]

Once all the components were ready, a prototype of the complete unit would then be assembled for testing. Upon satisfactory operation of the prototype, manufacturers would be called in to examine the unit, and production contracts would be drawn up. Production of the various components was generally assigned to the most appropriate and capable manufacturers, but one company alone rarely manufactured a complete unit. It was the general policy of the navy and its affiliated manufacturing firms that only the chief engineers of the contracted companies would have complete knowledge of the entire unit, its function and purpose. Subordinate engineers, who rarely had access to such information, were compelled to state after the war that "their secrecy prevented our best efforts."[77]

The Administrative Division of the NTRI determined priority of development and production, but when demand exceeded the capacity of the various manufacturers, a bottleneck was created that could only be relieved by negotiations with the army, which, in many cases, had contracted with the same firms for production. As previously discussed, a joint Army-Navy Technology Enforcement Committee was formed to address such problems, but the system failed, in part because of resistance from the lower echelons of the military services, and by the summer of 1945, assignments were being made on an individual basis. Early in the war, the military services used civilian engineers, university professors, and scientists in private laboratories as consultants on an as-needed basis, but as the war dragged on, assignments for these civilian scientists and engineers increasingly came about as a result of individual, personal relationships with either army or navy technical officers.[78]

One reason for the comparatively lackadaisical attitude of the Japanese military toward radar in the early years of the war was the shared perception of the technology as being primarily for defensive purposes. In those days, the military brass thought largely in terms of offensive weapons and did not yet perceive the great value radar could offer in defense, especially of the home islands.[79] In the Japanese navy, radar was thought to have a practical defensive application in the detection of approaching enemy aircraft by ships; thus, the first shipborne installations, the Model 2 Type 1 early warning radar sets, were installed onboard the battleships *Ise* and *Hyūga* for use in the attack on Midway and in the Aleutian Campaign at Kiska in June 1942.[80] But radar sets were not widely installed on navy ships at this time.

A few key events in the war changed navy policy toward radar. Navy brass in Japan—like their Italian counterparts—to a large extent attributed the defeat of Italian naval forces in the Battle of Cape Matapan in March 1941 to British advantage in radar. To that point, Japanese navy policy had precluded the use of radar in battle, opting instead for radio silence so as to prevent detection by the enemy. After Matapan, navy brass abandoned that doctrine and became more supportive of radar development and its use in combat.[81] The defeat of the Imperial Japanese Navy in the Battle of Midway in June 1942, however, was an even greater impetus for change as the navy brass came to believe that radar had played a significant role in the outcome of that engagement. This point was further underscored in October 1942 when, during the battle for Guadalcanal, Allied guns were able to find Japanese targets in the dark of night. These events eventually led to a complete reversal of attitude among navy brass toward radar.[82] In the spring of 1943, the decision was made to equip all types of warships with the more advanced microwave radar sets when possible. A factor accounting for the navy's initially less than enthusiastic support of microwave radar was that the earlier types required highly trained personnel to tune and maintain the receivers. From 1943 onward, however, engineers made a concentrated effort to simplify the technology so the sets could be used by less technically qualified personnel in the field.[83]

Because of the loss of ships and the paucity of materials, by early 1945, it became evident that a more concentrated effort was necessary in the research and development of radar and aviation electronics in general. In January, the Navy Ministry attempted to reorganize the navy's research and development infrastructure by creating the Second Navy Technical Arsenal, which was to consolidate navy electronics research projects at one facility and to provide a central office for their administration. The institute came under the primary direction of the Navy Aeronautics Department but was also made responsible to the Navy Technical Department. At this time, all electronics personnel at the NTRI and the Navy Aeronautics Research Department were transferred to the Second Navy Technical Arsenal. Some 350 technicians, including 80 engineers and scientists, were employed by the institute's electronics division operating with an annual budget of ¥100 million.[84] In this reshuffling of organizations, the Aeronautics Research Department was renamed the First Navy Technical Arsenal, which then became responsible for research and development of engines, air frames, armament, aviation instruments, and aviation ordnance. By this time, however, Japan was suffering from a lack of qualified electrical engineers, and there was no specific program to train additional engineers in problems concerning radio, radar, and sonar.[85]

Throughout World War II, the Japanese navy produced six basic series of radar sets with variant models, including land-based early warning sets (Mark

I, Models 1–4 series), shipborne early warning sets (Mark II, Models 1–2), shipborne surface fire control (Mark III, Models 1–3), land-based antiaircraft fire control (Mark IV), airborne ship-search radar (Mark V), and ground-controlled interception (Mark VI) (Appendix, Tables A9 and A10). These remained at a level comperable to British and American sets produced in 1942. The Japanese navy's negligent attitude toward this important new technology accounts, in large part, for the late and slow development of navy radar in World War II. Even so, where radar is concerned, the navy appears to have been more involved in research, development, and production than the army. Most radar sets were of navy design, including even some of the mobile and fixed land-based installations. Many of the sets installed in aircraft also originated with the navy.[86]

ARMY RADAR R&D IN WORLD WAR II JAPAN

Radar research and development in the Japanese army began to receive more attention and support after the return of the technical mission from Germany in 1941, but mobilization for radar research was not then considered urgent by any means. In the army, radar research, development, and production continued to operate through much of the war under a decentralized command structure similar to that of the navy. The two principal agencies concerned were the General Staff Headquarters and the Army Ministry. The General Staff Headquarters was required to submit research requests through the Army Ministry, which had the authority to approve or reject them. The Army Ministry consisted of a number of bureaus, the most important of which was the General Military Affairs Bureau (Gunmu-kyoku), under which, the Military Affairs Section (Gunkika) was responsible for oversight of research, procurement, and supply. (The Army Ministry also had jurisdiction over the Imperial Japanese Army Air Service Headquarters and the Ordnance Division.) Division One, Section Two of the General Staff Headquarters was responsible for equipment specifications. Section Three was responsible for requisitioning research, procurement, and supply. Division Three, Section Eleven of the General Staff Headquarters was responsible for supply logistics, planning, and operational use of radar.[87]

Until the early 1940s, radar related research in the army continued to operate under this relatively decentralized structure. (Even the Japanese army air service maintained separate laboratories from the army.) From the late 1930s, much of the army's electronics research was conducted at the Noborito laboratory of the Army Institute of Scientific Research (AISR). Located in

Kawasaki city, Kanagawa prefecture, the Noborito laboratory became the principal site for high-frequency electronics research.[88] Between 1940 and 1942, the organization and structure of the AISR laboratories underwent several changes, with the AISR being divided into ten separate research institutes (Rikugun Gijutsu Kenkyūjo), whereupon Noborito was redesignated the Ninth Army Technical Institute[89] (see Appendix, Table A2). But whereas the navy's policy was to perform as much of its own research as possible with in-house resources and personnel, where electronics was concerned, the army was more inclined to contract with outside research institutions such as universities and private firms.[90] The army relied extensively on such companies as Tokyo Shibaura Electric (Toshiba), Nippon Electric (NEC), Japan Radio (Nippon Musen), and Sumitomo Tsushin for its research and development.[91]

It was not until 17 June 1943 that the army established the Tama Technical Institute to coordinate the various radar related research projects that began to emerge in the early 1940s. The Tama Army Technical Institute, located on the outskirts of Tokyo in Tachikawa city in Kanagawa prefecture, then became the center for all army radar research conducted under the aegis of the Army Ministry. Tama, however, was not strictly or solely a research facility; it also acted as the central office for coordinating the research and production performed by universities and industry for the army. Much of the research itself was performed by civilian institutions and private firms, as noted above, according to specifications provided by the General Staff and the Army Ministry.[92] The Tama facility, like many other military research institutions during the war, generally established contracts with individual university scientists and industrial laboratories for basic research, and then completed development working with a select manufacturer.[93]

The Tama institute employed some 1,070 personnel, including 70 technical officers, 20 noncommissioned officers, 100 civilians redirected from the Army Ministry, and 880 other civilians taken into employment. The facility was inaugurated with an annual budget of ¥10 million (June 1943 to March 1944), which rose the following fiscal year to ¥15 million (April 1944 to March 1945). Some 80 percent of the budget was allotted for experimental work, and 20 percent went to basic research.[94] Research at the Tama facility was divided among seven sections working in different areas, including detectors and early warning equipment; locators, ground-control interception (GCI), fire control, and airborne radar; shortwave navigational aids; identification friend or foe (IFF); long-wavelength aids to navigation; warning and search receivers; and radio countermeasures.[95]

As a result of concerns over the vulnerability of the site to enemy bombing, in October 1944, selected elements of each section of the Tama radar research program were relocated to a site near Kobe, and these formed the Kansai branch of the Tama Technical Institute. In June 1945, the Kansai division was brought under the jurisdiction of the Imperial Japanese Army Air Service Headquarters. The Kansai branch also had access to the research facilities of Mitsubishi and Kawasaki as well as the laboratories of Osaka Imperial University.[96] On 3 April 1945, the original Tama laboratory suffered extensive damage from U.S. B-29 bombing raids, with nearly half of the facility being destroyed. Plans were underway to relocate what remained of the Tama institute to Nagano prefecture when the war ended.[97]

On the whole, army radar development and production lagged behind that of the Allies and Germany throughout the war, and to some extent trailed even the Japanese navy. The Japanese army developed three basic types of radar: fixed, mobile, and portable. Of these, several variant models were developed for land, sea, and air applications in the Tachi, Tase, and Taki series, including gun laying and searchlight control types and IFF (Appendix, Tables A9 and A11). Again, evaluations of these sets after the war determined that their technological level was roughly equivalent to Allied versions at the beginning of the war.

Applications of radar technology to other weapons systems and innovations, such as the proximity fuse, were also slow to develop in Japan. There was comparatively little research completed on the proximity fuse, and only one type was successfully developed. Designed in January 1944 by Asada Tsunesaburō at Osaka Imperial University for the army, and with support from the Technology Agency, this model, for use in aerial bombs, was composed of a photoelectric device that utilized the reflection of a pulsed beam of light emanating from a ground source. Apparently, a few hundred of these models were produced for experimental use, but none appear to have been successfully deployed in the field.[98] Research on acoustic proximity fuses and remotely detonated radar-tracked models for use in antiaircraft artillery shells and missiles had also been proposed, but there was apparently little research, and no notable progress on these types of weapons was made.[99] The major technical obstacle was the inability to produce a vacuum tube that could withstand the strains of the centrifugal forces involved.[100]

But there were other obstacles, perhaps greater still, to overcome. When the effort to develop a proximity fuse for an antiaircraft shell failed and attention was turned to development of the device for use in rockets and missiles, the military services appeared to be unreceptive to such fast-paced, innovative thinking. According to one report, failure in this line of research was partly because of "the inability of the armed forces to make up their minds" on such matters, which prompted Yagi Hidetsugu to remark after the war that "the military people generally behave[d] as if they did not want new weapons or ideas."[101] The Army-Navy Radio Wave Technology Committee (Riku-Kaigun Denpa Gijutsu Iinkai), established in August 1943, was formed to overcome such obstacles, but sectionalism in the military apparently proved too difficult for it to succeed.

Japan was certainly not unique in this regard. Scientists in Great Britain also encountered such wooden-headed attitudes from their military. Although radar had received a great deal of support from the War Ministry once Dowding had been convinced of its worth, the story of the proximity fuse in England was quite the contrary. The War Office, which had jurisdiction over development of the proximity fuse, gave this project such a low priority that it was all but abandoned. In this particular case, the War Office proved unreceptive to scientists attempting to initiate such projects and preferred that they "do what they were told."[102]

In Japan, the army was chiefly responsible for operating the radar network in the defense of the home islands, while the navy assumed control of radar installations overseas and throughout the Pacific. Before the outbreak of the Pacific War, the Japanese army had established an Air Defense System for the protection of the homeland. The Air Defense System was divided into three administrative districts with information centers in Tokyo, Osaka, and Fukuoka. Comprised mainly of a chain of Type A bistatic CW radar sets with a transmitter at one end and a distant receiver at the other, the Air Defense System was, in essence, an electronic fence that could detect whether an aircraft had penetrated the electronic beam between two radar stations. Local operators would then report the intrusion to the appropriate information center, which would, in turn, alert the airbases in the area, and fighter aircraft would be dispatched to intercept the intruder. As in Great Britain, women were commonly employed as switchboard operators and plotters at these communications centers, and by one estimate, occupied up to half of such positions.[103]

The navy also established a radar network for homeland defense of its own using primarily Type B sets. Although there was some overlap in the areas covered by the army's Air Defense System, the navy system operated entirely independent of the army and its chief purpose was to protect naval installations.[104] From around the end of 1942, the Japanese navy began to set up radar stations throughout the South Pacific. By about the end of 1944, the navy had erected an operational chain of early warning stations that stretched from New Guinea to Singapore, the Philippines to China, and from the Ryukyu Islands on to the home islands of Japan.[105]

The Japanese radar network, however, was no Chain Home system as found in Great Britain. The sets deployed mostly did not have the advanced technological capabilities of their British counterparts and could not usually give accurate information on the altitude and speed of approaching aircraft. The range of detection was also not as great. Moreover, the Japanese never developed the extensive central command structure of the Chain Home system as found in the operations center at Bentley Priory. Given the poor liaison between the army and navy, coordination of the two separate systems for early warning was difficult to manage, and consolidating the two into a central information office would have been problematic to say the least. In the words of one postwar U.S. intelligence report, "The inflexibility, uncoordination [*sic*], and poor organization of the Japanese Air Defense System saved the lives of many U.S. Airmen."[106]

Training in radar operations also lagged behind the West. The army did not establish a radar training facility until April 1944. Before this time, army technical officers were sent directly to the factories to receive training on the operation and maintenance of radar sets. The army eventually established five types of training programs, the facilities for which were located in sites near Tokyo, including Nagaoka, Ogawa, and Tachikawa. The army's training facility in Tachikawa city, for example, was capable of accommodating 1,200 students at a time, where radar operators received up to three months of training and maintenance personnel received up to six months. The navy began radar training in March 1942 at the Navy Communications School in Yokosuka and, in September 1944, established a more extensive training facility nearby at Atsugi in Kanagawa prefecture. This facility became the navy's primary radar training school. The navy program was more extensive than that of the army and was capable of accommodating up to 7,000 students with courses lasting from four to ten months.[107] A centralized administration for military training in radar was not established until as late as May 1945.[108]

THE MAGNETRON AND THE DEATH RAY

In Japan, both the army and navy attempted to develop a death ray. Progress on this weapon, however, depended on the development of a powerful magnetron capable of producing great amounts of microwave energy, a possibility that Wilkins had ruled out in England in 1935. The Japanese Army General Staff was the first to initiate a feasibility study on the death ray in 1930. In search of a decisive weapon, the General Staff was prompted by a newspaper article that briefly described an electric wave weapon allegedly invented by the German military in World War I. The General Staff officially requested the Army Ministry to initiate research on the subject at the Army Institute of Scientific Research. Their objective was to produce a weapon utilizing microwaves that could stop an internal combustion engine by means of the resonance effect or that could injure humans from a distance.[109] Such a device, they thought, might prove useful as an antiaircraft weapon because the equipment would not be easily portable and would not be suitable for mobile ground warfare. Other applications considered were for fixed-defense systems on land and for coastal defense in case of an attack by sea.[110] The AISR conducted a feasibility study and concluded, just as scientists in Great Britain had, that development of such a weapon would not then be possible because of its enormous energy requirements. No actual laboratory experiments appear to have been conducted at this time.[111]

With progress in the development of microwave-generating devices such as the magnetron, the means of focusing microwaves and utilizing the resonance effect became better known, and in 1936, the General Staff again considered the possibility of using microwaves as a weapon. When the Noborito laboratory was opened as a branch facility of the AISR in December 1937, it was assigned responsibility for research on microwave-producing equipment and its various applications. Research toward developing a weapon utilizing microwaves began around 1939 on a small scale with a team of thirty technicians. Their objectives were to determine how best to generate microwaves and how to stop an internal combustion engine by the resonance effect, and they sought to conduct basic research on the physiological effects of microwaves on live animals.[112]

But generating microwaves with sufficient power depended largely on the further development of the magnetron. Developed in the 1920s, the magnetron was to become the central component in such an electric wave weapons system. The team working under Yagi Hidetsugu at Tōhoku Imperial University in the late 1920s independently discovered the magnetron's capacity to produce ultrahigh-frequency waves and microwaves. Okabe worked on the problem of generating ultrahigh-frequency waves, while his colleague, Uda Shintaro, performed experiments on beam transmissions of 4.4-meter lengths. In 1927, Okabe reportedly produced "comparatively intense" electromagnetic waves with an experimental magnetron and obtained wavelengths of approximately 12 centimeters. With further modifications (applying the split-anode construction developed by German engineer Erich Habann in 1924), Okabe was able to increase output and obtain a wavelength of 40 centimeters. Adapting this design to communications equipment with directive antennae and a crystal detector, they were able to receive signals at a distance of one kilometer. Okabe's work on the split-anode magnetron inspired research on this technology throughout the world for several years to come, ultimately resulting in the development of the resonant cavity magnetron by Randall and Boot at the University of Birmingham in 1940. In the 1930s, the split-anode magnetron tube appeared to be the most capable technology for producing very short waves with significant power, even beyond the 1.5-meter to 50-centimeter range achieved in the decade after Okabe's research.[113]

Through 1940 and 1941, the army conducted experiments on animals to determine whether injury was caused by the heat generated or by other "special physiological effects of ultra-short waves" that were fatally damaging to the organs of the test animals. To determine the level of power and time necessary to cause injury, and to measure the precise amount of power absorbed by the test subject, animals were placed in the condenser field of the circuit and power was supplied from a one-kilowatt oscillator with wavelengths between 3 and 15 meters. But the power proved insufficient, and satisfactory results could not be achieved. Significant quantitative results were not obtained at this time.[114]

When the AISR underwent reorganization beginning in 1940, production of microwave oscillation equipment and experiments on internal combustion engines were assigned to the Seventh Army Technical Institute. Experiments there revealed that most internal combustion engines were well shielded and could not be affected by the resonance effect. As a result, army research on this subject was discontinued later that year.[115] In October 1941, the initial army working group for the death ray project was diverted to radar research, and the personnel were transferred to other military laboratories.[116]

But in 1943, research on the death ray was restarted at the Noborito laboratory. The Ninth Army Technical Institute, as it was now officially called, undertook research on the physiological effects of microwaves on live animals. Some progress was made in 1944 using wavelengths between 10 centimeters and 2 meters. As experiments began to show promising results, in 1944, additional funds were allocated for expanding research. Early in 1945, when, on the basis of the results of these experiments, the Army Ministry ordered this facility to develop a powerful new weapon, an additional ¥1 million was allocated for death ray research. By the end of the war, nearly ¥2 million (roughly $500,000) had been spent on the army's project.[117]

In 1945, the army's death ray project involved 116 military technicians under the command of Major General Kusaba Hideki.[118] Kusaba's personnel at Noborito included twenty technical officers, four civilian engineers, twelve part-time civilian consultants, and eighty technicians.[119] Among them were scientists and engineers with impressive credentials and research experience, such as Morita Kiyoshi, a doctor and professor of Electrical Engineering at the Tokyo Institute of Technology. Morita, who specialized in microwave radio communications engineering, became an assistant professor at the Tokyo Institute of Technology in 1934 and was promoted to professor in 1941. Yagi recommended him for the project at Noborito because of his specific interest in parabolic communications, energy concentration, and electromagnetic waves, as well as his expertise in the design of reflective mirrors.[120] Ikebe Tsuneto, who held a doctorate in physics, was another of the principal civilian consultants for the high-frequency research program at Noborito. From 1911 to 1913, Ikebe had served as an apprentice in the Siemens Brothers Corporation in London, and from May to November 1916, he was a researcher at the Sperry Gyro Company in New York. From 1935 to 1944, Ikebe conducted research for the army on antiaircraft fire control apparatus and was the chief engineer for the 80-centimeter magnetron development project.[121] Kusaba's team also included medical experts such as Matsuoka Shigeru, professor of medicine at Tōhoku Imperial University, and Minoshima Takashi, doctor and professor of medicine at Hokkaidō Imperial University. Minoshima was a graduate of the Tokyo Imperial University Faculty of Medicine, served as director of the First Physiological Laboratory, and was a member of the Research Institute of Applied Electricity. From 1940 to 1945, he worked as a consultant for the army conducting physiological and pathological research with microwaves.[122]

Throughout 1944 and 1945, experiments testing different wavelengths were conducted at Noborito using an operational prototype of the death ray. This experimental apparatus was a high-powered CW oscillator feeding a dipole antenna placed at the focus of an ellipsoidal reflector. The apparatus consisted of a 3-meter diameter ellipsoid mirror (full or less than half shape) with 5 to 10 meters' focal distance. Depth of the ellipsoid measured approximately 1.5 meters, with a power input of 1 to 2 kilowatts at 0.8-meter wavelength. The time of field application ranged between one to three minutes.[123] In some experiments, test subjects including various animals, such as mice, rabbits, marmots, and monkeys, were placed at the opposite focus of the ellipsoid. A systematic study was made of the physiological effects of the radiation as a function of the frequency. At each of the eight frequencies between 3 meters and 20 centimeters, twenty rabbits were subjected to radiation with a field strength intensity of one volt per centimeter for ten minutes. Japanese informants stated that monkeys were not used in the latter experiments because "they were difficult to get during the war." They also denied having conducted any such experiments on human beings.[124]

One experiment that used a 4-meter wave length with 50 kilowatts of continuous power with a Sumitomo 530-B tube proved capable of stopping a gasoline engine at close range and could kill a rabbit in thirty seconds to one minute at a distance of 3 meters. In another experiment, a monkey reportedly "the size of a medium dog" was killed in about three minutes.[125] Research at this time focused on building a larger, higher powered magnetron tube (80 centimeters), with a 10-centimeter wavelength, a power output of 200 to 300 kilowatts, and a reflector measuring 10 meters in diameter that would be capable of killing a rabbit at a distance of 30 meters from the reflector focal point. This apparatus remained under construction at the end of the war.[126] On the basis of previous experiments, in which rabbits were killed with 80-centimeter radiation in ten minutes at a distance of 30 meters, they calculated that a rabbit might also be killed in ten minutes from a distance of one kilometer. In trials utilizing wavelengths of 80 centimeters to 3 meters, postmortem medical examinations of animal subjects revealed the principal effect of exposure was hemorrhage of the lungs. Below the 80-centimeter wavelength, the primary effect was damage to the brain due to constriction of the arteries, and hemorrhage was again the chief cause of death.[127] This was apparently as far as the army's research on the death ray progressed by the end of the war.

Meanwhile, the Japanese navy was also engaged in development of a death ray, and navy scientists also understood that production of such a device depended on the further development of the magnetron. Magnetron research for the navy was carried out primarily under the direction of Captain Itō Yōji. Itō, a former student of Okabe, discovered independently through his study of the Kenelly-Heaviside layer that the reflection of waves from ships and aircraft became possible with a shorter wavelength. He submitted his results to the Science Research Committee of the Ministry of Education in March 1932, but after receiving no support, he set out to develop a magnetron oscillator himself. In 1933, Itō initiated research on the device at the Navy Technical Research Institute. In the following year, he began to collaborate with engineers at Japan Radio (Nihon Musen), who had undertaken magnetron research on their own in 1932. By 1937, their efforts had culminated in the development of the eight-split Tachibana (Mandarin Orange Blossom) type anode, the first stable microwave oscillator developed in Japan.[128] (It should be noted here that the close affiliation that came to develop between the NTRI and Japan Radio during the war may have had much to do with the fact that Nakajima Shigeru, an engineer and a high-level manager at Japan Radio Corporation, was the younger brother of none other than Itō Yōji himself![129])

At about the same time, the Japanese navy became interested in developing radar to improve night-fighting capabilities and to avoid collision of ships in battle formations in the dark. In September 1939, the NTRI and Japan

Electric Weapons: Radar and the "Death Ray" 115

Radio undertook research focusing on distance measurement for ships. Using a wavelength of 3 centimeters and a transmitter with sharp directivity and FM modulation, however, the research team was only able to detect the smokestack of a factory a few kilometers away because the power output of the transmitter was too low. But the team remained confident that an object as large as a warship could be detected at night using microwaves, and so research on microwave technology continued.[130] Meanwhile, by the end of the year, engineers at Japan Radio succeeded in producing a water-cooled cavity magnetron, the M3, having a 10-centimeter wavelength with a 500-watt continuous output of power.[131] By autumn 1941, the Japanese navy was able to produce 10-centimeter magnetrons with up to 5-kilowatt peak output.[132]

In the spring of 1943, with the tide of war turning, the navy high command decided that manufacture of microwave radar sets should be accelerated and that such equipment was to be installed on board all warships.[133] In 1944, the navy established a branch laboratory in Shimada city in Shizuoka prefecture for the specific purpose of conducting research on fundamental problems concerning magnetron tubes. Subsequent research at this facility revealed the theoretical mechanism of magnetron oscillation, which enabled Japanese researchers to develop various types of magnetron oscillators, although this line of research remained incomplete at the end of the war.[134] Engineers Itō Tsuneo (no relation to Yōji) and Takahashi Kanjiro worked in secret under the direction of Itō Yōji to develop a 6-centimeter magnetron capable of producing 30 watts.[135]

Two magnetron prototypes were developed at the Shimada laboratory. The first could generate a 15-centimeter wavelength with a 20-kilowatt continuous power output, while the second generated a 20-centimeter wavelength and a 100-kilowatt continuous power output. There were additional plans for a 10-centimeter wavelength magnetron with 500-kilowatt output, but the war ended before this model could be developed.[136] In all, the Japanese developed a variety of magnetron types, including both CW and pulsed models utilizing frequencies from 80 centimeters to 0.17 centimeters.[137] These devices were essentially on par with early models produced in the United States, but the United States quickly outpaced the Japanese after the arrival of the Tizard Mission.[138]

It was at the Shimada branch laboratory that an intensive effort toward the development of a death ray was undertaken for the navy. Generally classified under the heading of Z-Research, work on the electric wave weapon at Shimada was piecemeal at first, with much of the research being focused on development of a high-powered magnetron. But it was not until after Itō Yōji disbanded the Physics Committee in March 1943 that a more concentrated effort was given to development of the death ray under the navy. In the autumn of 1944, Z-Research received additional support and was upgraded with a new designation, Sei-gō Research or "Project Power."[139]

The death ray was one of the last, desperate hopes of the Navy General Staff for a new weapon that could turn the tide of war. The navy especially wanted a weapon with an effective range of over 10,000 meters to attack enemy ships. Moreover, it was hoped that such a weapon would offer an effective defense against the American B-29 bombers. Early plans envisioned a huge, rotating copper-plated reflecting dish to be installed on a tower larger than even one of the gun turrets of the superbattleship *Yamato*. Although navy brass were hopeful for its speedy development, not all scientists were as sanguine about the weapon's prospects. The venerable physicist Nagaoka Hantarō expressed doubt, indicating that even if such a weapon could be built, it would likely prove ineffective against airplane engines and crew, which were shielded by a metal fuselage. Yet despite such caveats, the navy proceeded with hope through the end of the war.[140]

Postwar U.S. military intelligence assessments of Japanese research and development of the death ray were mixed. Some investigators who examined the army's research data at the end of the war appeared not to have been very impressed with the project, stating, "While the results of the tests are interesting, there is nothing in them to indicate that Death Rays are likely to become an effective military weapon."[141] Yet others stated, "With the development of higher-power and shorter-wave length oscillators, which has become possible through the Allied research on radar, it is possible that a death ray might be developed that could kill unshielded human beings at a distance of five to ten miles if these Japanese experiments are reliable indications of the potentialities of the death ray."[142] One stated reason for the failure of the Japanese army program to develop a high-frequency electric wave weapon was that the Army Ministry and the army research staff did not give a "wholehearted effort" to this project. One impediment cited in U.S. postwar intelligence reports was the "improper dissemination of information by the army staff." Although competent civilian scientists had been brought into the project as consultants, they worked in "scattered localities" and were not kept informed of the development of the research. Moreover, Japanese informants stated that "a definite goal was not given to each scientist, and in some instances, the scientists did not know that the research was to develop a 'death ray' weapon."[143] Such observations appear not to have considered the fact that none of the other belligerents had succeeded in developing such a weapon either, or even whether any of the major powers could have done so during the war.

CONCLUSION

Postwar U.S. scientific intelligence reports judged Japanese research and development in radar up to August 1945 to be at a "very low level," comparable to that of England at the time of the Battle of Britain in 1940 or of the United States in 1942. Japanese night-fighter, GCI equipment, and antiaircraft fire control systems were sorely needed, and all were still under development at the end of the war. Japanese IFF equipment also remained in a rudimentary stage, and there was no standardization of IFF frequencies between the services. Earlier Japanese models apparently showed the influence of British and American equipment captured during the invasions of Singapore and the Philippines. Later models under development, however, were deemed more original. Some U.S. investigators were even impressed by individual Japanese scientists' achievements and noted Japan's "inherent capability of developing a modern radar program."[144] One report stated that the original work of many scientists was "first-class" and that with better organization, Japan could conceivably rise to the front rank of radar development.[145]

In particular, the Japanese were thought to have excelled in research on magnetrons, of which they had developed a greater variety of types and frequencies than had the United States during the war.[146] According to U.S. scientific intelligence investigators, Japanese research and development of magnetrons was "by far the most noteworthy development in their radar research," which they considered "almost entirely original" with only "a minor influence due to the recent capture of American magnetrons in the B-29 H2X radar."[147] Vacuum tube development at Japan Radio under the direction of engineer Nakajima Shigeru was also considered "outstanding."[148] Nonetheless, although Japanese research in magnetrons was recognized as being somewhat advanced, on the whole, all other equipment in use by the Japanese navy at the end of the war was judged to be obsolete by U.S. navy standards.[149] Negative assessments far outweighed the positive, and Japanese wartime research and development efforts were commonly described in less than flattering terms.[150]

Japan's comparatively low level of radar development was attributed largely to the "fundamental failure of the Japanese High Command to realize the operational importance of radar" early in the war. According to one assessment, "All of the weaknesses in Japanese radar may be traced to this basic cause."[151] As a result, radar research in Japan hardly had a chance to evolve into a viable program on par with those of the Allied forces. But there were numerous other factors. One U.S. report on the Japanese radar program emphasized the "lack of technical personnel, poor coordination of research and development, and [the] inability of production engineers to translate theory into practice," all of which combined resulted in a "halting, make-shift application of recognized microwave techniques."[152] The Japanese army and navy also carried out radar research independently of one another throughout most of the war, and there appears to have been little to no effective collaboration between them. No significant large-scale research program was initiated at the universities or any other government institution outside the auspices of the military services.[153]

The shortage of technical personnel remained a significant problem throughout the war. By one estimate, Japan had only between 5 to 10 percent of the research personnel that the United States found necessary to staff a "full-fledged" radar program.[154] Moreover, even the pool of scientific talent that was available during the war was poorly utilized. In stark contrast to the situation in the United States and Great Britain, the talents and efforts of civilian scientists in particular were not well directed or focused, and many researchers found themselves assigned arbitrarily to various military, industrial, and university laboratories and projects without apparent regard to their specialization.[155] There was no explicit policy for facilitating the systematic integration of civilian scientists and electrical engineers into radar research for the military. Many otherwise qualified and excellent technical personnel were left again to do "picayune jobs" often not related to war demands.[156]

Research and development on magnetrons and microwave systems was also slowed as a result of the diversity of effort and inadequate personnel and facilities. In general, the Japanese again had only about 10 percent as many scientists and engineers working on these research problems as worked on corresponding subjects in the United States.[157] There was also no set policy regarding the conscription of scientists and engineers throughout much of the war. According to Nakajima Shigeru, the aforementioned electrical engineer and participant in radar research for the navy, "Even engineers working on the development of weapons in a [private] company were drafted into the army as private enlisted soldiers . . . when war broke out, 800 engineers were working under my guidance at Japan Radio Company on research and development for magnetrons and radars. During the war, this staff was cut in half."[158]

To some extent, the shortage of technical personnel might have been addressed by better coordination. This point is indicated repeatedly throughout the U.S. intelligence reports, one of which explicitly cites the "lack of proper direction, organization, and coordination" to explain Japan's failure to meet the demands of war where radar was concerned.[159] The interservice rivalry between the Imperial Japanese Navy and Army, characterized as a state of "armed neutrality" during the war, was, again, a significant factor in retarding coordination of research and development of radar.[160]

In a few cases, private manufacturing firms ended up serving as the de facto liaison between the military services. In August 1943, manufacturers managed to convince the military to form a joint committee to coordinate production programs and to facilitate the exchange of radar technology and knowledge. The result was the Army-Navy Radio Wave Technology Committee (Riku-Kaigun Denpa Gijutsu Iinkai).[161] But the demands of secrecy still required manufacturers to maintain separate development and production sections for army and navy projects until late in the war. Permission was required before information concerning navy sets could be passed on to the army, and vice versa. In this environment, there were only a few isolated instances of cooperation. For example, magnetrons that were originally designed for the navy came to be used in some army radar sets, and some interservice cooperation in adapting the German Würzburg sets was achieved.[162] Until January 1944, when joint procurement and development of the German Würzburg antiaircraft radar system was undertaken by the military services, there had been no substantive effort to standardize radar equipment between the army and navy. Because the Würzburg was a German apparatus, neither service appeared to be reluctant to disclose information regarding its design.[163]

In another case, in January 1945, the army opted for procurement of the navy's 10-centimeter radar set for submarine detection when its own comparable 20-centimeter set for transport ships proved inferior. Planning for a joint research project to develop an airborne 5-centimeter set was underway in the last days of the war, and the Tase 6 set being planned for army antisubmarine applications was to be developed from a similar navy model, the Mark 22.[164] Beyond these minimal efforts, little more was accomplished.

The bizarre case of IFF development, although somewhat extreme, is perhaps one of the most egregious examples of the lack of technical cooperation between the military services during the war. The army originally took responsibility for the development of the IFF to be installed in aircraft, but the navy apparently became so dissatisfied with the army's slow rate of progress that it developed its own equipment. As a result, army and navy IFF sets ended up with different systems operating on entirely different frequencies. The refusal of the army and navy to standardize their IFF frequencies had the unfortunate result of rendering them incapable of distinguishing the friendly aircraft of their own military from those of the enemy.[165] It was reported that navy aircraft even had to identify themselves to the army by "wiggling their wings"![166]

The Technology Agency proved ineffective for coordinating R&D, and with the possible exception of the Army-Navy Radio Wave Technology Committee, no other top-down attempt was made to coordinate efforts between the services.[167] Because there was no oversight agency to coordinate radar research on a national scale, such as what existed in the United States under the OSRD, there was no means to manage efficiently the distribution of research among the numerous public, private, and military institutions available. Nor was there any effective means to avoid duplication of efforts between the military and the various research laboratories, nor any efficient way to oversee the recruitment and training of research personnel. The lack of cooperation between the services resulted in a detrimental degree of secrecy imposed on researchers and manufacturers, who were ordered, as a matter of policy, to maintain a separation of research for the army and navy projects. In short, manufacturers were ordered "not to let the left hand know what the right was doing."[168]

In addition to poor coordination, concerning both policy and organization of research and development, another explicitly stated problem was "production allocation methods."[169] Here, the policy of compartmentalization was again identified as a key factor. According to one report, until January 1945, "research and production were carried out on a component basis rather than on a complete equipment basis. The research group and the company assigned to produce a unit were given little insight into the design and manufacture of the other components of the equipment and little information on how the equipment would later be used in the field. This fact, coupled with an apparent total lack of provision for informing research and production personnel of service deficiencies, resulted in a very poor modification program."[170]

This "unbridgeable gap" between research and production existed throughout much of the war.[171] Civilian engineers and technicians in private firms contracted to work on electronics and radar for the military services often were not informed as to how the equipment they developed was performing in combat, nor were they allowed to visit radar installations in the field. They were also generally not allowed to go aboard military ships to inspect installed equipment or to observe such apparatuses in operation. As a result, the designers of the equipment had little to no opportunity to make necessary adjustments to adapt design to function, which was a significant obstacle to development.[172] Engineers from Japan Radio were only occasionally permitted to visit army and navy laboratories to consult on the development of equipment under joint development.[173] This policy may have contributed to the Japanese penchant for more simplistic designs, which obviated the need for precision work in production as well as specialized skills in maintenance. This practice made it possible for the equipment to be mass-produced by untrained laborers, thus addressing the shortage of skilled workers, as well as reducing the need for advanced technicians in the field.[174]

The lack of adequate test equipment and parts, and the destruction of manufacturing facilities toward the end of the war, further complicated development and production.[175] Good vacuum tubes, for example, were critically in short supply. To address this need, universities and technical schools transformed their laboratories into research centers for the development of radar tubes, but these remained of poor quality, and some 58 percent of all such tubes were still being manufactured by a single company, Japan Radio Corporation.[176] Allied bombing later in the war also had a very detrimental impact on production. By one estimate, about 80 percent of the productive capacity for microwave equipment, for example, had been destroyed or was being relocated to avoid destruction by the end of 1944.[177]

Finally, another explanation for Japan's comparatively low level of radar development during the war was Germany's reluctance to share more advanced technology. Throughout the 1920s and 1930s, the Japanese government and the navy imported from Germany, particularly from the firm Telefunken, various types of radio communications equipment, including azimuth instruments and direction finders.[178] But during the war, German assistance in radar was minimal, in part because of the prevailing view that Japan was a weak ally that might be defeated quickly and, thus, advanced technology might thus fall into enemy hands. For that reason, Germany provided Japan with very little information on radar and other advanced weapons technologies.[179]

German policy toward technology transfers to Japan, at least where radar was concerned, began to change somewhat in late 1943, but even then, only information that the Germans believed the Allies already possessed was provided to the Japanese.[180] Colonel Satake Kinji, who had traveled to Germany with the army's technical mission in 1940, apparently made a second trip in 1943. On that occasion, the Germans showed Satake all the radar systems then in production, but they did not share any of the technology currently under development. As a result of Satake's visit, the Japanese arranged to duplicate the Würzburg type radar. The Würzburg radar proved to be one of the very few exceptions to Germany's miserly technology transfer policy, and it was the only set for which they provided the Japanese complete specifications.[181]

In December 1943, Satake returned to Japan via submarine accompanied by two German radar specialists, Heinrich Foders of Telefunken and Emil Brinker from GEMA. They brought with them plans for the Würzburg radar sets C and D, as well as some blueprints for the Riese, Freya, Wasserman, Wismar, and other GEMA-designed equipment, including also a radar intercept receiver (Athos). Foders came to assist in the production of the Würzburg, but progress was slow, and of the three sets built, only one was put into operation on an experimental basis by the end of the war.[182] Foders, who remained in Japan briefly after the war, had a low opinion of his Japanese colleagues. In an interview conducted after the war, he stated, "the Japanese would not have known how to use information on advanced technical developments if it had been given to them."[183] Other Germans in Japan were "unanimous in their scorn and dislike of the Japanese and felt that their missions had accomplished very little." Likewise, some of the Japanese engineers appeared to have resented the Germans' presence as well.[184] When Brinker arrived at the Second Navy Technical Arsenal to help in the production of the German radar, his Japanese colleagues apparently regarded him as "an unwelcome arrival."[185]

After the war, Japanese scientists, engineers, industrial representatives, and military technical officers all adamantly claimed that, with few exceptions, Japan received very little technical aid from Germany or Italy. The exchange of technical personnel between Japan and Germany in radar research was minimal, with only the two radar specialists, Foders and Brinker, and a few technicians having visited during the war. Although some Japanese technical officers visited Germany on observation missions, and were permitted to inspect German operational radar, new technologies under development remained off limits to them and were not shared. According to Satake, the Germans were liberal in showing him equipment that had been in field use, but denied him access to laboratories where research and development was in progress on new systems.[186] Similarly, Itō Yōji toured German high-frequency research and experimental stations during a trip in the winter of 1943–1944, but German scientists interviewed after the war stated that "he was not shown everything" and that most of their "very important developments" were not revealed.[187]

Aside from direct exchange through technical personnel, the foreign trade offices of business firms and the diplomatic services also provided channels for liaison with Germany. Considerable technical information, including design specifications for a 10-centimeter airborne set, apparently was also exchanged by radio late in the war. But such contact proved insufficient to enable the Japanese to make much practical use of the German know-how at that stage.[188]

In the end, none of the radar systems developed by the Japanese military appears to have been capable of solving one of Japan's greatest and most urgent problems: how to defend against the U.S. B-29 bombers. Japan lacked accurate radar for ground-control intercept and fire control, as well as an integrated system for making effective use of the operating installations. To make matters worse, by May 1945, Allied radar jamming technology was also proving so effective that in most instances, Japanese antiaircraft batteries had to make visual contact before opening fire.[189] Where electric weapons were concerned, Japan had no means by which to successfully attack and destroy the B-29 Superfortresses or to interfere with Allied bombing raids over Japan. Even the United States with its superior radar technologies for interception, fire control, and perhaps even proximity fuses, would likely have found such a mission very difficult.[190]

In his official history of wartime scientific research, James P. Baxter attributed the comparative success and productivity of the U.S. radar development program at the MIT Radiation Laboratory to "a highly flexible and effective administration, extensive research in fundamentals, steady improvement of components, and close liaison with the army and navy, and the British."[191] Many of these factors were missing from the Japanese experience, just as they were in the German and Soviet cases. In contrast to the Japanese system, in which the military would turn over a design to a manufacturer for production, in the U.S. system, the Rad Lab served as a central hub of information exchange and training to which manufacturers would send their engineers and from which experts could be dispatched to industry for consultation as needed.[192] Although the Japanese army's Tama or Noborito laboratories, or the navy's NTRI, could have fulfilled such a role, their efforts remained divided throughout the war. There was no such common institute available to both military services in Japan.

4
AERONAUTICAL WEAPONS: ROCKETS, GUIDED MISSILES, AND JET AIRCRAFT

The technological gap in aeronautics between Japan and the West widened considerably during World War I, but Japan was able to catch up by the outbreak of World War II. The interwar years proved to be a time of rapid development for Japan. Corporations such as Mitsubishi, Kawasaki, and Nakajima all became involved in the aviation industry in the late 1910s, and by the 1930s, with generous military support and cooperation with the private sector, not to mention continuous importation of technology from the United States and Europe, Japan had again reached parity with the nations of the West. The Mitsubishi A6M5 (Zero), with its high performance capability, and the Model 97 reconnaissance plane, an earlier commercial version of which set a new world record for long-distance flight in 1938, both demonstrated that Japan's aeronautics industry had reached a level of sophistication on par with many western nations.[1]

Although the airplane proved its value as a weapon in World War I, other types of aeronautical weapons awaited development of additional technologies, such as new fuels and sophisticated electronics. Advanced rockets, guided missiles, and jet aircraft did not emerge until late in World War II, and while other nations progressed in the production of these, Japan remained at a comparatively low level of development. Largely cut off from technological exchange and international trade with the United States and Europe during the war, even the aircraft industry in Japan was unable to keep pace with its counterparts in the West after 1942.[2]

In contrast to Nazi Germany, where research on advanced aeronautical weapons had begun in earnest in the early 1930s, Japan made little progress in this field. In part, the discrepancies between Germany and Japan in development, effort, and interest can be explained by considering the different purposes for which rockets and missiles, in particular, were to be used. In the case of Germany, these weapons were developed as part of the arsenal for the offensive against England, and later in the war, potentially the United States, whereas in Japan, they were designed to address specific defensive needs late in the war. As a result, serious research, especially on guided missiles, did not begin until well after the tide of war had turned against Japan and the defense of the home islands with new weapons became a military priority. By that time, however, Japan had neither the material resources nor the engineering base necessary to produce such advanced weapons.

The Japanese military used conventional rockets extensively throughout the Pacific theater, and few improvements were made to these standard weapons during the war. Chronic shortages of materiel and technical personnel slowed research and development of guided missiles and jet aircraft, and fierce interservice rivalry stymied any hope of collaboration between the army and navy until late in the war. Moreover, the military services generally did not use the civilian pool of scientific and technical talent to its full potential. Although the Technology Agency came to have a hand in aeronautical research for the army, its overall impact was marginal. Japan's system for advanced aeronautical weapons R&D remained decentralized and divided among the laboratories of the military, the imperial universities, and private industry throughout the war. On the whole, Germany's R&D infrastructure in the aeronautics industry also remained decentralized, with the critical exception of Peenemünde, the highly centralized and vertically integrated production facility where Germany produced the V-2, advanced guided missiles, and rocket- and jet-powered aircraft. The Japanese never attempted to build a large-scale research and development complex such as Peenemünde, nor would they likely have had the industrial and engineering base to do so during the war. Japan was able to copy some German designs and quickly bring them to the prototype stage, and it also invented some promising weapons of its own. But for the most part, the lack of resources, industrial capacity, and poor mobilization kept Japanese innovations in advanced aeronautical weapons near prewar levels.

THE ROCKET IN MODERN WARFARE

The rocket had been used as a weapon long before it ever saw action on the modern battlefield. The origin of the rocket can be traced to tenth-century China with the invention of the "fire arrow." The first rockets were simple explosive projectiles made of wood, bamboo, or paper and were propelled by a rudimentary form of gunpowder, known as "black powder." Arab traders and invading Mongol armies brought black powder to Europe around 1240, and the introduction of the rocket soon followed. By the sixteenth century, rockets were in common use as fireworks and weapons throughout Europe and Asia.³

The modern version of the combat rocket emerged in the early nineteenth century. In 1805, William Congreve, a technician working at the Woolwich Arsenal in England, developed a barrage rocket based on projectiles of Indian design confiscated by the British army in 1790. Although the fundamental design was almost identical, Congreve constructed his rockets with metal, which increased both their destructive power and range. By 1810, the Congreve rockets were being used throughout Europe.⁴ Despite some improvements, however, the rocket remained a notoriously inaccurate weapon in combat until the 1840s, when William Hale, an English inventor, improved accuracy by developing a spin-stabilized type rocket. But by the 1850s, advances in artillery technology, which offered greater range and accuracy, began to eclipse the rocket. By the end of the nineteenth century, the rocket had fallen out of common use as a weapon.

Three visionaries, Konstantin Tsiolkovsky, Robert H. Goddard, and Hermann Oberth, revived interest in the rocket in the early twentieth century. Tsiolkovsky, a self-made expert in rocketry who came to be called the Father of Soviet Space Flight, was the first to conceive of a multistaged rocket for space travel. In the United States, Goddard, who held a doctorate in physics, was the first to develop a working liquid-fuel rocket motor, making the first significant design change to the rocket since the days of Congreve and Hale. Oberth, a physics teacher from Hungary, captured the imagination of Weimar Germany with his books on space flight.⁵

The Soviet Union jumped to an early lead in rocketry largely as a result of Tsiolkovsky's influence. Throughout the 1920s, his work remained mostly theoretical and focused on the development of rocket engines for interplanetary flight. In 1924, when Tsiolkovsky went public with his design for a multistaged rocket, the concept was so far ahead of its time that it went largely unnoticed by all but a few hearty enthusiasts. But in his capacity as a teacher, Tsiolkovsky had sparked the imaginations of a new generation of Russian rocketeers, both military and civilian. They in turn professionalized rocket engineering and assisted in the creation of the first government-supported rocket programs in the Soviet Union. By the late 1920s, the USSR led the world in the formation of research laboratories and academic institutions devoted to aeronautics and rocketry, including the Central Aero and Hydrodynamics Institute (Tsentralyni Aero-Gidrodinamichescky Institut, TsAGI), established in 1918, and the Leningrad Gas Dynamics Laboratory (Gazodinamicheskaia Laboratoriia, GDL), founded in 1928 with financial and technical support provided by the government's Revolutionary Military Council, the predecessor of the Soviet Ministry of Defense. The Group for the Study of Reactive Motion (Gruppa Izucheniia Reaktivnogo Dvizheniia, GIRD), a quasi-military organization comprised mostly of civilian rocket enthusiasts, was established in 1931, assuring the USSR of a growing body of young talent from which to draw.[6]

Rocket research, development, and production progressed rapidly in the USSR during the 1930s. The GDL began to produce aircraft-launched rockets from 1930 and produced the Soviet Union's first liquid-propellant rocket motor, the ORM-1, which was stand-tested in 1931. Throughout the decade, over a hundred liquid-fuel engines of various types were developed at the GDL, and thousands of static and flight tests were conducted. It also continued to enjoy successful production of solid-fuel rockets as well. In September 1933, Army Commander and Chief of Armaments Mikhail Tukhachevskii helped to bring together the GDL military facility and the mostly civilian GIRD to form a new central government organization for rocket research, the Reactive Scientific Research Institute (Reaktivnyi Nauchno-Issledovatel'skii Institut, RNII). In the same year, GIRD launched the Soviet Union's first liquid-fueled rocket, the GIRD-09. In the shadow of such progress, Tsiolkovsky died in 1935, long before his revolutionary concepts for space flight were realized.[7]

In the United States, Robert Goddard, a professor of physics at Clark University in Massachusetts, was among the first to develop functioning rockets. Goddard's research during World War I led to the development of the bazooka as well as improvements on barrage and antiaircraft rockets. In 1926, Goddard launched the world's first rocket powered by a liquid-fuel engine. From 1941, he worked on liquid-propellant jet-assisted takeoff rockets (JATO) for the military. But an ignorant press and an equally naive public, who often ridiculed Goddard for tinkering with "moon rockets" and such, overlooked his sound scientific achievements. Goddard was labeled an eccentric, but he obtained over 200 patents on new rocket and engine designs before his untimely death in 1945.[8]

The British had no Tsiolkovsky or Goddard of their own. Rocketry in England languished after the Explosives Act of 1875 banned private research, citing concerns over public safety, and it was not until the work of Goddard and others became well known that the general public again became interested in the rocket. In 1933, the British Interplanetary Society was formed, and a founding member, Phil Cleator, hoped to design and build a rocket-propelled car. Lacking financial support and government approval, however, the car was never built.[9] The British military did not resume rocket research until late in 1934, after news of German activities in this field compelled officers at the Woolwich Arsenal to begin investigating rocket propulsion for antiaircraft defense.

In July 1936, the Imperial Defense Committee's Subcommittee on Air Defense Research assumed authority over rocket development, but throughout the decade research in this field remained a low priority.[10]

In Germany, Hermann Oberth had proposed development of a liquid-fuel, long-range rocket to the German War Department as early as 1917, but the military rejected the idea as too impractical for the time. Rockets were still unreliable. During World War I, rockets had been used mainly for signal flares, and rockets launched from airplanes were used to destroy barrage balloons. As yet, the rocket had not otherwise proved to be of much use. In 1923, Oberth published a pamphlet on manned space flight, *Die Rakete zu den Planetenräumen* (The Rocket into Planetary Space), which generated great public interest and made him a national celebrity. Public enthusiasm for the rocket resulted in the formation of the Society for Space Travel (Verein für Raumschiffahrt, VfR), in 1927, which named Oberth its president in 1929. Director Fritz Lang promoted his film *Frau im Mond (Woman in the Moon)* by contracting Oberth to launch a rocket at its premier. Such stunts drew numerous space travel enthusiasts to the VfR, including a young Wernher von Braun, the engineer who was to lead development of the V-2 rocket for Nazi Germany.[11]

In 1930, the VfR established a headquarters in Berlin and constructed a modest testing ground, the Raketenflugplatz, where members of the society could launch rockets. One VfR member, Rudolf Nebel, a former World War I pilot and amateur rocket enthusiast who had worked with Oberth on the *Frau im Mond* project, attempted to interest the military in their work. From early as 1930, Nebel began to write letters to Hermann Göring, Josef Goebbels, and even Hitler, trying to obtain financial support for their experiments, but it came to nothing. For several months, Nebel attempted to solicit aid from various government ministries, science institutions, and corporations. He soon gained a reputation for being "more of a salesman and con artist than an engineer," but he eventually managed to wrangle some 5,000 marks (about $1,200) from the army's Ordnance Division.[12]

Karl Becker, then a lieutenant colonel and chief of the Ballistics and Munitions Section of the Army Ordnance Division, was already aware of the VfR and followed its activities with some interest. Becker, who held a doctorate in engineering, had himself considered the rocket a potential alternative to heavy artillery, which was then forbidden to Germany under the terms of the 1919 Treaty of Versailles. He visited the Raketenflugplatz and observed small-scale rockets being launched. Becker subsequently invited Nebel to conduct a demonstration at the army's weapons range at Kummersdorf. Nebel brought along von Braun. The launch, conducted on 22 June 1932, was a failure, but it resulted in the meeting of Becker and von Braun. Becker quickly assessed that von Braun was a more capable technician than Nebel, and by December, von Braun was working for Becker at Kummersdorf. In April 1934, the Propaganda Ministry issued a decree banning all publications concerning technical details or military uses of rockets, hoping to hide Germany's interest in the long-range ballistic missile from the world. The VfR and other German rocket societies folded one after another as the rocket became an official military secret.[13]

Nothing of the sort was happening in Japan. There were few, if any, real enthusiasts and no genuine rocket societies like the VfR to support private research. The origins of modern rocketry in Japan are comparatively obscure, but it is almost certain that the first substantive research efforts began with the military. Technical officers at the Seventh Army Technical Institute of the Army Technical Department in Tokyo began theoretical studies of rocket projectiles in 1931 and started experimenting with rudimentary solid-fuel rockets in the following year.[14] The first rocket type performed poorly in field tests, and after several failed experiments, research on this design was terminated. In September 1932, a second series of experiments was undertaken to develop a rocket-propelled artillery shell in order to improve the range of conventional artillery shells. From 1936 to 1940, the Army Technical Department also worked to develop a small fin-stabilized rocket, but as a result of its erratic flight characteristics, this model proved unsuitable for military use and the project was canceled.[15]

Research on liquid-fuel propellants in Japan began at the Army Technical Department around 1936. The first test of a liquid-fuel rocket occurred near Tokai in Ibaraki prefecture in May 1937. This model utilized a mixture of liquid oxygen and alcohol, and of the five tested, only one was launched successfully. After this series of tests, the project was canceled because of the high cost of the experiments.[16] In general, rocket research in the military did not begin in earnest until 1940, when more intensive development of combat rockets became desirable for the war in China.

The first known civilian effort to develop a rocket in Japan was recorded in 1935. A photograph of the rocket appeared in the June 1935 edition of *Astronautics,* a publication of the American Rocket Society. The journal attributed the design and construction of the rocket to Obara Tsunendo, a purported amateur enthusiast from the Nippon Rocket Society. The journal provided little information on either the designer or the obscure organization. According to one observer, the experiment was "not worth mentioning," however, because the rocket was "of such a primitive construction [that it used] gun powder for the fuel," and it apparently was not even capable of flight.[17]

The absence of such a pioneering figure as Tsiolkovsky, Goddard, or Oberth, coupled with a lack of enthusiasm for rocketry in the general public and the military, explains to some extent Japan's slow entrance into this field of research. In contrast to Germany, where the military was able to recruit talent from among the nation's several rocket societies and amateur enthusiasts, the military services in Japan could only look to their technical officers, who had little or no real expertise in rocket design or construction. As a field of study, rocketry in Japan remained undeveloped until the exigencies of war provided a sufficient military imperative to push technological progress further.

ADVANCED AERONAUTICAL WEAPONS IN WORLD WAR II

When World War II erupted in Europe in September 1939, the Soviet Union and Nazi Germany were well ahead in the development of rockets. Pioneering research in jet-engine technology was also being undertaken in Nazi Germany and Great Britain. But of all the principal belligerents, it was Germany that took the lead in nearly every area of rocketry and jet propulsion. Although the Soviet Union and the United States would dominate in these fields in the postwar period, they both fell behind Germany during the war. The Soviets arguably retained their lead only in solid-fuel rocket technology. The reasons for this development vary and merit closer attention.

Despite its early lead in rocketry, the USSR eventually fell behind in most areas of rocket-related research during World War II. The Soviet Union was one of the first nations to use modern rockets in combat with some success when it deployed aircraft-launched rockets (Type RS-82) to the front in the border war against the Japanese Kwantung Army at Khalkin-Gol (Nomonhon) in the summer of 1939.[18] But rockets were not a high priority weapon at the time, and although development of the Katiusha series barrage rocket proceeded apace thereafter, it was not until the eve of the German invasion on 22 June 1941 that mass production was actually authorized.[19] The Soviet Union then became the first of the belligerents to adopt barrage rockets for wide-scale use in combat. As the war's leader in rocket artillery, the Soviets produced and used more solid-fuel barrage rockets than any other nation in the war, with the BM-13 Katiusha being the most extensively used from 1941.[20]

Beyond rocket artillery, however, the Soviets did not excel due to several factors. As a relatively poor nation with an undeveloped economy, resources were scarce. And, during the war, priority in weapons development went to those projects having greater potential for immediate use on the battlefield.

Time and resources for longer-term projects, such as long-range liquid-fuel missiles, were luxuries the Soviets could not afford. Moreover, there were institutional constraints. Although on the whole the Soviet economy rejected competition in industry, the military R&D system remained an exception to this policy and encouraged competition and pluralism among rival agencies in weapons development. But this policy was only good insofar as resources allowed and, thus, it applied almost exclusively to development of conventional weapons. In the scheme of the general military R&D system, rockets were still considered a secondary or "peripheral" weapon at best, and so more innovative models were not readily accepted.[21]

Finally, the political purges beginning in 1936 deprived the USSR of its leading advocates and engineers in rocketry. In 1937, Tukhachevskii, who had risen to the rank of marshal and was the leading proponent of rocket research in the military, was arrested and executed under suspicion of being a traitor. The purges extended even to the designer of the Katiusha rockets, Georgii Langemak, and I. T. Kleimenov, director of the RNII. (The RNII itself was dissolved in that year and the NII-3 division of the Commissariat for Ammunition assumed responsibility for rocket development.) The purges were incited, to some extent, by preexisting hostilities between factions of engineers engaged in heated "technical debates," such as favoring liquid-fuel over solid-fuel rocket development, as well as between those whose interests in rockets were more utilitarian and directed toward the war effort versus those who were known to have had an interest in developing rockets for space travel. Under the purges, preexisting institutional rivalries and professional jealousies surfaced with a vengeance, resulting in the unfortunate loss to the Soviet Union of many of its preeminent scientists and engineers in rocketry.[22]

With the invasion of the German army, many research centers and factories were evacuated to the east, and resources had to be directed toward immediate military needs. Development of liquid-fuel rockets was brought to a near standstill as resources were concentrated instead on the mass production of the more cost-effective solid-fuel barrage rockets.[23] For the remainder of the war, the USSR was not a significant competitor in the fields of advanced rocketry, guided missiles, and jet propulsion. Like the United States, it would not take a lead in these areas until reaping the harvest of captured German technology in the postwar period.

The United States got off to a much slower start than the USSR, despite Goddard's contributions in World War I and after. The military services in the United States did not become much interested in rocket development until 1940, when Dr. Clarence Hickman, an associate of Goddard and one of the few American scientists specializing in rocketry, penned a letter to NDRC chair, Vannevar Bush, advocating a government supported rocket development program. High-ranking officers in the military services were skeptical of the proposal, because rockets were inaccurate and inefficient compared to guns. But the rocket appeared to offer a solution to a problem that was vexing the Bureau of Ordnance and the navy. Both desired a projectile with great explosive power that could be fired with little recoil from aircraft and light surface vessels. The rocket appeared to hold the greatest potential for such an application.[24] In July, Bush appointed Hickman chair of a newly created NDRC department under the Division of Armor and Ordnance. Called Section H after Hickman, this branch was to conduct rocket research in collaboration with the army, navy, and the NDRC. The navy provided Hickman with a small laboratory at the Naval Powder Factory at Indian Head, Maryland, together with a corner of the Naval Proving Ground at Dahlgren, Virginia, on the Potomac River.[25]

Rocket research in the United States got a small boost from data provided by the Tizard Mission in the summer of 1940, which may have saved the Americans a few additional months of experimentation. By the spring of 1941, several new rocket weapons were under development at Section H, including antiaircraft rockets, artillery and aircraft-launched rockets, and a rocket-accelerated armor-piercing bomb.[26] Close cooperation with British scientists and engineers proved helpful to the progress of American R&D in rocketry during this formative stage, but it was not nearly as significant as the assistance received in nuclear fission and radar research. The British simply were not as far ahead of the United States in rocketry as they were in basic research in these other areas.

In the summer of 1941, Dr. Charles C. Lauritsen of the NDRC visited England to observe progress in antiaircraft rocket research. Upon his return to the United States, Lauritsen used information he had gathered in England to help convince the NDRC to expand the rocket program. As a result, the NDRC began to supplement research at Indian Head with contracts from Bell Telephone Laboratories and George Washington University. The NDRC also established a new research group, designated Section L for Lauritsen, which was subsequently housed at the California Institute of Technology (Caltech) in Pasadena and placed under his supervision. Caltech was a logical choice because research on rockets for jet-assisted takeoff had been undertaken there at the Guggenheim Aeronautical Laboratory since 1939. Renamed the Jet Propulsion Laboratory (JPL) in November 1943, research and development of long-range solid-fuel rockets and jet engines was begun there in 1944.[27] From this point forward, Caltech and JPL became integral to rocket development, and after the war, they became major contributors to the U.S. space program.

Research accelerated after the United States entered the war in December 1941. In 1942, the NDRC designated additional facilities to support rocket research, including Wright Field in Dayton, Ohio, the U.S. Army Air Force Base in Dover, Delaware, and the Naval Ordnance Test Station at Inyokern, California. When the NDRC was restructured in late 1942, Sections H and L were placed under the aegis of the newly formed Division Three, which became responsible for rocket ordnance, and Lauritsen was appointed its director in June 1943. These changes helped to reduce duplication of research efforts and facilitated greater cooperation among the military services and university laboratories. From 1942 to 1943, laboratories affiliated with the NDRC and its Sections H and L worked to improve solid-fuel propellants and produced several types of rockets, including an improved bazooka antitank rocket.[28] With the cooperation of Caltech and the NDRC, in 1943, the Navy Bureau of Ordnance and the Bureau of Aeronautics produced a series of fin-stabilized, aircraft-launched antisubmarine and antishipping rockets and rocket launchers.[29] Division Three also developed a series of ship-to-shore fin-stabilized barrage rockets for the navy.[30]

In less than four years, the U.S. military began to produce some of the most effective combat rockets introduced in World War II. By the end of the war, the army and navy together were spending some $1 billion per year on rockets alone. (This was perhaps not a tremendous sum in view of the U.S. War and Navy Department annual budget of $60 billion, but on a comparative scale, it was considerably more than the $2 billion total budget of the Manhattan Project.) Such rapid development and production were made possible not only by the close technical cooperation between the United States and Britain, but much more importantly, by the extraordinary degree of collaboration between the military services, civilian scientists, and private industry.[31] By 1943, the United States had even outpaced its British ally.

For their part, the British army and the Royal Air Force (RAF) both stepped up rocket production with the outbreak of war. A special department was established in the Ministry of Aircraft Production to expand research and development. By the summer of 1944, British Typhoon fighter aircraft were flying thousands of sorties using rockets against German tanks and personnel, with great success.[32] The British Admiralty also developed notable rocket types, but beyond the sharing of technology and concomitant technical data, there was no extensive collaboration with the RAF and the army. All British rockets developed at this time used solid-fuel propellant, as liquid-fuel propellants for rockets never advanced beyond the research stage in England during the war. Guided missile development was also minimal.[33]

Although the Tizard Mission and subsequent British technical assistance had helped to advance the fledgling U.S. rocket program, they were of little help in developing guided missiles. For its part, the U.S. military also had done almost no research of its own in this area by the start of the war. It was not until August 1943 when Germany successfully used a radio-controlled missile in combat that high-ranking military officers in the United States began to recognize the potential of this new weapon. From that point forward, the military services worked in conjunction with the OSRD and NDRC to expand projects for the development of guided missiles as quickly as possible.[34]

One of the first guided missiles designed in the United States was the Dragon, a radio-controlled aerial torpedo with a television camera mounted in the nose. Development proved difficult, however, when private television and electronics related firms attempted to merge their designs with the airframes developed by the military. To overcome some of the ensuing technical difficulties involved in systems integration, the NDRC enlisted the aid of the National Bureau of Standards, which formed a special research group for the project. But before development advanced to the production stage, the project became sidetracked when the navy requested the National Bureau of Standards to design an effective antisubmarine guided missile. Using a scaled-down version of the Dragon, late in 1944, the National Bureau of Standards produced the Pelican, a radar-guided antisubmarine missile.[35]

By this time, however, the German U-boat threat had subsided greatly, and despite its excellent performance in flight tests, the navy scrapped the Pelican, declaring that the missile was of "no operational use."[36] The technical knowledge gained from the development of the Pelican was subsequently applied to a more advanced model, the SWOD Mk 9 air-to-surface guided missile, also known as the Mk 57 Bomb, or Bat. The Bat, developed by the Navy Bureau of Ordnance in cooperation with the Radiation Laboratory at MIT, was a low-angle glide bomb equipped with a radar bombsight for active homing. The Bat entered service in January 1945 and was first used on 23 April 1945 at Balikpapan, Borneo. Although the Bat was the only completely automatic target-seeking missile developed during the war, its efficacy in combat proved less than satisfactory.[37]

Nazi Germany expended far more effort and resources on rockets and guided missiles than any other belligerent during the war. As early as June 1933, Wernher von Braun had completed drawings for the Aggregat-1 (A-1), the first in the series of liquid-fuel, long-range ballistic missiles developed by the German army. The A-1 never flew, but improvements on the design led to the development of the A-2, two of which performed successfully in experiments conducted in December 1934. These and subsequent launches compelled von Braun to seek a more suitable firing range, one that would accommodate long-distance tests as well as provide the necessary secrecy. To meet these requirements, von Braun chose Peenemünde, a small fishing village on the remote island of Usedom on the Baltic Sea. With cooperation from the Luftwaffe, which was interested in developing rocket-propelled aircraft and aerial torpedoes, construction of the Peenemünde Experimental Center was completed in May 1937. The new facility brought together much of the rocket development staff from Kummersdorf as well as former members of the VfR and selected engineers from private industry.[38]

The Luftwaffe and the army divided Peenemünde between them. The Luftwaffe's testing facility, Peenemünde-West, occupied about 4 square miles and included landing fields and hangars for experimental aircraft, such as the Messerschmitt rocket-propelled Me 163 and the Me 262 twin-jet fighter-bomber. Peenemünde-East, the army's rocket development center, occupied 18 square miles and employed approximately 17,000 engineers and workers.[39] It was here under the direction of General Walter Dornberger that the most technologically advanced rockets of World War II were built. Dornberger's management philosophy of "everything under one roof" concentrated R&D as much as possible at this single establishment. Dornberger ran Peenemünde-East like a private company. The heads of all departments, divisions, and branches were civilians, and Dornberger was able to secure some 4,000 soldiers with educational backgrounds in engineering to round out the research staff. According to Dornberger, "the most significant factor in the successful development of the rockets proved to be that the research institutes, the engineering departments, the static test facilities, the oxygen generating plants, the work shops, and the launching sites were all at the same location and under one management."[40]

The rockets and guided missiles developed by the German army at Peenemünde-East are too numerous to discuss in much detail here, but Hitler's two "vengeance weapons," the Vergeltungswaffe-Eins (V-1) and the Vergeltungswaffe-Zwei (V-2), merit attention. The FZG-76, or V-1, also known as the buzz bomb or doodlebug among Londoners, was the forerunner to the modern cruise missile and the first operational guided missile produced in Germany. The V-1 was simple in design. It was essentially a midwing monoplane propelled by a pulse jet engine mounted above the fin, and as such, it was really more a flying bomb than a guided missile. But it was unlike anything ever seen before, and it had a significant psychological impact when it first appeared in the skies over London late in 1943. During the war, Germany launched 9,251 V-1s against England and 6,551 against Belgium. The V-1, however, proved to be rather slow and inaccurate. British fighter planes and antiaircraft fire—aided by the Chain Home network of radar installations along the southern coast of England—were eventually able to destroy scores of them before they could reach their targets.[41]

Germany's most advanced guided missile, the Aggregat-4, or V-2, was much faster. It could reach London within five minutes after launch and proved nearly impossible to destroy in the air.[42] The first V-2 prototypes were completed in February 1942, and test launches were conducted in the following June. On 8 September 1944, Germany launched the first V-2 against England. By 27 March 1945, over 1,100 of the missiles had fallen on London, resulting in 2,742 dead and over 6,000 injured. In all, Germany fired more than 2,100 V-2s against Antwerp, Liège, and Brussels on the Continent. Although the V-2 proved to be a formidable weapon of terror, it was far more expensive to produce and on the whole much less effective than the heavy bombers it was intended to replace. The V-2 was less accurate than hoped, and its rate of failure was high. Ultimately, the psychological impact of the V-2 on the people of London was perhaps greater than the actual damage it inflicted on the city.[43]

Production of rockets and missiles by the German navy paled in comparison to the army, and there was little collaboration between the two services in the development of these weapons.[44] The most significant missile developed by the German navy was the Henschel Hs-293, a radio-guided monoplane equipped with a 1,100-pound (500 kilogram) warhead. It was launched from a parent aircraft and guided to target by radio control. The Hs-293 proved somewhat effective in combat and was responsible for sinking several cargo vessels and warships.[45]

At the beginning of the war, there was a significant amount of cooperation between the German army and the Luftwaffe in the development of rockets and guided missiles at Peenemünde. By the spring of 1942, however, the situation had changed. As the Luftwaffe struggled to regain priority among the services, it began to siphon much-needed resources from the V-2 program for development of its own missiles and jet aircraft. There was even less collaboration with the navy. And from about spring 1943, the SS began to meddle in the affairs of Peenemünde, adding yet another authority competing for resources and control, as well as another burdensome layer of bureaucracy, when the decision was made to exploit slave labor for the manufacture of the rockets. Allied bombing raids on Peenemünde, beginning in August 1943, also forced the decentralization and dispersal of the V-2 production program, much of which was taken underground until the end of the war. Despite such drawbacks, the engineers at Peenemünde were able to produce the most technologically advanced rockets and guided missiles of the war. That they were able to do so is indicative not only of their collective engineering talent, but also of the organizational efficiency provided early on by Dornberger's "everything under one roof" management philosophy.[46]

JAPANESE ROCKETS AND GUIDED MISSILES

Compared to Germany, Japan had far less collective engineering talent, and until research was begun on advanced types of guided missiles later in the war, there was simply no need for the level of organizational efficiency such as that found at Peenemünde. First, the rocket did not become a priority weapon for either of the Japanese military services until late in the war. Throughout most of the conflict, development and production of rockets remained limited to simple models that were easy and inexpensive to manufacture in quantity. The military did not attempt to mobilize civilian scientists on a large scale for rocket development, and compared to the other belligerents, Japan had virtually no experts in this field. It could not draw from such a large pool of civilian talent as Germany had at the beginning of the war. Rocket R&D, limited as it was, remained the exclusive purview of the military, which contracted with private firms only on an as-needed basis for further development and production. And as might be expected, there was not much interservice collaboration, with the exception of sharing a few basic designs, until late in the war.

Within the Japanese army, the Seventh Army Technical Institute of the Army Technical Department was responsible for basic research while models with promising designs were turned over to the First Army Technical Institute for further development and testing. The Second Army Arsenal in Tokyo produced the propellant powder, and the army's Osaka Arsenal constructed the rockets. In 1942, the army began production of several types of spin-stabilized rockets (SSR) for use in close combat, including antitank and antiaircraft rockets. A 90-mm antitank rocket was developed, presumably derived from designs of the U.S. bazooka and German antitank weapons.[47] And according to one report, by March 1945, the Japanese army may actually have produced "the world's largest barrage rocket"[48] (Appendix, Table A12).

The Imperial Japanese Army Air Service began research on aircraft-launched rockets in 1938 at the Third Army Aeronautical Technology Research Institute in Tachikawa, but it was not until the early part of 1944 that an operational aircraft rocket, the Ro-3 Type I, was produced. Based on the design of the army SSR types, this rocket proved rather ineffective in combat because of its excessive high speed, which rendered it erratic and impractical as a tactical weapon. The Third Army Aeronautical Technology Research Institute otherwise conducted only minimal research on fin-stabilized rockets[49] (Appendix, Table A13).

The Japanese navy began research on solid-fuel rockets on a very small scale in 1936, but development of rockets as weapons did not occur until 1942, and mass production of combat rockets did not begin until 1944. After observing the test firing of an army rocket in early 1942, navy officers resolved to build similar rockets of their own. The naval arsenals at Kure and Sasebo became the centers for this field of research. Technical officers at the Kure Naval Arsenal copied the design of the army's 40-cm SSR type rocket, and production began in the spring of 1944. By April 1945, technical officers at Kure, with help from technicians at the First Navy Technical Arsenal in Kanazawa, had developed several additional types of rockets (Appendix, Table A14). Design of rocket launchers and fabrication of metal parts for navy rockets were generally conducted at the Kure Naval Arsenal. Solid propellants for navy rockets were manufactured at the Second Navy Powder Arsenal in Hiratsuka city in Kanagawa prefecture, and test firing was conducted on a small island near Kure.[50]

The navy also produced various types of combat rockets for aircraft. Research on aircraft-launched rockets began in 1935 with the goal of developing high-velocity ordnance capable of penetrating the metal plating of enemy warships. Preliminary designs of this type of rocket were available as early as 1939, but production did not begin until 1943. Among the rockets designed by the navy in 1944 and 1945 were those for use against aircraft carriers, submarines, landing craft, and large airplanes[51] (Appendix, Table A15). The navy also attempted to develop a rocket-propelled torpedo, but the project was abandoned after the weapon was determined to be impracticable at that time.[52]

Rockets came to be used more frequently by the Japanese toward the end of the war. Production of combat rockets for the navy doubled from 50,000 units in 1944 to 100,000 in 1945 as a result of efforts to increase defensive strength in the central Pacific.[53] Although ship-launched rockets were in common use by 1944, it was not until the landing on Iwo Jima in February 1945 that U.S. forces first encountered Japanese navy ground-based barrage rockets in combat. Bottlenecks in production, as well as the difficulty of transport due to the increasingly effective blockade of the Japanese home islands by the U.S. navy, often resulted in a significant lag time between production and use in combat.[54]

Both the army and navy undertook designs for long-range solid and liquid-fuel rockets toward the end of the war. A 90-mm spin-stabilized rocket with an estimated range of 2,000 meters was under development by the Army Technical Department, and a navy version was undergoing wind-tunnel tests by engineer Sugimoto Masao at the Second Navy Technical Arsenal when the war ended.[55] Navy technicians designed a 2-meter-long, 20-cm-diameter rocket using a hydrogen-peroxide and alcohol fuel mixture that was to have an effective range of 10,000 to 20,000 meters carrying an explosive charge of 50 kilograms. Work on this rocket did, however, not progress beyond the design stage, and no models were produced before the end of the war.[56] In February 1945, research was begun on another high-altitude, ground-launched antiaircraft rocket at the First Navy Technical Arsenal, but it did not reach the development stage.[57]

As the Allied forces advanced further across the western Pacific, the Japanese army and navy grew desperate for new weapons to halt their progress. The military needed weapons with much greater range, accuracy, and firepower than existing conventional weapons, such as the rocket, could deliver. Guided missiles appeared to hold such a potential, and in the last two years of the war, both services started research programs for their development. Although a few of these would eventually come under the purview of the Army-Navy Technology Enforcement Committee in autumn 1944, most R&D efforts in guided missiles were conducted by the military services independently of one another. What little interservice collaboration there was in missile development was much too little and came too late to have had any significant impact on the outcome of the war.

I-GŌ SERIES AIR-TO-SURFACE MISSILE

The Japanese army began research on guided missiles comparatively late in the war. Initial efforts to produce guided missiles relied largely on radiowave remote-control technology, which had become fairly common by the 1940s.[58] In the spring of 1943, the army initiated the Sa-gō project, the purpose of which was to develop a radio-guided, antiaircraft rocket designed to explode in midair. Later, the objective of the project changed to development of an antiship missile. In May 1944, when the Army Aeronautics Department realized a need to develop a special purpose weapon for attacking Allied warships at a great distance. Allied shipborne antiaircraft fire was proving very effective against Japanese airplanes, and the Imperial Japanese Army Air Service needed to reduce the losses of its pilots and aircraft. Toward that end, the Sa-gō project was abandoned in favor of developing a long-range radio-guided, air-to-surface missile, designated I-gō. The Second Army Aeronautical Technology Research Institute was designated the research center for the project, and Colonel Arimori Mitsuo, chief of the Aircraft Section of the Technical Division of the Army Aeronautics Department, was made project leader. Arimori was permitted to recruit several technical experts from the First and Fifth Army Aeronautical Technology Research Institutes as well.[59]

Responsibility for the design of the stabilization mechanism, the radio-control system, and the overall direction of the flight tests of the I-gō were assigned to Major Omori Masuo of the First Army Aeronautical Technology Research Institute.[60] Airframe design and construction of the I-gō model 1A was assigned to a Mitsubishi team under engineer Ozawa Hisanojo. Technicians and engineers from the army air service, Mitsubishi's Nagoya Engine Research Division, and the Nagasaki Ordnance Works collaborated in the production of the rocket engines for both the I-gō-1A and I-gō-1B models. The Tokyo Aircraft Instrument Company was assigned development and manufacture of the pneumatic systems to power the gyro and to operate the control surfaces.[61]

The I-gō-1A was a simple monoplane with a cruciform wing configuration and constructed primarily of wood. It was to be equipped with a 1,760-pound (800 kilogram) warhead and transported by the Mitsubishi Ki-48 and Ki-67 (Peggy) bombers[62] (Appendix, Table A16). The I-gō-1A and its sibling, the I-gō-1B, were to be launched from the parent aircraft about seven miles from the target at an altitude between 2,300 and 3,000 feet. The missiles were to sustain flight through a short burn of the rocket engine, which was to be fueled by a mixture of hydrogen peroxide and sodium permanganate. The parent aircraft was to follow the missile and guide it by radio control to within 2.5 miles of the target. A bombardier positioned in the nose of the parent aircraft was responsible for tracking both the distance from the target as well as the line of flight. By means of optical sighting equipment and radio control, the bombardier was then to visually direct the missile to its target.[63]

Mitsubishi built a total of fifteen I-gō-1A missiles, ten of which were delivered to the army by November 1944. The army conducted the first series of drop tests at Point Manazuru, near Atami in Kanagawa prefecture, later that month. A second series of drop tests was conducted at Lake Biwa near Kyoto and at Wakasa Bay, near Maizuru city on the Japan Sea. These tests proved the I-gō-1A ineffectual for use in combat: engineers determined that U.S. antiaircraft would be able to shoot down the parent aircraft before the missile could be deployed. As a result, development of the I-gō-1A was terminated and the missile did not enter service during the war.[64]

The I-gō-1B was similar to the I-gō-1A in design and construction, although slightly smaller, with wooden wings and a fuselage composed of tin. The I-gō-1B was designed to fit under the Kawasaki Ki-67 bomber, the Kawasaki Ki-48-II bomber, and the Ki-102b assault aircraft for transport. It was to be equipped with a 660-pound (300 kilogram) armor-piercing warhead.[65] Manufacture of the I-gō-1B was assigned to the Kawasaki Aircraft

Corporation, where Kitano Jun served as chief engineer for the design of the airframe. Engineers Hayashi Teruo and Nagamori Kyūzo at the Sumitomo Communication Machine Corporation developed the radio-control system and collaborated with the Hokushin Electric Works to develop the electrical system for the gyro and the surface controls. As with the I-gō-1A, design of the rocket engine for the I-gō-1B was assigned to Mitsubishi.[66] Some 150 I-gō-1B missiles were built by the end of the war.[67]

The first 1B model was ready for testing by the end of October 1944. The first tests were conducted near Ajigaura in Ibaraki prefecture in November and focused on launching and gliding. The initial results seemed promising, and a second battery of test drops was begun at Point Manazuru to attempt radio control under powered flight. A subsequent series of tests continued until July 1945, during which time the engineers worked to improve the control and stabilizing systems. Test drops with targets were conducted at the Yokaichi Army Air Field in Shiga prefecture, where the army used the large Shiraishi rock in Lake Biwa as a target. The results of these tests indicated that the radio-control system and flight characteristics of the I-gō-1B missile were satisfactory and promising for operational use in combat. The development team estimated that the missile could have as high as a 75 percent accuracy rate on strikes against aircraft carriers and battleships.[68] Although the I-gō-1B performed well in drop tests, project engineers again concluded that the parent aircraft would likely prove too vulnerable to enemy attack in combat. Even as improvements were being considered, U.S. B-29 air raid attacks began to decimate the factories manufacturing the missiles, and production was brought to a halt. The army was forced to suspend the project, and the I-gō-1B never saw combat.[69]

Under the direction of the army, engineers at Tokyo Imperial University's Aeronautical Research Institute began research on a third type, the I-gō-1C, in the spring of 1944. The I-gō-1C replaced the radio guidance system of its predecessors with equipment capable of homing on shock waves emitted by the large guns on enemy warships. Three I-gō-1C missiles were test-launched from a Mitsubishi Ki-67 (Peggy) heavy bomber at the Kujihama Bombing Test Ground near Mito Air Base in March 1945. After the sound-homing device proved successful in these tests, the Army Aeronautics Department increased support for the I-gō-1C missile program. Twenty of this model were produced while still in the experimental phase, but only six were flight tested. Just before the next phase of scheduled tests, Allied air raids damaged some of the equipment and forced the relocation of the testing grounds to a site in Akita prefecture. The war came to an end while these preparations were underway. Thus, although it had performed with considerable success in preliminary tests, the I-gō-1C did not reach the mass-production stage by the end of the war.[70]

Although the I-gō missile did not enter service in combat, its rapid pace of development was impressive to at least one U.S. military intelligence investigator, who noted after the war, "the fact that this missile was designed, built, and tested within four months is remarkable and indicates a close organization between the army and its contractors."[71] It is difficult to assess whether army-industry cooperation on this particular project was really more remarkable than that of others. Researchers at the Sumitomo Corporation stated after the war that army officers were often indifferent toward the civilian engineers, which put a constant strain on working relations between the two groups.[72] This was by far the more common experience.

KE-GŌ HEAT-HOMING AIR-TO-SURFACE MISSILE

The Ke-gō infrared, heat-homing missile was one of the few advanced aeronautical weapons that came to be developed under the auspices of the Army-Navy Technology Enforcement Committee.[73] In May 1944, the Army Weapons Administrative Department (Rikugun Heiki Gyōsei Honbu) initiated a program for research on a long range, heat-homing missile, and in July, it established a special research group at the Army Institute of Scientific Research for its development. Colonel Nomura Yasuo of the Second Army Technical Institute was put in charge of the project, which was designated Ke-gō.[74] Praised by U.S. intelligence investigators as "the most important guided missile on which the Japanese are known to have worked," the Ke-gō B-1 model in particular was perhaps the most technologically sophisticated guided missile that Japan attempted to produce during the war.[75] In theory, it was capable of detecting a large ship from an altitude of over 4 miles (7,000 meters) under clear weather conditions, and it could even detect the heat radiated from a person's face from a distance of about 100 yards (100 meters).[76]

Under the aegis of the Army Weapons Administrative Department, R&D on the Ke-gō B-1 proceeded at a number of research facilities, including the Seventh Army Technical Institute and Tokyo Imperial University's Aeronautical Research Institute, where Professor Itokawa Hideo, an aeronautical engineer, was contracted to conduct studies in aerodynamics. The Communications and Engineering Department of Osaka Imperial University was contracted to design the electrical system, and the Hitachi Corporation signed on to produce gyros. The Nagoya Arsenal assumed responsibility for manufacturing the airframe. In all, over 300 scientists and engineers from the military, universities, and industry were involved in the project.[77]

Nine different types of the B-1 model were designed, from series designation 101 to 109, but of these, only four reached the development stage. As few as ten of the 101 type and five of the 102 were completed. Of the 106 type, 50 were produced, and 30 of the 107 types were completed by the end of the war. Several test flights were conducted involving the latter two models.[78] The Ke-gō B-1 106 and 107 missiles shared the same basic design and dimensions. Each had a torpedo-shaped body measuring approximately 9.8 feet (3 meters) in length and 1.64 feet (50 centimeters) in diameter with two sets of cruciform wings, one fore and one aft, with the former measuring over 8 feet (2.4 meters) in length. The head of these missiles consisted of a parabolic reflector to collect heat from the target for the infrared sensors. At the center of the reflector was a bolometer, a type of extremely sensitive thermometer, which produced electrical resistance according to the thermal radiation measured. The heat-seeking homing device utilized fluctuations of electric current transmitted by the bolometer as it responded to the heat source to indicate changes in flight direction.[79]

Flight tests of the Ke-gō B-1 106 and 107 were conducted at Lake Hamana and Hamamatsu Bay in Shizuoka prefecture beginning in October 1944 and lasting through the summer of 1945. Of the fifty to sixty Ke-gō missiles tested, only six successfully homed on the heat source and functioned as designed. All others failed. Although the experiments met with minimal success, project engineers decided that the heat-seeking apparatus had operated satisfactorily and that changes in the design of the missile itself might improve performance. Further flight tests were canceled in July 1945 as engineers began to revise the design of the missile. These revisions resulted in the B-1 108 model, but subsequent laboratory experiments on this type revealed that the control surfaces on all previous models were too small for effective flight control and that a much larger model would have to be built.[80]

The last model in the series, the Ke-gō B-1 109, was almost twice as large as its predecessors. It measured 18 feet (5.5 meters) in length and 1.7 feet (50 centimeters) in diameter. The 109 was to carry a warhead ranging in weight from 440 to 660 pounds (200 to 300 kilograms). Improvements were also made to the empennage, including a braking system to allow more time for the operation of guidance controls. Additional tests were scheduled for September 1945, but the war ended before these could be conducted. The Ke-gō B-1 109 model never advanced beyond the experimental stage.[81]

Although the Ke-gō missile showed potential for further development, it was not made operational by the end of the war. Despite the laudatory comments made by U.S. intelligence investigators about the missile after the war, some Japanese engineers derided the project. According to Yagi Hidetsugu, who served as president of the Technology Agency until May 1945, the Ke-gō project was typical of the poor coordination that plagued new weapons development. The high level of secrecy imposed on such programs resulted in an extreme degree of compartmentalization that ultimately obstructed progress in research. After the war, Yagi stated, "One scientist would be asked to develop the most sensitive possible thermopile; another, the most sensitive bolometer; another, a sensitive amplifier, and so on. None of these scientists were [*sic*] told what was the purpose of the development, nor were they told anything about the other components of the system in which their special device had to work. As a result, when the equipment was all put together in the army or navy laboratories, it generally failed to function. Then, the scientists were called on to make modifications but still without being told the purpose or nature of the total equipment."[82] Apparently, the Army-Navy Technology Enforcement Committee had little impact on the Ke-gō project's ultimate outcome.

FUNRYŪ SURFACE-TO-AIR MISSILE

Development of the first surface-to-air missiles in Japan was prompted by the appearance of the U.S. B-29 Superfortress in the skies over northern Kyūshū in the summer of 1944. The Imperial Japanese Army and Navy were at a loss as to how to defend the home islands against this formidable new bomber. Japanese fighter aircraft could not reach the high altitudes necessary to engage the B-29, and antiaircraft fire proved largely ineffective for the same reason. To meet the air defense crisis posed by the B-29, the navy initiated development of the Funryū, or Raging Dragon, series of surface-to-air missiles.[83]

Development of the Funryū proved quite difficult, as there were great organizational and technical obstacles to overcome. The Funryū missile began as the brainchild of Yoshida Ryū, a navy technical lieutenant serving with Division Four of the Navy Department of Ships, which was responsible for the design of warships. As a member of Division Four, Yoshida did not have the authority to develop a missile, which generally fell within the jurisdiction of the ordnance group in Division One. As an aeronautical weapon, however, development for the missile also came under the authority of the Navy Aeronautics Department, which was in direct competition with the Department of Ships for resources. Cooperation between the two was unlikely. Even among the various branches of the Department of Ships, collaboration was uncommon. Each department jealously guarded its own projects. For one division to take on the work of another without consent was taboo, even insubordinate. Consequently, Yoshida had to approach his superior officers with great care when proposing development of the Funryū.[84]

On 2 July 1944, Yoshida presented his design to the commanding officers of Division Four. The officers were initially incensed by his proposal, and Yoshida was nearly dismissed. His idea struck them as brash, perhaps even radical at first, but the situation was desperate. After careful consideration, the commanding officers informally granted Yoshida permission to begin work on the missile. To avoid potential strife between the departments, Yoshida was ordered to work under Dr. Sugimoto Masao in the Third Section of the Physics Department at the Navy Technical Research Institute, which was under the direct authority of the Department of Ships. When Yoshida arrived at the NTRI, engineers there were already in the early stages of developing a liquid-fuel, rocket-propelled antiship missile, which had been designated simply the Special Propulsion Missile. The basic design of the Special Propulsion Missile was then adopted in order to expedite Yoshida's plan, whereupon it was designated the Funryū Model 1. Further B-29 attacks, however, resulted in Yoshida's surface-to-air missile being given priority of development over the antiship missile, and research on the Special Propulsion Missile was thus terminated. Development proceeded thereafter under the new designation, Funryū Model 2[85] (Appendix, Table A17).

Research and development duties were apportioned to several navy facilities. Primary responsibility for developing the missile's guidance system was assigned to the Electronics Department at the NTRI, airframe construction was assigned to the Navy Shipyard at Yokosuka, and production of the solid-fuel rockets for the experimental prototype became the duty of the Naval Powder Arsenal in Yokosuka. Division Four of the Department of Ships was made responsible for contracting with private companies for production. Among them were the Nagasaki Ordnance Works of Mitsubishi Heavy Industries, the Kawasaki Aircraft Corporation, the Tokyo Aircraft Instrument Company, and the Technical Research Institute of the Nippon Broadcasting Company.[86]

A significant step forward in the coordination of R&D for the Funryū was taken in March 1945 with the formation of the Propulsion Research Department at the Navy Technical Research Institute. It had taken a formal inquiry before the general-director of the Department of Ships, as well as an investigation by the Military Affairs Bureau of the Navy Ministry, before the Cabinet and the Minister of the Navy officially sanctioned the formation of the new department. The Propulsion Research Department was set up as a special, temporary task force to coordinate development, and it brought together some forty engineers and technical officers from the various departments of the institute, including specialists in physics, electronics, engines, and navigation. Technical officer and Rear-Admiral Oyagi Shizuo was appointed department manager, and Yoshida was appointed chief designer. Including workers, the department numbered over 300 members.[87]

The formation of the Propulsion Research Department helped to expedite the pace of research on the propulsion systems for Funryū models 2 and 3. Because it was intended primarily for experimental use in launch and guidance tests, the Funryū Model 2 was equipped only with a simple solid-fuel rocket while work continued on the liquid-fuel engine. The Model 2 was gyro stabilized and equipped with a radio-control guidance system commonly used in remote-controlled drones and target vessels. The first operational prototype was completed in April 1945. From April to June 1945, ten of the Model 2 missiles were test-fired on Mount Asama near the city of Karuizawa in Nagano prefecture. Although the radio guidance system worked according to design, poor stability in rolling, particularly at the slower speeds encountered after launch, prevented accurate guidance. Project engineers determined this model to be a failure, and by the middle of summer 1945, development of the Model 2 was abandoned in favor of the Model 4, which was to have a more advanced guidance system and improved stability controls.[88] The Model 3 was essentially the same as the Model 2, but was intended to be the first liquid-fuel, rocket-propelled version of the Funryū series missile. Research and development proceeded in parallel with the Model 2. Only one prototype of the Model 3 was built, however, and it was never flight tested. With the cancellation of the Model 2 program in favor of the Model 4, work on the Model 3 was also terminated, and it never reached the production stage.[89]

In design, the Model 4 was the most advanced of the Funryū series. It was considerably larger than the previous models, and its radar-tracking guidance system was a significant technological step beyond the radio-guided, remote-control systems of its predecessors. The guidance system for the Model 4 consisted of two ground-based radar sets feeding signals to the airborne missile. According to the design, the first radar set was to track the target as the second radar set traced the missile and transmitted control signals for course corrections. Data from the two sets were to be fed into a comparator-computer—a basic adding machine—whereupon changes in the missile path would then be calculated and relayed to the second radar set. The Model 4 was to be powered by a Toko Ro-2 liquid-fuel rocket engine (based on the German Walther type) utilizing a mixture of hydrogen peroxide, methanol, and hydrazine hydrate with 3,307 pounds' (1,500 kilograms) thrust.[90]

Development of the Model 4 required the involvement of several research facilities and manufacturers. The Kawasaki Aircraft Company was contracted to develop the airframe, and the Nagasaki Ordnance Works of Mitsubishi Heavy Industries was assigned responsibility for the design and manufacture of the propulsion units. Professor Tani Ichirō of Tokyo Imperial University's Aeronautical Research Institute was contracted to design stabilization equipment and to analyze the performance of the airframe. The Technical Research Institute of the Nippon Broadcasting Company assisted in the testing of the guidance system.[91]

Although the Propulsion Research Department of the NTRI brought together engineers and technicians from the navy and private industry to collaborate on the development of the Funryū series missiles, sectionalism within the navy continued to obstruct production. When Yoshida requested 2 metric tons of duralumin from the Navy Aeronautics Department to manufacture a lighter airframe for the missile, his request was flatly rejected. According to Yoshida's memoirs, the Navy Aeronautics Department repeatedly replied, "For something like a pilot-less, four-wing airplane, not one piece of duralumin will be handed over."[92] Because of such organizational and technical obstacles, manufacture of the airframe and the guidance system was further delayed, and only two of the rocket motors—one produced by Mitsubishi's Nagasaki Ordnance Works and the other by the NTRI—were completed by 15 August 1945. Ground tests for the new engines, scheduled for 16 August, were never conducted. Although nearly ready for mass production, the Funryū Model 4 remained under development at the end of the war.[93]

ROCKET PLANES AND JET AIRCRAFT IN THE WEST

As might be expected, Germany took the lead in developing rocket- and jet-propelled aircraft. The Heinkel He 176 became the world's first true rocket-propelled aircraft when it successfully completed its brief maiden test flight on 15 June 1939. Because of erratic flight characteristics, the difficulty of control, and the volatility of its fuel, the He 176 was abandoned in favor of the more promising Messerschmitt Me 163 Komet, a small, tailless delta-winged plane, development of which the Reich Air Ministry (Reichsluftfahrtministerium, RLM) supported at Peenemünde-East. Engineers Alexander Lippisch, designer of the first delta-wing aircraft, and Helmut Walther, designer of early ramjets and hydrogen peroxide–burning rocket engines, were brought in to develop the Me 163. In order to retain a measure of independence in its R&D capacity from the army, the RLM also supported development of rocket-propelled aircraft at facilities outside Peenemünde, such as at Trauen under Dr. Eugen Sänger. Such a radical design, however, would likely not have progressed beyond the drawing board without the ardent support of Wolfram Freiherr von Richtofen, cousin of the Red Baron, Manfred von Richtofen, and head of the Development Division of the Luftwaffe's Technical Office.[94] Versions of the Me 163 were developed in time to see combat near the end of the war, but they proved ineffective because of the limited burn time of the rocket and their difficult maneuverability.[95] The Soviets also produced a rocket fighter, the BI, which made its first successful test flight on 15 May 1942, but was not used in combat.[96] The Northrup Corporation in the United States was also designing a delta-wing rocket-propelled aircraft, but it remained in the design stage at the end of the war.[97]

Like nuclear weapons and radar, the jet engine was an invention whose time had come. Limitations of the conventional piston-engine propeller aircraft led engineers in England, Germany, and the United States to develop an entirely new approach to propulsion, leading to the "turbojet revolution" in the late 1930s.[98] Frank Whittle, a Royal Air Force cadet, was the first to conceive of the jet engine, but he was unable to interest the British Air Ministry in supporting his idea in the late 1920s and had to raise his own funds for research and development. He was soon surpassed by Dr. Hans von Ohain, a German physicist, who quickly attracted the attention and support of the leading German aircraft manufacturer, Ernst Heinkel. On 27 August 1939, the Heinkel He 178 became the world's first turbojet aircraft to fly.[99] Other German engineers, such as Herbert Wagner and Max Adolph Muller of the Junkers Aircraft Company, were also working to develop the jet engine, and helped to advance turbojet technology with the official sponsorship of the RLM.[100] Other models of jet aircraft, such as the Messerschmitt Me 262 twin jet-engine fighter, soon eclipsed the He 178.[101] The RLM provided Messerschmitt a contract for a series of five experimental aircraft, and by July 1941, the Me 262 had successfully completed its first flight test using the twin turbo engines. The Me 262 had a maximum speed of 540 mph and was armed with four 30-millimeter cannons and rockets fitted in the nose section. A total of 1,433 Me 262s were manufactured, and of these, between 100 and 200 were used in combat by the end of the war.[102]

The Allies also attempted to develop jet aircraft for the war. Whittle finally won official support from the British Air Ministry in June 1939. His engines powered the first British jet aircraft, the Gloster E.28/39, which made its maiden flight on 15 May 1941, and subsequently evolved into the twin-engine Gloster Meteor. The development of jet aircraft may be the most notable technological endeavor in which the United States lagged behind the other principal belligerents during the war. Feasibility studies in jet propulsion were conducted under the Bureau of Standards as early as the 1920s, but evaluations made on the basis of technologies available at that time led to the erroneous conclusion that jet propulsion would never be of practical value for military purposes. Years later, with war approaching, a special committee to study rocket and jet propulsion was established under the NDRC in February 1941, and in April, a Special Committee on Jet Propulsion was established and began investigation of rocket-assisted takeoff (RATO).[103]

In the United States, basic research on jet engines had been left largely to the National Advisory Committee for Aeronautics (NACA), and private firms were reluctant to invest the capital for R&D in the turbojet. With the outbreak of the war, the U.S. Army Air Corps, which was severely deficient in its quality and quantity of modern aircraft, placed priority on the production of airplanes that could be delivered for combat use within six months. Such radical new technologies as the jet engine were set aside. Even with generous technical aid from the British, the United States was unable to put an operable jet aircraft into service by the end of the war. However, it had made significant technological strides in the three years between 1942 and 1945 and was poised to take the lead in the aerospace industry in the postwar period.[104] The USSR also was unable to develop a jet aircraft in time for the war, but it became the United States's greatest competitor in aerospace during the years of the cold war, borrowing, as the Americans did, numerous designs from the Germans in this field.[105]

OHKA ROCKET-PLANE

With the success of General Douglas MacArthur's Island Hopping campaign and further encroachment of U.S. military forces into Japan's defense perimeter, the Japanese navy became increasingly desperate to find an effective strategy to halt the enemy's advance. In October 1944, Admiral Onishi Takajirō introduced the "special attack" strategy, which called for young pilots to crash their explosive-laden aircraft into enemy warships. The newly formed special attack units were designated Divine Wind Special Attack Forces (Shinpū Tokubetsu Kōgekitai), often abbreviated as Tokkōtai, but more commonly known as kamikaze.[106] The Ministry of Munitions began to divert materials and resources to the production of "special attack aircraft" (Tokkōki), which were little more than fighter planes modified to accommodate larger explosive loads. Many conventional aircraft were used for this purpose, but new models were also designed solely for suicide missions.

Perhaps the most infamous of the special attack aircraft was the Ohka rocket-plane. During the airlift at Rabaul in 1944, Naval Ensign Ohta Mitsuo of the 405th Naval Air Group witnessed several Allied air attacks against Japanese forces.[107] Seeing first hand that the Japanese navy was increasingly less capable of defending itself, Ohta conceived an idea for an expendable aircraft for use in suicide attacks against enemy warships. He consulted Professor Ogawa Taichirō, an aeronautical engineer at Tokyo Imperial University's Aeronautical Research Institute, for assistance in the design. Ogawa passed the duty on to engineer Kimura Hidemasa, who completed the design and constructed a small model. Professor Tani Ichirō performed tests in the institute's wind tunnel, and turned over the data and sketches to Ohta.[108]

On 5 August 1944, Ohta submitted to his superior officers at the First Navy Aeronautical Technology Arsenal the drawings of the rocket-propelled suicide aircraft. Ohta's idea initiated a debate among high-ranking navy brass, who, in desperation, were willing to consider sacrificing a small aircraft—and a life—for the successful destruction of an Allied warship. In response to Ohta's proposal, on 16 August 1944, the Japanese Naval General Staff ordered engineers at the Navy Aeronautics Research Department in Yokosuka to begin development. Ohta may have violated protocol by taking his idea to civilian engineers before proposing the design to his superiors, but it may be indicative of the extent of the navy's desperation that such an infraction was overlooked when the military stood to benefit.[109]

At the beginning of the Pacific War, the Navy Aeronautical Technology Arsenal (Kaigun Kōkū Gijutsushō) and its affiliated branches comprised one of the most advanced facilities for aeronautics research in the world, employing some 2,000 technicians and 32,000 laborers. The heart of the laboratory was the Design Department of the Aircraft Division, then headed by Technical Lieutenant Commander Yamana Masao. Yamana directed development of the Ohka, with Technical Major Miki Tadanao as chief designer, Lieutenant Commander Hattori Rokurō in charge of structural design, and Lieutenant Washizu Kyūichirō in charge of performance calculations.[110] The navy designated the project Marudai, taken, in part, from the first ideograph in Ohta's name, and development continued under complete secrecy. In less than a month, the engineers completed the first prototype, the Yokosuka MXY7 Model 11.[111] The MXY7 series rocket-propelled suicide aircraft came to be more commonly known as the Ohka, meaning "cherry blossom." It was an appropriate and significant moniker for such an aircraft, as the cherry blossom was traditionally a poetic symbol of the ephemeral nature of human life.[112]

Designing an aircraft for the exclusive purpose of conducting suicide missions weighed heavily on the minds of the engineers, as well as some of the naval officers who ordered the Ohka into production. When Rear Admiral Saba Jirō, director of the Aircraft Division of the Navy Aeronautical Technology Arsenal, visited the Ministry of Munitions to discuss subcontracting production of the Ohka to private firms, Lieutenant Commander Matsuura Yokei, director of production for the Ohka, sharply rebuked him for raising the issue. Matsuura stated that there was no way to assign production of the Ohka to private firms. Not only might it result in a breach of security, but also, Matsuura argued, "they would think the navy had gone crazy."[113] As a result, production was initially confined exclusively to military facilities.

Given the limitations of the Japanese economy toward the end of the war and the purpose for which the Ohka was designed, construction had to be done as cheaply as possible. One of the first Ohka types to reach the production stage was the Model 11. This model was constructed primarily of aluminum and plywood, as the engineers had designed it to be mass produced by unskilled laborers using readily available and expendable materials. The Model 11 was a midwing monoplane with a wingspan measuring 16 feet 5 inches (5 meters). The wing and tail assemblies were made of plywood. The fuselage, made of aluminum, measured about 19 feet 10 inches (6 meters), and was fitted with a Plexiglas, bubble-type canopy enclosing the cockpit to protect the pilot during flight. The Model 11 was equipped with only a rudimentary instrument panel, including a speedometer, altimeter, and attitude indicator. A 2,640-pound (1,200 kilogram) warhead was to be installed in the nose section, and three Type Four K-1 Model 20 solid-fuel rocket engines were to provide a combined thrust of 1,764 pounds (800 kilograms). Ten of the Ohka Model 11 types were built by the end of September 1944.[114]

Glide tests were begun in October 1944 at Sagami Bay south of Tokyo, and powered flight trials began the following month, but the navy ordered full production of the Ohka Model 11 to commence without waiting for the results. The navy had ordered 150 Ohkas to be produced by the end of the month, but the Navy Aeronautical Technology Arsenal was unable to meet the demand. Despite the strong sentiment that production of the Ohka should remain strictly a military matter, eventually the navy had no choice but to subcontract with private firms to manufacture parts of the aircraft. The Nippon Aircraft Company and Fuji Aircraft were thus contracted to produce the wings and tail sections of the Ohka.[115]

The Model 11 was designed for transport by the Mitsubishi G4M2e (Betty) bomber, which had to be modified to carry the Ohka. Adjustments to the wings and fuel system were made, and additional protective armor for the bomber crew was added. The G4M2e bombers were to carry the Ohka to within 55 miles of the target and release it at 27,000 feet. Upon release, the

Ohka was to glide for 52 miles at an average speed of 229 mph. Within 3 miles of the target, the Ohka pilot was to engage the three solid-fuel rockets to accelerate the aircraft to a speed over 600 mph. In actual combat, however, the Ohka rarely performed as expected. During the Okinawa campaign the effective range of the Ohka proved less than 10 miles, which made the cumbersome G4M2e bomber extremely vulnerable to Allied antiaircraft fire.[116]

The Ohka Model 11 first entered combat on 21 March 1945, when eighteen G4M2e bombers, escorted by thirty fighter planes, took off from Kanoya Air Base in southern Kyūshū to engage the approaching U.S. fleet. Sixteen of the eighteen bombers were loaded with an Ohka, but about 60 miles from the target, fifty U.S. fighter aircraft intercepted the Japanese bombers. The bomber crews had little choice but to jettison the heavy Ohka in order to escape. All eighteen of the bombers were lost, together with sixteen of the Ohkas, and only four of the escort fighters returned to Kanoya.[117]

The first successful Ohka attacks occurred on 1 April 1945 at Okinawa when the U.S. battleship *West Virginia* and three transport ships were hit, each sustaining extensive damage. American servicemen, who had their first glimpse of the Ohka on this day, dubbed it the *Baka*, meaning "fool," in Japanese. Although some Ohka attacks were successful, as in the sinking of the destroyer *Mannert L. Abele* on 12 April 1945, such strikes were few. The Ohka proved to be practically ineffective in the defense of Okinawa, and its continued use began to wear on the morale of Japanese naval officers. Approximately 755 Model 11 Ohkas were manufactured by March 1945 when production of this type ceased. Although production was stopped, they continued to be used in desperation until the end of the war.[118]

Meanwhile, the engineering team at the Navy Aeronautical Technology Arsenal moved on to develop the successor of the Model 11, the Ohka Model 22. The Model 22 was practically identical to its predecessor, with the exception of being fitted with a Hatsukaze Tsu-11 Campini-type jet engine and an additional single Type 4 Model 21 solid rocket booster slung under the fuselage. The designers of the Ohka originally intended the Model 11 to be equipped with a liquid-fuel rocket or jet engine, but development of these engines had proceeded too slowly. The Aichi Aircraft Company began production of the Campini jet engine for the Model 22 in March 1945, and the Murakami, Jiguro, and Fuji Aircraft companies were contracted to manufacture parts.[119] To improve the speed and range of the Ohka, the engineers not only replaced the engine, but also reduced the weight of the explosive warhead to 1,323 pounds (600 kilograms). Project engineers also selected a faster mother aircraft, the Yokosuka P1Y1 Ginga bomber (Frances), to transport the Ohka. The Model 22 was first test flown on 12 August 1945. Upon separation from the parent aircraft, however, auxiliary rockets installed under the wings ignited accidentally, causing the Ohka to stall and crash. About 50 Model 22 types were under production, and preparations for a second test flight were underway when the war came to an end.[120]

Other Ohka types were also under development at the end of the war. The Model 33 was slightly larger than the Model 22 in design. It was to be powered by an Ne-20 turbojet engine with a 1,764-pound (800 kilogram) warhead. Trial manufacturing of the Ne-20 progressed slowly, and in July 1944, the Navy Aeronautical Technology Arsenal discontinued development. The Ohka Model 43A was to be launched by catapult from surfaced submarines, and its variant, the Model 43B, was to be launched by catapult from caves along the southeast coast of Japan. Both the Model 43A and 43B were to be powered by the Ne-20 turbojet. Design of the Ohka Model 53, which was to be towed aloft rather than dropped from a transport aircraft, was also underway. None of these models reached production by the end of the war.[121]

BAIKA AND SHINRYŪ "SPECIAL ATTACK" PILOTED MISSILES

Among the other "special attack" piloted missiles under development at the end of the war were the Baika and Shinryū. A piloted version of the German V-1 missile, dubbed the Kawanishi Baika, or Plum Blossom, by the navy, was among the few army-navy cooperative ventures undertaken late in the war. Professor Ogawa Taiichirō at Tokyo Imperial University's Aeronautical Research Institute and his colleague Professor Tani Ichirō were contracted as chief engineers for the project. Basic designs for the airframe and pulse-jet engine were completed in July 1945 and submitted to the Army Aeronautics Department. The navy agreed to collaborate in development of the engine and tests were conducted at the First Navy Aeronautical Technology Arsenal. The Kawanishi Aircraft Corporation was assigned responsibility for trial production of the airframe, and work on the fuselage was undertaken at the Second Munitions Arsenal. Because materials were scarce, design and construction had to be simplified and substitutions made. Turpentine was even suggested as an alternate fuel.[122] Another important substitution was using a human pilot in place of the original guidance system. In the words of a Japanese technical officer, "The V-1 lacked eyes. In view of the lessons learned from our study of the robot bomb of our friendly Ally (Germany), we must give the V-1 eyes. However, not *every* country can manufacture the eyes for this destructive weapon."[123] By this time, U.S. military intelligence understood the reference to Japanese suicide tactics and expected large-scale production of the Baika. But the war ended before development was completed.

Plans for the Shinryū piloted missile were developed by the navy in collaboration with the Transportation Ministry's Aeronautics Testing Facility in early 1945. The Shinryū was to be a type of rocket-launched glide-plane loaded with a 100-kilogram bomb intended for use in destroying enemy tanks during the anticipated invasion of the Japanese mainland. The first model was test-fired at the Kasumigaura base in southeastern Ibaraki prefecture just before the end of the war. It suffered damage on landing, and the war ended before the Shinryū could be readied for a second test.[124]

SHŪSUI ROCKET-PROPELLED INTERCEPT FIGHTER

Development of a fast-climbing intercept fighter became desirable with the arrival of the B-29 Superfortress over the home islands of Japan. The ceiling and speed of the Zero proved no match for the high-altitude American bomber, and the Raiden, the next best hope, was still in the early stages of production.[125] Knowing of its success in producing jet- and rocket-propelled interceptors, Japan turned to Germany for technical assistance. Late in 1943, the Japanese military attaché in Berlin obtained a license to manufacture the Messerschmitt Me 163 rocket-propelled fighter and its Walther HWK 109-509 engine. Months passed before arrangements could be made to send blueprints and a partially assembled engine for the Me 163 to Japan. On 31 March 1944, the U-512 *Satsuki*, the first of two Japanese submarines carrying engine parts and diagrams, departed the port of Kiel. The second submarine, the *I-29*, departed Lorient, France, on 16 April. On board the *I-29* was Iwatani Eiichi, a navy commander and engineer, who carried with him notes and drawings of the Me 163.[126] The *Satsuki* was sunk en route in the Atlantic on 13 May with all cargo, while the *I-29* arrived safely in Malaysia on 14 July. Iwatani disembarked in Penang and returned to Japan by airplane, but his submarine was sunk near Taiwan about a week later. All that remained of the critical materials concerning the Me 163 were the papers Iwatani had carried with him. Japanese engineers had to build the aircraft nearly from scratch.[127]

The Japanese version of the Me 163 was to be produced jointly under the August 1943 Army-Navy Aeronautical Technology Committee accord, under which the services agreed to collaborate in the development of advanced aeronautical weapons.[128] The army assumed primary responsibility for the development of the liquid-fuel rocket engine while the navy was to produce the airframe, but the navy also began work on a turbojet engine as an alternate. Mitsubishi accepted responsibility for design and production of the aircraft, which was to be completed under the direction of engineer Takahashi Mijiro together with the collaboration of the First Navy Aeronautical Technology Arsenal. Three additional aircraft manufacturers were also contracted for the project. The Japanese versions of the Me 163 were designated the J8M1 Shūsui ("Sword Stroke") by the navy, and Ki-200 by the army.[129]

Although development of the airframe progressed rather quickly, several difficulties were encountered as the aircraft entered the production stage. Manufacturers that had contracted with the army, such as Yokoi Aircraft, found the expedited production schedules difficult to meet. Mitsubishi also experienced difficulty because the navy continuously requested modifications and added design features. Morale among workers at Mitsubishi was low, as they had little hope for the successful production of the aircraft's engine. Some project engineers even began to suggest that another German plane, the Me 262 twin-engine jet fighter, the plans for which Iwatani had also acquired in Germany, was a more promising intercept aircraft and that efforts should be concentrated on its development instead.[130]

But work on the Shūsui went forward. The first successful combustion tests were conducted in November 1944 at the Mitsubishi arsenal in Nagasaki, and the first full static engine test took place on 19 January 1945 at the Oppama rocket test site at the Yokosuka naval base. In the meantime, R&D on the fuselage was underway at the First Navy Aeronautical Technology Arsenal.[131] On 8 January 1945, the test-glider prototype, designated MXY8 Akigusa ("Autumn Grass"), was successfully flown for the first time. U.S. bombing raids did not seriously damage the Mitsubishi assembly plant in Nagoya where the first rocket-powered Shūsui prototype was being completed, but they did cause delays in the production schedule. Despite these setbacks, the first powered versions of the Shūsui were delivered to the testing grounds at Yokosuka in March. Flight tests were readied in July 1945. With a wingspan measuring just over 32 feet (9.5 meters), the Shūsui, a tailless Lippisch (delta-wing) aircraft, was somewhat smaller than the German model on which it was based. Powered by a single Toko Ro-2 liquid-fuel rocket engine, it was designed for a maximum speed of 559 mph (900 kph) over a five-minute burn cycle.[132]

The maiden flight of the navy's J8M1 Shūsui took place on 7 July 1945 but ended in disaster. Because of a design flaw in the fuel injection system, the engine stalled during a steep climb at an altitude of 1,100 feet. The aircraft crashed, and the pilot died from injuries sustained in the impact. The navy scheduled a second test flight for 2 August 1945, but a delay in engine construction caused the flight to be postponed, and the flight never took place. The army conducted a test flight of its own on 10 August 1945, but it too met with failure.[133]

Plans were also underway to convert the Shūsui into an unmanned radio-guided missile for use against enemy warships and large aircraft. Engineers at the NTRI under the supervision of Major Okamoto Masahiko developed a guidance system, which was to utilize two VHF beams with an effective range of 10,000 feet (3,048 meters). The guidance system was tested in July 1945 and met with limited success; however, the war ended before it could be made operational for combat.[134]

Given the usual production cycle of three years for a new Japanese aircraft during the war, it is noteworthy that the Shūsui went from design to test flight in only about a year. Considering the many great obstacles to its completion, the feat is even more impressive. Although the Army-Navy Aeronautical Technology Committee, later subsumed under the Army-Navy Technology Enforcement Committee, ostensibly united the military services in the effort, in fact, the army and navy projects proceeded almost independently of one another, and communication between the two was poor. Allied bombing raids caused factories to be relocated out of the major cities, further delaying production. Jurisdiction over aspects of the project blurred, and priorities in development changed during the transfers. Matériel and personnel were always in short supply. At the Nippon Aircraft plant in Yamagata, for example, schoolgirls were conscripted to work on the aircraft, and women, still a comparatively untapped segment of the labor force, were trained to weld the propellant tanks.[135] Although the Shūsui had shown promise as a much needed intercept fighter, it never reached the mass-production stage.

KIKKA AND KARYŪ TWIN JET-ENGINE FIGHTERS

Production of jet aircraft was also desired to meet the defense challenge posed by the B-29 bombers. But development of jet engines also came comparatively late to Japan and followed a familiar pattern of technological development. The origins of jet engine research in Japan may be traced to the mid-1930s. While in Europe on a study tour for the navy, Captain Tanegashima Tokiyasu learned of the development of the continuous-feed gas turbine in France and other early jet engine technologies emerging at that time. Tanegashima returned to Japan in 1937 with information he had gathered, hoping to initiate research on the new technology. But serious R&D efforts in jet engines did not get underway until after the attack on Pearl Harbor. From around December 1941, Tanegashima began to make the rounds to various engine manufacturers to initiate research. Experiments on a turbine exhaust system (YT-15) were undertaken at the First Navy Aeronautical Technology Arsenal, but by the end of 1942, little progress had been made. Collaboration with several manufacturers, including the Mitsubishi Engine Works in Nagoya, Nakajima and Ishikawajima Aircraft Corporations, and the Ishikawajima Shibaura Turbine Corporation proved more fruitful, however, and resulted in June 1943 in the production of three axial flow (TR-10) type turbojet engines.[136]

Meanwhile, the army had also begun research into jet engines. In October 1942, the Second Army Aeronautical Technology Research Institute, with assistance from Nakanishi Fujio, then director of Tokyo Imperial University's Aeronautical Research Institute, began research on a type of turboprop engine (Ne-201), development of which was assigned to the Ishikawajima Shibaura Corporation. This line of research paralleled other projects that were being conducted in collaboration with the Kawasaki Aircraft Corporation, which resulted in the production of a type of ramjet, designated Ne-0, which was successfully ground tested in July 1943.[137] Other engines to emerge in this series included the Ne-1 through Ne-4 models. Research and development of the Ne-3 and Ne-4 was successful in the early half of 1944, but it was discontinued later in the year. Development of the Ne-1 also ended in July 1944 as parts became unavailable.[138] Interservice collaboration under the Army-Navy Aeronautical Technology Committee may have stimulated development and production of jet engines, as several indigenous types were produced.[139] But the real boost in development came in July 1944 with the arrival of blueprints and photos of the Jumo 004B and BMW 003A jet engines, which Iwatani had obtained in Germany.

As previously stated, Iwatani had returned to Japan not only with designs for the jet and rocket engines, but also for the German aircraft in which they were to be installed. The Japanese military services quickly adopted the design of the Me 262 twin jet-engine fighter to produce replicas of their own. Under the auspices of the Army-Navy Technology Enforcement Committee, the navy produced the Kikka ("Orange Blossom"), and the army the Ki-201 Karyū ("Fire Dragon").[140] In September 1944, the Navy Department of Ships assumed responsibility for the production of the Kikka in collaboration with the Nakajima Aircraft Company, where primary responsibility for design and production was assigned to engineers Ohno Kazuo and Matsumura Kenichi. The Kikka was an impressive replica of the Me 262, though somewhat smaller, with a wingspan measuring nearly 33 feet (10 meters). The Kikka was to be powered by two Ne-20 axial-flow turbojets, which were modeled after the German BMW 003 jet engine.[141]

The Kikka made its maiden flight on 7 August 1945 at the Kisarazu Naval Air Base in western Chiba prefecture, making it Japan's first fully operational jet aircraft. The first flight was considered only a limited success, however, and a second test was scheduled as soon as possible. But the second test flight on 11 August was aborted because of the improper installation of the RATO wing rockets, which had been attached to improve acceleration on take off. A second prototype was nearly ready for flight, and eighteen additional prototypes were under production, but the war ended before these could be made operational.[142] The army's Ki-201 Karyū also remained under development at the end of the war.[143]

EXPERIMENTAL FUEL RESEARCH AND DEVELOPMENT

Paralleling the research in rocket and jet engines was the R&D conducted on the fuels to power them. Lieutenant Commander Hino Kumao directed much of the navy's research on solid-fuel propellants for rockets at the NTRI in Tokyo. Hino held a doctorate in engineering from Tokyo Imperial University, where he served on the faculty from 1936 to 1941. From 1941 to 1943, he served as a section chief in the research department for high explosives at the Second Naval Powder Arsenal. In 1943, he became director of research in solid propellants for rockets and guns at the Navy Technical Research Institute.[144] About the time he became director, in 1943, technical officers at the NTRI were working to develop more effective propellants, as well as RATO for heavy bombers. Limited research was also underway to improve barrage and aircraft-launched rockets. No significant improvements had been made in solid-fuel propellants in Japan since the introduction of ortho-tolylurethane in 1933, which gave black powder greater stability in handling. Having reached an impasse, Hino began to investigate liquid propellants. But little progress was made at the NTRI at this time.[145]

While Hino worked away at the NTRI in Tokyo, technicians at the Nagasaki munitions factory were developing a working model of a rocket engine that would utilize a mixture of hydrogen peroxide and sodium permanganate as fuel. The research team proposed test production to the authorities at the Navy Department of Ships, but no one in the navy's chain of command expressed much interest in developing liquid fuel propellants for rockets at that time. Rockets were still considered no more than secondary weapons, and navy officials had grave concerns about the safety and reliability of the highly volatile chemicals that such an engine would require for fuel. A more practical propellant was yet to be developed.[146]

Opinions changed, however, with the introduction of the V-1 rocket into combat in the European theatre in late 1943. The V-1 stimulated research on new rocket types and liquid fuels in Japan. Research on alternative fuels to be used in rockets, torpedoes, the Shūsui, and various other weapons, such as the Kaiten minisubmarine, which was also designed for suicide attacks, began almost simultaneously in June 1944 at the First Navy Aeronautical Technology Arsenal, the Navy Technical Research Institute, and at the First Navy Fuel Arsenal in Ofuna in Iwate prefecture. Technicians first tried a concentrated hydrogen peroxide and sodium permanganate solution as a new rocket fuel, but the sodium permanganate solution proved too volatile for practical use. Experiments were continued with a hydrogen peroxide and hydrazine hydrate–methanol combination instead.[147]

In order to facilitate interservice cooperation in liquid fuels R&D, on 16 September 1944, the Ro-gō Z-stoff Committee (Ro-gō Z-yaku Iinkai) was established to serve as a coordinating and liaison council for the further investigation of alternative liquid fuels.[148] A Special Fuels Division was also established in the Munitions Ministry. Chemical propellants appeared to offer a practical alternative to conventional fuels, such as gasoline, which were becoming extremely limited in supply as the war continued.[149] Consequently, great efforts were expended to increase production of such alternatives as hydrogen peroxide and hydrazine hydrate, which required mostly ample amounts of water, electric power, and sulfuric acid to produce. Yet even these seemingly simple ingredients were not always available in great abundance in wartime Japan.[150]

The navy had several companies to help produce the chemical propellants needed for the new liquid-fuel rocket and jet engines. Among these were the many manufacturers brought under the aegis of the Special Fuels Division at the Navy Fuel Arsenal, including: Mitsubishi Synthetic, Mitsui Chemical, Hodogaya Chemical, Sumitomo Chemical, and Nihon Chissō, for example. But given deficiencies in special metals, such as platinum for electrodes, and electrolytic cells, which were necessary for use in the production process, in Japan, all the pertinent manufacturing facilities of the Japanese empire had to be brought to bear on the problem. Fortunately for Japan, it had extensive industrial facilities in China, Manchuria, and Korea.[151]

Korea offered the best hope. When, in 1938, Japan faced an embargo from the United States on high-octane aviation fuel, the Navy Fuel Arsenal investigated a new process to manufacture iso-octane from synthesized butanol and turned to the Nitchitsu Konzern in Korea to mass produce it. Nitchitsu was a large conglomerate and a manufacturer of butanol with several factories operating in the port city of Hungnam (called Kōnan by the Japanese), Korea. Together with Noguchi Jun, founder and president of Nitchitsu, the navy established Nitchitsu Fuel Industries in 1941 and subsequently built a factory for the production of iso-octane. Designated the NA plant, it was to be the first of several secret industrial sites established jointly by Noguchi and the navy and erected in Hungnam. (The "N" was to signify "navy, Noguchi, and nitrogen," and the "A" was a reference to aircraft fuel.) Navy officials called the NA plant the "jewel of the Japanese navy" and gave it the highest order of military secrecy. Access to the plant was severely restricted, and only selected personnel from the navy and Nitchitsu were permitted entry.[152]

The NA plant was only the beginning for Noguchi. In May 1941, Nitchitsu Fuel Industries established the ND plant to produce acetaldehyde, and in November 1941, it erected the NB factory to expand manufacturing of butanol.[153] The last factory to be built in this series, the NZ plant, was constructed in less than a month in August 1944 and was on par with the NA factory in the level of secrecy imposed on those who worked there. The NZ plant was set up to manufacture hydrazine hydrate and hydrogen peroxide, the primary ingredients of Z-stoff, the highly volatile liquid rocket fuel that German engineers had developed for use in the V-2. (The "Z" in the factory's acronym stood for "Z-stoff."[154]) The navy desperately wanted the new fuel for use in the Shūsui and Kikka aircraft then under development.

By early October 1944, the NZ factory was able to produce one metric ton of hydrazine hydrate on a daily basis.[155] But there were problems. The Nitchitsu technicians had no previous experience mass-producing hydrogen peroxide, the other key ingredient of Z-stoff, and further delays occurred while equipment from other facilities was being diverted and retooled for its production. By the end of the following month, the equipment was in place, and hydrogen peroxide was being manufactured on an industrial scale in Hungnam. But it soon became obvious to the engineers there that manufacturing was proving too costly and the quality of the product itself was unsatisfactory. By the end of the year, serious shortages of hydrazine and other materials contributed to further delays in the production of the Z-stoff. As a result, the decision was made to cease hydrogen peroxide production at Hungnam, and the equipment was retooled and converted for other needs.[156]

Meanwhile, additional factories for the manufacture of hydrogen peroxide were being erected in Japan. The objective was to construct a series of hydrogen peroxide concentration plants that would be capable of producing a total of 3,000 tons of 80 percent hydrogen peroxide per month. One plant, located at the First Navy Fuel Arsenal in Ofuna, began production in November 1944 and reached a capacity of 90 tons per month. Another plant at the same site did not begin manufacture until August 1945. Construction of additional plants was underway at other locations throughout Japan, but only one of these, the Yamagita Edogawa factory of Mitsubishi, was able to produce hydrogen peroxide during the war.[157]

For its part, the Japanese army began research in experimental rocket fuels at the Seventh Army Technical Institute in August 1944, where tests of chamber and thrust pressures were conducted. It was the navy that dominated efforts in this area, however, particularly after receiving technical information from Germany on the process of manufacturing the hydrogen-peroxide alcohol fuel mixture. The navy provided the army with some information on the proper handling of the fuel, but apparently little else.[158] Despite the efforts of such organizations as the Army-Navy Technology Enforcement Committee, the Ro-gō Z-Stoff Committee, and the Army-Navy Technical Control Committee, cooperation between the services remained limited because of persistent rivalry and bureaucratic sectionalism, and the war ended before effective use could be made of any of the new fuels.

CONCLUSION

Throughout World War II, Japan lagged well behind Nazi Germany and the Allied nations in the development of rockets, guided missiles, and jet aircraft. Germany took the lead in rocketry and the turbojet revolution largely because of the advocacy of ranking military officers and civilian engineers of talent, such as von Richtofen, Becker, and von Braun, among others. Given the restrictions of the Versailles Treaty, the German military services were open to such technologies, which appeared to offer paths to new weapons development without violating the 1919 agreement. Germany also had a high level of scientific and engineering competence in aeronautics, owing in no small part to the experience gained in World War I and the cadre of civilian enthusiasts and amateurs in the VfR, which provided a solid foundation on which the military could build (not to mention the "ideological enthusiasm" of many of these who were eager to support Hitler and the Reich).[159] Where the successful development of such weapons as the V-1 and V-2 were concerned, Dornberger's "everything under one roof" management philosophy was also an important factor. As for the Allies, while research in the Soviet Union was hindered by the political purges and the German invasion, progress in the United States was accelerated early in the war by technical assistance from Great Britain. Thereafter, the close cooperation among the OSRD, the military services, the universities, and private industry enabled the United States to advance rapidly in research, development, and production, although never equaling the efforts or results of Germany during the war.

In Japan, development of rockets, guided missiles, and jet aircraft did not become a priority until late in the war, and the final results of the military's efforts were comparatively negligible. The general technology policy of the military services was largely to blame. Neither the army nor the navy initiated new weapons projects in earnest until Japan was put on the defensive in the Pacific. Furthermore, until the formation of the Army-Navy Aeronautical Technology Committee, established in August 1943, and the Army-Navy Technology Enforcement Committee, formed in September 1944, cooperation between the services remained minimal. But even after these committees were established, collaboration on such projects as the Shūsui and Kikka was limited largely to the sharing of technical data. The army and navy generally hoarded technical information from one another and passed along only what was deemed necessary to designers and private manufacturers at any given time. This policy of compartmentalization imposed by the military caused delays in development and production. And, at no point did the military foresee the necessity of creating a centralized complex like Peenemünde.

Unfortunately for Japan, it also had no comparable pool of civilian talent from which to draw, such as existed in Germany in the 1930s. Personnel and resources were stretched to the limit, and both were used inefficiently. University scientists and engineers were contracted on an as-needed basis and were often required to perform double duty for the military, conducting tests on demand for both the army and navy. Professor Tani Ichirō at Tokyo Imperial University's Aeronautical Research Institute, for example, was contracted to carry out aerodynamic tests on both the Funryū and the Shūsui. Civilian scientists and engineers were prohibited from sharing data with other researchers working on separate projects, and the lack of collaboration only further strained human resources.

The quality and quantity of labor was yet another factor. Although the engineers at Peenemünde had at their disposal a large workforce to manufacture the V-2s—comprised mainly of enslaved Jewish laborers at the Mittelwerk facility in Nordhausen—in Japan, the army and navy resorted to conscripting high school boys, physically challenged college students, and various "nonessential personnel" to replace the skilled workers who had been drafted into the military. The military demand for able-bodied men reduced personnel with production experience in the factories to near extinction. Women, however, remained a comparatively unexploited segment of the labor force in Japan, and unlike their Rosie the Riveter counterparts in the American aircraft industry, Japanese women never comprised more than 20 percent of the total workforce.[160] By the time the military services began to cooperate under the Technology Enforcement Committee agreement, however, Japan's failing industry likely could not have supported the mass production of such technologically sophisticated weapons at any rate.

Finally, Japan received little assistance in the way of technology exchange with Nazi Germany. There were few notable exceptions. As previously mentioned, in 1943, the Japanese obtained the rights to manufacture the rocket-propelled Me 163 interceptor and the jet-propelled Me 262 fighter aircraft, and blueprints and parts were sent to Japan via submarine in 1944. Information on production methods for the hydrogen peroxide fuel was provided as well.[161] Germany also furnished technical data on a few guided missiles, such as the Hs-293 antiship missile, the Hs-294 air-to-surface missile, the Hs-298 air-to-air missile, and the Hs-117 radio-controlled antiaircraft rocket. However, it is unlikely that this information was of any benefit to the Japanese at all, because these missiles did not become operational even in Germany until late in the war. Japan simply had too little time and resources to make much practical use of such data.[162]

A few German technicians were sent to Japan toward the end of the war, but most of these were specialists in mechanical design, plant construction, and production, rather than in research and development. Among them was Kurt Schmidt, an aeronautical engineer for Heinkel Aircraft, who traveled to Japan aboard the *I-29* in June 1943.[163] Schmidt's mission was to help with aircraft plant construction. When interviewed by U.S. intelligence officers after the war, Schmidt stated that no means of communication with Germany had been available to him, and the aura of secrecy surrounding his work was such that it negated any useful purpose he might have served outside the scope of his mission. Consequently, Schmidt felt his mission was a failure.[164] Other German technicians echoed his sentiments.[165] No formal agency had been established to facilitate scientific and technical exchange between Germany and Japan, such as there had been under the OSRD with the United States and Great Britain. All communications from Germany were delivered to the Japanese Embassy in Berlin and passed through "regular channels."[166]

The exchange of technical information between Germany and Japan was minimal and largely one way. Hitler refused to share data on the V-2 and was reluctant to entrust to Japan technical information on other "wonder weapons" until the tide of war had turned against Germany.[167] Japan also was not in a position to offer Germany much in return, especially in terms of advanced technology. Toward the end of the war, Japan could only provide gold or limited amounts of raw materials for trade.[168]

Under these circumstances, it is not surprising that Japan trailed far behind Germany in the development of advanced aeronautical weapons during the war. Although U.S. navy intelligence officers assessed Japanese naval rockets as "formidable, satisfactorily performing weapons," they also noted that these "were developed and put into production too rapidly for much refinement."[169] More sophisticated weapons than these standard combat rockets required far more time and resources for successful development. But as has been previously discussed, this was not a problem unique to Japan; the USSR suffered similar constraints. Although collaboration between the army and navy proved moderately beneficial and had a noticeable impact on quickening the pace of research and development of the Shūsui and the Kikka, such cooperative efforts were far too few and came far too late to result in successful production of such advanced weapons before the end of the war.

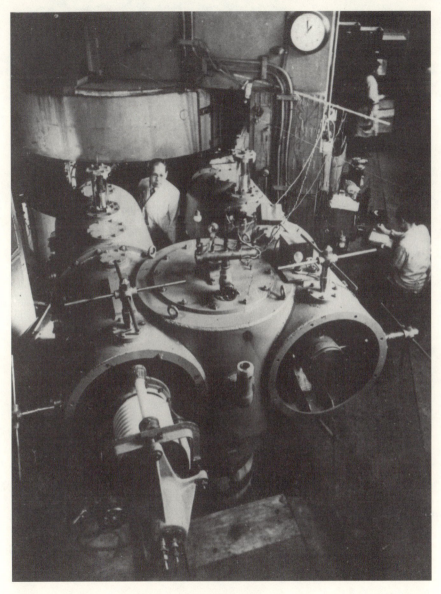

Figure 1. Dr. Nishina Yoshio with the 210-ton 60-inch cyclotron at the Riken. Courtesy of the Harry C. Kelly Collection, North Carolina State University.

Figure 2. Navy Commander Itō Yōji (ca. July 1941). Courtesy of Itō Yoshimasa.

Figure 3. Navy radar Mark 1 Model 1 Type 2 Designation 11. Daito Naval Experimental Facility Collection. Courtesy of Kawamura Yutaka.

Figure 4. Navy radar Mark 1 Model 3 Type 3 Designation 13. Daito Naval Experimental Facility Collection. Courtesy of Kawamura Yutaka.

Figure 5. Navy radar Mark 2 Model 2 Designation 22. Daito Naval Experimental Facility Collection. Courtesy of Kawamura Yutaka.

Figure 6. Army radar Tachi 18. Courtesy of the U.S. National Archives (331-SCAP-09A).

Figure 7. Army radar Tachi 24 (Würzburg Type). Courtesy of the U.S. National Archives (331-SCAP-30A).

Figure 8. Japanese magnetron. All metal type. Daito Naval Experimental Facility Collection. Courtesy of Kawamura Yutaka.

Figure 9. I-Gō Radio-Guided missile (I-gō rocket bomb). Courtesy of the National Air and Space Museum, Smithsonian Institution (SI 73-10612).

Figure 10. I-Gō Radio-Guided missile (I-gō rocket bomb) loaded under Ki-48 bomber. Courtesy of the National Air and Space Museum, Smithsonian Institution (SI 73-10615).

Figure 11. Front view of Mitsubishi J8M Shūsui (MXY 8 Akigusa). Courtesy of the National Air and Space Museum, Smithsonian Institution (SI 81-14324).

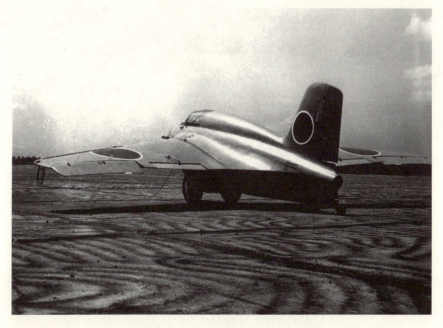

Figure 12. Rear view of Mitsubishi J8M Shūsui (MXY 8 Akigusa). Courtesy of the National Air and Space Museum, Smithsonian Institution (SI 81-14326).

Figure 13. Nakajima G8N1 Kikka under construction. Courtesy of the National Air and Space Museum, Smithsonian Institution (SI 73-5677).

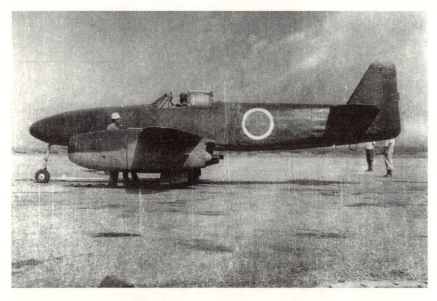

Figure 14. Nakajima Kikka (Orange Blossom). Courtesy of the National Air and Space Museum, Smithsonian Institution (SI 73-5676).

Figure 15. Chemical weapons storage area, Okunoshima, Japan. Courtesy of Clark Hultquist.

Figure 16. Power plant, Okunoshima, Japan. Courtesy of Clark Hultquist.

Figure 17. Lieutenant General Ishii Shirō, director of the Unit 731 Pingfang compound. Courtesy of the Unit 731 Museum, Pingfang, China.

Figure 18. Aerial view of Pingfang compound. Courtesy of the Unit 731 Museum, Pingfang, China.

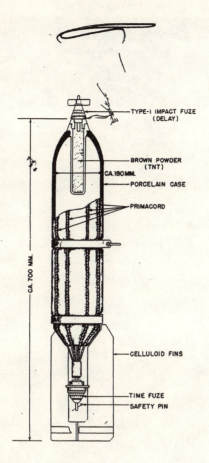

Figure 19. Line drawing of the Type 50 Uji bomb. U.S. National Archives (Thompson Report).

Figure 20. Nishina Yoshio and U.S. military at the destruction of the Riken cyclotrons, November 1945. Courtesy of the Harry C. Kelly Collection, North Carolina State University.

5
CHEMICAL AND BIOLOGICAL WARFARE

Japan had much greater success in the production of chemical and biological weapons than it did with the atomic bomb, radar, and guided missiles. Much of the production technology for chemical weapons was already well known by the end of World War I, and the industrial infrastructure for their production was already in place in Japan by the outbreak of World War II. Although the productive capacity of Japan's chemical industry was certainly not on par with that of Germany or the United States, it was at least comparable to that of France and Italy. All of these nations continued research and development in chemical warfare (CW) after World War I. But although most nations chose to abide by the Geneva Protocols of 1925, which prohibited the use of chemical and biological weapons, Japan did not. Many Japanese army officers were allegedly initially opposed to the use of CW, but by the late 1930s, the army was widely deploying various poison gases throughout China.

The production of biological weapons did not require the allocation of great amounts of natural resources, large capital investments, or even a strong industrial capacity. Nor was there a need for extensive collaborative research or the integration of various institutions or additional laboratories. Properly equipped, a single laboratory and supporting facility could manufacture millions of lethal pathogens on its own. Unlike nuclear weapons development, no complex managerial structure or centralization of oversight was necessary to create and sustain a viable biological weapons development program. Considering Japan's poor factor endowments during the war—namely the lack of natural resources and a limited industrial capacity—it is understandable that Japan undertook biological weapons research with such intensity. Although the Japanese program was not as extensive as that of the United States, it surpassed the American program in various aspects of "research" because of the willingness of the army doctors to use human subjects in their experiments.

As a result, the Japanese biological warfare program emerged as one of the most advanced of all the belligerents of World War II.

MODERN CHEMICAL AND BIOLOGICAL WARFARE AND WORLD WAR I

Chemical and biological warfare (CBW) can be dated to the earliest recorded battles. One of the first known uses of rudimentary chemical weapons occurred in 431 BCE, when the armies of Sparta used toxic clouds of sulfur fumes in the siege of the Athenian city of Platea. Ancient armies commonly used smoke in combat. A primitive form of biological warfare (BW) was to foul enemy water supplies with the corpses of dead men and animals, a common practice of the Persian, Greek, and Roman armies and so on through the American Civil War and the South African Boer War. Another early form of BW was to catapult the bodies of dead soldiers, excrement, and corpses infected with various diseases, especially bubonic plague, into enemy fortresses. But the development of chemistry and biology as modern fields of science, the growth of the chemical industry, and advances in medicine and hygiene were all necessary before chemical and biological weapons could become a practical part of any modern military arsenal.[1]

The Geneva Convention of 1864 and the Hague Conventions of 1899 and 1907 were among the first efforts to codify humane behavior in modern warfare. The Hague Conventions even led to specific limitations on the use of chemical weapons. In spite of these agreements, however, it was only a matter of time before chemical weapons were being developed and produced on an industrial scale for use in combat. In 1912, chemists in France invented a tear gas grenade that French police freely used to quell civil unrest. Soon after, engineers in England began research on a chemical-laden artillery shell. Not surprisingly, the prohibition against chemical weapons was largely ignored during World War I. As fighting bogged down in trench warfare, the belligerents looked to new weapons to break the deadlock. The horrors of CW were still unknown in modern combat, and chemical weapons offered a terribly effective alternative to more conventional weapons.[2]

France was the first nation to use chemical weapons in World War I, when in August 1914, the French army fired tear gas grenades against German troops at the front. It did not take long for Germany to respond with new chemical weapons of its own. With stocks of conventional artillery munitions dwindling, German military authorities readily accepted the proposal of chemist Fritz Haber of the prestigious Kaiser Wilhelm Institute to use chlorine gas against the Allies. On 22 April 1915, Germany seriously escalated CW in battle by attacking French troops at Ypres with chlorine gas. The single attack at Ypres killed some 5,000 soldiers and left 10,000 more wounded. After Ypres, the Allies became determined to retaliate in kind. In England, chemists were organized into a special military unit to deploy chemical weapons at the front. But Germany continued to employ chlorine gas and escalated its use on the eastern front, while German chemists at home worked to develop even deadlier chemical agents. By 1916, chemical weapons had become the subject of intense military research among all the principal combatants of World War I.[3]

In January 1916, the British government established the Porton Down Experimental Station to develop and test chemical weapons. Located on the southern edge of the Salisbury Plain, Porton Down employed over 1,000 scientists and soldiers. Several new chemical weapons were developed at this facility. But even with Porton Down, Britain's entire chemical industry was no match for the mighty German Interessen Gemeinschaft cartel, known as IG Farben. Carl Duisberg, head of the IG Farben cartel, was a strong advocate of CW and assisted Haber's foray into chemical weapons development. Germany's chemical industry was the most advanced in the world at the outset of World War I and thus held significant advantages in chemical weapons production. Dye factories, for example, were quickly converted to produce mustard gas. In contrast, it took France nearly nine months and Britain fourteen to construct a single mustard gas plant. Only the United States, with its as yet untapped industrial capacity and vast resources, could potentially match Germany in the production of chemical weapons.[4]

The United States entered the war and the chemical weapons race comparatively late. The army did not begin CW research or establish chemical combat units until early 1917. With the United States' entry into the war appearing imminent, on 3 April 1917, the National Research Council formed the Subcommittee on Noxious Gases, composed of officers from the army and navy, members of the NRC Chemistry Committee, and the director of the U.S. Bureau of Mines. A plant for producing CW artillery shells was built at Edgewood, Maryland, in the autumn of 1917, and within a year, additional factories were erected there for the manufacture of chlorine, chloropicrin, and phosgene. In May 1918, the Army Ordnance Department designated this facility the Edgewood Arsenal.[5] On 28 June, the U.S. War Department established the U.S. Army Chemical Warfare Service (CWS), which was charged with the task of coordinating the R&D efforts of the various agencies of the government and military involved in chemical weapons production.[6]

As for Japan, when World War I broke out in Europe, it joined the Allies in the war against the Central Powers and took advantage of the opportunity to seize Germany's leased territories in China. But Japan largely avoided the war. Japanese troops remained in Asia, and only military attachés and official observers were dispatched to Europe. Japanese soldiers did not directly experience the horrors of chemical weapons in the war and there arose no immediate need for the Japanese army to develop offensive or defensive capabilities in CW at this time. As a result, Japan took a somewhat lackadaisical approach to CW research, and it did not keep pace with the western powers in this field. But the efficacy of chemical weapons in World War I did not go unnoticed. In 1915, the Army Technology Review Board began to investigate new weapons being used on the battlefield in Europe. Among the many items of interest were gas masks and poison gas launchers. The board established committees to investigate development of these, but little progress was made. Elsewhere, in the Army Medical College (Rikugun Gun'i Gakkō), army physician Koizumi Chikahiko had begun some parallel investigations of his own. His research interests were soon to intersect with those of the Army Technology Review Board, and his involvement was to prove critical to the formation of Japan's CW program.[7]

Koizumi Chikahiko was perhaps the person most qualified for taking the leading role in launching Japan's CW research. After graduating from the College of Medicine at Tokyo Imperial University in 1908, Koizumi joined the army. Within a year he was commissioned as a first lieutenant with a corresponding rank of second surgeon and was assigned to the Tokyo Army Arsenal as an industrial physician, a position he held for two years. In 1911, Koizumi transferred to the Army Medical College, where he worked in the hygienics laboratory. Among his first research projects was a study of the relationship between nutrition and the gross income of workers, which he conducted at the army arsenal where he formerly worked. His paper on the subject was named best article of the year (1911) by the Medical Society of Tokyo. Koizumi's general interest in biochemistry also led him to study the specific problem of the absorption and expulsion of chemical materials in the human body. In 1914, the opportunity arose to investigate picric acid poisoning among factory workers in the munitions industry. This experience led him to pursue additional research on the medical effects of hazardous industrial materials on human beings. As a physician, Koizumi's research interests were focused on the preservation of the general health and welfare of industrial workers, and he appears not to have been interested in researching chemical weapons just yet. Ironically, however, it was his work with toxic substances that led him to consider the potential of CW.[8]

After learning of Germany's use of poison gas against the Allies at Flanders in April 1915, Koizumi consulted a report by the Industrial Toxins Research

Committee of Germany, which he had obtained from the German chemist Arnold Sommerfeld sometime shortly before the war. The report listed numerous chemical agents, discussed research on the toxicity of various compounds, and explained methods to reduce the harmful effects of toxic materials used in industrial manufacturing.[9] Realizing the potential of chemical weapons for Japan, Koizumi proposed the initiation of CW research to the Army Technology Review Board, and later that year, the board authorized him to begin research. From 1915, his work focused on developing asphyxiating gases, which were the compounds most commonly used by Germany in World War I.[10] Because he lacked a laboratory of his own for such research, Koizumi had to conduct experiments with dangerous chemicals and gases in a designated laboratory of the Army Medical College's hygienics school.[11] This situation was far from being conducive to advanced research. The time for expansion had come.

The Japanese army made significant advances toward the formation of a CW program at this time. In September 1917, construction of a new Chemical Weapons Laboratory was approved for the Army Medical College, and in May 1918, the Army Ministry established a Provisional Committee on Poison Gas Research to provide oversight of the fledgling chemical weapons research program there. Koizumi was named chief of research on protective devices, and by the end of the year, he had at his disposal a modest two-story brick building housing a special laboratory for research. It was here that Koizumi was able to conduct experiments with several toxic chemicals and poison gases, and it was here that he subsequently developed a gas mask that came to be widely used by the army. But the real leap for the army came in April 1919, when the Army Technical Department (Rikugun Gijutsu Honbu) established the Army Institute of Scientific Research (Rikugun Kagaku Kenkyūjo) as its primary research institution. Within a few years, its Third Department, which later became the Sixth Army Technical Institute, would take over responsibility for Japan's official CW program.[12]

In comparison to other countries, however, chemical weapons research, development, and production in Japan during and after World War I remained on a relatively small scale. Germany alone used approximately 57,600 tons of toxic gases—including chlorine, phosgene, and mustard, to name only a few—which accounted for nearly half of the total tonnage of gases used by all combatants. By the end of the war, chemical artillery shells accounted for an astonishing 35 percent of the total of French expenditures on ammunition. In England they accounted for 25 percent, and in the United States, 15 percent.[13] Of the principal combatants of World War I, however, the United States produced the most poison gases, nearly four times the amount of

Germany and almost as much gas as England and France combined.[14] Japan, on the other hand, did not produce chemical weapons on an industrial scale during World War I, nor did it use them. Such conditions were to change greatly in Japan's next war.

In contrast to CW, the principal belligerents employed BW on only a very limited scale during World War I. In Germany, in April 1916, the Sanitary Corps advocated an intensive BW campaign against England and submitted a plan to the War Department suggesting the use of dirigibles to drop glass balloons filled with a highly virulent plague culture over London and various English seaports. The planners hypothesized that the element of surprise and panic produced by the appearance of plague, in addition to the extensive loss of human life, would have a profoundly devastating and demoralizing effect on the British. Although this plan met with approval from a number of the top-ranking officers in the War Department, it was flatly rejected by the Army Medical Department, which feared retaliation in kind.[15]

Similar fears may have acted as a deterrent to BW being used more widely during the war. None of the principal combatants established an official biological weapons R&D program during World War I, and the few instances of BW known to have occurred were limited to acts of sabotage. For example, in 1915, German saboteurs in the United States inoculated a shipload of horses and cattle bound for England with glanders. Once discovered, the animals were dumped into the ocean, thus foiling the plan to spread disease among livestock in England. The French also alleged that German agents attempted to infect horses and cattle along the western front with glanders and anthrax. France also accused Germany of dropping bacteria-laden fruit, chocolate, and toys into Romanian cities from airplanes.[16] On the whole, however, BW efforts were minimal in World War I, and it was not until the 1930s that formal, large-scale R&D programs were established.[17]

CHEMICAL AND BIOLOGICAL WEAPONS IN WORLD WAR II

Chemical weapons had proven effective in World War I, but they also resulted in horrific casualties and left survivors with previously unknown injuries and chronic ailments. Around the world, public opinion concerning CW was divided. On the one hand, military leaders argued that continued R&D in chemical weapons was necessary for national defense. On the other hand, civilians and humanitarian groups, such as the Red Cross, denounced chemical weapons and called for an international prohibition on their development and use. In response to such pressures, the Washington Conference on Arms Limitations in 1922 banned chemical weapons. Compliance, however, depended largely on the strength of public opinion against CW, and the treaty provided no safeguard against future violations. The League of Nations Disarmament Conference in 1925 led to the creation of the Geneva Protocols, which reaffirmed the ban on chemical weapons as defined by the Washington Treaty and—at the behest of the Polish delegate—added a prohibition against biological weapons as well. But the protocols did not prohibit R&D or the stockpiling of CBW weapons, nor did they provide penalties for violations. In sum, the protocols were simply a ban on the "first use" of chemical and biological weapons. Forty-one nations signed the agreement, but there were important stipulations and a few exceptions. Some nations reserved the right to retaliate in kind if attacked with chemical or biological weapons. The United States refused to ratify the protocols altogether, arguing that ratification would make it impossible to develop and maintain adequate defensive measures against CBW.[18] Japan also abstained from ratifying the protocol.[19]

Public opposition to chemical weapons, as well as military demobilization after World War I, had a significant impact on the CW program in the United States. Industrial and university laboratories largely abandoned military-related research, and in 1918, the army dissolved its Subcommittee on Noxious Gases. By June 1919, nearly 97 percent of the U.S. Army's Chemical Warfare Service personnel had been demobilized. The CWS itself only narrowly escaped dissolution and was spared by the National Defense Act of 1920, which made the CWS a permanent branch of the army. The CWS was saved largely by the efforts of Brigadier-General Amos A. Fries, who feared that without it, the United States would fall dangerously behind in CW research. In March 1920, Fries established the Chemical Warfare Technical Committee to serve as a liaison organization to other divisions of the army. Later that year, he formed the Chemical Warfare Branch Committee, which became responsible for producing and handling CW matériel. Fries also oversaw the reorganization of the Edgewood Arsenal, adding the Medical Research Department and the Chemical Research and Development Division, among others. In 1923, Fries further revamped the U.S. chemical weapons program by forming the Chemical Warfare Board to manage CW R&D and policy, and to coordinate the technical developments of the CWS with the tactical doctrines and needs of the army. Despite Fries's efforts, however, the CWS remained a low priority and received little funding or support at this time.[20]

CW programs elsewhere in the world fared better. Not only did the British keep the Porton Down facility operational after the armistice, but they intensified offensive R&D efforts and campaigned to attract the best and brightest scientists in the country to the program. The British also continued to use chemical weapons in the interwar period. In 1919, the Royal Air Force dropped canisters of arsenic smoke during the intervention in the Russian Civil War and allegedly used phosgene and mustard gas in Afghanistan. In France, the Atelier de Pyrotechnie du Bouchet near Paris became the central installation for CW research. Italy formed the Military Chemical Service (Servizio Chemico Militare) in 1923. In the Soviet Union, the Red Army established a chemistry agency and opened the Higher Military School for Chemistry in Moscow in 1920. In 1922, the Red Army began collaborative R&D with the Germans on chemical weapons, which was later to become the Tomka Project.[21] And in August 1925, the Military-Chemical Agency of the Red Army was established while troop-training programs in CW were initiated at designated institutions throughout the nation. By the start of the war, the Soviets had built up a sizable arsenal and were capable of manufacturing 8 tons of poison gases per month, of some fourteen types in all.[22] As for Germany, the Versailles Treaty of 1919 prohibited it from engaging in chemical weapons R&D, but clandestine research in CW continued nonetheless.[23]

The Geneva Protocols did not stop further R&D, nor could they prevent chemical weapons from being used again. During the invasion of Abyssinia (Ethiopia) in 1935, the Italian air force used mustard gas bombs to kill some 15,000 Abyssinian soldiers. Despite the protests of Emperor Haile Selassie to the League of Nations, there was little that could be done short of declaring war against Italy. In its defense, the Italian government claimed that it had not violated the 1925 Geneva Protocols because the agreement did not expressly prohibit chemical weapons when used in retaliation for illegal acts of war, which it alleged the Abyssinians had committed. Italy claimed its soldiers had been tortured and decapitated by the Abyssinians, thus rationalizing the use of chemical weapons.[24]

The Italian war in Ethiopia was a clear signal that the short era of peace enjoyed after World War I was drawing to an end. Throughout Europe in the 1920s and 1930s, the nations that were to form the Axis alliance began to rearm, and in the fervor of rearmament, the Geneva Protocols were largely ignored. Production of chemical weapons increased throughout Europe and the United States, as well as in Japan. In 1936, the French built a phosgene factory at Clemency, and the British began to build a mustard gas factory at Sutton Oak. In the following year, the Soviet Union opened new chemical factories at Brandyuzhsky, Kuibyshev, and Karaganda. The United States reactivated its phosgene and mustard gas plants at Edgewood. In Germany, a separate CW section was established in the Army Department (Ordnance) in 1935. The next year, the Army General Office created the Chemical Troops and Gas Defense Inspectorate. The Army Gas Defense School was opened in 1938, and large-scale production of CW agents was under way by the end of the year. By the time World War II began, Germany had amassed some 12,000 tons of CW agents, some 80 percent of which was mustard gas. By the late 1930s, Japan also had developed a significant CW capacity, and it began to use chemical weapons against the Chinese in battles on the Asian continent.[25]

The Geneva Protocols also did not prevent nations from engaging in BW research. Great Britain, for example, began a BW research program within only a decade of signing the agreement. Responding to reports that the Germans were engaged in BW research, in February 1934, Sir Maurice Hankey, Secretary to the Cabinet and the Imperial Defense Committee, argued to the Chiefs of Staff that the potential of biological weapons should be investigated. Hankey was not immediately successful in gaining much support for BW research, but he managed to persuade Dr. Paul Fildes, Britain's leading microbiologist, to get involved. In October 1936, the Imperial Defense Committee established the Microbiological Warfare Committee under its jurisdiction and appointed Hankey as chair. Defensive measures, such as stockpiling vaccines, fungicides, and insecticides, were taken the following year by the recommendation of the committee. In April 1938, a Public Health Laboratory was established to investigate suspicious outbreaks of diseases and to distribute vaccines. Britain also engaged in offensive BW research. A modest BW laboratory was established at Porton Down in 1940 under Fildes. His team, never more than forty-five members, remained small throughout the war. From 1942, Great Britain and the United States began to collaborate in BW research much in the same way that they cooperated in the development of nuclear weapons and radar. The British disclosed the results of all their BW research to the United States by 1944, and in 1945, they offered tropical research stations in Australia and India for large-scale testing.[26]

The outbreak of war in Europe in September 1939 prompted increased support for CBW R&D in the United States and among most of the principal belligerents as well. The U.S. Congress raised the annual budget for the Chemical Warfare Service from $2 million in 1940 to more than $60 million in 1941, and to over $1 billion in 1942. The CWS also expanded from 1,128 in 1940 to 20,225 affiliated military personnel by 1942.[27] Also in that year, the National Defense Research Committee (NDRC) subsumed oversight for CW R&D in Division B, under the supervision of James Conant. In August 1942, the NDRC and CWS established the Technical Committee to coordinate CW R&D and to serve as the liaison between the two agencies. After the reorganization of the NDRC in December 1942, the majority of CW research came under the aegis of Divisions Nine, Ten, and Eleven.[28]

New facilities were built and university laboratories were mobilized for R&D in chemical weapons. In 1942, the CWS built a new laboratory at the Massachusetts Institute of Technology (MIT) and occupied laboratories at Columbia University. The NDRC established a toxicity laboratory at the University of Chicago, and a proving ground for CW munitions was established in Dugway Valley, Utah, which became the primary facility for field-testing CW agents and munitions in the United States. In the autumn of 1942, the Combined Chiefs of Staff established the U.S. Chemical Warfare Committee (USCWC) to coordinate all CW research activities by the military. To facilitate greater cooperation between the Allies, a joint U.S.-Canadian Advisory Committee was formed, which was later expanded to include Great Britain.[29] Such cooperation among the Allies greatly stimulated and advanced the CW program in the United States. In 1944, the CWS established an experimental station on San José Island off the western coast of Panama, where the CWS, the NDRC, Canada, and Great Britain collaborated in research on CW weapons under tropical conditions.[30]

The CWS also began to investigate biological weapons from the 1920s, but a formal BW program was not established until 1943. In July 1941, Harvey H. Bundy, special assistant to the Secretary of War, brought together representatives of the CWS, the OSRD, Army Intelligence, and the Surgeon General to discuss the coordination of BW research. In November, the Secretary of War, Henry L. Stimson, established the War Bureau of Consultants (WBC), a committee of twelve scientists led by Dr. Frank Jewett, then President of the National Academy of Sciences, to further examine U.S. needs in BW defense. As a result of recommendations from the WBC, in May 1942, President Roosevelt approved the formation of the Federal Security Agency, which was to prepare defensive measures and procedures for BW retaliation. The agency, later renamed the War Research Service (WRS), came under the direction of George W. Merck. From that point forward, general supervision of BW research in the United States was assigned to the WRS, and development was carried out primarily under the auspices of the CWS.[31]

In April 1943, the CWS established the BW Research and Development Center at Camp (later Fort) Detrick in Frederick, Maryland, where pilot plants for large-scale production of biological agents were put into operation. A production plant for BW agents was also installed at the Vigo Ordnance plant near Terre Haute, Indiana, and two proving grounds, one on Horn Island in Mississippi Sound and the other at Granite Peak adjacent to the Dugway facility, were established. The annual budget for BW R&D was set at approximately $2 million.[32] In January 1944, the entire BW program was transferred from the WRS to the Special Projects Division under the CWS. In October

1944, the U.S. Biological Warfare Committee was established with Merck as its chairman. The purpose of the committee was to make recommendations on policy to the Secretary of War and to serve as a liaison with its British counterpart, the London Interservice Subcommittee on Biological Warfare.[33] The BW program in the U.S. became a large undertaking with extensive collaboration among government agencies, universities, and branches of the military. Between 1942 and March 1945, over $40 million were invested in plant construction and equipment. At the apex of its organizational strength in August 1945, the Special Projects Division included 396 army officers, 124 navy officers, over 3,000 enlisted men, and 206 civilians.[34] Much of the documentation on the U.S. BW program remains classified, but it appears to have been much larger in scale than that of any other nation during World War II.[35]

The Soviet Union's foray into BW research began in 1925 with the formation of the Military Chemical Agency (MCA). Under the directorship of Jacov Fishman, the MCA became responsible for managing the Soviet BW program, while the Ministry of Defense coordinated research with the Ministry of Health, which in turn was responsible for overseeing BW-related research at thirty-five institutions throughout the Soviet Union. As with most everything else, the Politburo sat atop the Soviet BW program hierarchy. Among the primary research facilities in Moscow were the Moscow Institute of Epidemiology and Microbiology; the Charkov Scientific Research Institute of Microbiology, Vaccine, and Serum Studies; the Red Army Scientific Research Institute; and the Scientific Research Institute of Health. Facilities in Leningrad included the Zlatogrov-Maslokovich Laboratory of the Leningrad Veterinary and Zoological Technical Institute and the Leningrad Bacteriological Institute. The principal Soviet testing grounds for BW research included Tomka (near Shikhany); Gorodomlia Island (Lake Seliger), which included the outpost of the Red Army Biochemical Institute and the testing grounds of the Public Health Institute of Dneipropetrovsk University; and Vozrozhdeniya Island in the Aral Sea.[36]

According to U.S. navy intelligence documents, Professor Maslokovich of the Zlatogrov-Maslokovich Laboratory (Leningrad Veterinary and Zoological Technical Institute) was the leading figure in early Soviet BW research. Soviet scientists experimented with plague, anthrax, tularemia, typhoid, glanders, cholera, and foot-and-mouth disease. Many experiments were moved away from populated areas, like Moscow and Leningrad, to isolated areas, such as Gorodomlia Island, for the maintenance of secrecy and greater protection of the populace. Maslokovitch is also reported to have developed an airplane-launched bomb for the dissemination of anthrax and encephalitis.[37] But as with so many other areas of science, BW research also suffered under the

Stalinist purges of the late 1930s, resulting in the arrests of numerous capable scientists, including even MCA director Fishman.[38]

By the outbreak of war in 1939, the Axis powers were also involved in various aspects of CBW R&D and production. Throughout World War II, Italy's Military Chemical Service managed CW R&D, preparedness, and deployment. British intelligence estimated that Italy was capable of producing 25 tons of mustard gas and 5 tons of Lewisite per day, as well as other poison gases such as phosgene and diphenylchlorarsine, to name a few.[39] Italy was well equipped to launch a chemical weapons attack, but as with other belligerents during the war, the fear of retaliation in kind served as a restraint. Late in the spring of 1942, Churchill and Roosevelt both made grave threats to the Axis nations that the use of chemical weapons would bring about retaliation "on the largest possible scale."[40] Italy appears not to have established a formal BW program during the war.[41]

Germany ratified the 1925 Geneva Protocols in 1929. Despite the ban on CBW, however, and regardless of other weapons development prohibitions imposed by the Versailles Treaty, by the early 1940s, Germany had rebounded in CW R&D and production, owing largely to its substantial manufacturing base in the nation's powerful chemical industry. There were in Germany at least nineteen factories capable of producing some 12,000 tons of poison gas per month.[42] In addition to the nerve gases sarin and tabun, German factories also produced for the military two types of mustard gas as well as chlorine trifluoride, or N-Stoff, which was so volatile that it could cause clothes, hair, and asphalt to combust upon contact. Research on CW agents was conducted at Spandau and Raubkammer, which together employed about 1,200 people.[43] Although Germany did not use poison gases against the Allies in combat during the war, large quantities of poison gas were utilized to murder Jews, Gypsies, and "political prisoners," among others, in German death camps. Initially, carbon monoxide gas produced by engine exhaust was employed to kill the prisoners, but when this proved inefficient, the pesticide Zyklon B was used. Some victims at these camps were also exploited in experiments to test the efficacy of such CW agents as mustard gas, tabun, and sarin. By the end of the war, the Nazis had killed over 4.5 million people at the Auschwitz camp alone.[44]

Throughout the interwar years and early in the war, various offices of the German military services managed oversight of CW and BW related R&D together. From 1924, an office of the Inspectorate of the Artillery in the Army Ordnance Office assumed responsibility for CBW research. In 1935 and 1936, the Chemical Warfare Defense Section and the Inspectorate of Smoke Screen Forces and Gas Defense were created and took over responsibility for CBW.

In 1941, the head of the Army Ordnance Office, General Walter Leeb, redistributed CBW duties among various institutions. For example, the Surgeon General's Office of the Army Medical Inspectorate assumed responsibility for research in bacteriology and defense, the Veterinary Inspectorate took on responsibility for animal affairs, and the Chemical Warfare Defense Section assumed control over field trials and dissemination procedures. Numerous institutions were involved in some level of BW research in wartime Germany, but none of these emerged as a central establishment comparable to Camp Detrick in the United States.[45]

Not surprisingly, two independent and competing organizations emerged as the primary forces in Germany's BW program. In 1943, all army units concerned with BW related research were to be combined under the aegis of the Blitzableiter Committee under the direction of Professor Dr. Heinrich Kliewe, a leading bacteriologist with his own laboratory at the Institute for General and Military Hygiene in Berlin. As director of German BW research in the Office of the Surgeon General of the Wehrmacht, Kliewe studied anthrax, plague, cholera, tularemia, and glanders, among others, and conducted research on the development of mask filters. Various types of mustard-anthrax shells and bombs were also studied in an attempt to enhance their effectiveness and durability. Kliewe's BW research facilities were quite limited, however, and he had at his disposal only one office and five rooms. Outside laboratories had to be used for designated experiments.[46] Dissatisfied with the Kliewe group, later in 1943, Reich Marshal Hermann Göring, then president of the Reich Research Council, appointed Professor Kurt Blome, director of the Kaiser Wilhelm Institute's Center for Cancer Research, to head a rival BW program. Blome's network conducted BW related research at the Posen Military Medical Academy and used concentration camps at Buchenwald, Dachau, and Natzwieler to conduct experiments on inmates. But the German BW program at Posen never got very far. In March 1945 the facility was abandoned because of the advance of the Soviet army.[47]

Germany's BW program was comparatively minimal in scale and suffered from a lack of funding and adequate personnel. There was considerable dissension within the Blitzableiter Committee on Biological Warfare, whose members could not agree on procedures for research, and cooperation among the various branches of the armed forces was poor. Furthermore, the German BW program was limited by a general prohibition on offensive BW research that came from no less than Hitler himself. According to a U.S. navy intelligence report, the inadequacy of the German BW program was "undoubtedly less due to the inability of German scientists successfully to develop such a program than to Hitler's personal opposition to the use of BW."[48] Defensive research, however, was generally supported. There was apparently no central location for human experimentation because tests were conducted at the numerous death camps.[49]

On the whole, BW research in Germany appears to account for a relatively small percentage of the murders committed by Nazi doctors in World War II. Human experimentation was mostly conducted under the general program of "racial purification," including the sterilization program (eugenics), the killing of the mentally ill and the retarded (euthanasia), and the eradication of Germany's racial minorities, especially the Jews (the Final Solution).[50] Of the Axis powers, it was Japan that employed CW most widely in combat and emerged as arguably the most advanced nation in BW R&D, perhaps even surpassing the United States.

CHEMICAL WEAPONS R&D IN WORLD WAR II JAPAN

Chemical weapons research in Japan initially focused on defensive measures. But concern over the possibility of the Soviet Red Army using poison gas against Japanese troops on the Asian continent compelled the Japanese army to expand its investigation into offensive measures as well. (The threat of retaliation in kind was considered the best deterrent by most countries at the time.) Japanese military leaders had observed how widely poison gas was used as a tactical weapon in Europe during World War I, and they sought to add chemical weapons to their arsenal in the buildup of national defense in the post–World War I era. The aforementioned Provisional Committee on Poison Gas Research, established in May 1918 by the Army Ministry, was assigned to investigate chemical weapons and their industrial manufacturing processes. The committee was composed of thirty experts, including Koizumi Chikahiko, who traveled abroad to study CW programs in the West.[51]

In March 1919, Koizumi left Japan for a tour of the United States and Europe. In the United States, he visited army hospitals and studied the American system of conscription and methods of training relevant to military medicine. While in Europe over the summer, Koizumi visited battlefields where poison gas warfare had been employed, and he gathered information on CW from authorities in each country. He returned to Japan later that year hoping to continue his research on gas warfare with the many publications and research materials that he had acquired while abroad. But when he returned to Japan, Koizumi found that the Army Institute of Scientific Research had taken over much of the responsibility for CW research. Furthermore, during his absence, his mentor, Professor Inaba Ryōtaro, had died, leaving Koizumi to become the successor to his position as chief of the hygienics laboratory. Thereafter, Koizumi assumed mostly administrative duties and was unable to devote his attention to publishing the results of his research. In 1923, the Great Kantō Earthquake destroyed several buildings of the Army Medical College, and any CW research still being conducted there all but ceased. When Koizumi was named Army Surgeon General in 1934, this promotion further removed him from conducting CW-related research himself, and he spent much of the rest of his career as a bureaucrat.[52] His personal involvement in developing CBW programs in Japan, however, was far from over.

Since its foundation in 1919, the Army Institute of Scientific Research—the research branch of the Army Technical Department—and its affiliated personnel played an increasingly larger role in the development of Japan's fledgling CW program. Primary responsibility for the program there was delegated to a career officer, Lieutenant Colonel Hisamura Taneki. Hisamura visited Europe in 1918 and 1919 to study German and French deployment of chemical weapons, and in 1919, he served as a representative of the Japanese Ministry of Foreign Affairs in Berlin and as a member of the Allied Committee on the Enforcement of the Versailles Treaty, which was charged with the responsibility of investigating and dismantling chemical weapons production facilities in Germany. Upon his return to Japan, Hisamura reported everything that he had learned about German CW and poison gas manufacturing to his superior officers. In 1921, he was sent abroad once more to investigate the CW programs in the United States, France, and Germany. Hisamura found these to be "considerably advanced," and when he returned to Japan, he lobbied his superiors to invest more in CW technology so that Japan would not fall too "far behind." The army responded quickly, providing Hisamura with ¥50,000 for research and ¥25,000 for the construction of a new laboratory in Tokyo. Hisamura also invited Koizumi to join his CW research group around this time, but, likely because of his other obligations, Koizumi did not accept the offer.[53]

Japan's CW program matured steadily during the 1920s and 1930s. Research and development on poison gases was underway at the Army Institute of Scientific Research by November 1922.[54] In June 1925, the army promoted Hisamura's CW research group to departmental level, designating it the Third Department of the Army Institute of Scientific Research. Additional funds were also allocated. In that year, the Third Department received ¥300,000 for research, and an additional ¥1.2 million was provided for the expansion of research facilities. By 1928, Hisamura's Third Department included forty laboratories and twenty affiliated workshops occupying two large buildings and an annex, staffed by a hundred researchers and technicians.[55]

Around this time, Japan also began to receive technical assistance from Germany in the formation of its fledgling CW program. In 1926, a German scientist and expert on chemical weapons, identified in a U.S. intelligence report only as "Dr. Mezner," went to Japan and stayed for two years as a guest lecturer and consultant on poison gases at the Army Institute of Scientific Research.[56] Research on the manufacturing of the known principal poison gases began "in earnest" shortly thereafter.[57]

To a large extent, Japan's progress in CW-related research depended on such foreign assistance. Mezner's lectures, together with information gathered abroad by Hisamura and others, not only helped to complete Japan's knowledge of CW on the battlefield in Europe in World War I, but also assisted significantly in the formation of Japan's own CW program. Throughout the interwar period, Japanese military personnel enjoyed what can only be considered rather liberal access to western CW-related facilities, and they made several trips abroad. For example, in April 1924, Hisamura, on yet another trip to the United States, this time accompanied by a Japanese engineer, was able to inspect the Edgewood Arsenal in Maryland.[58] Thus, by the late 1920s, the Japanese army had at its disposal extremely detailed information ranging from the organization of the CW services in the United States, France, and Germany, to maps depicting the areas and terrain in which chemical weapons had been used and how they had been deployed, to the design of specific weapons, such as chemical-laden shells and gas grenades, as well as protective devices for humans and horses.[59] Even well into the 1930s, Japanese military technical missions continued to gain access to federal laboratories in the United States.[60] With such information at hand, CW R&D in Japan was able to keep up with that of other nations.

Throughout the war years, three institutions served as the principal R&D sites for Japan's CW program: the Sixth Army Technical Institute in Tokyo, the Sagami Naval Research Department, and the Third Army Aeronautical Technology Research Institute. The largest and most advanced of these was the Sixth Army Technical Institute, which conducted the majority of Japan's CW research. In 1941, the army significantly expanded the research branches of the Army Institute of Scientific Research, and the Third Department was upgraded and renamed the Sixth Army Technical Institute. This facility comprised some twenty buildings with over 700 personnel on staff. Of this number, about fifty were army scientists, forty were civilian technicians, and the rest were laborers. Toward the end of the war, the Sixth Army Technical Institute operated on an average annual budget of approximately ¥3 million (about $750,000/1944 base year). Although this facility conducted intensive research and synthesized over 1,000 compounds, it failed to produce any new chemical weapons.[61] The Sixth Army Technical Institute also operated a branch station in Manchuria, designated the Chichihara (Tsitsihar) Laboratory, which employed about 300 technicians and workers.[62]

The Japanese navy began CW R&D at the Navy Technical Research Institute in 1923. In 1931, responsibility for CW R&D was transferred to the Navy Powder Arsenal at Hiratsuka in Kanagawa prefecture. In 1934, a separate Chemical Research Division was established to subsume the former CW R&D duties of the Hiratsuka Arsenal. The navy expanded the Chemical Research Division in May 1943 and renamed it the Sagami Naval Research Department, at which time it became responsible for all of the navy's CW R&D. The Sagami Naval Research Department employed some 300 staff members, of which only 30 were scientists with advanced training, while the rest were laboratory technicians and laborers. Only a small percentage of the work was assigned to university and industrial laboratories. By the end of the war, about ¥1.3 million ($330,000) annually was appropriated for research at the Sagami Naval Research Department. Research on new chemical agents was conducted on a very small scale, and about one hundred compounds or so were synthesized at Sagami.[63]

The third, and smallest, facility for CW R&D was the Third Army Aeronautical Technology Research Institute located at the Tachikawa airfield in central Tokyo prefecture. This facility conducted research on aerial spray technologies and chemical bombs. It occupied only two floors of a nondescript wooden building and employed a total staff of approximately 300, of which only two officers and seventeen technical officers were exclusively dedicated to CW research. Only ¥30,000 ($7,500) annually was allocated for CW R&D at this comparatively diminutive facility.[64]

The primary site of chemical weapons production in Japan was the small island of Okunoshima. Nestled in the Inland Sea in Hiroshima prefecture between Japan's main island of Honshū and the island of Shikoku, Okunoshima provided secrecy and protection against any accidental release of toxins into the general population. The army appropriated the island under the Military Secrets Act in August 1927 and established a branch of the Army Arsenal Bureau in the city of Tadanoumi on the main island directly across the Inland Sea from Okunoshima. In May 1929, the Okunoshima arsenal began production of selected chemicals, concentrating on the manufacture of tear and mustard gases. The complex consisted of several factory buildings, a power plant, warehouses, office buildings, and a hospital, with convenient access to its own harbor. Lieutenant Colonel Hisamura Taneki, who had served an important leadership role in establishing Japan's CW research program at the Army Institute of Scientific Research, also assisted in the founding of the

Okunoshima plant. The initial staff of eighty workers included seven engineers, all of whom were graduates of industrial or pharmaceutical colleges. Over the years, the staff expanded significantly, from 225 in 1935 to 2,645 in 1937, and peaking at over 6,000 between 1937 and 1944, when the arsenal operated at full capacity to meet war production demands.[65]

On a monthly basis, Okunoshima was capable of producing 200 tons of mustard gas, 50 tons of lewisite, 80 tons of diphenylcyanoarsine, 50 tons of hydrocianic acid, and 2.5 tons of chloroacetophenone.[66] In addition to Okunoshima, army arsenals in Osaka and Oji, and naval arsenals at Maizuru and Hiratsuka also produced mustard and tear gases. From the early 1930s, private firms also produced poison gases for the military, including the Hodogaya Chemical Company, which manufactured phosgene, chlorine, bromine, and benzoic acid, and the Sumitomo Chemical Company, which made arsenic derivatives.[67]

In the formative years of Japan's CW program, the Army Medical College was responsible for training in chemical weapons. But with the growth of the program, in 1933, the army established a new CW training school at Narashino in northwestern Chiba prefecture. Placed under the direction of the Inspector General of Military Education, Narashino became the principal CW training facility for both services. According to a postwar U.S. intelligence report, Narashino was "splendidly equipped, well staffed and effective in the fulfillment of its mission until the end of the war."[68] Between 1939 and 1945, a total of 3,074 officers were graduated from Narashino.[69] Upon graduation, these line officers returned to their respective units to disseminate knowledge gained during CW training.[70]

Although Japan's CW program paled in comparison in scale and scope to those of the other principal belligerents in World War II—especially the United States—it was Japan, more than any other nation, that relied most frequently on the deployment of chemical weapons in combat. Not long after the Marco Polo Bridge Incident in July 1937, the Japanese army began to use chemical weapons against Chinese military forces and civilians. At first, non-lethal lacrimators, such as tear gas, were used. Some Japanese field commanders had initially been reluctant to deploy chemical weapons, ostensibly fearing their troops might grow overly dependent on them. With increased Chinese resistance, however, from about 1938, the Japanese army used chemical weapons, especially poison gases, with increased frequency.[71]

In 1938, Chinese delegates to the League of Nations presented evidence of the Japanese army having used tear and mustard gases on the Shanghai front and elsewhere. Subsequent investigations by U.S. and British intelligence supported their claims.[72] Later that year, President Roosevelt issued the first of a series of statements condemning Japan's use of chemical weapons, but at the time, there was little the United States could do short of a declaration of war. Throughout the war with China, the Japanese army used poison gases on as many as 2,091 occasions, with estimates of casualties ranging from 36,968 to 80,000, including both military and civilians.[73] In 1942, after the United States' entry into the Pacific War, Roosevelt again denounced Japan's CW attacks on China and declared that the United States would retaliate in kind if Japan did not cease using chemical weapons. For the most part, however, Roosevelt's warning was an empty threat, as the United States did not yet have sufficient stocks of chemical weapons in the Pacific to retaliate on a large scale.[74]

In general, it was the policy of the Imperial Japanese Army to restrict use of poison gases as a tactical weapon, and they supposedly were never considered part of the army's "conventional" arsenal. Throughout the war, the Japanese army limited the use of chemical weapons almost exclusively to operations in China. When interrogated after the war, General Tōjō claimed that although Japan had conducted CW research during the war, it was in a "defensive sense" and that the use of chemical weapons was "forbidden" because, if used, it "would have been disastrous for Japan." He cited three reasons for Japan to abstain from CW: international law (which prohibited CW); the United States' strength vis-à-vis Japan; and Japan's vulnerability as an island nation. Tōjō insisted that he himself had forbidden the use of chemical weapons, even stating, "I made tremendous fuss about this," and arguing that CW was prohibited on the basis of policy and strategy.[75] Given the Imperial Japanese Army's extensive use of poison gases in China, however, the first factor listed can be disregarded as a ruse. Logically, only the threat of retaliation in kind by a technologically equal or superior military force prohibited further use of chemical weapons by Japan. Thus, one can argue that Roosevelt's threat of massive retaliation appears to have prevented the spread of CW attacks by Japan more widely throughout the Pacific.[76] Perhaps, as a result, chemical weapons did not play a significant role in the outcome of the war.

BIOLOGICAL WEAPONS R&D IN WORLD WAR II JAPAN

Of all Japan's wartime weapons of mass destruction projects, the BW program can be considered to have been the most successful. Unlike the development of nuclear weapons, radar, guided missiles, and chemical weapons, biological weapons did not require the allocation of scarce natural or technological resources, nor did their production depend on a significant industrial capacity.

To produce vast amounts of biological weapons, it was not necessary to mobilize scientists on a large scale or to coordinate R&D efforts across many institutional boundaries, as was often the case with other advanced weapons projects. Biological weapons could be produced on a large scale by the army alone, and comparatively cheaply. Biological weapons were thus a suitable alternative for a nation with few natural resources and a limited industrial and scientific capability, as Japan was during the war.

The primary force behind the initiation and formation of Japan's BW program was Lieutenant General Ishii Shirō. Ishii graduated from the Medical Department of Kyoto Imperial University in 1920 and enlisted as an army surgeon the following year. In April 1921, he was commissioned as an officer at the rank of surgeon–first lieutenant and assigned to the Imperial Guards Division. He was transferred to the First Army Hospital in Tokyo in August 1922, but returned to Kyoto Imperial University in 1924 to pursue postgraduate studies in bacteriology, serology, pathology, and preventative medicine. In August 1924, he was promoted to captain, and later that year, he was sent to Shikoku to study the outbreak of a new strain of encephalitis that had reached epidemic proportions. Ishii attempted to devise an effective filtration system for isolating the virus suspected to be the cause of the disease. This assignment brought him into research on epidemic prevention and water filtration early in his career. From that point forward, these subjects were to become the primary focus of his research.[77]

After taking his doctorate in microbiology in 1926, Ishii was posted to the Kyoto Army Medical Hospital. In the course of his research there, Ishii read the report on CBW prepared by Japan's representative to the 1925 Geneva Conference. He saw potential in the development of a BW program and began to lobby superior officers in the Army Ministry and the Army General Staff to support research in this field.[78] But at that time, army brass found his proposal disagreeable and offered no support. Undaunted, in 1928, Ishii set out to investigate BW programs in other nations. He embarked on a world tour that was to last for two years, taking him across Asia, into Europe, and on to the United States.[79]

Following his return to Japan in 1930, Ishii was promoted to the rank of major. In August of that year, he was appointed professor of immunology in the Department of Epidemic Prevention at the Army Medical College in Tokyo, where he taught as an instructor by day and conducted clandestine BW research by night. Around this time, Ishii again began to lobby superior officers on the General Staff and in the Army Ministry to support BW research, arguing that the most powerful nations were already preparing for bacteriological warfare, and that if Japan did not do the same, it would find itself in "serious difficulties" in the future.[80] Emphasizing Japan's vulnerability because of the comparative lack of raw materials and mineral resources, Ishii argued that biological weapons were more economical to produce than conventional weapons. Furthermore, he argued, BW must have great potential—otherwise, it would not have been forbidden by the Geneva Protocols of 1925.[81]

Ishii made his appeal to a senior colleague at the Army Medical College, none other than Koizumi Chikahiko, the progenitor of Japan's CW program. Koizumi, now a colonel, was receptive to Ishii's plan, perhaps as a consequence of having been unable to fulfill his own ambitions in chemical weapons research. Ishii won him over, and Koizumi's patronage soon brought with it the additional support of other high-ranking army officers.[82] But Ishii was also making a name for himself on his own. In 1931, he developed the first functional prototype of a ceramic water filter and purification system for use by troops in the field. Ishii made the rounds within the army, demonstrating the machine and convincing army brass of its efficacy. He took out a patent on the apparatus, and the Japanese army and navy both adopted it for field use.[83]

Japanese military expansion in northeast China after the Manchurian Incident in 1931 brought about new opportunities for Ishii's agenda. In 1932, Ishii set out on a tour of the region. The remoteness of China's northeast and its strategic location between Japan and its potential rival, the Soviet Union, appealed to him. Ishii thought Manchuria would be an ideal environment in which to develop a BW program, and army brass agreed. By the end of the year, Ishii was able to garner support for the establishment of a small-scale BW research operation there. A special detachment of the Kwantung Army, the Tōgō Unit, was created to oversee the program. The Tōgō Unit was to operate in complete secrecy, and detachment members were given aliases and prohibited from mingling with the civilian population. Two modest laboratories were set up under Ishii's direction, one in the city of Harbin and the other in a nearby village called Beiyinhe (Hainga). The laboratory in Harbin housed "defensive" research in vaccines, while the Beiyinhe site was to have a more sinister purpose, for "offensive" research. Back in Tokyo at the Army Medical College, in August of that year, an Epidemic Prevention Laboratory was also established with Ishii as its director.[84]

Although the evidence is sketchy, it appears that around this time (1932–1933) Ishii began BW-related research using live human subjects both in Tokyo and in Manchuria. Certainly, engaging in such work in Tokyo was risky. Manchuria was the more logical site for this type of activity. Manchuria not only provided security and safety from contaminating the domestic population, but it also provided other important advantages for Ishii's research agenda. For example, the climate was similar to the far eastern regions of the

Soviet Union, where Ishii anticipated using BW most, and thus offered almost identical weather conditions for testing. Because of the close proximity to the Soviet border, the Tōgō Unit would also be in a strategic forward position to deploy biological weapons rapidly against the Soviet Red Army or Chinese forces if necessary. Manchuria also provided a certain "moral space" in which Ishii could expand his BW research into more nefarious realms.[85] Unlike Japan, there was plenty of space in Manchuria in which to build and operate BW research facilities without as much attention having to be given to safety or secrecy. Under the protection of the Kwantung Army, Ishii could also advance his agenda without much concern for civilian detection or interference, as might be encountered domestically. Moreover, Ishii intended to exploit the racially and ethnically diverse population of China's northeast for its vast supply of "human material" for use in BW experiments—another advantage Manchuria held over Japan.[86]

Harbin was an ideal place to start. Located in the heart of the Manchurian territory in Heilongjiang province, Harbin was a cosmopolitan city on par with most developed cities of Asia for the time. Throughout its history, the city had been a contested space, settled and populated alternately by Manchus, Russians, and ethnic Han Chinese. By the early twentieth century, Japanese colonialists and various expatriates from Europe and Central Asia had also made it their home. From the splendor of St. Sophia Cathedral, with its characteristic Russian-style onion-shaped domes, and the numerous Christian churches, Jewish synagogues, and Islamic mosques, to the former Russian commercial district, Harbin was a unique blend of East and West, surrounded by vast stretches of small farms, traditional villages, and undeveloped grasslands.[87]

But after the Japanese arrived, the ambiance of Harbin radically changed. Japan's wartime gendarmerie, the Kempeitai, ruled the streets, and under Japanese occupation, anyone living in or around Harbin was subject to arrest with little or no evidence. All that was needed to detain a person was to accuse him of being a spy, a communist, a Soviet sympathizer, an anti-Japanese dissident, or a "bandit," a frequently used euphemism for various undesirables.[88] The accused could be imprisoned without trial. In this manner, many people simply disappeared and were never seen again. Many of them, it is now known, were turned over to Ishii at Beiyinhe, Ishii's first colonial outpost for human experimentation. Secrecy surrounded the site as much as its high mud walls.[89] There, Ishii conducted research to test human resistance to various diseases and toxins. Ishii and his colleagues injected their subjects with active strains of viruses and bacteria and carefully documented the effects over time. When the subjects died, they disposed of the bodies in a high-pressure electric furnace.[90]

Ishii worked hard to impress the top brass with his "research." Sometime in the mid-1930s, he even began to film his experiments to show superior officers back in Tokyo, attempting to impress them with the films as much as the research data he amassed.[91] Ishii gained a reputation for being something of a sycophant among his peers for constantly trying to curry the favor of army brass, but his efforts paid off. In 1934, no less than Major General Nagata Tetsuzan, the leading figure in the Control faction (Tōseiha), then Chief of the Military Affairs Division of the Army Ministry, allocated ¥200,000 for Ishii's fledgling BW program.[92] Ishii became quite an admirer of Nagata and was said to have kept a bust of his likeness in his office.[93]

From that point forward, Ishii and his BW agenda advanced quickly. In August 1935, the same month Nagata was assassinated, Ishii was promoted to lieutenant colonel. The loss of his favored patron, however, did not slow Ishii or the burgeoning momentum of Japan's BW program. In August 1936, army brass sanctioned the formation of the Kwantung Army Epidemic Prevention and Water Supply Unit (Bōeki Kyūsuibu), later to become infamously known by its numerical designation, Unit 731, and Ishii was appointed its commander.[94] Also around this time, the Kwantung Army Hippo-Epizootic Administration, a subsidiary unit, was formed and placed under the command of Major General Wakamatsu Yujirō of the Veterinary Service. Later designated Unit 100, the Hippo-Epizootic detachment primarily conducted BW research on horses and cattle, specializing in the production of animal-related diseases, such as anthrax and glanders.[95]

Problems at the Beiyinhe compound, however, caused a temporary setback. In autumn 1934, a riot had broken out among captives at the Beiyinhe prison, and some managed to escape. Soon after, an ammunition dump nearby exploded in what appeared to be a well-executed act of sabotage. As a result, Ishii was compelled to abandon his laboratory at Beiyinhe. He moved the unit headquarters to a new location at the Harbin Military Hospital, but this facility proved to be much too small for the greater BW research program that Ishii had in mind. Frustrated with the limited accommodations in Harbin, Ishii surveyed the northeast countryside in search of a more remote area in which to establish a new research center.[96] About 17 miles (27 kilometers) south of Beiyinhe, between Harbin and Hsinkiang, he discovered a cluster of small villages collectively known as Pingfang.[97] Late in the autumn of 1936, Ishii confiscated the area under the authority of the Kwantung Army and evacuated its inhabitants. It was here that Ishii established one of the largest biological weapons facilities constructed during World War II.[98] Pingfang was also to become the largest death camp in all of East Asia.

Construction of the Pingfang compound began in 1937. With the full support and cooperation of the Kwantung Army, and by the harsh exploitation of local Chinese laborers, Ishii's BW research facility was completed within two years.[99] The Pingfang site included over 150 buildings, with several production areas and laboratories. At the center of the compound was the main research facility, the Ro block, so called because of its resemblance to the Japanese phonetic character of the same pronunciation. The Ro block doubled as the central laboratory and a high-security prison capable of holding up to 300 captives. The Pingfang facility also included a power station, a railway siding, hangars for several small, light aircraft, a meteorological station, an administration building, a machine shop, stables for both "infected" and "control" livestock, and housing for the staff and its garrison of 3,000 assorted military personnel. Pingfang was entirely self-sufficient, even to the extent of providing its own food supply by raising vegetables and livestock.[100] By the late 1930s, the Pingfang facility was capable of producing some 21 million doses of various types of vaccines in a single year. In the course of one production cycle, which required only a few days, Pingfang could produce billions upon billions of microbes. The production rate of pathogens was so high that output came to be measured in kilograms.[101]

Ishii staffed Pingfang with the most capable personnel he could get. The core staff consisted of 35 medical officers, 18 pharmacists, 22 sanitation engineers, 11 technicians, 29 engineers with a supporting crew of 175 assistant engineers, an interpreter, 5 paymasters, and nearly 100 noncommissioned officers in various support positions.[102] But the elite of the staff were the doctors and scientists. With the collaboration of his former mentors at Kyoto Imperial University, Ishii was able to recruit young talent from his alma mater to begin to staff the Pingfang research facility. Among those recruited by Ishii early on were Yoshimura Hisato, lecturer on the Faculty of Hygiene, Okamoto Kōzō, lecturer in Pathology, Assistant Professor Ishikawa Tachiomaru, and Kyoto Medical School graduate Doctor Naitō Ryōichi, to name a few.[103]

With Pingfang as a central anchor, Ishii's BW program rapidly expanded throughout Asia. By the summer of 1938, there were eighteen additional units operating throughout China, with some 300 individuals assigned to each detachment. By 1939, there were approximately 5,000 people engaged in various aspects of BW research under Ishii's command, with the majority stationed at Pingfang and the remainder scattered from south China to Indonesia in euphemistically designated army "water purification" units.[104]

Ishii grew eager to test the capabilities of his BW research in combat. The first opportunity came in the summer of 1939, when Kwantung Army troops clashed with Mongolian forces at Nomonhan on the border between Manchuria and Outer Mongolia. The Mongolians called on the Soviets for assistance, and the Japanese soon found themselves overwhelmed by the Red

Army in what was becoming a full-scale war.[105] With Japanese troops facing certain defeat, a small detachment from Unit 731 attempted to halt the advance of the enemy by contaminating the Khalkin-Gol River with typhus, paratyphus, and cholera while the remaining Japanese forces retreated. The effort met with only minimal success, but it was encouraging enough for Ishii to continue with his research agenda.[106] His superiors agreed, and by December 1940, Unit 731 was further expanded with the formation of additional subunits in Hailar, Songo, Linkou, and Hailin (Mudanchiang). Throughout the war, Unit 731 and its affiliated branches conducted small-scale BW operations on at least six different occasions in China, in one instance resulting in a limited outbreak of cholera and bubonic plague in Changteh in the autumn of 1942.[107]

Although the atrocities committed by Unit 731 at Pingfang and elsewhere in China are generally not as widely known as those committed by Nazi doctors at Auschwitz and other death camps in Europe, they were certainly no less gruesome or evil. Like their Nazi counterparts, Ishii and his staff also committed horrible acts of torture and murder in the name of science. As previously noted, Ishii and his collaborators routinely infected human subjects with various pathogens, usually to observe the progression of a given disease, but also to provide data on the efficacy of the cultures that were being developed for vaccines. In one series of experiments involving smallpox, samples of the virus were obtained from a naturally occurring case in Manchuria, then dried and prepared for dissemination. Victims of the tests were forced to inhale the dried samples from a paper bag. In another case, subjects were simply injected with blood from guinea pigs infected with typhus.[108] In another series of experiments, subjects were taken to the nearby airfield at Anta and tied to stakes with various parts of their bodies exposed. Bacteriological bombs were dropped from various altitudes near the subjects, infecting the victims with the shrapnel that penetrated their bodies. The victims were subsequently returned to Pingfang for observation and later were either dissected or vivisected.[109] Most of the vivisections were performed in a specially designated room in the cellar of Ro block. The vivisection room was top secret, and only selected researchers were permitted to know of its existence. It was strictly off limits to anyone not directly involved in its operations.[110]

There were also torturous freezing experiments in which subjects were exposed to the extreme cold of the Manchurian winters. The purpose of such research was ostensibly to develop treatments for frostbite and various other afflictions that Japanese soldiers might encounter during combat in extremely cold climates. Victims of these experiments were exposed to subzero temperatures, and in some cases, water was even poured over the bare arms and legs of subjects left outside chained to posts or locked in stockades. Fans were set up next to them to increase the flow of freezing air over their exposed limbs. An arm or leg might be considered sufficiently frozen if it emitted a dull thud when struck with a club. Although a treatment for frostbite was successfully developed, victims were rarely cured. Most often, gangrene set in, and the subjects either died an agonizingly slow death or were simply shot.[111] The Unit 731 staff also conducted pressure chamber tests similar to those performed by Dr. Sigmund Rascher at Dachau. But Ishii's favorite research topic was the genetic susceptibility of the different races to various diseases.[112] In all of these "experiments," subjects were routinely dehumanized, commonly referred to as *maruta* (meaning "log") in order to perpetuate the charade that the victims were mere objects, simply matériel for the research agenda of the Unit 731 BW program.[113]

Beyond the experiments with human subjects and the production of bacteriological agents, Ishii and his Pingfang organization also attempted to develop effective weapons and methods for the dissemination of BW agents, including bombs, artillery shells, and dispersal by aircraft. By far the greater effort was invested in the development of several types of bombs to deliver the various biological pathogens. Designated according to the army's I-Ro-Ha (that is, A-B-C) system, few of the bombs in this series actually proved to be practicable (Appendix, Table A18). Among the more potentially effective types was the Uji Type 50 bomb. The Uji series models were constructed of a porcelain casing with celluloid fins that combusted upon explosion, which destroyed evidence of the bomb and its use. A timer fuse installed in the nose exploded at a predetermined height for maximum dispersal of pathogens. Some 1,100 to 2,500 Uji-model bombs were produced between 1938 and the end of the war.[114] Of the other several biological bombs developed at Pingfang and its affiliated sites, only the Ha bomb, designed to inflict anthrax-infected wounds, was drop tested from the air and judged sufficiently effective for aerial attacks.[115] An effort was also made in 1944 to develop a rudimentary cluster bomb. Euphemistically called the "mother and daughter bomb," it was designed to explode at a predetermined altitude by radio control and to disperse smaller bombs for a wider distribution of pathogens. But the project was eventually abandoned because of the high costs involved, and only one type of this weapon was produced.[116] Although many of the bacteriological bombs were field tested, it is unknown if any were used in actual combat.

By the end of the war, Japan's BW program had become one of the most advanced of all the principal belligerents in World War II. Largely because of the free use of human subjects for research, Ishii and his staff at Pingfang were able to surpass other national BW programs whose doctors worked within the confines of the western medical tradition steeped in the Hippocratic Oath and its primary precept of "first, do no harm." Ishii and his collaborators had no such moral restraint. U.S. intelligence officers investigating Japan's BW program after the war emphasized this aspect of Ishii's research and noted its potential "value." As one investigator stated:

> Evidence gathered in this investigation has greatly supplemented and amplified previous aspects of this field. It represents data which have been obtained by Japanese scientists at the expenditure of many millions of dollars and years of work. Information has accrued with respect to human susceptibility to these diseases as indicated by specific infectious doses of bacteria. Such information could not be obtained in our own laboratories because of scruples attached to human experimentation. These data were secured with a total outlay of ¥250,000 to date, a mere pittance by comparison with the actual cost of the studies.[117]

Despite his relative "success" and the support Ishii enjoyed from the army, however, his grandiose vision of biological agents as the ultimate weapons for Japan never came to fruition. And despite even strategic plans to conduct BW against the continental United States using various types of transoceanic balloons to carry disease-laden payloads, Ishii's biological war remained limited to small-scale tactical uses in Asia.[118] As with CW, the prospect of retaliation in kind prevented more wide-scale use of biological weapons. Although, relatively speaking, Ishii's BW program can be considered to have been a success for having developed numerous lethal pathogens for potentially devastating use in combat, in the end, it had no effect on the outcome of the war.

CONCLUSION

Most of the principal belligerents had some capability in CBW during the war, but only Japan is known to have used both chemical and biological weapons in actual combat. Japan's CW program, such as it was, however, remained on a comparatively limited scale, and chemical weapons were only a minor factor in the war. One U.S. intelligence report, completed after the war, evaluated Japan's CW program as "sub-standard and inadequate to the needs of a modern first-class military power," and "at no time during the war were the Japanese capable of participating in large-scale chemical warfare with a first-class military power."[119] This report attributed Japan's comparatively weak

CW capacity to the army's failure to establish a separate Chemical Warfare Service charged with the responsibility of developing an "integrated, balanced, and coordinated program."[120] Instead, the Army General Staff Office remained responsible for CW policy and implementation throughout the war.[121]

Moreover, qualified officers with experience in CW research and development did not have much influence over policy at the level of the General Staff, and responsibility for CW in general was apparently assigned to those "who either had little or no knowledge of the subject, little or no interest in it, or both."[122] This shortcoming was apparently also true of the navy, where the organization of CW research lagged even further behind that of the army. The sole organization for formulating plans and policy for CW in the navy was the Chemical Warfare Committee, established as late as April 1945. The late date of the formation of this committee is evidence of the navy's low priority for CW, suggesting that it was formed only when the war became so desperate for Japan that such unconventional weapons were considered necessary to stop the Allies' advance in the Pacific.[123] Chemical weapons also likely had a low priority for the navy from the beginning, because they were not generally as useful in combat at sea as they would have been for the army's forces on land.

There were also other significant, and by now, familiar problems. As was the case with other advanced weapons development programs in wartime Japan, there was minimal collaboration between the military services. In the early stages of the war, the Imperial Japanese Army and Navy shared information on chemical munitions and CW defense, and naval officers were permitted to train at the army's CW school at Narashino.[124] But this appears to have been the extent of army-navy collaboration in this area. An official liaison organization between the army and navy for CW R&D, policy, and deployment was totally lacking. According to U.S. intelligence investigations conducted after the war, "This situation seemed to stem from the personal feelings of one service for the other, which ranged from mere coolness, as in the case of CW, to almost open hostility. The result was that there was relatively little interchange of information between the two services."[125]

The military services also failed to make much use of university scientists for R&D in chemical weapons. The army even refused requests by its own scientists and technicians in the Sixth Army Technical Institute to bring civilian chemists into the program, stating that it was "too dangerous" to do so.[126] Although the Sixth Army Technical Institute consulted a few university professors on occasion, none was taken into full confidence for CW research. For example, among some of the few university scientists consulted on an as-needed basis were Horiuchi Jirō and Shibata Zenichi of Hokkaido Imperial University; Hara Rienzaburō of Tohoku Imperial University; Samejima

Taesaburō and Ishitate Morizō of Tokyo Imperial University; and Chitani Toshizō of Osaka Imperial University, who pulled double duty for the military by studying development of artificial arsenic acid for the army and conducting research on heavy water for the navy's F-gō nuclear weapons project.[127]

Civilian research institutes also went largely untapped by the military services during the war. Neither the army nor navy appear to have recruited chemists from the prestigious Institute of Physical and Chemical Research (Riken) for R&D in chemical weapons.[128] Moreover, most civilian scientists arguably were not interested in CW R&D, and with the exception of a few private firms involved in manufacturing poison gases, there appears not to have been any further interest in CW R&D in the civilian sector during the war.[129]

Collaboration between Japan and its Axis allies was also lacking. Although Japan had received some important technical information from Germany before the war, Germany provided little or no such information during the war itself, despite the Japanese army having requested assistance through the embassy in Berlin.[130] The Japanese navy received some chemical spray tanks from Germany around the beginning of the war, but little or nothing else.[131] There were apparently no German CW specialists sent to Japan during the war, and Japan had no such experts of its own in Germany.[132] Japan also had no CW liaison with Italy, and no information was exchanged between them on this subject during the war.[133]

Although nearly 1,000 types of CW agents were manufactured by Japan during the war, the CW program itself remained a relatively low priority for the military. As a result, Japan produced no new poison gases or chemical weapons beyond those extant at the outset of the war, and there were no significant advances in chemical weapons or CW technology. With the exception of the China theater, chemical weapons played no significant role in the outcome of the Pacific War.

In contrast, Japan's BW program became one of the most formidable among the principal belligerents in the war. Under the auspices of the Kwantung Army, Lieutenant General Ishii Shirō had wide-ranging authority and autonomy to build a strong BW program in northeast China, and Unit 731 received substantial support from the army.[134] From 1937 to 1945, Unit 731 alone was allocated an annual budget of some ¥6 million through the Kwantung Army.[135] Moreover, at Pingfang, Ishii had assembled a highly secretive and well-disciplined research group sustained by an extensive and self-supporting infrastructure. Once established, Ishii did not need much contact with university scientists outside of his own laboratories, as he was able to bring in selected physicians and specialists from his own alma mater. Finally, the comparatively low level of technology involved in the development of biological weapons also obviated the need for massive capital expenditures, the allocation of scarce resources, reliance on a weak industrial sector, and the integration of scientists and engineers from numerous diverse fields, as was necessary with other projects, such as nuclear weapons. Given Japan's limited factor endowments during the war, and Ishii's apparently relentless advocacy of BW, it is understandable why Japan pursued biological weapons development to such a degree.

The command structure and hierarchy of control into which Ishii's BW program fit was also an important factor. The Army General Staff, Second Operations Section, was solely responsible for BW policy, and the Army Ministry retained general supervisory authority over BW research and development. The commander of the Kwantung Army, General Umezu Yoshijirō, had authority over all operations in Manchuria, including that of Unit 731.[136] But at Pingfang, it was Ishii who ruled. Ishii was able to advance his BW program virtually unfettered by the sort of bureaucratic and organizational constraints that obstructed research in other fields of advanced weapons development. The budget for Unit 731 was channeled directly through the Kwantung Army, which operated independently under its own authority in Manchuria and was accountable only to the emperor.[137] Thus, with the support of the commanding officer of the Kwantung Army, Ishii had virtual carte blanche to conduct his BW program in any manner he wished.

Although Ishii enjoyed more influence than did scientists in Japan's other weapons of mass destruction programs, and although the BW program generally succeeded where the others had failed, it was still not without problems of its own. Because of its highly secretive nature, some of the research conducted at Pingfang was necessarily compartmentalized. According to a U.S. intelligence report, only Ishii and his assistant director, Colonel Masuda Tomosada, had full knowledge of the entire BW operation at Pingfang. Doctors and scientists at Pingfang were generally restricted to research in their own fields and were not permitted access to other areas.[138] This level of compartmentalization and secrecy sometimes created difficulties. For example, technicians at the army arsenal in Mukden (now Shenyang) who were responsible for developing a bomb to deliver the biological pathogens were kept ignorant of the complete purpose of the weapon. Consequently, the appropriate experts were not brought into the project and deficiencies in design and production were not overcome.[139] According to Colonel Masuda, "organizational difficulties, petty jealousies, and poor equipment" also disrupted the effort to produce a more practical bacteriological bomb.[140]

After the war, Japanese army officers attempted to trivialize the BW program, claiming it had been a "failure" because they were "unable to obtain the necessary supplies and cooperation with other branches of the military," and ostensibly because the project was "forbidden by the Emperor."[141] Subsequent investigations by U.S. military intelligence, however, proved such claims to be largely false. Although no substantive evidence exists to indicate that there was significant interservice collaboration in BW R&D during the war, one curious artifact exists suggesting that the navy may have been more involved in BW research than is presently known. After the war, U.S. naval intelligence officers found experimental models of a bacteriological bomb at the Second Naval Arsenal in Kanagawa. It was apparently developed as one in a series of other conventional bomb types. But American investigators were unable to find further evidence of BW research conducted by the Japanese navy during the war. After the war, high-ranking navy officers disavowed any knowledge of the army's activities at Pingfang, and it appears that the navy did not establish a BW program of its own.[142] It would seem that Japan's wartime BW program was entirely an army-dominated enterprise, and so the point concerning "cooperation with other branches of the military" in this instance may be moot.

The question of the emperor's knowledge of the subject, however, is somewhat more problematic. Although all Japanese military officers interrogated after the war initially avowed that the emperor knew nothing of BW research, some later revealed that there were close ties between Pingfang and the imperial family. For example, Prince Takeda Tsuneyoshi, the emperor's cousin, known during the war pseudonymously as Lieutenant Colonel Miyata Tsuneyoshi, was Deputy Chief of the Strategic Division of the Kwantung Army and served as a finance officer. Takeda is alleged to have been in charge of issuing visitors' passes to Unit 731 and its facilities.[143] In 1982, members of Japan's Communist Party claimed to have uncovered state documents revealing that Hirohito, himself a biologist, not only approved the formation of Unit 731, but had allegedly even taken a keen interest in the production of BW agents at Pingfang.[144] Given the support Ishii's program came to enjoy at the highest levels of the government and the army, it is questionable whether the emperor would have remained in complete ignorance of its existence.

Perhaps one of the worst miscarriages of justice from the war was that neither Ishii nor most of his collaborators were ever brought to trial for war crimes. With the exception of a dozen or so Unit 731 members who were captured and tried by the USSR at Khabarovsk in 1949, the remaining personnel were able to parlay their advanced knowledge of BW into immunity from prosecution from the Allies, which was granted by U.S. occupation authorities under Supreme Commander for the Allied Powers in the Pacific (SCAP), General Douglas MacArthur, in Japan. The key to the deal was the extensive data on human experimentation produced by Unit 731 researchers. As one U.S. official stated after the war, "Information of Japanese BW experiments will be of great value to the U.S. BW research program . . . The value to the U.S. of Japanese BW data is of such importance to national security as to far outweigh the value accruing from 'war crimes' prosecution."[145] As a result, some of the worst perpetrators of crimes against humanity went unpunished after the war. In fact, as will be seen in the next chapter, many of Unit 731's leaders went on to enjoy profitable careers after the war.

EPILOGUE
THE IMPACT OF WORLD WAR II ON SCIENCE IN JAPAN

The preceding discussion would begin to suggest that the impact of science on the war for Japan was minimal, at least in the areas of the advanced weapons projects examined above. Japan lacked the natural and human resources as well as the industrial capacity to produce nuclear weapons. Radar development remained at a comparatively low level, and although radar proved somewhat useful for Japan during the war, Allied progress in this field far outpaced the Japanese, especially after the British invention of the resonant cavity magnetron. A "death ray" was a pipe dream for all the belligerents, and although other nations ruled out its development early in the war, the Japanese continued to pursue this very impractical technology throughout. In the latter stages of the war, Japan was developing some innovative guided missiles and jet aircraft, but most of these remained beyond the nation's capacity to mass produce, while others were derivative of German designs and barely reached the production stage by the end of the war. The Japanese army used chemical weapons on a limited scale in China but did not use them more widely against Allied forces in the Pacific. Likewise, the Kwantung Army used biological weapons throughout China, mostly in the northeast, but they also do not appear to have been used against the Allies in the Pacific theater. For the most part, Japan fought the war with the same weapons that it had had at the outset, and no new, decisive technology was produced to change the tide of war in Japan's favor. Ironically, throughout much of the war, it was indeed the indomitable fighting spirit of the common soldier that proved to be Japan's most formidable weapon.

Japan's failure to develop such advanced weapons as discussed above can largely be attributed to the failure of wartime science policy. Science and technology mobilization policy in WW II Japan was ineffective, which resulted in the failure of advanced weapons R&D programs and prevented Japan from experiencing a Big Science revolution at this critical time. Beyond the problems of resource deficiencies and insufficient industrial capacity, advanced weapons projects were plagued by organizational difficulties at every level. Because of sectionalism in the government and conflict with the military, the Technology Agency was stripped of its power and proved incapable of uniting or coordinating the scientific resources among the government, military, industrial, and academic sectors. The army and navy refused to cooperate with one another on any significant scale until late in the war. University scientists remained grossly underutilized, and the military tended to rely on them only when their own technical officers proved incapable of doing the work. Research was commonly impeded by a rigid and often unnecessary policy of compartmentalization. Moreover, many civilian scientists were ambivalent toward conducting research for the military. Under these circumstances, science had not much opportunity to make a significant impact on the war for Japan.

But what of the *impact of the war on science* in Japan? It can be argued that the war had both a positive and negative impact. For some, the war years proved to be a golden age, during which funding for research became more plentiful than ever before. University scientists, for example, largely continued to conduct research in areas of their own interest, and those research topics having some relevance to the war usually received a greater amount of funding than perhaps would have been forthcoming during peacetime.[1] Second, once the government changed its policy of drafting university students in the sciences and engineering, between 1941 and 1945, the number of graduates in these fields tripled.[2] Moreover, the war offered many important lessons regarding the organization and mobilization of the nation's science infrastructure.[3]

The significance of science to the outcome of the war became apparent to almost all of Japan's leaders. The scientific and technological superiority of the United States was horrifyingly demonstrated in the nuclear bombings of Hiroshima and Nagasaki. Not only had the United States produced atomic bombs, but it had also created a complex aeronautical weapons system, the B-29 Superfortress, to deliver them. Despite what historians may now believe about the role of science in World War II, in postwar Japan, science became a favored explanation for the Japanese to understand why they had lost the war. Japan's first postwar prime minister, Prince Higashikuni Naruhiko, for example, stated that science and technology had been the nation's greatest weakness during the war. When one general was asked what he thought was the primary reason for Japan's defeat, he responded simply, "science."[4] Their defeat in war revealed to the leaders of Japan just how decisive science had been in the dark years of the past and how vital it was to be for the nation's bright future.

The lessons of the war were taken to heart. As the nation's leadership came to reflect on the experience of the war, some eventually realized that at least where science mobilization was concerned, the war had not been entirely in vain. Science historian Hiroshige Tetsu has argued, "The experience acquired, the systems set up and continued in the post-war years, the realization of the necessity to reinforce Japan's scientific power and to renovate the academic system, all served as a background to the development of science in Japan after World War II."[5] In the postwar period, Japan's leaders brought forth a new system capable of directing science and technology resources toward national reconstruction and the promotion of economic growth.[6] They did so largely by retaining—where possible—those institutions and methods that best served them during the war and discarding those that did not.[7] It was in this environment that Japan finally was able to experience a Big Science revolution. But it was to be a long and uneasy road.

The physical infrastructure of science in Japan suffered a great deal during the war with the destruction of laboratories and affiliated research and development facilities from the U.S. bombing campaign, but the negative impact of the war on science did not end with surrender in August 1945. By the end of the month, U.S. forces under General Douglas MacArthur, the Supreme Commander of Allied Powers in the Pacific (SCAP), began to arrive in Japan. In September, MacArthur established SCAP headquarters in Tokyo, and from there, he set out to implement the occupation's primary objectives of demilitarizing and democratizing Japan. Where science was concerned, the policies enforced under these objectives proved to be particularly harsh. In most cases, scientists in Japan were able to resume their teaching responsibilities as well as their prewar research activities at the universities. Many scientists applied themselves to conducting research that would be of some use in the reconstruction of the nation or in solving the more immediate problems of poverty and food shortages.[8]

As part of the demilitarization policy, on 22 September 1945, SCAP issued a directive forbidding the manufacture of every type of aircraft, warship, ammunition and armaments, and any of their concomitant parts. The directive also required all scientific and technical institutions to submit reports identifying the nature of the research being conducted in their laboratories. And it prohibited all research and laboratory experiments involving the separation of radioactive elements, especially uranium.[9] Not long after, on 1 October 1945, the Technology Agency was dissolved.[10]

At the Riken, Nishina Yoshio and his colleagues were busy restoring order and attempting to get back to the business of basic research. In compliance with the directive, Nishina applied for permission to operate his cyclotrons for research on neutrons and radioactive elements, which he hoped to apply to various problems in the fields of biology, medicine, chemistry, and metallurgy.

SCAP approved Nishina's request on 17 October 1945, with the proviso that he abide by the restrictions stated in the directive. Ten days later, SCAP corrected itself and issued a second memorandum to Nishina limiting his research on radioactive substances and neutrons to the fields of biology and medicine only.[11] Less than a month later, on 19 November 1945, Nishina was surprised with orders from SCAP to terminate all experiments requiring the use of the cyclotrons.[12] It was a portent of worse things to come. On 24 November 1945, U.S. occupation personnel seized all the cyclotrons in Japan, including those at the Riken, and proceeded to cut them to pieces with torches. The parts were subsequently dumped into the deepest part of Tokyo Bay.[13]

The destruction of the cyclotrons came as a great shock to Nishina as well as physicists throughout the United States and Europe, who were quick to protest the incident, calling it a "wanton and stupid" act.[14] Subsequent investigations proved that the order to destroy the cyclotrons had not originated with SCAP but had come from Washington under the direction of the Secretary of War, Robert P. Patterson. Patterson denied having seen the order and argued that it had been mistakenly issued by someone else in the War Department.[15] Long after the incident, in his memoir, *Now It Can Be Told*, General Leslie Groves explained that the order had come from his office, but that it was a mistake resulting from a misunderstanding of a new subordinate on his staff.[16] This explanation seems unlikely, especially in light of Grove's response at the time, in which he stated, "While it is recognized that a cyclotron may also be used for scientific research in other fields, it is essential to the carrying out of effective atomic bomb research which our government believes should be prohibited to naturally belligerent and dishonest nations."[17] The incident remains shrouded in controversy even to this day, but one thing is certain: the loss of the cyclotrons effectively paralyzed the development of nuclear physics in Japan for several years to come.

Research conditions for applied physicists in the immediate postwar years in Japan were extremely poor. Laboratories often could not procure necessary materials for experiments, as people everywhere struggled to obtain even the most basic necessities to live. The Riken, for example, had to struggle not only with shortages, but also with the dissolution of its network of affiliated industries under SCAP's economic policy, which sought to break up Japan's monopoly corporations and cartels. Moreover, U.S. intelligence officers under SCAP even advocated closing down Nishina's laboratory.[18] Physicists directly related to applied nuclear research remained under suspicion throughout the early years of the occupation.[19]

Thus, to a large extent, it was the theoretical physicists who brought Japan back into the international community of scientists. In 1947, J. Robert Oppenheimer offered theoretician Yukawa Hideki a position as a visiting professor at the Institute for Advanced Study in Princeton in recognition of his pioneering work on the meson particle theory, for which Yukawa won the Nobel Prize in physics two years later. After his return to Japan, in 1953 Yukawa was appointed the director of a newly established research institute in Kyoto, which today bears his name as the Yukawa Institute for Theoretical Physics.[20] In 1949, Oppenheimer also invited Yukawa's junior colleague, Tomonaga Shinichirō. Physicist Freeman Dyson of the Institute for Advanced Study credited Tomonaga for having "maintained in Japan a school of research in theoretical physics that was in some respects ahead of anything existing elsewhere at that time" despite the turmoil of the war.[21] Tomonaga was later to share the Nobel Prize in physics with Harvard University physicists Julian S. Schwinger and Richard Feynman in 1965 for their contributions to the development of quantum electrodynamics.[22]

Kikuchi Seishi, who participated in the navy's feasibility study on the atomic bomb, also played an important role in reestablishing scientific relations with the United States. From 1950 to 1952, Kikuchi was a visiting lecturer at Cornell University and at the University of California at Berkeley. Later, he became the first director of Tokyo University's Institute for Nuclear Studies, and he directed the construction of two new cyclotrons at Osaka University.[23] Nishina Yoshio, considered "the father of Japanese nuclear physics," was among the most active of scientists involved in the reconstruction of Japanese science immediately after the war, even after the destruction of the Riken cyclotrons. But sadly, Nishina died of cancer in 1951, thus cutting short the life and career of one of Japan's most brilliant and capable scientists.[24]

With the end of the American occupation of Japan and the signing of the San Francisco Peace Treaty in 1952, Japanese applied physicists were again free to pursue nuclear research. As the nation's politicians pushed for the establishment of an atomic energy industry in Japan, prominent physicists were brought in to advise on the formation of atomic energy policy. The Japan Atomic Energy Commission was established in December 1955, and physicists Yukawa Hideki and Fujioka Yoshio were among the scientists included as first members.[25] As might be expected, many of Japan's leading wartime physicists played a central role not only in the rebuilding of the nation's physics infrastructure, but in the formation of Japan's nuclear power industry as well (Appendix, Table A19). Finally, the era of Big Science in physics had begun in Japan.

Research in aeronautics was also forbidden by the SCAP directive, and it was not until after the end of the occupation that scientists and engineers again became active in this field in Japan. It should not be surprising to find that the postwar leaders in aeronautics were active during the war and gained much valuable experience at that time. For example, Itokawa Hideo, Hino Kumao, Tani Ichirō, and Takagi Noboru all emerged as leading figures in Japan's early postwar rocket research in the 1950s and 1960s. Itokawa, an engineer for the Nakajima Aircraft Company during the war, was a member of the army's Ke-gō B-1 missile project and also contributed to the development of the Yokosuka P1 Y1 Ginga bomber. In 1949, Itokawa became a professor in the Department of Engineering at Tokyo University. In 1951, he began research on high-speed projectiles and rockets at Tokyo University's Institute of Industrial Science. His experiments with the Pencil Rocket in 1955 drew the attention of several private corporations, such as Nippon Electric and Fuji Precision, which later became a division of the Nissan Corporation. Itokawa pioneered the field of rocketry in postwar Japan, and his numerous contributions to the Baby, Kappa, Lambda, and Mu series of rocket experiments earned him the appellation of "the Wernher von Braun of Japan."[26]

Hino Kumao was deeply involved in research on high explosives and rocket propellants for the navy from 1941 to 1945, and by the end of the war he was serving as director of research in solid propellants for rockets and guns at the Navy Technical Research Institute. Hino remained involved in rocket research after the war by participating in a series of international symposia on rockets and astronautics held in Tokyo throughout the late 1950s and early 1960s.[27] Tani Ichirō became a professor of aeronautical engineering at Tokyo Imperial University in 1943, and during the war conducted wind tunnel experiments at the Army Aeronautical Technology Research Institute, where he also served as a regular consultant to such aircraft manufacturers as Kawanishi and Kawasaki. From March 1944 to March 1945, Tani served as chair of the Aeronautical Research Group under the Science Mobilization Council. After the war, he applied his advanced knowledge of aeronautics to the development of the first rockets produced in Japan in the postwar period.[28]

Takagi Noboru, an electrical engineer, became an important figure in Japan's early postwar rocket research because of his contributions in electronics and telemetry. Takagi became a professor of engineering at Tokyo Imperial University in 1942. During the war he conducted research on quartz filters and Rochelle salt oscillators for the army, and he studied ultrahigh-frequency waves at the Navy Technical Research Institute. He also received funding from the Ministry of Education for research on piezoelectric crystals. After the war, Takagi was appointed director of the Radio Educational Research Institute and became a leading researcher in rocket telemetry, working closely with Itokawa on the Kappa and Lambda series of rockets.[29] Drawing on their collective education and wartime experience, Itokawa, Hino,

Tani, and Takagi, among others, formed the organizational nucleus and completed the early experiments that laid the foundation for the creation of Japan's National Aeronautics and Space Development Agency (NASDA) in 1969. (For additional examples, see Appendix, Table A20.) Thus was the age of "Big Engineering" in aeronautics born in Japan.

Wartime aeronautics research also led to important commercial spin-offs. Dr. Miki Tadanao, who served in the navy as a technical officer and was the principal designer of the airframe for the Ohka Model 11, went on to become a pioneer in the development of the Shinkansen bullet train. After the war, Miki took a position with the Japan Railway Technical Reserve Institute (RTRI) of Japan National Railways, hoping to rebuild the nation's devastated rail system. Drawing on his knowledge of aeronautics from his wartime experience, he sketched a design for a high-speed train, and together with his colleagues at the RTRI, Miki produced what were to become the plans for Japan's Shinkansen. On 25 August 1964, Miki witnessed the maiden journey of the *Hikari*, the express bullet train running between Tokyo and Osaka, the streamlined cars of which he had conceived and helped to develop.[30]

Perhaps as much as any industry, the railroad helped to launch the era of Big Engineering in Japan. With aeronautical research prohibited after the war and many aeronautical engineers facing unemployment, RTRI director Nakahara Juichirō made it company policy to actively recruit jobless engineers of various types from the disbanded military institutes. By the end of 1946, Nakahara had hired over 1,000 workers from the former Central Aeronautical Research Institute (Chūō Kōkū Kenkyūjo), which was about 73 percent of that institute's total workforce during the war. Among them were such engineers as Miki Tadanao, wind tunnel expert Yamamura Tatsuo, Kumezawa Ikurō, and Dr. Matsudaira Tadashi, a chief engineer in the development of the famous Zero. All four became laboratory leaders at the RTRI and made important contributions to the development of the Shinkansen.[31]

As historian John Dower has noted, such "linkages and influences" from wartime to the postwar period are "apparent almost everywhere one looks." Dower states, "In ways we only now are beginning to understand, developments that took place in conjunction with Japan's fifteen-year war proved to be extremely useful to the postwar Japanese state."[32] Scholars have only recently begun to examine the extent to which the wartime experience of Japan's scientists and engineers can be linked to national reconstruction and economic growth in the postwar period.[33] And as previously noted, more than one Japanese winner of the Nobel Prize gained valuable experience during the war.[34]

Perhaps nowhere were such links more visible, or more important to the postwar economy, than in the electronics industry in Japan. Many of the electrical engineers who played important roles in the growth of Japan's electronics industry in the postwar period gained valuable experience during the war while employed at the Navy Technical Research Institute. For example, Nippon Electric Company (NEC) executives Ouchi Atsuyoshi and Ogata Kenji served as technical lieutenants, as did Japan Victor executives Takayanagi Kenjirō, Shinji Ichirō, and Takano Shizuo, who came to be known after the war as "Mr. VHS" for his contribution to the development of videotape technology. With Takayanagi's help, some fifty technical officers found employment at the NHK Broadcasting Technology Research Institute just after the war. But perhaps the most famous examples are Ibuka Masaru and Morita Akio, the former NTRI technical lieutenants who formed the Totsuko Corporation (Tokyo Communications Industry), which became known around the world as Sony. No fewer than seven senior executives at Sony had served at the NTRI during the war.[35] (For additional examples, see Appendix, Table A21.)

But the connection between wartime and postwar research in Japan also has a dark side. Few of the scientists and physicians of Unit 731 were ever brought to justice. Although the Soviet Union tried several of the perpetrators who were apprehended in Manchuria and Korea after the war, not a single one was tried for war crimes by the United States or the Allied International Military Tribunal.[36] Many returned to Japan and eventually established lucrative private practices, while others became professors at prestigious universities and medical schools. A few even profited from the knowledge gained during the war by starting business ventures in the medical and pharmaceutical industries. Six of the eight men named directors of Japan's National Institute of Health between 1947 and 1983, for example, had some ties to Unit 731.[37] Their leader, Ishii Shirō, apparently died of throat cancer in 1959, but several of his colleagues and subordinates from Unit 731 went on to prosper in the postwar period. (For a cursory list, see Appendix, Table A22.) Because most of the physicians and scientists of Unit 731 evaded public scrutiny even long after the war, Japan's medical community never faced quite the level of criticism and restructuring experienced by so many other fields of science in postwar Japan.[38]

The examples given above suggest that there was great continuity in institutions and personnel from the war into the postwar period. In particular, the experience and training gained during the war provided many scientists and engineers the means to make significant contributions to the reconstruction of Japan and its economic growth after the war. In this way, one might argue that the war, on the whole, had a positive impact on science in Japan, despite even all the tragedies the war had brought about. Perhaps, when viewed in this light, it had been a "useful war" after all.[39]

APPENDIX

Table A1. Principal Military Research Institutions in World War II Japan

Year	Research Institution
1915	Navy Technical Department (Kaigun Gijutsu Honbu)
1918	Navy Aeronautics Laboratory (Kaigun Kōkūki Shikensho)
1919	Army Technical Department (Rikugun Gijutsu Honbu)
	Army Institute of Scientific Research (Rikugun Kagaku Kenkyūjo); research institution of the Army Technical Department
	Army Aeronautics Division (Rikugun Kōkūbu)
1920	Navy Department of Ships (Kaigun Kansei Honbu)
1923	Navy Technical Research Institute (Kaigun Gijutsu Kenkyūjo)
1924	Army Aeronautics Department (Rikugun Kōkū Honbu); formerly the Army Aeronautics Division (est. 1919)
1925	Army Aeronautical Technology Department (Rikugun Kōkū Gijutsu Honbu); expanded office of the Army Aeronautics Department
1927	Navy Aeronautics Department (Kaigun Kōkū Honbu)
1931	Navy Technical Research Institute Short-Wave Laboratory (Tanpa Kenkyūshitsu)
	Navy Aeronautical Technology Arsenal (Kaigun Kōkū Gijutsushō); abbreviated as Kūgishō (Naval Air Arsenal), with affiliated Navy Aeronautics Research Department (Kaigun Kōkū Kenkyūbu) branches
1935	Army Aeronautical Technology Research Institute (Rikugun Kōkū Gijutsu Kenkyūjo)
	Institute of Bacteriological Warfare, Manchuria (Rikugun Saikinsen Kenkyūjo)
1938	Navy Fuel Arsenal Division of Experiments and Research (Kaigun Nenryōshō Jikkenbu)
1939	Central Aeronautical Research Institute (Chūō Kōkū Kenkyūjo); affiliated with Ministry of Communications
1940	Army Aeronautics Arsenal (Rikugun Kōkū Kōshō)
	Army Fuels Arsenal (Rikugun Nenryōshō)
	Navy Aeronautical Technology Arsenal (Kaigun Kōkū Gijutsushō)
1942	Army Weapons Administrative Department (Rikugun Heiki Gyōsei Honbu)

	First through Ninth Army Technical Institutes (Dai-Ichi—Dai-Kyū Rikugun Gijutsu Kenkyūjo); former research institutes of the Army Technical Department
	First through Eighth Army Aeronautical Technology Research Institutes (Dai-Ichi—Dai-Hachi Rikugun Kōkū Gijutsu Kenkyūjo); former research institutes of the Army Aeronautical Technology Department
	Army Aeronautical Testing Division (Rikugun Hikō Jikkenbu)
1943	Tama Army Technical Institute (Tama Rikugun Gijutsu Kenkyūjo)
	Navy Technical Arsenal (Kaigun Gijutsushō)
	First Navy Technical Arsenal (Dai-Ichi Kaigun Gijutsushō)
	Second Navy Technical Arsenal (Dai-Ni Kaigun Gijutsushō)
	Shimada Navy Technical Research Institute (Shimada Kaigun Gijutsu Kenkyūjo)
	Army Fuels Institute (Rikugun Nenryō Kenkyūjo)

SOURCE. Hiroshige Tetsu, *Kagaku no shakai shi: (ue) Sensō to kagaku* [Social History of Science: Part I: War and Science] (Tokyo: Iwanami Shoten, 2002), 115, 215. Hiroshige Tetsu, *Kagaku no shakai shi: (shita) Keizai seichō to kagaku* [Social History of Science: Part II: Economic Development and Science] (Tokyo: Iwanami Shoten, 2003), 38. Chikayoshi Kamatani, "The History of Research Organization in Japan," *Japanese Studies in the History of Science* 2 (1963): 1–79.

Table A2. Principal Imperial Japanese Army Ground Force Research Institutions

Institute	Research Areas
First Army Technical Institute	Swords, bayonets, rifles, guns, ammunition, harnesses for drawing and pack horses, trajectory, 40 mm antiaircraft machine gun, 10 cm gun for tank, 15 cm self-propelled gun, 10 cm non-reacting gun, 7.5 cm antitank gun, 10 cm antitank gun, 7.5 cm heavy antiaircraft gun, 20 cm short self-propelling gun
Second Army Technical Institute	Intelligence, observation, surveillance, balloons, observation apparatus, aiming glasses for guns, meters, calculators, and water-surveying apparatuses
Third Army Technical Institute	Explosive powder and firing accessories, large searchlights, gearing for searchlights, equipment for close fighting on seashore, equipment for close attack, superheavy raft pontoon for bridging, railway tractor, river-crossing equipment for railway
Fourth Army Technical Institute	Tanks, motor cars, tractors, armored cars, fuels, oil, medium tanks (A, B), carriage of 10 cm self-propelled gun, medium tractor, carriage of 7.5 cm antitank gun and 10 cm antitank gun, steam tractor, amphibious-track, civilian motor car, small Type Four maneuverable wheeled motor car
Fifth Army Technical Institute	Signal ordnance, movable signal and telephone, composition of waves of moveable wireless apparatuses, air transport of fixed wireless apparatuses, wireless equipment, air-defense signal equipment, aviation intelligence, heavy signal apparatus of super shortwave, simple signal equipment
Sixth Army Technical Institute	Chemical weapons, medical and veterinary research concerning chemical warfare, poison gas detection and defense, sanitary research for precaution and cure
Seventh Army Technical Institute	Physics of ordnance, fundamental research on new ordnance, research on physiology of ordnance, rocket ordnance, utilization of liquid fuel, nonreacting gun, study of piercing shell, militarization of nocturnal vision and electric detector, underwater sound detection, oceanic meteorology, magnet ordnance and submarines, wireless operation, television
Eighth Army Technical Institute	Ordnance materials, materials for the chemical industry, research on the quality and preservation of materials for ordnance, springs, qualities of various steels, bulletproof steel, rubber, compound resin and batteries
Ninth Army Technical Institute (aka Noborito)	Ultrashort waves (microwave), investigation and manufacture of materials and equipment for forward troops, equipment for propaganda and military police (MP), microwaves, simple signal equipment, incendiary agents, photography agents and equipment, equipment for MP, equipment for forward troops

Tenth Army Technical Institute	Transportation, motorboats, personal landing boats, escort boats, transport boats, submarine attack boats, driving boats, submersible pillboxes, basic torpedo, engines for boats
Tama Army Technical Institute	
Army Fuels Institute	
Army Weapons Administrative Department	Weapons concerning heat ray and radiant ray, ship detectors, night radar, autocharge boat, autoglider

SOURCE. General Headquarters, United States Army Forces, Pacific, Scientific and Technical Advisory Section, "Report on Scientific Intelligence Survey in Japan: September and October 1945," 1 November 1945, vol. 2, U.S. National Archives, College Park, MD, RG 165, box 2056, appendix 2-A-1 to 2-A-3, 2-B-a-1, 1-D-1 to 1-D-7.

Table A3. Principal Imperial Japanese Army Air Service Research Institutions

Institute	Research Areas
Army Aeronautics Department	Testing of aircraft, ordnance, parachutes; flight tests of aircraft ordnance, fuel, oil; experimentation of reactive propelling machinery; experimentation on reactive propellant machinery; experimentation on weapons, ammunition, cannon and rifle mounting, tools for guns, accessories; instruction in the use of new planes; flight tests
Army Meteorological Department	Meteorology
Army Aeronautical Technology Research Institutes	
First	Fuselage, propellers, wind tunnel tests; use of nonmetal materials
Second	Engines, parts and accessories, experimentation on fuel and lubricating oil, engine testing
Third	Bombs, air gas defense equipment, bombing apparatus (except optics), experimentation on bombing weapons, arms for air chemical war, related apparatus
Fourth	Signal ordnance, wireless apparatus, experimentation of same and searchlights
Fifth	Aerial sights, aerial photography, gauges, navigational apparatuses, experimentation on same
Sixth	Metal materials, basic research on metals
Seventh	Clothing, foods, related items, experimentation on same
Eighth	Hygienic psychology, oxygen inhaler, tests on same
Tama Army Technical institute	Electric wave ordnance

SOURCE. General Headquarters, United States Army Forces, Pacific, Scientific and Technical Advisory Section, "Report on Scientific Intelligence Survey in Japan: September and October 1945," 1 November 1945, vol. 2, U.S. National Archives, College Park, MD, RG 165, box 2056, appendix 2-A-1 to 2-A-3, 2-B-a-1, 1-D-1 to 1-D-7.

Table A4. Principal Imperial Japanese Navy Research Institutions

Institute	Research Areas
Navy Department of Ships	Division 1: Guns; Division 2: Torpedoes; Division 3: Electronics; Division 4: Naval Architecture (Shipbuilding); Division 5: Engines; Division 6: Mines
Navy Technical Research Institute (NTRI)	Institute established under the aegis of the Navy Department of Ships with oversight of the following research divisions: Physics, Chemistry, Electronics, Radio, Naval Architecture (Shipbuilding), Materials, Acoustics, Experimental Psychology
First Navy Technical Arsenal* (Dai-Ichi Kaigun Gijutsushō)	Aeronautics, aeronautical weapons
Second Navy Technical Arsenal* (Dai-Ni Kaigun Gijutsushō)	Acoustics, surgical, light and heat, magnetic, radar, and communications

SOURCE. General Headquarters, United States Army Forces, Pacific, Scientific and Technical Advisory Section, "Report on Scientific Intelligence Survey in Japan: September and October 1945," 1 November 1945, vol. 2, U.S. National Archives, College Park, MD, RG 165, box 2056, appendix 2-A-1 to 2-A-3, 2-B-a-1, 1-D-1 to 1-D-7. Kawamura Yutaka, "Kyū-Nihon kaigun no dempa heiki kaihatsu katei o jirei toshita dai-niji taisenki Nihon no kagaku gijutsu dōin ni kan suru bunseki" [A Case Study of Electric Wave Weapons Development Process in the Former Japanese Navy: An Analysis of Japanese Science and Technology Mobilization in World War II] (PhD diss., Tokyo Institute of Technology, 2002), 22–23.

*The First and Second Navy Technical Arsenals were established as a result of the reorganization of the Navy Aeronautical Technology Arsenal (Kaigun Kōkū Gijutsushō) and the Navy Technical Research Institute (Kaigun Gijutsu Kenkyūjo) in February 1945.

Appendix   211

Table A5. Organizational Hierarchy for Science and Technology Policy

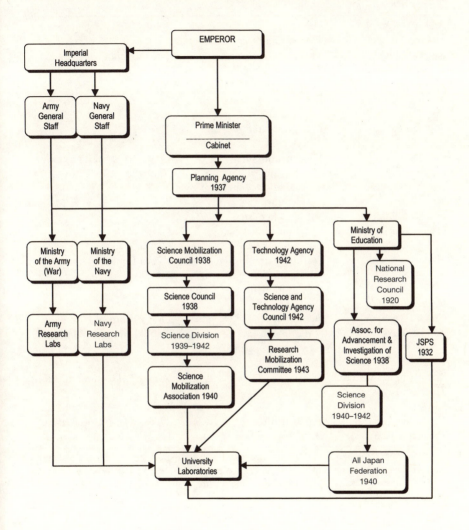

Table A6. Principal Researchers of the Imperial Japanese Navy F-gō Project

Researcher	Assignment	Affiliation
Arakatsu Bunsaku	Director, General Research	Kyoto Imperial University
Yukawa Hideki	Theory of atomic nucleus	"
Sakata Shōichi	Theory of neutron	Nagoya Imperial University
Kobayashi Minoru	Theory of uranium separation	Kyoto Imperial University
Kimura Kiichi	Basic measurements with cyclotron	"
Shimizu Sakae	Isotope separation with cyclotron	"
Ota Takeshi	Mass measurements	Osaka Imperial University
Sasaki Shinji	Manufacture of uranium hexafluoride, chemical radiation	Kyoto Imperial University
Horiba Shinkichi	Nuclear chemistry	"
Okada Shinzō	Uranium extraction, uranium metal	"
Hagiwara Tokutarō	Quality of uranium hexafluoride, basic measurements	Kyoto Imperial University
Ishiguro Masao	Deuteride	"
Chitani Toshizō	Deuterium	Osaka Imperial University
Kanda Eizō	Fluorine, fluorinated hydrogen, oscillator for cyclotron	Tōhoku Imperial University
Kobayashi Masatsugu	"	Sumitomo Communications
Miyazaki Kiyoshi	"	"
Niwa Yasujiro	"	"
Nitta Shigeharu	Ultracentrifuge	Tokyo Meter Corporation
Takahashi Isao	Oscillator circuit	Japan Radio Corporation

SOURCE. Table translated from Nippon Kagakushi Gakkai [Japan History of Science Society], ed., "Butsurigaku to senji kenkyū" [Physics and Wartime Research] in *Nippon kagaku gigutsusi taikei* [Outline of History of Science and Technology in Japan] (Tokyo: Daiichi Hōgen Shuppan, 1970), 13:468.

Table A7. Principal Researchers of the Imperial Japanese Army NI-gō Project

Group	Researcher	Assignment	Affiliation
Planning	Major Koyama Kenji	Progress of research concerning general planning and matters related to outside organizations	Army Aeronautics Department
Theoretical Calculations	Tamaki Hidehiko Fukuda Nobuyuki	Theoretical calculations in physics	Riken
First Isotope Separation Group	Takeuchi Masa 1st Lt. Sachi 2nd Lt. Hashitaka 2nd Lt. Mori Sakata Tamio	Isotope separation by thermal diffusion	Riken
Second Isotope Separation Group	Major Suzuki 1st Lt. Kimoto Ozaki Seinosuke	Isotope separation by thermal diffusion	Osaka Imperial University
Chemistry	1st Lt. Ishiwatari Ogoshi Kunihiko 1st Lt. Sekihara 1st Lt. Wanibuchi 2nd. Lt. Kawamura 2nd. Lt. Funatsu	Chemical reactions and refining	Riken
Physics	Nishina Yoshio Shinma Keizō Sugimoto Asao Tajima Eizō	Determination of fundamental constants	Riken
First Detection Group	Nishina Yoshio Yamazaki Fumio 1st Lt. Kinoshita 1st Lt. Nakane Nariamoto Takahiro	Measurements of degree of isotope separation	Riken
Second Detection Group	Asada Tsunesaburō Ota Takeshi Ogata Tadaichi	Measurements of degree of isotope separation	Osaka Imperial University
Raw Materials	Iimori Satoyasu Hata Shin 1st Lt. Nakane Nakajima Otokichi	Resource investigation and manufacture of uranium oxide from materials	Riken

SOURCE. Table translated from Nippon Kagakushi Gakkai [Japan History of Science Society], ed., "Butsurigaku to senji kenkyū" [Physics and Wartime Research] in *Nippon kagaku gigutsusi taikei* [Outline of History of Science and Technology in Japan] (Tokyo: Daiichi Hōgen Shuppan, 1970), 13:465.

Table A8. Laboratory Equipment for Nuclear Research

Research Institution	Apparatus	Leading Personnel
Riken-Nishina Laboratory	Two cyclotrons, Clusius tube, Wilson cloud chamber, Van de Graaff generator	Nishina Yoshio
Tokyo Imperial University	Cockcroft-Walton accelerator	Sagane Ryōkichi
Kyoto Imperial University	Cyclotron, Cockcroft-Walton accelerator, Wilson cloud chamber	Arakatsu Bunsaku
Osaka Imperial University	Cyclotron, Cockcroft-Walton accelerator, Van de Graaff generator, mass spectrometer, Clusius tube	Kikuchi Seishi
Kyūshū Imperial University	Van de Graaff generator	Shinohara Kenichi
Tōhoku Imperial University	Van de Graaff generator	Matsumoto (f.n.u.)

SOURCE. Compiled from G-2 to Economic & Scientific Section, 13 May 1946, "Papers on 'Budget for Atomic Nuclear Research,'" U.S. National Archives, College Park, MD, RG 331, Entry 224, Box 1, Folder: "Research, Nuclear, Japan"; and Headquarters IX Corps, "Atomic Research," 15 October 1945, U.S. National Archives, College Park, MD, RG 331, Entry 224, Box 1, Folder: "Research, Nuclear, Japan."

Table A9. Imperial Japanese Navy and Army Radar Nomenclature

Imperial Japanese Navy radar sets were designated according to Mark (Go), Model (Kei/Kata/Gata), Modification (Kai), and Type (Shiki). Numerals in the tens digit space indicated Mark based on the following:
Mark 1 Series: Ground-based Search/Early Warning
Mark 2 Series: Shipboard Search/Air Warning
Mark 3 Series: Shipboard Fire Control
Mark 4 Series: Antiaircraft Fire and Searchlight Control
Mark 5 Series: Panoramic Indication/Airborne/Search
Mark 6 Series: Guiding Type (Ground Controlled Interception)
Numerals in the single digit space (second digit) indicate type according to the following:
Type 1: Fixed
Type 2: Mobile
Type 3: Portable

Japanese Imperial Aarmy radar sets were given acronymic designations wherein the prefix *Ta* represented the Tama Research Institute where the sets were designed and suffixes indicated type, such as *chi* (ground/earth), *se* (water/sea), and *ki* (air).
Only specifications of principal radar sets used during the war are given. Experimental radar sets not used during the war and units not in production generally have been omitted. Date completed indicates termination of research. Many sets became avaiable prior.

SOURCE . Some discrepancies exist in the sources concerning radar nomenclature. An attempt was made to resolve these by comparing the accounts given in the primary and secondary sources listed below. For secondary sources used, see Henry E. Guerlac, *Radar in World War II: Sections D–E, Appendices, Glossary, Indexes, The History of Modern Physics, 1800–1950* (New York: Tomash/American Institute of Physics, 1987), 917–24. Sean S. Swords, *Technical History of the Beginnings of RADAR* (London: Peter Peregrinus, 1986), 299–304. Nakagawa Yasuzo, *Japanese Radar and Related Weapons of World War II,* English edition edited by Louis Brown, John H. Bryant, and Naohiko Koizumi (Laguna Hills, CA: Aegean Park Press, 1997), 83–91. Roger I. Wilkinson, "Short Survey of Japanese Radar—I," *Electrical Engineering* 65 (August–September 1946): 370–77. Roger I. Wilkinson, "Short Survey of Japanese Radar—II," *Electrical Engineering* 65 (October 1946), 455–63. These appear to be based largely on the following primary sources: General Headquarters, "Japanese Wartime Military Electronics and Communications," Section VI, *Japanese Army Radar,* 1 April 1946, prepared by Technical Liaison and Investigation Division, Office of the Chief Signal Officer, General Headquarters, United States Army Forces, Pacific, U.S. National Archives, College Park, MD, RG 331, Box 7428, Folder 15. General Headquarters, United States Army Forces, Pacific, Scientific and Technical Advisory Section, "Report on Scientific Intelligence Survey in Japan, September and October 1945," vols. 1 and 2, U.S. National Archives, College Park, MD, RG 165, Box 2056; see especially 1:21–22; vol. 2, appendixes 1-A-b-3 to 1-A-b-12. U.S. Naval Technical Mission to Japan, December 1945, "Electronics Targets: Japanese Submarine and Shipborne Radar," table 2, report no. E-02, microfilm. See also Nippon Kagakushi Gakkai [Japan History of Science Society], ed., "Senjika no tsūshin gijutsu" [Wartime Communications Technology], in *Nippon kagaku gijutsusi taikei* [Outline of History of Science and Technology in Japan] (Tokyo: Daiichi Hōgen Shuppan, 1970), 19:374–76, 19:377–78.

Table A10. Imperial Japanese Navy Radar Sets

Ground-Based Early Warning

Mark 1 Model 1 Type 2 (series 0–3) Designations 11, 11-1, 11-2, 11-3
Comments: Also known as the "Type-B" pulsed radar. Known generally among Allied forces as the "Guadalcanal type" as a result of its having first been encountered there, it was the first type of Japanese radar to have been captured by Allied forces.
Purpose: Ground-based, fixed antiaircraft
Date Completed: July 1943
Number Manufactured: 30
Manufacturers: Toshiba, NEC, Nihon Onkyo
Wavelength (cm): 300
Frequency: 100 MHz
Pulse length: 20–25 μs
Pulse rate: 1,000 and 500 Hz
Peak power output (kw): (Models 0–1) 5; (Models 2–3) 40
Transmitter/Receiver: Parallel two wire/UN954, RE-3 Detector
XM antenna: 14 x 29 ft array, five elements of half-wave dipoles
Weight (kg): 8,700
Max range (search distance/km): 130 (single plane), 250 (group)

Mark 1 Type 3 (series 3–11) Designation 11-K
Purpose: Shore-based
Date Completed: October 1943
Number Manufactured: unknown
Manufacturers: unknown
Frequency: 150 MHz
Pulse length: 20 μs
Pulse rate: 500 Hz
Peak power output (kw): 10
XM antenna: double array of five dipoles
Max range (search distance/km): 150

Mark 1 Model 2 Type 2 (series 0–3) Designation 12, 12-Kai-2, 12-Kai-3
Comments: The Japanese dubbed this model the "mobile mattress" and considered it to be the best search radar in general use.
Purpose: Ground-based, mobile antiaircraft
Date Completed: April 1944
Number Manufactured: 50
Manufacturers: Toshiba, Nihon Onkyo
Wavelength (cm): 200/150
Frequency: 200 and 150 MHz
Pulse length: 10 μs
Peak power output (kw): 5
Transmitter/Receiver: Parallel two wire/UN954, RE-3 Detector
XM antenna: 14 x 29 ft array, five elements of half-wave dipoles

Weight (kg): 6,000
Max range (search distance/km): 50–100

Mark 1 Model 3 Type 3 Designation 13
Purpose: Ground-based, also ship and submarine-based, antiaircraft
Date Completed: March 1943
Number Manufactured: 1,000
Manufacturers: Toshiba, Anritsu
Wavelength (cm): 200
Frequency: 150 MHz
Pulse length: 10 μs
Pulse rate: 500 Hz
Peak power output (kw): 10
Transmitter/Receiver: Parallel two wire/UN954
XM antenna: vertical dipole, Yagi receiver (submarine); two dipole arrays (ship or land)
Weight (kg): 110
Max range (search distance/km): 50–100

Mark 1 Model 4 Designation 14
Purpose: Ground-based, long-range antiaircraft
Date Completed: May 1945
Number Manufactured: 2
Manufacturer: Toshiba
Wavelength (cm): 600
Frequency: 50 MHz
Pulse length: 20 μs
Pulse rate: 250 Hz
Peak power output (kw): 100
Transmitter/Receiver: Parallel two wire/UN954
XM antenna: four two-element Yagi
Weight (kg): 30,000
Max range (search distance/km): 250–450

Shipborne Early Warning Radar

Mark 2 Model 1 Type 2 Designation 21
Purpose: Ship-based, antiaircraft
Date Completed: August 1943
Number Manufactured: unknown
Manufacturers: Toshiba, Nihon Onkyo
Wavelength (cm): 150
Frequency: 200 MHz
Pulse length: 10 μs
Peak power output (kw): 5
Transmitter/Receiver: Parallel two wire/UN954, RE-3 Detector
XM antenna: two horizontal sets of four dipoles
Reverse ant: two horizontal sets of three dipoles
Max range (search distance/km): 70–100

Surface Search and Fire-Control Radar

Mark 2 Model 2 Type 1–4 Designation 22-Kai-3 and 22-Kai-4
Purpose: Ship and submarine-based, antisurface warning and fire control
Date Completed: September 1944
Number Manufactured: 300
Manufacturers: Nihon Musen (Japan Radio Corporation), Hitachi
Wavelength (cm): 10
Frequency: 3,000 MHz
Pulse length: 10 μs
Pulse rate: 600 and 2,500
Peak power output (kw): 2
Transmitter/Receiver: Magnetron/Crystal
XM antenna: horn; Reverse antenna: horn
Weight (kg): shipborne 1,320; submarine 2,140
Max range (search distance/km): 17–35

Shipborne Surface Fire-Control Radar

Mark 3 (Models 1–3) Designation 31, 32, 33
Comments: Units 31 and 32 remained under experimental use. Unit 33 was not used during the war. Operation of these sets was generally considered unsuccessful.
Purpose: Shipborne, antiship
Date Completed: (31) March 1945; (32) September 1944; (33) January 1945
Number Manufactured: (31) unknown; (32) 60; (33) unknown
Manufacturers: Nihon Musen, Hitachi
Wavelength (cm): 10
Frequency: 3,000 MHz
Pulse length: 10 μs
Pulse rate: 2,500
Peak power output (kw): 2
Transmitter/Receiver: Magnetron/Crystal
XM antenna: parabolic (31); horn (32–33)
Weight (kg): (31) 1,000; (32) 5,000; (33) 800
Reverse ant: common (31); double horns (32–33)
Max range (search distance/km): 12–35

Land-Based AA Fire-Control Radar

Mark 4, Models 1 and 2 Designation 41, 42, 43
Comments: A copy of the U.S. SCR-268. NEC manufactured 50 sets. Research on Model 2 was undertaken between January 1943 and October 1944. NEC, Nihon Onkyo, and Hitachi produced 60 sets.
Purpose: Ground-based, antiaircraft; (43) searchlight control
Date Completed: (41) August 1943; (42) October 1944; (43) July 1945
Number Manufactured: (41) 50; (42) 60; (43) 121
Manufacturers: Sumitomo, Nihon Musen, Nihon Onkyo, Hitachi
Wavelength (cm): 150
Frequency: 200 MHz
Pulse length: 3 μs
Pulse rate: 1,000 Hz

Peak power output (kw): 13
Transmitter/Receiver: Ring Parallel two wire/UN954
XM antenna: 2 x 4 dipoles (S3); 4 Yagi complex (S24)
Weight (kg): (41) 5,000; (42) 5,000; (43) 500
Receiving (azimuth and elevation) ant: 2 x 4 dipoles, 6 dipoles, or 8 horizontal Yagi, lobe-switched
Max range (search distance/km): 20–40

Airborne Ship-Search Radar (Air Mark 6) H-6

Mark 6, Model 4
Research completed in August 1942. JRC and Kawanishi manufactured 2,000 sets.
Purpose: Airborne, search and warning
Date Completed: August 1942
Number Manufactured: 2,000
Manufacturers: Nihon Musen, Kawanishi
Wavelength (cm): 200
Frequency: 150 MHz
Pulse length: 10 μs
Peak power output (kw): 3
Transmitter/Receiver: Parallel two wire/UN954
XM antenna: four nose-mounted Yagi
Reverse ant: two wing-mounted reflected dipoles
Weight (kg): 110
Max range (search distance/km): 100 (fleet)

Airborne Air-Search Radar

Type 51, 10 cm "Pathfinder"
Comments: Called the "Rotterdam" type by the Japanese, who apparently were unaware of the origin of the name, although they claimed not to have received any technical information for this set from the Germans or captured Allied sets.
Purpose: Airborne search
Date Completed: not completed, not used
Number Manufactured: estimated 3
Manufacturer: Nihon Musen
Wavelength (cm): 10
Peak power output (kw): 10
Transmitter/Receiver: Magnetron/Crystal
Antenna: parabola, SR
Weight (kg): 200
Max range (search distance/km): 20

Mark 1 Designation 61, 62, 63 (Joint Army-Navy Würzburg), Army Tachi 24
Comments: Intended as a reproduction of the German Würzburg D. Plans and components were brought to Japan from Germany in January 1944. German technicians and engineers from Telefunken assisted the Japan Radio Corporation (Nihon Musen) with assembly, but only three sets were under construction at the end of the war. The army set, designated Tachi 24 (Radio Locator, Würzburg Type; Type 4 Radio Locator) was intended for use in detection and early warning against U.S. B-29s. Reengineering according to Japanese specifications resulted in delays, and only three sets were in production at the end of the war.

220 Secret Weapons and World War II

Table A11. Imperial Japanese Army Radar Sets

Type-A (Ko) Continuous Wave (CW) Doppler (Ultrashortwave Detector) Radar
Comments: In the initial stage of the war, the Air Defense System of the Imperial Japanese Army depended largely on the "Type-A" (Ko) set, which was the earliest air-warning equipment developed in Japan. The Type A operated with a continuous wave modulation (1,000 cycle note) using the Doppler effect to register a beat note in the receiver when the line of transmission was broken between transmitter and receiver. This system did not allow for precise location of enemy aircraft. Many of these were erected in Japan, Korea, and Formosa. Later, these systems relied on the fixed Tachi 6 type radar.

Purpose: Ground-based, detection
Date Completed: January 1941
Number Manufactured: uncertain
Manufacturers: Toshiba, various others
Wavelength (cm): 500–750
Frequency: 40–60 MHz
Peak power output (kw): 0.003, 0.01, 1, 4
Transmitter/Receiver: not listed
Dipole antenna: some with 3 reflectors in parabola, some with single reflector
Weight (kg): 100–2,000
Max range (search distance/km): 20–300

Tachi 6: Mk 229 Model 4 Model 50–2 (Fixed Ultrashortwave Warning Device B)
Comments: Also called Wewak Radar, this set was considered the most important and reliable early warning type radar available to the Japanese. In addition to its limited ability to determine altitude, its chief disadvantage was its great weight and bulk, which made erecting sets in remote locations difficult.

Purpose: Ground-based early warning, defense of strategic locations
Date Completed: June 1942
Number Manufactured: 300–350
Manufacturers: Sumitomo, Nihon Musen, Matsushita
Wavelength (cm): 442, 417, 395, 375
Frequency: 65–83 (68, 72, 76, 80) MHz
PRF, cps MCW (550 or 1,000 switched)
Pulse length: 10–70 μs
Peak power output (kw): 50
Transmitter/Receiver: TR-594A x 2/ME664A
XM antenna: a) box, non directional; fixed b) crossed v dipoles 4–6 high, fixed
Reverse antenna: 2 x 2 dipoles with reflectors, fixed b) 4 x 2 dipoles with reflectors, rotating
Weight (kg): 10,000
Max range (search distance/km): 300 (planes)

Tachi 7 (Radio Detector Field Use Type)
Purpose: Ground-based, mobile for "field use," aircraft early detection
Date Completed: May 1943
Number Manufactured: 60
Manufacturers: Iwasaki Tsūshin

Wavelength (cm): 300
Frequency: 100–116 MHz
PRF, cps MCW (750)
Pulse length: 20–40 μs
Peak power output (kw): 50
XM antenna: 4 x 3 dipoles with reflectors
Transmitter/Receiver: RT-323 x 2/UN-954
Reverse antenna: Common T-R
Weight (kg): 18,000 (transported in four trucks)
Max range: 300 km

Tachi 18 (Radio detector, carrier type) Type 4 Early Warning Radar
Comments: Intended as a more portable replacement for the bulky Tachi 7. The Tachi 18 was the most portable of the Japanese army early warning sets.
Purpose: Ground-based, mobile, aircraft early detection
Date Completed: January 1944
Number Manufactured: 400
Manufacturers: Iwasaki Tsūshin, Toshiba Tsūshin
Wavelength (cm): 283, 294, 307, 320,
Frequency: 92–108 (94, 98, 102, 106) MHz
PRF, cps 375
Pulse length: 10–70 μs
Peak power output (kw): 50
Transmitter/Receiver: RT-323 x 2/UN-954
XM antenna: 4 x 6 with reflectors
Reverse antenna: Common T-R
Weight (kg): 4,000
Max range (search distance/km): 250–300

Tachi 20 (Radio detector for elevation angle measures)
Comments: The Tachi 20 was designed for use in conjunction with Tachi 6 fixed installations with an improved receiver for altitude finding having both lobe switching in azimuth and elevation. This unit was found only in the home islands, and few saw operational use.
Purpose: Ground-based, long distance high altitude detection
Date Completed: May 1944
Number Manufactured: 20
Manufacturers: Anritsu
Wavelength (cm): 375, 395, 417, 442
Frequency: 68, 72, 76, 80 MHz
PRF, cps 500 or 1000 switched
Peak power output (kw): 50
Transmitter/Receiver: RT-323 x 2/UN-954/Tachi 6
XM antenna: 4 x 6 with reflectors
Reverse antenna: 4 groups of 2 x 2 dipoles in diamond formation with reflectors
Weight (kg): 2,000
IF, 11 μs
Max range (km): 100 (planes)

Tachi 24 (Würzburg Type): see Navy radar Mark 1 Designation 61

Tachi 35 (Radio detector for elevation angle measure) Type 5 Warning Device
Purpose: Ground-based high altitude aircraft detection and position finder
Date Completed: March 1945
Number Manufactured: 3
Manufacturers: Sumitomo
Wavelength (cm): 367
Frequency: 82 MHz
PRF, cps 500
Pulse length: 10–70 μs
Peak power output (kw): 50
Transmitter/Receiver: TR-1501 x 2/ME-644A
XM antenna: 4 x 4 dipoles with reflectors
Reverse antenna: 4 groups of 2 x 2 dipoles in diamond formation with reflectors
Weight (kg): 4,000
Max range (km): 100

Tachi 1: Model 1 Mark TA Model 1 (Radio Locator)
Comments: Apparent copy of the British SLC set, a complete set of drawings and specifications of which were captured in Singapore in 1942. Designed for use as a searchlight control locator, the Tachi 1 performed poorly because it could not generate sufficient power as originally designed.
Purpose: antiaircraft
Date Completed: January 1943
Number Manufactured: 25
Manufacturers: Sumitomo
Wavelength (cm): 150
Frequency: 200 MHz
PRF, cps 1000
Pulse length: 1–2 μs
Peak power output (kw): 10
Transmitter/Receiver: T-1500 A x 2/UN-954
XM antenna: Yagi
Receiver antenna: 4 horizontal Yagis in diamond formation with screen reflector; "conical" scan by phasing.
Weight (kg): 2,500
Max range (km): 15–20

Tachi 2: Model 2 Mark TA Model 2 (Radio Locator)
Comments: An improved version of the Tachi 1, the Tachi 2 remained inaccurate in determining elevation but generally performed satisfactorily otherwise.
Purpose: antiaircraft
Date Completed: January 1943
Number Manufactured: 25
Manufacturer: Toshiba
Wavelength (cm): 150
Frequency: 200 MHz
PRF, cps 1000

Pulse length: 2 µs
Peak power output (kw): 10
Transmitter/Receiver: ST-5 x 2/UL-6306
XM antenna: Yagi
Receiver antenna: 4 horizontal Yagis in diamond formation with screen reflector
Weight (kg): 2,500
Max range (km): 20–40

Tachi 3: Model 3 Mark TA Model 3 (Radio Locator)
Comments: Modeled after British gun-laying Mark II sets captured in Malaya, the Tachi 3 became the army's primary fixed installation set for searchlight and gun control and was the preferred apparatus for the defense of important sites. Installed in parallel with the Tachi 2, these sets were used to control six 120 mm guns and six 88 mm guns in circular and semicircular patterns, respectively.
Purpose: antiaircraft
Date Completed: November 1943
Number Manufactured: 120–150
Manufacturer: Sumitomo
Wavelength (cm): 385
Frequency: 78 MHz
PRF, cps 1875
Pulse length: 1–5 µs
Peak power output (kw): 50
Transmitter/Receiver: TR-1501 x 2/ME-664 A
XM antenna: Single Sterba, 4 x 2 with reflectors
Receiver antenna: 5 dipoles in horizontal diamond formation
Weight (kg): 4,000
Max range (km): 40–60

Tachi 4: Model 4 Mark TA Model 4 (Radio Locator)
Comments: A mobile midsize set, the Tachi 4 was designed to replace the Tachi 1 and 2 models primarily for use in searchlight control and early warning in mountainous areas. The Tachi 4 suffered from poor performance in determining azimuth and elevation, and the fire control computer failed to operate the attached guns.
Purpose: antiaircraft
Date Completed: November 1943
Number Manufactured: 70
Manufacturer: Toshiba
Wavelength (cm): 150
Frequency: 200 MHz
PRF, cps 1000
Pulse length: 2 µs
Peak power output (kw): 10
Transmitter/Receiver: ST-5 x 2/UL-6306
XM antenna: Yagi, 4 elements
Receiver antenna: four 3 element Yagis with screen reflector
Weight (kg): 2,500
Max range (km): 20

Tachi 31 Modified Model 4 (Radio Locator)
Comments: The Tachi 31 was designed to address enemy radar jamming countermeasures and was a modified version of the Tachi 1, 2, and 4 lightweight gun-laying radar sets.
Purpose: radar countermeasures
Date Completed: August 1944
Number Manufactured: 40
Manufacturer: Toshiba
Wavelength (cm): 150
Frequency: 200 MHz
PRF, cps 3750
Pulse length: 2 μs
Peak power output (kw): 10
Transmitter/Receiver: SY-5 x 2/UL-6306
XM antenna: four 3 element vertical polarized Yagis mounted on a rectangular screen
Receiver antenna: Common T-R
Weight (kg): 2,500
Max range (km): 18–25

Airborne Radar

Taki 1 (Models 1–4)
Comments: Four models of the Taki I were developed, but only two (Models 2 and 4) saw extensive use. The Taki I was originally designed for use on heavy bombers. Models 1, 2, and 3 were essentially identical in design with variations in power and antennae.
Purpose: Airborne detection of ships and submarines
Date Completed: September 1943; Model 4 June 1945
Number Manufactured: 1,200 (Total Models 1–4)
Manufacturers: Nihon Musen, Toshiba
Wavelength (cm): 150, Model 4 200
PRF, cps 1,000; Model 4 PRF, cps 250
Pulse length: 5 μs
Peak Power output (kw): 10
Transmitter/Receiver: T-311 x 2/UN-954; Model 4: T-319 x 2/UN-954
Antennas: Model 1: 3 Yagis mounted on nose and wings; Model 2: 1 element Yagi on nose and 2 x 2 array mounted on either side of fuselage; Model 3: same as Model 1 with faster lobing rate; Model 4: 4 element Yagi on nose, 2 x 2 array on either side of fuselage
All models use common T-R
Max range (km): submarines, 15; large ships, 60; ship groups 100

Taki 13
Purpose: Airborne
Date Completed: January 1944
Number Manufactured: 1,500
Manufacturers: Toshiba

Wavelength (cm): 80
Peak Power output (kw): 0.1
Transmitter/Receiver: T-304 A x 1 or T-332 x 2/UN-955
Antennas: doublette
Weight (kg): 20
Max range (km): 120

Taki 4
Purpose: Airborne identification
Date Completed: December 1943
Number Manufactured: 10 (?)
Manufacturers: Tōyō Tsūshin
Wavelength (cm): 7–0.8 m
Receiver: UN-954
Antennas: Reverse L
Weight (kg): 150
Max range, altitude (km): 4,000/200

Taki 5
Purpose: Airborne position finder
Date Completed: December 1943
Number Manufactured: 30
Manufacturers: Tōyō Tsūshin
Wavelength (cm): 4.5–1 m
Receiver: UN-954
Antennas: Yagi dipole
Weight (kg): 50
Max range, altitude (km): 4,000/250

Shipborne Radar

The Japanese army developed—independently of the navy—several types of radar sets for use on their own transport ships and submarines. Research on antisubmarine radar was undertaken in 1942. The army eventually adopted the navy's Mark 2 Model 2 set for surface searching. U.S. intelligence judged Japanese army shipborne radar development as unsuccessful because the intended results were not achieved and comparatively few sets were actually used.

Tase 1 Mark 235 "Ultrashortwave Warning Device B"
Comments: Production of this set was terminated on the belief that Allied planes were able to home in on the transmitted signal, resulting in many Japanese army ships being discovered and sunk. Remaining sets were erected on land.
Purpose: Shipborne (army transports), aircraft detection, early warning position finder
Date Completed: February 1943
Number Manufactured: 30
Manufacturers: Toshiba
Wavelength (cm): 260–286
Frequency: 110 MHz
PRF, cps 375

Pulse length: 20–60 μs
Peak Power output (kw): 50
Transmitter/Receiver: RT-323 x 2/UN-954
XM Antenna: box type, four vertical sets of dipoles in a quadrant, nondirectional
Receiver antenna: 2 x 2 dipoles with reflectors
Weight (kg): 4,000
Max range (km): 200–300

Tase 2 Type 4 (Antisubmarine Radar)
Comments: The Tase 2 was designed for use on troop transports in detection of submarines and was one of the army's first efforts to produce centimetric type radar. This set was installed on only two ships. Tests proved these sets had insufficient range for use at sea and were subsequently designated for use on land.
Purpose: Shipborne, submarine detection and position finding
Date Completed: December 1943
Number Manufactured: 80
Manufacturers: Nihon Musen, Toshiba
Wavelength (cm): 15.7
PRF, cps 1875
Pulse length: 3 μs
Peak power output (kw): 1
Transmitter/Receiver: MP-15/BK-15
XM Antenna: Horizontal dipole with 2.5 meter parabola
Receiver antenna: Common T-R
Weight (kg): 2,000
Max Range (km): Submarine periscope, 2; surfaced sub, 10; large ships, 30

Table A12. Imperial Japanese Army Rocket Ordnance

Rocket Type, caliber (cm)	Total Length (mm)	Total Weight (kg)	Weight of Explosive (kg)	Maximum Range (m)	Year Produced
7	359	4.070	0.710	750	Not indicated
9/8	508	8.600	1.730	1,080	1942
15	782	30.685	5.180	3,000	Not indicated
20	1,019	83.700	16.540	2,400	1943
24/30	975	110.700	24.700	2,940	1943
40	1,874	507.600	79.280	3,700	1943
60	Unknown	2,130	300	Unknown	Under development

SOURCE. Table compiled from Nihon Heiki Kōgyōkai, *Rikusen heiki sōkan* (Tokyo: Shuppansha, 1977), 144–45 and General Headquarters, United States Army Forces, Pacific, Scientific and Technical Advisory Section, "Report on Scientific Intelligence Survey in Japan: September and October 1945," 1 November 1945, vol. 2, U.S. National Archives, College Park, MD, RG 165, box 2056, appendixes 1-F-1 to 1-F-3. Data given in these sources are inconsistent and cannot be reconciled. Preference is given to the Japanese source, which is more comprehensive.

Table A13. Imperial Japanese Army Aircraft-Launched Rocket Ordnance

Type	Diameter (mm)	Length (mm)	Weight (kg)	Explosive (kg)	Year Produced
Ro-3 Type I	87	470	8.7	1	May 1944
Ro-3 Type II	101	540	10.5	2.4	Oct 1944
Ro-7	300	1,400	250	35	Oct 1944
Ro-8	200	1,000	80	9.5	Oct 1944, design only
Ro-Ta	200	1,200	75	9.5	Oct 1944
Ro-5 Type I	202	1,000	80	9.7	Oct 1944
Ro-5 Type II	240	1,400	130	13	Jun 1944 (fin-stabilized)
Rocket bomb motor	180	1,000	35	12	Aug 1944

NOTE. Figures for range not given. Table compiled from Air Technical Intelligence Group, "Aircraft Rockets," Report No. 307, 15 December 1945, appendix B, NASM. File: "Japan, Missiles (WW II)."

Table A14. Imperial Japanese Navy Rocket Ordnance

Rocket Type cal. (cm)	Total Length (mm)	Total Weight (kg)	Weight of Explosive (kg)	Maximum Range (m)	Intended Use	Month/Year Developed
8 (SCR) Ro-Ta	350	5.9	0.53	1,200	Antitank	Sep 1944
10 (SCR) Ro-Ta	435	10.3	1.59	1,200	Antitank	Mar 1945
12 (ISR) Ro-Se	735	24	4.5	4,500–4,800	Antiaircraft/ Barrage	July 1944
12 (HER) Ro-Tsu	735	24	1.63–2.5	4,500–4,800	Barrage	Jan 1945
20 (SCR) Ro-Ta	800	50	8	1,200–1,500	Antitank	Apr 1945
20 (ISR) Ro-Tsu	1,020	80–88.9	11	3,000–3,700	Antiaircraft/ Barrage	Nov 1944
20 (HER) Ro-Tsu	1,080	90–91	61	1,800	Barrage	Mar 1944
+Model 1	same	84.65	15.7(?)	4,500	Barrage	Jan 1945
45	1,760	600–660	100–167	1,500–1,600	Barrage	Apr 1944
Type 3, Model 1	1,800	370	250	5,000	Barrage	Not indicated
Type 3, Model 2	1,100	102	60	3,000	Barrage	Not indicated

SCR = shape charge rocket; ISR = incendiary shrapnel rocket; HER = high-explosive rocket.
SOURCE. Table compiled from U.S. Naval Technical Mission to Japan, December 1945, "Table I: Salient Features of Japanese Naval Rockets," Report No. 0-09, 7, U.S. Navy Archive, Washington, DC, Naval History Division, microfilm. Fukui Shizuo et al., eds. *Kimitsu heiki no zembō: Waga gunji kagaku gijutsu no shinsō to hansei* (Tokyo: Kōyōsha, 1953), 254–55, 296.

Table A15. Imperial Japanese Navy Aircraft-Launched Rocket Ordnance

Type	Diameter (cm)	Total Length (m)	Total Weight (kg)	Explosive Weight (kg)	Intended Target
Type 3, No. 25, MK 4, Model 1	30	1.9	315	3.5	Aircraft carriers
Type 5, No. 1, MK 9	10	0.9	15	1	Surfaced submarines
Type 3, No. 6, MK 27, Model 1	20	1.7	66	2.5	Large aircraft
Type 3, No. 1 MK 28, Model 1	10	0.7	9	0.6	Large aircraft
Type 3, No. 6, MK 9 (experimental)	20	1.7	84	10	Landing craft

NOTE. Table compiled from Air Technical Intelligence Group, "Aircraft Rockets," Report No. 307, 15 December 1945, appendix B, table II, Japanese Naval Aircraft Rockets, NASM, File: "Japan, Missiles (WW II)."

Table A16. I-gō Series Missile

Type/Model	1A	1B	1C
Wingspan (ft/m)	19.8/6	13.2/4	Not available
Length (ft/m)	18.9/5.8	13.4/4.08	11.5/3.5
Total weight (lb/kg)	3,300/1,500	1,650/750	Not available
Warhead (lb/kg)	1,760/800	660/300	Not available
Maximum speed (mph/kph)	342/550	342/550	Not available
Maximum range (mi/km)	7/11	7/11	0.5/0.8
Date completed	Nov 1944	Oct 1944	Not available

SOURCE. Table compiled from Air Technical Intelligence Group, "Japanese Radio Controlled Flying Bomb 'I-gō,'" Report No. 114, 20 November 1945, appendix A, NASM, File: "Japan, Missiles (WW II)." U.S. Naval Technical Mission to Japan, "Japanese Guided Missiles," Report No. 0-02, U.S. National Archives, College Park, MD, Operational Archives, U.S. Naval History Division, microfilm. Martin Caidin, "Japanese Guided Missiles in World War II," *Jet Propulsion* 26 (August 1956): 691–96.

Table A17. Funryū Series Missile

Dimensions	Model 2	Model 3	Model 4
Wingspan (ft/m)	3.15/1	Same as Model 2	5.25/2
Length (ft/m)	7.9/2.2	"	13.2/4
Diameter (in/cm)	12/30	"	33.5/60
Total weight (lb/kg)	815/370	"	4,190/1,905
Warhead (lb/kg)	110/50	"	440/200
Maximum speed (mph/kph)	525/845	Not tested	684/1,100
Maximum altitude (ft/m)	16,405/5,000	Not tested	49,215/15,000
Engine type	Solid fuel	Liquid fuel	Toko Ro-2 liquid fuel
Completion date	Apr 1945 (prototype)	Apr 1945 (prototype not tested)	Under development

SOURCE. Table compiled from Martin Caidin, "Japanese Guided Missiles in World War II," *Jet Propulsion* 26 (August 1956): 691–96. René Francillon, *Japanese Aircraft of the Pacific War*, 4th ed. (Annapolis, MD: Naval Institute Press, 1994), 532–34.

Table A18. Japanese Bacteriological Bombs

Bomb Type	Year Produced	Number Produced (Approximate)	Description	Conclusions
I	1937	300	Iron; 44 lb/20 kg	Unsuitable for dropping from plane
Ro	1937	300	Iron; 44 lb/20 kg	Unsuitable for dropping from plane
Ha	1938	500	Iron; 88 lb/40 kg	Probably effective
Ni	1939	200	Iron; 110 lb/50 kg	Probably effective
U	1939	20	NA; 66 lb/30 kg	Not usable
Uji* (old type)	1938	300	Porcelain; 55 lb/25 kg	Effectiveness poor
Uji* (Type 50)	1940–1941	500	Porcelain; 55 lb/25 kg	Best among Uji bombs; effectiveness questionable
Uji (Type 100)	1940–1942	300	Porcelain; 110 lb/50 kg	Effectiveness poor
GA	1940	50	Glass/NA	NA/NA

SOURCE . Sources give conflicting production numbers and years. I have opted in favor of the "Thompson Report" listings because this investigation appears most credible. Arvo T. Thompson, "Report on Japanese Biological Warfare (BW) Activities," 31 May 1946, Army Service Forces, Camp Detrick, Frederick, Maryland, U.S. National Archives, College Park, MD, RG 319, Box 2097, File: "Japanese Biological Warfare Activities, Army Defense Forces," 10–16. "Table of Japanese Experimental BW Bombs," Military Intelligence Division, War Department, Washington, DC, "Biological Warfare: Activities & Capabilities of Foreign Nations," 30 March 1946, U.S. National Archives, College Park, MD, RG 319, 1946–1948, P&O Files, P&O 381, "Biological Warfare," TS, Case 67/3.

*For the Uji series, low internal explosive pressure and lack of metallic effect are advantageous for preserving bacterial viability. Livestock eating grass in breeze within range of 33 to 65 feet were killed as follows: horses 50–90 percent, sheep 90–100 percent.

Table A19. Leading Figures in Nuclear Research

Name	Wartime Activities	Postwar Activities
Arakatsu Bunsaku	Led navy's F-gō atomic bomb project	President of Konan University
Fujioka Yoshio	Professor of physics at Tokyo Imperial University, conducted research in ultraviolet rays, infrared, radiation	Central figure in atomic power development, led mission to inspect atomic power plants in United States and Europe (1954), member of JAEC (1955)
Kikuchi Seishi	Participant in navy's Committee on Research in the Application of Nuclear Physics	Director of Tokyo University's Institute for Nuclear Studies, professor of physics concurrently at Osaka and Tokyo University
Kimura Kenjirō	Professor of geochemistry at Tokyo Imperial University, director of Rare Elements Research Project	President of the Radioactive Isotope Research Committee
Kimura Kiichi	Participant in navy's F-gō atomic bomb project, conducted basic measurements using cyclotron	Professor of physics at Kyoto University, assisted in construction of cyclotron (1953)
Kimura Motoharu	Assistant research fellow at Riken, participant in army's NI-gō	Professor of physics at Tohoku University, first Japanese to study atomic energy abroad in postwar Japan
Nishina Yoshio	Head of army's NI-gō	President of Japan Science Research Institute (Riken), died 1951
Sakata Shōichi	Professor of Physics at Nagoya University, participant in navy's F-gō project, studied nuclear theory	Professor of Physics at Nagoya University, developed Sakata model of atomic structure (1956), prominent nuclear peace activist
Sugimoto Asao	Participant in army's NI-gō at Riken, study of fundamental constants	Japan Scientific Development Council representative on the Nuclear Reactor Design Subcommittee (1955)
Takeda Eiichi	Participant in army's NI-gō at Riken, research on isotope separation	Japan Society for the Promotion of Science representative on the

Tomonaga Shinichirō	Participant in army's NI-gō at Riken	Nuclear Reactor Design Subcommittee (1955) President of Tokyo Kyōiku University (1956–1962), Nobel Prize winner (1965)
Yukawa Hideki	Professor at Kyoto Imperial University, consultant to army and navy atomic bomb projects as theorist	Professor at Columbia University (1949), Nobel Prize winner (1949), director of Institute for Fundamental Physics at Kyoto University, member of JAEC (1955)

SOURCE. Compiled from The Japan Biographical Research Department, *The Japan Biographical Encyclopedia & Who's Who* (Tokyo: Rengo Press, 1958), passim. General Headquarters, United States Army Forces, Pacific, Scientific and Technical Advisory Section, "Report on Scientific Intelligence Survey in Japan: September and October 1945," 1 November 1945, vol. 3, U.S. National Archives, College Park, MD, RG 165, Box 2056, passim. "Brief History of Research during the War," U.S. National Archives, College Park, MD, RG 331, Box 7416, File: "Research Wartime." U.S. Department of State, *Confidential U.S. State Department Central Files: Japan Internal Affairs, 1950–1954* (Frederick, MD: University Publications of America, 1984), microfilm.

Table A20. Leading Figures in Rocketry and Aeronautics Research

Name	Wartime Activities	Postwar Activities
Hattori Rokurō	Navy technical officer, participant in Ohka project	Engineer for Bridgestone Tire
Itokawa Hideo	Aeronautical engineer at Tokyo Imperial University's Aeronautical Research Institute, helped design Ginga bomber, participant in Kego B-1 missile project	Professor at Tokyo University, leading figure in Japan's early rocket and space development efforts, pioneered rocket research with Baby, Kappa, and Lambda series rockets
Kimura Hidemasa	Doctor of Engineering, participant in Ohka and Shūsui projects	Professor of engineering at Nihon University, helped design software for aircraft flight simulators
Hino Kumao	Led navy research on rockets fuels, participant in Funryū missile project	Director of Japan Chemical Corporation, participant in international symposia on rockets and astronautics
Miki Tadanao	Aeronautical engineer for navy, participant in Ohka project	Engineer with the Japan Railway Technical Reserve Institute, helped design first Shinkansen
Ogawa Taiichirō	Professor of aeronautical engineering at Tokyo Imperial University, leading engineer on Baika project, consultant on Ohka project	Professor of aeronautical engineering at Meiji University
Sugimoto Masao	Dr. of Engineering, participant in Funryū missile project	Director of the Board of Industrial Technologies (1954), lecturer at Tokyo University
Tani Ichirō	Professor of engineering at Tokyo Imperial University, conducted research on high-speed aerodynamics, participant in Ohka project	Professor of engineering at Tokyo University

SOURCE. Compiled from *Gendai jinbutsu jiten* [Contemporary Who's Who] (Tokyo: Sun Data Systems, 1982). Monbusho daigaku gakujitsukyoky, ed., *Daigaku kenkyūsha* [University Researchers] (Tokyo: Nihon gakujutsu shinkōkai, 1971). *Kodansha Encyclopedia of Japan* (Tokyo: Kodansha, 1983). "Biographical Files of Japanese Scientists," U.S. National Archives, College Park, MD, RG 331, Box 7439.

Table A21. Leading Figures in Electronics and Radar Research

Name	Wartime Activities	Postwar Activities
Asada Tsunesaburō	Death ray	University professor
Asami Yoshihirō	Death ray	Director of Applied Electricity Research Institute at Hokkaido University from 1946
Hayashi Kiyoshi	Death ray; specialized in applications of magnetrons to microwave research; designed magnetrons from 1934 to 1945	Engineer at Kawanishi Factory (Kobe)
Ibuka Masaru	NTRI	Cofounder of Sony
Ikebe Tsuneto	Death ray; chief engineer on 80 cm magnetron development	Chief engineer at Nippon Koshuha K.K. (Ikeda Laboratory) in microwave research
Kato Nobuyoshi	Promoted radar research in navy	Promoted semiconductor industry
Kikuchi Seishi	Death ray	See Table A19
Kotani Masao	Atomic Nucleus Project research, electronics and communications, magnetron theory, Tokyo Imperial University	Professor of physics at Tokyo University, recipient of Japan Academy Prize (1948), member of Japan Science Council
Kusaba Sueki [Hideki]	Death Ray; director of army ultrashortwave research, 1941–1945	Employed by Nippon Koshuha K.K. (Ikeda Laboratory)
Matsuoka Shigeru	Death ray; Tohoku University, conducted microscopic examination of animals killed by exposure to microwave radiation; fields of interest included medicine, pathology of the brain and nerves, cerebral hemorrhages, tuberculosis, and malignant tumors	Professor of medicine at Nagasaki University (1949)
Minoshima Takashi	Death ray; physiological studies of ultrashort waves	Hokkaidō University medical faculty, director of the First Physiological Laboratory; medical faculty and member of the Research Institute of Applied Electricity at Hokkaido University (1949)

Morimoto Shigetaki	Death ray; designed triode oscillators	International Telecommunication Co. (Kokusai Denki) (1949)
Morita Kiyoshi	Death ray; research in microwave radio communications	Professor at Tokyo Technical College (1949); vice chairman of the Television Academy
Morita Akio	NTRI	Cofounder of Sony
Nakajima Shigeru	Death ray; assisted in manufacture of magnetrons at navy's Shimada Laboratory	Employed as chief technician at Doitsu Bosch Corporation and Japan Radio Corporation; became director of JRC in 1947; awarded Purple Ribbon Medal (1963) and Third Class Order of the Sacred Treasure (1977) for his work in electronics
Ogata Kenji	NTRI	NEC
Okamura Sōgo	Ship detection with microwave radar	University professor
Ouchi Atsuyoshi (Lt.)	NTRI	NEC
Ozawa Yasutomo	Death ray	Technical research engineer at Nippon High Frequency K.K.; adjunct staff at Hokkaido University (1946); assistant at the Research Institute of Applied Electricity
Sasada Sukesaburō	Death ray; doctor of medicine Hokkaidō University	Employed by Nippon High-Frequency Company; also experimented on the use of anaesthetic rays to cure venereal disease and rheumatic fever
Shinji Ichiro (Lt.)	Radar and electronics, NTRI	JVC (Japan Victor Corporation)
Takano Shizuo (Lt.)	Radar and electronics, NTRI	"Mr. VHS," JVC
Takayanagi Kenjiro	Chief of Airborne-Radar Technology section, NTRI	"Father of Japanese television"; JVC
Watanabe Yasushi	Professor, Tōhoku Imperial University, electronics	Promoted semiconductor industry, specialist in telephony engineering, Tōhoku University
Yagi Hidetsugu	Death ray	University research

| Yoshihiro Asami | Death ray | Director of the Applied Electricity Research Institute, Hokkaido University (1946); member of the Radio Wave Technical Council, Radio Wave Scientific Research Council, and Hokkaido Scientific and Technological Council |

SOURCE. *Japanese Research on High-Frequency Electric Wave Weapons,* U.S. National Archives, College Park, MD, RG 319, Entry 82. The Japan Biographical Research Department, *The Japan Biographical Encyclopedia & Who's Who* (Tokyo: Rengo Press, 1958). Nakagawa Yasuzo, *Japanese Radar and Related Weapons of World War II,* English edition edited by Louis Brown, John H. Bryant, and Naohiko Koizumi (Laguna Hills, CA: Aegean Park Press, 1997). Nakajima Shigeru, "General Outline of Japanese Radar Development up to 1945," in Erich Pauer, ed., *Papers on the History of Industry and Technology of Japan, Volume 2: From the Meiji Period to Postwar Japan* (Marburg: Frderverein, 1995), passim.

Table A22. Careers of Leading Unit 731 Personnel

Name	Wartime Activities	Postwar Activities
Dr. Andō Koji	Head of Unit 731 vaccine-producing detachment at Dairen	Professor at Tokyo University's Infectious Diseases Research Institute
Dr. Asahina Masajirō	Participant in typhus vaccine production	Employed by National Institute of Health
Dr. Futagi Hideo	Vivisection team leader	Cofounder of Japan Green Cross
Dr. Hayakawa Kiyoshi	Member of Singapore detachment, veteran of Nomonhan BW activities	Manager of Hayakawa Medical Company
Dr. Hayashi Ichirō	Unit 731 researcher	Professor at Nagasaki University Medical School
Dr. Ishikawa Tachiomaru	Unit 731 pathologist	Professor at Kanazawa University, President of Kanazawa University Medical School
Dr. Kanazawa Kenichi	Performed experiments with Songo ticks	Chief of the research section of Takeda Pharmaceutical Company
Dr. Kitano Masaji	Participant in research on frostbite and epidemic hemorrhagic fever	Cofounder of Japan Green Cross, member of Special Committee for Antarctic Research
Dr. Masao Kusami	Leader of Unit 731 pharmacology squad	Professor of pharmacology at Shōwa University
Dr. Masuda Tomosada	Deputy to Ishii at Pingfang	General practitioner; died 1952
Dr. Naitō Ryōichi	Researcher at Pingfang	Cofounder and president of Japan Green Cross
Dr. Ogata Tomio	Participant in research on communicable diseases	Professor in medical faculty at Tokyo University
Dr. Ogawa Tōru	Researcher with Nanking Detachment of Unit 731, specialist in typhoid	Staff member of Nagoya Prefecture Medical University
Dr. Okamoto Kōzō	Pathologist at Pingfang, performed vivisections	Professor at Kyoto University, Director of Kyoto University Medical Department
Dr. Tabei Kazu	Researcher at Pingfang, specialist in dysentery and typhoid	Professor of Bacteriology at Kyoto University
Dr. Tamiya Takeo	Recruit director for Unit 731	First general director of Japan National Cancer Center, president of the Japan Medical Association

Dr. Tanaka Hideo	Flea expert	Director of Osaka Municipal University's School of Medicine
Dr. Yamada Toshikazu	Director of Denken bacteriological unit	Professor at Kumamoto University, director of hygiene in Yokohama city
Dr. Yamanaka Taboku	Attached to Nanking Unit	Dean of Osaka Medical School, director of Japan Bacteriological Association
Dr. Yoshimura Hisato	Participant in frostbite experiments	President of Kyoto Prefectural Medical College, president of the Japan Meteorological Society, consultant to fisheries and frozen food companies

SOURCE. This is a partial listing of known Unit 731 members and collaborators. Compiled from Tsuneishi Keiichi, *Igakushatachi no sōshiki hanzai: Kantōgun dai-731 butai* [The Systematic Crimes of the Physicians: Kwantung Army Unit 731] (Tokyo: Asahi Shimbunsha, 1994), 204–9. See also Peter Williams and David Wallace, *Unit 731: Japan's Secret Biological Warfare in World War II* (New York: Free Press, 1989), 235–43. Hal Gold, *Unit 731 Testimony* (Tokyo: Yen Books, 1996), 142–43.

NOTES

INTRODUCTION

1. For example, crude forerunners of the modern submarine were built and used to limited effect during the U.S. Civil War, but nothing approached the destructive capacity of the *Nautilus*, featured in Jules Verne's *20,000 Leagues Under the Sea* (1870), until World War I. Verne described enormous cannons in *From the Earth to the Moon* (1865) and *The Begum's Fortune* (1879), presaging the development of long-range artillery, such as the "Paris Gun," developed by Germany during World War I. (Ironically, the oversized cannon described in the latter novel was designed by the sinister Professor Schultz, a German leader who intended to use the new invention to force the world to meet his demands.) *Begum's Fortune* also described the use of a "carbonic acid gas," portending the introduction of chemical weapons in World War I. In the novel *For the Flag* (1896), Verne even described a device called the "fulgurator," a self-propelled guided missile capable of enormous destructive power akin to the modern nuclear ballistic missile—a weapon not to be realized until well after World War II.

2. *The Shape of Things to Come* was made into a film and presciently released in 1939, the year of the outbreak of World War II in Europe. The impact of Wells's novels on scientists at the time is also noted in Richard Rhodes, *Making of the Atomic Bomb*, 24; and David E. Fisher, *Race on the Edge of Time*, 139.

3. Frank H. Winter, *Prelude to the Space Age*, 15, 37–39, 75. Donald E. Tarter, "Peenemünde and Los Alamos."

4. For an example, see in particular *Flash Gordon Conquers the Universe*, chapter 1, episode 1, "The Purple Death Strikes Earth" (King Features, 1934). The pestilence depicted here was to be simulated five years later as the "walking death" in the film version of *Things to Come*.

5. Hiromi Mizuno, "Science, Ideology, Empire," 283–304.

6. The role of science in World War I is still being debated among historians. Daniel Kevles has written much to challenge the characterization of World War I as a chemist's war, arguing that the role of the physicist has been understated and that the submarine was actually more significant in the war effort than were chemical weapons. See Daniel J. Kevles, *Physicists*, 137–38. See also Everett Mendelsohn, "Science, Scientists, and the Military"; and Louis Morton, "War, Science, and Social Change."

7. Richard Overy, *Why the Allies Won*, 180–207. See also Mark Harrison, *Economics of World War II*. Alan S. Milward, *War, Economy and Society*.

8. Overy, *Why the Allies Won*, 242. See also Roland, "Science and War," 265. Morton, "War, Science, and Social Change," 53–54.

9. Fisher, *Race on the Edge of Time*, x.

10. Guy Hartcup, *Effect of Science*, xii.

11. Michael J. Lyons, *World War II*, xi.

12. Benjamin H. Kristy, "Science, Technology, and Weapons Development," 200. Three books, written for a popular audience and published in Japanese, provide basic narratives of the development of some of the advanced weapons produced by Japan during the war, but they do not offer much insight into the impact of science on the war or vice versa. See Tokuda Hachirōe, *Ma ni awanakatta heiki*; Naitō Hatsuho, *Kaigun gijutsu senki*; and Fukui Shizuo et al., *Kimitsu heiki no zembō*.

13. Alex Roland, "Science, Technology, and War."

14. Neither of these subfields of history was considered in the mainstream of American historiography in 1985 when Roland first offered this observation. See Roland, "Science and War," 247.

15. See for example, Michael J. Neufeld, *The Rocket and the Reich*; Mark Walker, *German National Socialism*; and Robert Buderi, *Invention that Changed the World*, to name only a few. There are also several excellent studies of the Manhattan Project, far too numerous to list here, but Richard Rhodes's *Making of the Atomic Bomb* is one of the most popular.

16. On the United States, the books in the series *Science in World War II* remain standards. See especially James P. Baxter, *Scientists Against Time;* Lincoln R. Theismeyer and John E. Burchard, *Combat Scientists;* and Irvin Stewart, *Organizing Scientific Research for War*. For a more recent study concerning U.S. industrial mobilization for the war effort, see Peter Neushul, "Science, Technology and the Arsenal of Democracy." Regarding the United Kingdom and the Allies more broadly, see Hartcup, *Effect of Science;* R. V. Jones, *Most Secret War;* M. M. Postan, D. Hay, and J. D. Scott, *Design and Development of Weapons*. See also Donald H. Avery, *Science of War;* David Zimmerman, *Great Naval Battle of Ottawa;* and Roy M. MacLeod, *Science and the Pacific War*. Regarding National Socialist Germany, see Margit Szöllösi-Janze, *Science in the Third Reich;* and Kristie Macrakis, *Surviving the Swastika*. On the Soviet Union, see Lennart Samuelson, *Plans for Stalin's War Machine;* and John Barber and Mark Harrison, *Soviet Defence-Industry Complex*. For general context, see Loren R. Graham, *Science in Russia and the Soviet Union*.

17. The most numerous by far are the books on Japan's biological warfare program and Unit 731. In English, see Sheldon H. Harris, *Factories of Death;* Peter Williams and David Wallace, *Unit 731;* and Hal Gold, *Unit 731 Testimony*. The latter two, written by journalists, appear to have been intended for a more popular audience, and although Harris's book is perhaps the more reliable, it also is not without its flaws. A truly satisfactory account—which would require the exploitation of Japanese-, Chinese-, and English-language sources—has yet to be published in English. There are far more publications in Japanese on the subject. Historian Tsuneishi Keiichi in particular has written extensively on Unit 731 and Japan's BW research. See, for example, Tsuneishi Keiichi, *Kieta saikinsen butai*. On other weapons projects, see Ishizawa Kazuhiko, *Kikka;* Naitō Hatsuho, *Kimitsu heiki Funryū;* and Yamamoto Yōichi, *Nihonsei genbaku no shinsō*.

18. Despite the existence of two collections that are very rich in primary materials on the subject, there are few works that focus extensively on science and technology mobilization in wartime Japan. See *Minobe Yōji Monjo;* and the official documents collection of the first president of the Technology Agency, Inoue Tadashirō, in Kokugakuin daigaku toshokan, *Inoue Tadashiro Monjo*. The recently published books by Hiroshige Tetsu, *Kagaku no shakai shi: (ue) Sensō to kagaku*, and *Kagaku no shakai shi: (shita) Keizai seichō to kagaku*, a revised and expanded version of a previous publication, provide a general overview. The multivolume series Nippon Kagakushi Gakkai, *Nippon kagaku gijutsusi taikei*, endures as a standard reference work. On science mobilization, see especially vol. 4. Oyodo Shōichi, *Miyamoto Takenosuke to kagaku gijutsu gyōsei*, is an excellent source on science and technology mobilization and policy through the early war years, but it does not address specific military topics in detail. The recently completed dissertation by Kawamura Yutaka offers a chapter on wartime mobilization and is perhaps the most thorough study of Japan's wartime navy radar development available anywhere. See Kawamura Yutaka, "Kyū-Nihon kaigun no dempa heiki kaihatsu katei o jirei toshita dai-niji taisenki Nihon no kagaku gijutsu dōin ni kan suru bunseki." English-language materials on wartime science and technology policy and mobilization in Japan are limited to a few journal-length articles. See especially Yamazaki Masakatsu, "Mobilization of Science and Technology"; and Kamatani Chikayoshi, "History of Research Organization." See also selected chapters in Nakayama Shigeru, David L. Swain, and Eri Yagi, *Science and Society in Modern Japan*. A comprehensive examination of wartime science and technology mobilization is beyond the scope of the present study, however, and such a work remains to be published in English.

19. Nakayama Shigeru, "History of East Asian Science."

20. Although few in number, scholars in this area of specialization are generally known for the exceedingly high quality of their work. See in particular the publications by Alvin D. Coox, John W. Dower, Edward J. Drea, David C. Evans, Morris F. Low, Mark R. Peattie, Richard J. Samuels, and Tessa Morris-Suzuki, for example. Clearly not all would consider themselves military historians or exclusively historians of science and technology.

21. Notable exceptions are Hiroshige Tetsu, Tsuneishi Keiichi, Yamazaki Masakatsu, and Kawamura Yutaka, whose representative works are cited above.

22. As James Bartholomew has demonstrated, support for Yukawa's Nobel award nomination began to emerge in the late 1930s and continued to build even through the war. The postwar discovery of the pi-meson by Cecil F. Powell and Guiseppe Occhialini, confirming Yukawa's theory, likely cinched his nomination for the award. See James R. Bartholomew, "Japanese Nobel Candidates," 238–84. On Yukawa's research during wartime, see Satio Hayakawa, "Development of Meson Physics."

23. Nakajima Hideto, "Categorization of Technology."

24. Ibid., 42.

25. James H. Capshew and Karen A. Rader, "Big Science." Helmuth Trischler, "Aeronautical Research Under National Socialism"; Angelo Baracca, "'Big Science' vs. 'Little Science'"; and Derek J. De Solla Price, *Little Science, Big Science*. It has been argued that the essential elements of Big Science were already in place in the Soviet Union as early as 1921. See Alexei Kojevnikov, "Great War." For several informative essays on the history of Big Science, see especially Peter Galison and Bruce Hevly, eds., *Big Science*.

26. The debate over whether some projects are more properly called "Big Science" or "Big Engineering" need not concern us here, as the elements required are essentially the same. See Trischler, "Aeronautical Research Under National Socialism," 82–83. On broader themes concerning the historiography of Big Science, see especially Bruce Hevly, "Reflections on Big Science and Big History."

27. Martin van Creveld, *Technology and War*, 161.

28. See especially selected essays in Nakayama Shigeru, *Social History of Science and Technology*. See also Richard Samuels, *Rich Nation, Strong Army;* and Andrew J. Robertson, "Mobilizing for War."

29. For arguments on this point, see John W. Dower, "Useful War"; and Morris F. Low, "Useful War."

30. See especially General Headquarters, United States Army Forces, Pacific, Scientific and Technical Advisory Section, "Report on Scientific Intelligence Survey in Japan: September and October 1945," 1 November 1945, vols. 1–5, U.S. National Archives, College Park, MD, RG 165, Box 2056, which was conducted under the direction of Karl T. Compton after the war. On this source, see R. W. Home and Morris F. Low, "Postwar Scientific Intelligence Missions to Japan." See also Yukuo Sasamoto, "Scientific Intelligence Survey."

CHAPTER 1. MOBILIZING SCIENCE AND TECHNOLOGY FOR WAR

1. On this subject, see especially the relevant essays in Mark Walker, ed., *Science and Ideology*.

2. The DSIR remains today as an important agency in the administration of science and technology in Great Britain. David Zimmerman, *Top Secret Exchange*, 22. Kiyonobu Itakura and Eri Yagi, "Japanese Resarch System."

3. M. M. Postan, D. Hay, and J. D. Scott, *Design and Development of Weapons*, 433–39. On the British research system and science mobilization for weapons development in World War II, see also Guy Hartcup, *Challenge of War*.

4. As the official OSRD historian, James P. Baxter noted, "The British, it is true, never created as simple an organization of science for war as that established in the United States in 1940 and 1941, but it is one of their qualities which have stood them in good stead that they can operate, under pressure, what seems to us an enormously complicated structure and get results which elsewhere could be hoped for only from simpler and better coordinated administrative machinery." James P. Baxter, *Scientists Against Time*, 11–12.

5. Robert A. Lewis, "Some Aspects of the Research and Development Effort."

6. Lennart Samuelson, *Plans for Stalin's War Machine*, 152–53.

7. Loren R. Graham, *Science in Russia and the Soviet Union*, 180–81.

8. See the section on Soviet mobilization by Eduard Kolchinsky in Walter E. Grunden et al., "Laying the Foundation for Wartime Research."

9. Zhores A. Medvedev, *Soviet Science*, 32–41; Paul R. Josephson, *Totalitarian Science and Technology*.

10. Samuelson, *Plans for Stalin's War Machine*, 19, 186–87.

11. For a brief historical overview of the Soviet Union's central policy-making bodies during this period, see David Holloway, "Innovation in the Defense Sector," 296–303.

12. Kolchinsky, in Grunden et al., "Laying the Foundation for Wartime Research."

13. David Holloway, "Soviet Style of Military R&D."

14. Baxter, *Scientists Against Time*, 12–14.

15. On the history of the NDRC and OSRD, see especially Irvin Stewart, *Organizing Scientific Research for War;* and Baxter, *Scientists Against Time*, passim.

16. Quoted from Stanley Goldberg, "Inventing a Climate of Opinion." See also Stewart, *Organizing Scientific Research for War*, 5–6.

17. Baxter, *Scientists Against Time*, 14.

18. Baxter, *Scientists Against Time*, 13–18. Stewart, *Organizing Scientific Research for War*, 7. See also Daniel Kevles, *Physicists*, passim.

19. Carroll Pursell, "Science Agencies in World War II."

20. Goldberg, "Inventing a Climate of Opinion," 434. Kevles, *Physicists*, 299–301. Stewart, *Organizing Scientific Research for War*, 35–38, 53.

21. Helmut Maier, in Grunden et al., "Laying the Foundation for Wartime Research."

22. Kristie Macrakis, *Surviving the Swastika*, 11–48.

23. See the classic study by Alan Beyerchen, *Scientists Under Hitler*.

24. Macrakis, *Surviving the Swastika*, 76–84, 88.

25. Leslie E. Simon, *German Research in World War II*, 63–98. Macrakis, *Surviving the Swastika*, 90–91.

26. Macrakis, *Surviving the Swastika*, 90–94. Simon, *German Research in World War II*, 79–80. Baxter, *Scientists Against Time*, 3–7.

27. Macrakis, *Surviving the Swastika*, 93–94. Simon, *German Research in World War II*, 79–80, 105–6.

28. Maier, in Grunden et al., "Laying the Foundation for Wartime Research."

29. Hartcup, *Challenge of War*, 30.

30. Richard Rhodes, *Making of the Atomic Bomb*, 241–42, 248–50.

31. Vera Zamagni, "Italy."

32. Kawamura Yutaka, "Tairiku kagakuin setsuritsu." For a comprehensive survey of Japanese science and technology history throughout this period, see especially Hiroshige Tetsu, *Kagaku no shakai shi: (ue) Sensō to kagaku*, passim.

33. Masakatsu Yamazaki, "Mobilization of Science and Technology." The Technology Agency is also referred to in various sources as the "Board of Technology" and the "Technology Board."

34. Kiyonobu Itakura and Eri Yagi, "Japanese Research System." See also Hiroshige, *Kagaku no shakai shi*, 117–30.

35. Hiroshige, *Kagaku no shakai shi*, 105–11. Kamatani Chikayoshi, "History of Research Organization."

36. The Japan National Research Council is alternately referred to in English-language sources as the "Japan Scientific Research Council." It should not be confused with the Japan Science Council (Nihon Gakujutsu Kaigi) formed in the post–World War II era. On this important period in the history of science and technology in Japan, see especially James R. Bartholomew, *Formation of Science in Japan*, passim. See also Tuge Hideomi, *Historical Development of Science and Technology*, passim. Hiroshige Tetsu, "Role of the Government."

37. Michael A. Cusumano, "Scientific Industry." Itakura and Yagi, "Japanese Research System," 194–96. Kamatani, "History of Research Organization," 33.

38. Shimao Eikoh, "Some Aspects of Japanese Science."

39. These included the Petroleum Industry Law (1934), the Automobile Manufacturing Industry Law (1936), the Synthetic Petroleum Manufacturing Law (1937), the Law for Iron and Steel Manufacturing Industries (1937), the Aircraft Manufacturing Law (1938), the Machine Tool Industry Law (1938), and the Shipbuilding Manufacturing Law. Tessa Morris-Suzuki, *Technological Transformation of Japan,* 145–46. See also Kamatani, "History of Research Organization," 40–56.

40. Nearly fifty such research facilities were established from 1927 to 1939, including the Japan Synthetic Chemical Research Institute (1927), Tokyo Electric Company Research Laboratory (1928), the Department of Research at Sumitomo Electric (1930), the Muto Institute of Physical and Chemical Research (1933), Toyota Motor Research Laboratory (1936), the Chemical Research Laboratory for Natural Resources and the Precision Instrument Research Laboratory at the Tokyo Institute of Technology (1939), the Industrial Science Research Laboratory at Osaka University (1939), and the Central Aeronautical Research Institute under the Ministry of Communications, to name a few. See the more complete lists in Kamatani, "History of Research Organization," 1–79; Hiroshige, *Kagaku no shakai shi: (ue),* 115, 215; and Hiroshige Tetsu, *Kagaku no shakai shi: (shita),* 38.

41. Shimao, "Some Aspects of Japanese Science," 86.

42. JSPS awards also supported graduate research in the humanities and social sciences. For annual budget allocations, see Kagaku gijutsu seisakushi kenkyūkai, *Nihon no kagaku gijutsu seisakushi,* 34–36. See also General Headquarters, Supreme Commander for the Allied Powers, Economic and Scientific Section, "Science & Technology in Japan: Scientific and Technological Societies of Japan, Part I," October 1947, Harry C. Kelly Papers, North Carolina State University, Raleigh, North Carolina, P. P. 72.40, Bowen Dees, Report No. 10, 81–82. Some tables from this source are also reproduced in Hiroshige, *Kagaku no shakaishi: (ue) Sensō to kagaku,* 161–62. The yen/dollar rate fluctuated significantly throughout the interwar years. From about 1941, and throughout much of the war, the rate averaged about four yen to the dollar. For the annual averages, see Japan Statistical Association, Statistics Bureau, Management and Coordination Agency, *Historical Statistics of Japan,* table 10-11-a, "Foreign Exchange Rates (1874–1943)." For historical background and an informative comparison of related U.S. and Japanese government expenditures at this time, see William D. O'Neil, "Interwar U.S. and Japanese National Product and Defense Expenditure." I am indebted to Arthur Alexander and William D. O'Neil for bringing these sources to my attention.

43. General Headquarters, United States Army Forces, Pacific, Scientific and Technical Advisory Section, "Report on Scientific Intelligence Survey in Japan: September and October 1945," 1 November 1945, vols. 1–5, U.S. National Archives, College Park, MD, RG 165, Box 2056, vol. 1, 2. [Hereafter cited as GHQ, "Scientific Intelligence Survey."]

44. Hiroshige Tetsu, "Social Conditions for Prewar Japanese Research."

45. Kamatani, "History of Research Organization," 34.

46. Ibid., 38–39. Thomas A. Bisson, *Japan's War Economy,* 3–11, 22.

47. Michael A. Barnhart, *Japan Prepares for Total War,* 22–23.

48. Ibid., 23–25.

49. Leonard Humphreys, *Way of the Heavenly Sword,* 43–46, 79–89.

50. Ibid., 89–101.

51. Ibid., 99–107.

52. Alan S. Milward, *War, Economy and Society*, 175.

53. On factionalism in the army, see James B. Crowley, *Japan's Quest for Autonomy*, passim; and James B. Crowley, "Japanese Army Factionalism in the Early 1930s."

54. On the impact of the dispute over the London Naval Treaty, see especially Crowley, *Japan's Quest for Autonomy*, 35–81.

55. Humphreys, *Way of the Heavenly Sword*, 102.

56. On the role of the SMR, see Ramon H. Myers, "Japanese Imperialism in Manchuria." Concerning the impact of Japanese imperialism and Japan's military and political hegemony on the economic development of the region, see the additional relevant essays in Peter Duus, Ramon H. Myers, and Mark R. Peattie, *Japanese Informal Empire*, as well as Louise Young, *Japan's Total Empire*, passim.

57. For a concise but informative essay on the history of the Kwantung Army, see Alvin D. Coox, "Kwantung Army Dimension."

58. Young, *Japan's Total Empire*, 30–31, 38–40, 140–49. Crowley, *Japan's Quest for Autonomy*, 110–21.

59. The latter was created ostensibly to facilitate collaborative research between Chinese and Japanese scientists, but it remained a Japanese dominated facility. See Morris F. Low, "Architecture of Japanese Colonial Science."

60. Kawamura, "Tairiku kagakuin setsuritsu," 132–37.

61. On the decline of political party power and the rise of military influence in the Japanese government during the 1930s, see especially Gordon Mark Berger, *Parties out of Power*, 86–93. The Cabinet Research Bureau is alternately called the Cabinet Investigative Bureau. See Barnhart, *Japan Prepares for Total War*, 67–75.

62. Barnhart, *Japan Prepares for Total War*, 74–75. Crowley, *Japan's Quest for Autonomy*, 256–73.

63. Barnhart, *Japan Prepares for Total War*, 42–47.

64. More specifically, it was the Tientsin Garrison of the Japanese North China Army against the Chinese 29th Army under Sung Che-yuan. See Lincoln Li, *Japanese Army in North China*, 3–4, 41–43.

65. Barnhart, *Japan Prepares for Total War*, 75–76, 85–90.

66. As quoted from the translated text in Jerome B. Cohen, *Japan's Economy*, 10.

67. "Statutes Indicating Revision in the Organization and Functions of the Planning Office and the Planning Board, 1937," as reprinted in Bisson, *Japan's War Economy*, 208–11. On the political fallout resulting from the formation of the agency and the subsequent decline of Ishiwara's influence, see Barnhart, *Japan Prepares for Total War*, 93–100; and Berger, *Parties out of Power*, 88, 133–34, 149. (Berger refers to the *Kikaku-in* as the "Cabinet Planning Board.") Much of the following account is based on Nippon Kagakushi Gakkai, "Senji taisei to kagaku dōin," vol. 4, *Tsūshi*, 315. [Hereafter cited as *NKGT*.]

68. *NKGT*, 315.

69. For a discussion of the significance of the terminology and the traditional separation of "science" (*kagaku*) from "technology" (*gijutsu*), see Hiromi Mizuno, "Science, Ideology, Empire." See especially chap. 4, "A New Order for Science-Technology," 200–253.

70. *NKGT*, 315–16.

71. The first of these conflicts began in August 1938 with forces of the Kwantung Army confronting Soviet troops at the northeast border of Manchuria and the Soviet

Union. The government in Tokyo prevented further escalation, but nearly a year later, in May 1939, the Japanese Kwantung Army again engaged Soviet forces in a border dispute, this time on the northwestern border of Manchuria and Mongolia at Khalkin-Gol. This little-known conflict, which grew into a full-scale war, is often called the Nomonhan Incident more broadly. The conclusion of the German-Soviet Nonaggression pact, coupled with great losses suffered by the Kwantung Army, brought about a diplomatic resolution and the conflict ended on 15 September 1939. On the Nomonhan Incident, see especially Alvin D. Coox, *Nomonhan*.

72. *NKGT*, 316. Kamatani appears to be in error on this date, stating that the Science Section was newly established in the Cabinet Planning Board (Agency) in October 1937. At this time, however, within the Planning Agency, science and technology policy was handled mainly by the Science Office operating under the Industrial Bureau, one of the six main departments of the Planning Agency. Kamatani, "History of Research Organization," 48. For clarification, see also Gijutsuin kōetsu, Kagakudōin kyōkai hensan, *Kagaku gijutsu nenkan*, 1.

73. GHQ, "Scientific Intelligence Survey," vol. 3, appendix 8-A-1.

74. The Science Mobilization Association was also intended to help facilitate coordination of research between civilian and military institutions by forming joint projects. Toward that end, in October 1941 it conducted a national survey of individual scientists and their research interests in the military, public, private, and academic sectors, and grouped them accordingly into several thousands of "Neighborhood Research Associations," which were to be managed under the aegis of the Science Mobilization Association. What impact these Neighborhood Research Associations may have had on the war effort in general remains uncertain, but they appear not to have contributed to advanced weapons research in any apparent or significant way. *NKGT*, 315, 320. Hiroshige, "Role of Government," 334.

75. *NKGT*, 316.

76. *NKGT*, 316. See also James R. Bartholomew, "Science in Twentieth Century Japan." On the resignation of Araki, see Crowley, *Japan's Quest for Autonomy*, 201–6.

77. Hiroshige, "Role of the Government," 330–35. Kamatani, "History of Research Organization," 48–49. See also GHQ, "Scientific Intelligence Survey," vol. 3, appendix 8-A-1.

78. GHQ, "Scientific Intelligence Survey," vol. 3, appendix 8-A-1.

79. Morris-Suzuki, *Technological Transformation of Japan*, 147–49. For more on the history of this movement, see Oyodo Shōichi, *Miyamoto Takenosuke to kagaku gijutsu gyōsei*, 375–91.

80. Erich Pauer, "Japan's Technical Mobilization."

81. Sawai Minoru, "Kagaku gijutsu shintaisei."

82. *NKGT*, 317–19.

83. Most of the revisions came from the Planning Agency. For a listing of the drafts and amendments, see Sawai, "Kagaku gijutsu shintaisei," 368. Copies of the original documents can be found in *Minobe Yōji Monjo*. [Hereafter cited as "Minobe Yōji Files."] On the "New Order of Science and Technology," see especially registration nos. 6588, 6590, 6592, 6597, 6599, 6602, 6604, 6606, 6608, 6609, 6610, 6589, 6591, 6593, and 6188.

84. *NKGT*, 319.

85. *NKGT*, 320–21, 346–47. Kagaku gijutsu seisakushi kenkyūkai, *Nihon no kagaku gijutsu seisakushi*, 39.

86. *NKGT,* 321.

87. The response to the Technology Agency proposal may be considered typical of Japan's polycratic bureaucracy and closely paralleled the experience of the formation of the Imperial Rule Assistance Association (*Taisei yokusankai*), a government body established in 1940 to concentrate political power under a national unified, mass-based party. Intended as a political umbrella organization to facilitate implementation of the broader New Order agenda in Japan, the association instead remained fractured among existing party lines as interest groups vied for control at the national, regional, and local levels. The association thus became little more than a national organization for controlling resources and morale. For more on the Imperial Rule Assistance Association, see especially Berger, *Parties out of Power,* 315–40.

88. Major General Suzuki Teiichi assumed the presidency of the Planning Agency, and Admiral Toyoda Teijirō became Minister of Commerce and Industry. The Planning Agency became heavily staffed with army officers thereafter. See Barnhart, *Japan Prepares for Total War,* 172–73, 200–201, 240.

89. The Planning Agency's Science Division study surveyed science and technology related policies and institutions with a particular emphasis on Germany, but including also the United States, Great Britain, and Italy. See "Kagaku gijutsu seisaku ni kan suru chōsa (1)" ["Survey Concerning Science and Technology Policy (1)"], May 1941, Minobe Yōji Files, 6541, 6549.

90. GHQ, "Scientific Intelligence Survey," vol. 3, appendix 8-A-2. Kagaku gijutsu seisakushi kenkyūkai, *Nihon no kagaku gijutsu seisakushi,* 39.

91. GHQ, "Scientific Intelligence Survey," vol. 3, appendix 8-A-3. Kamatani, "History of Research Organization," 58. A summary of the 27 May 1941 proclamation can be found in "Kagaku gijutsu shintaisei kakuritsu kōyō jisshi ni kan suru ikensho" [Statement Concerning the Administration of the Outline of the Establishment of a New Order of Science and Technology], Minobe Yōji Files, 6542.

92. Yamazaki, "Mobilization of Science and Technology," 167–81.

93. According to Hiroshige, the Technology Agency's annual budget for research support was ¥1.3 million in 1942, and just over ¥1 million in 1943, with figures for 1944 and 1945 uncertain. The "Scientific Intelligence Survey" gives a much higher figure for the agency's annual budget—about ¥20 million—which probably includes the budget for all divisions of the agency, such as the Central Aeronautical Research Institute, which was transferred from the Ministry of Communications in 1942. (Hiroshige lists these figures separately.) All research proposals submitted to the Technology Agency for funding, regardless of their office or institution of origin, were to be considered by a designated committee within the agency itself. If approved, grants were awarded, ranging in amount from a few hundred yen to several hundred thousand yen. Such grants were the sole source of funding for many research projects. See Hiroshige, *Kagaku no shakai shi: (shita),* 67. GHQ, "Scientific Intelligence Survey," vol. 3, appendix 8-B-2. Kamatani, "History of Research Organization," 42, 56. Oyodo, *Miyamoto Takenosuke,* 212, 448–49.

94. GHQ, "Scientific Intelligence Survey," vol. 3, appendix 8-A-3.

95. *NKGT,* 321–22. Yamazaki, "Mobilization of Science and Technology," 170–79. A survey of Technology Agency approved research projects bears out the dominance of army aeronautics, with 64 of the 158 subjects considered during the first session concerning aviation. See Ichikawa Hiroshi, "Empirical Study." Original documents can be found in the files of Count Inoue Tadashirō, who served as president

of the Technology Agency from January 1942 to December 1944. See Kokugakuin daigaku toshokan, *Inoue Tadashirō Monjo*.

96. *NKGT*, 321–22.

97. Nihon kaigun kōkūshi hensan iinkai, *Nihon kaigun kōkūshi*, 3:112–14. [Hereafter abbreviated as *NKKS*.]

98. "Riku-Kaigun gijutsu iinkai no ichibu" [The Role of the Army-Navy Technology Committee], Bōeichō kenkyūjo toshokan, Meguro-ku, Tokyo, Japan, Kaigun 22, Gijutsu Kankei—Gijutsu, Zenpan 6, Zenpan 2.

99. These committees also had been preceded by the much more tentative "Army-Navy Aeronautics Cooperation Committee" (Riku-Kaigun kōkū kyōtei iinkai), which was formed in 1921 for the purpose of facilitating interservice consultation on issues concerning the development of the military aviation industry. It lasted for only two years. *NKKS*, 3:104–12. See also Bōeichō bōei kenshūjo senshibu, *Rikugun kōkū heiki no kaihatsu, seisan, hokyū*, 427–29.

100. These measures also included proposals to support more basic research, whereas, at this point in the war, one might have anticipated a preponderance of calls for increased funding of applied research, which might arguably have been more expedient in accelerating the development of some types of military technology. Hiroshige, *Kagaku no shakaishi (shita)*, 50–55. See also Kamatani, "History of Research Organization," 57–58.

101. Kamatani, "History of Research Organization," 58.

102. Presumably, the Army-Navy Aeronautics Committee was also dissolved at this time. See *NKKS*, 3:105, 112. Bōeichō Bōei Kenshūjo Senshibu, *Rikugun kōkū heiki*, 427.

103. Bōeichō Bōei Kenshūjo Senshibu, *Rikugun kōkū heiki*, 427–29, 457.

104. Kawamura Yutaka, "Kyū-Nihon kaigun no dempa heiki kaihatsu katei o jirei toshita dai-niji taisenki Nihon no kagaku gijutsu dōin ni kan suru bunseki," 48–49. See also Bōeichō Bōei Kenshūjo Senshibu, *Rikugun kōkū heiki*, 457. It may also be called the Army-Navy Technology *Application* Committee. See Yamazaki, "Mobilization of Science and Technology," 177–78.

105. GHQ, "Scientific Intelligence Survey," vol. 2, appendix 8-A-1 and 8-A-3.

106. Yagi later resigned from the committee to attend to his duties as director of the Technology Agency. Longacre et al., Interview with Dr. H. Yagi, 17 October 1945, GHQ, "Scientific Intelligence Survey," vol. 3, appendix 3-b-2.

107. Major H. K. Calvert to Major F. J. Smith, "Japanese Militarists Want Miracle Weapon," 29 May 1945, U.S. National Archives, College Park, MD, RG 77, Entry 22, Box 173, Folder 44.70: "Japan, Misc."

108. Ibid.

109. Congleton, O'Keefe, and Mastick interview with General Tada, 14 September 1945, "Atomic Bomb Mission, Japan: Final Report, Scientific and Mineralogical Investigation," U.S. National Archives, College Park, MD, RG 77, Entry 22, Box 172.

110. S. Watanabe, "How Japan Has Lost a Scientific War," September 1945, U.S. National Archives, College Park, MD, RG 38, Box 111, File: "Historical Information."

111. Ibid.

112. GHQ, "Scientific Intelligence Survey," 1:53.

113. Ibid. See also Nakagawa, *Kaigun gijutsu kenkyūjo*, 32–33.

114. GHQ, "Scientific Intelligence Survey," 1:52.

115. Ibid., 1:51.

116. Berger attributes the rise of sectionalism, in part, to the waning influence of the political parties in the early 1930s. See Berger, *Parties out of Power*, 80.
117. GHQ, "Scientific Intelligence Survey," vol. 3, appendix 8-B-2.
118. GHQ, "Scientific Intelligence Survey," 1:17–18.
119. Ibid.
120. GHQ, "Scientific Intelligence Survey," vol. 3, appendix 8-B-3.
121. Kamatani, "History of Research Organization," 56–57.
122. According to one account, there was considerable tension between the Japan National Research Council, under the Ministry of Education, and the Cabinet's Technology Agency. See Daily Report, Ensign B. J. O'Keefe, 12 September 1945, "Atomic Bomb Mission, Japan: Final Report, Scientific and Mineralogical Investigation," U.S. National Archives, College Park, MD, RG 77, Entry 22, Box 172.
123. Moreland interview with Dr. Hantarō Nagaoka, 16 October 1945, "Scientific Intelligence Survey," vol. 3, appendix 25-1, 25-3.
124. Bartholomew, "Science in Twentieth Century Japan," 889.
125. Baxter, *Scientists Against Time*, 22.
126. Moreland interview with Dr. Hantarō Nagaoka, 16 October 1945, GHQ, "Scientific Intelligence Survey," vol. 3, appendix 25-1, 25-3.
127. GHQ, "Scientific Intelligence Survey," vol. 3, appendix 8-A-1.
128. GHQ, "Scientific Intelligence Survey," 1:16.
129. Ibid., 51.
130. Karl T. Compton interview with Yagi Hidetsugu, 11 September 1945, GHQ, "Scientific Intelligence Survey," vol. 3, appendix 3-A-1.
131. GHQ, "Scientific Intelligence Survey," 1:51.
132. Mitsuo Taketani, "Methodological Approaches in the Development of the Meson Theory."
133. GHQ, "Scientific Intelligence Survey," 1:52.
134. Ibid., 16–18.
135. S. Watanabe, "How Japan Has Lost a Scientific War," September 1945, U.S. National Archives, Washington, DC, RG 38, Box 111, File: "Historical Information." See also Sakata Shōichi, "Kenkyū to sōshiki." Kamatani, "History of Research Organization," 68. Hiroshige, "Role of the Government," 334–35. For a deeper historical analysis of the alleged impact of "feudalistic" traditions on the sciences in Japan, see especially James R. Bartholomew, " 'Feudalistic' Legacy of Japanese Science"; and James R. Bartholomew, "Japanese Culture and the Problem of Modern Science."
136. GHQ, "Scientific Intelligence Survey," 1:14.
137. GHQ, "Scientific Intelligence Survey," vol. 3, appendix 8-A-1 to 8-A-3.
138. GHQ, "Scientific Intelligence Survey," 1:7–8, 11.

CHAPTER 2. NUCLEAR ENERGY AND THE ATOMIC BOMB

1. Although not specifically identified by Groves, he was most likely referring to two Japanese physicists, Sagane Ryōkichi and Yasaki Tameichi, who went to Berkeley in 1935 to study cyclotron design and construction under Ernest O. Lawrence. See Leslie R. Groves, *Now It Can Be Told*, 187. See also J. L. Heilbron and Robert W. Seidel, *Lawrence and His Laboratory*, 317–20.
2. G-2 to Economic and Scientific Section, 13 May 1946, "Papers on 'Budget

for Atomic Nuclear Research,'" U.S. National Archives, College Park, MD, RG 331, Entry 224, Box 1, Folder: "Research, Nuclear, Japan."

3. Lawrence Badash, Elizabeth Hodes, and Adolph Tiddens, "Nuclear Fission," 196–231.

4. Ibid, 197.

5. Richard Rhodes, *Making of the Atomic Bomb*, 209–16. Richard G. Hewlett and Oscar E. Anderson Jr., *New World*, 12.

6. Seisan gijutsu kyōkai [Production Technology Committee], *Kyū-kaigun gijutsu shiryō, Dai 1-hen*, (3) *Dai 5-shō*, Bōeichō kenkyūjo toshokan, Meguro-ku, Tokyo, Japan, Kaigun 6, Zenpan 5, 303–22.

7. Rhodes, *Making of the Atomic Bomb*, 250–64.

8. Rhodes, *Making of the Atomic Bomb*, 250–71. Hewlett and Anderson, *New World*, 12–13.

9. Szilard filed several patent applications in Britain regarding the neutron chain reaction, the production of radioactive materials, and the chemical separation of radioactive elements from nonradioactive isotopes. See Badash et al., "Nuclear Fission," 208–9. On the life and career of Leo Szilard, see William Lanouette with Bela Szilard, *Genius in the Shadows*.

10. On the life and career of Enrico Fermi, see Laura Fermi, *Atoms in the Family*.

11. Lanouette, *Genius in the Shadows*, 175–88. Hewlett and Anderson, *New World*, 13–15.

12. George Pegram, a physicist and dean of the graduate faculties at Columbia University, arranged the meeting with Fermi and the navy representatives. The navy's Bureau of Engineering presented the money to the Carnegie Institution, which refused the funding "for reasons of internal policy," but agreed to do the research nonetheless. See Hewlett and Anderson, *New World*, 15; Badash et al., "Nuclear Fission," 213; and Rhodes, *Making of the Atomic Bomb*, 292–96.

13. Szilard called for self-censorship concerning fission research within the international scientific community and tried to convince the French team to delay publishing their results. See Spencer Weart, *Scientists in Power*, 75–92.

14. Rhodes, *Making of the Atomic Bomb*, 296; David Irving, *Virus House*, 38–40. For a more current account of the history of nuclear fission research in Nazi Germany, see Mark Walker, *German National Socialism*, 17–19.

15. Which of these responses is more representative of "German bureaucratic efficiency" is a matter of debate among historians. Concerning the government's response to the scientists, Badash et al. state that the Reich Ministry of Education reacted "with famed German efficiency, rather than bureaucratic bumbling." David Irving, however, refers to the handling of the Harteck/Diebner letter as an example of German bureaucratic ineptitude. Walker provides many examples to support both views. See Badash et al., "Nuclear Fission," 215. David Irving, *Virus House*, 32–34. Walker, *German National Socialism*, 17–21. For a comparative discussion of the influence of political ideology on nuclear weapons research, see Mark Walker, "Comparative History of Nuclear Weapons."

16. Rhodes, *Making of the Atomic Bomb*, 296.

17. Paul R. Josephson, "Early Years of Soviet Nuclear Physics." On nuclear research in the Soviet Union, see especially David Holloway, *Stalin and the Bomb*, 49–56.

18. Sachs insisted that the letter also bear Einstein's signature. Szilard promptly complied and returned with a second draft as requested. Rhodes, *Making of the Atomic*

Bomb, 303–9. Badash et al., "Nuclear Fission," 218–20. Hewlett and Anderson, *New World*, 15–17.

19. Irving, *Virus House*, 39.
20. Badash et al., "Nuclear Fission," 215–16.
21. Nippon Kagakushi Gakkai, "Butsurigaku to senji kenkyū," vol. 13, *Butsuri Kagaku*, [Hereafter cited as *NKGT*.]
22. Vincent C. Jones, *Manhattan*, 14–15, 21–22.
23. Hewlett and Anderson, *New World*, 22–23. Rhodes, *Making of the Atomic Bomb*, 282–88.
24. Rhodes, *Making of the Atomic Bomb*, 329–31, 340–41. Concerning nuclear research in England, see Margaret Gowing, *Britain and Atomic Energy*, 389–93.
25. Irvin Stewart, *Organizing Scientific Research for War*, 7–9. Hewlett and Anderson, *New World*, 24–26. On the Tizard Mission, see David Zimmerman, *Top Secret Exchange*.
26. Walker, *German National Socialism*, 25–41.
27. In June 1940, the German army had also confiscated the cyclotron at the Joliot-Curie laboratory in Paris. Though the apparatus was not completely assembled at the time, it soon would be. See Weart, *Scientists in Power*, 153–62; and Kristie Macrakis, *Surviving the Swastika*, 169–75.
28. That Japanese scientists considered themselves to be in a nuclear arms race is an unsubstantiated premise of the book, Robert K. Wilcox, *Japan's Secret War*.
29. Yomiuri Shimbunsha, "Nihon no genbaku." [Hereafter cited as *SSNT*.] Yamashita Nobuo, "Ma ni awanakatta Nihon no genbaku."
30. On the early history of modern physics in Japan, see Koizumi Kenkichirō, "Emergence of Japan's First Physicists"; and Kim Dong-Won, "Emergence of Theoretical Physics."
31. Account of Arakatsu Bunsaku, *SSNT*, 221–25.
32. Although Arakatsu had conducted most of the research, the announcement was made under Hagiwara's name in the 6 October 1939 edition of the *Review of Physical Chemistry of Japan*. See Arakatsu, *SSNT*, 226.
33. Account of Suzuki Tatsusaburō, *SSNT*, 78–79. See also Tsuneishi Keiichi, "Riken ni okeru uran bunri no kokoromi." Sources do not wholly agree on the exact origin or timing of the initiation of the army project. Suzuki states that Yasuda made the request shortly after he arrived at his post at the Army Aeronautics Department in April 1940. In another account, Yasuda claims to have first discussed nuclear research with Riken physicist Nishina Yoshio and a colleague during a chance meeting on a train in Tokyo in late June 1940. According to Yasuda, on this occasion, Nishina said he could begin experimental research toward development of a nuclear weapon, which would suggest the impetus came not from the military, but from a scientist. See Yasuda Takeo, "Nihon ni okeru genshibakudan seizō ni kansuru kenkyū no kaiko." See also Yamazaki Masakatsu, "Dainiji sekai taisenji no Nihon no genbaku kaihatsu."
34. Suzuki, *SSNT*, 78. For background on Japan's wartime nuclear weapons research in English, see the account in The Pacific War Research Society, *The Day Man Lost*, passim. [Hereafter cited as PWRS.] Much of this version is based on the accounts given in *SSNT*. See also John W. Dower, " 'NI' and 'F' "; and Morris F. Low, "Japan's Secret War?" For a direct comparison of the German and Japanese nuclear weapons projects, see Walter E. Grunden, Mark Walker, and Yamazaki Masakatsu, "Nuclear Weapons and Nuclear Energy in Wartime Germany and Japan."

35. The companies included Mitsubishi, Nakajima, and Japan Jyūyū Metals and Special Steel. Suzuki, *SSNT,* 78–79.

36. *SSNT,* 82; and *NKGT,* 442.

37. *SSNT,* 87–88. The Atomic Nucleus Research Project, supported by the Japan Society for the Promotion of Science, focused on basic research, but was not directly involved in nuclear weapons research for the military. See "Brief History of (Atomic) Research During the War," U.S. National Archives, College Park, MD, RG 331, Box 7416, Folder: "Research, Wartime." On the life and career of Nishina Yoshio and background on the history of his research laboratory at the Riken, see Tamaki Hidehiko and Ezawa Hiroshi, *Nishina Yoshio.*

38. PWRS, *The Day Man Lost,* 30; Dower, "'NI' and 'F,'" 74. This version of events would seem to contradict Yasuda's account. It is possible Nishina only suggested such research could be undertaken, but then was less sanguine when the responsibility for the work actually fell to him.

39. Rhodes, *Making of the Atomic Bomb,* 375.

40. The Clusius tube was actually codeveloped by Klaus Clusius and Gerhard Dickel and is more accurately known as the Clusius-Dickel tube. Walker, *German National Socialism,* 29–31.

41. Hewlett and Anderson, *New World,* 29–32.

42. Arnold Kramish, *Atomic Energy in the Soviet Union,* 48–62; Holloway, *Stalin and the Bomb,* 72–79.

43. Hewlett and Anderson, *New World,* 41.

44. Edwin McMillan and Philip Abelson discovered plutonium in 1940. Its potential use as a fuel in nuclear weapons was yet to be conceived. Hewlett and Anderson, *New World,* 33–34.

45. Rhodes, *Making of the Atomic Bomb,* 424–28. Hewlett and Anderson, *New World,* 81–83.

46. Walker, *German National Socialism,* 84–85; Irving, *Virus House,* 54, 73–79, 105–11.

47. Albert Speer, *Inside the Third Reich,* 226–29. The subject of Hitler's attitude concerning physics and wartime nuclear fission research is explored in greater detail in Mark Walker, *Nazi Science.*

48. *SSNT,* 178–79. Fukui et al., *Kimitsu heiki no zembō,* 160–61.

49. Nakagawa Yasuzō, *Japanese Radar,* 6–8, 21–22. Nakajima Shigeru, "General Outline of Japanese Radar," 269–94. *SSNT,* 178.

50. *SSNT,* 178–79.

51. *SSNT,* 177–79. Fukui et al., *Kimitsu heiki no zembō,* 160–61.

52. See Itō's account in Fukui et al., *Kimitsu heiki no zembō,* 161–65. Original documents can be found in Kakubutsuri ōyō kenkyū iinkai, *Kyū-Nihon kaigun gijutsu kenkyūjo denki kenkyūbu.* [Hereafter cited as *Tōshin Shiryō.*]

53. According to Nakajima Shigeru, younger brother of Itō Yōji, Yamamoto personally asked Itō to develop a new weapon in April 1941. At the time of this alleged meeting, however, Itō still would have been in Germany. In this account, Nakajima is also in error on the date Itō left for Germany, stating January 1940 rather than 1941. See William Aspray, interview with Nakajima Shigeru, 26 May 1994, Center for the History of Electrical Engineering, IEEE, available at http://www.ieee.org/history-center, "Oral Histories: Japanese Interviews." For clarification regarding Yamamoto's order

for new weapons and the formation of the "Physics Committee," refer to the account based on the memoirs of Mizuma Masaichirō as found in Kawamura Yutaka, "Kyū-Nihon kaigun no dempa heiki kaihatsu katei o jirei toshita dai-niji taisenki Nihon no kagaku gijutsu dōin ni kan suru bunseki," 93 (see especially footnotes 68 and 69).

54. Minutes from the committee meetings can be found in *Tōshin Shiryō*. Discussions from the first meeting are partially reproduced in Fukui et al., *Kimitsu heiki no zembō*, 161–65. See also *SSNT*, 178–79. Some published accounts concerning the formation of this committee erroneously give the designation for this program as "A-Research" or "Project A," which actually entailed research on radar and the death ray. Most of these versions appear to be based on the recollections of Asada Tsunesaburō, who served as a project member, and who began to give interviews on the subject in the 1960s and 1970s. See specifically Seisan gijutsu kyōkai, *Kyū-kaigun gijutsu shiryō, Dai 1-hen*, (3) *Dai 5-shō*, Bōeichō kenkyūjo toshokan, Meguro-ku, Tokyo, Japan, Kaigun 6, Zenpan 5, 303–22; and Thomas M. Coffey, *Imperial Tragedy*, 246–47.

55. This account has Nishina making the request to Major General Kawashima Toranosuke, who did not become a liaison to the Riken until spring 1943. But the request was certainly made while the navy's Physics Committee was still active. See the reference in *SSNT*, 180.

56. As director, Nishina proposed changing the name to the Physics Committee, which was officially adopted in late June 1942. Nishina Yoshio to Itō Yōji, 25 June 1942, *Tōshin Shiryō*, 12:A12. For the most current and accurate account of these events and a discussion of the original documents, see Kawamura Yutaka and Yamazaki Masakatsu, "Butsuri kondankai."

57. *SSNT*, 180; and *NKGT*, 442.

58. *SSNT*, 180–81.

59. As quoted in Coffey, *Imperial Tragedy*, 244. To some degree, it might be argued that the initiation of nuclear weapons research in Japan was prompted by concerns over research activities in the United States—just as the fear of German atomic bomb research had stimulated the formation of the Manhattan Project. But it would be overstating the case to argue that Japanese scientists felt they were in an actual "race" with the United States to develop nuclear weapons.

60. Fukui et al., *Kimitsu heiki no zembō*, 308.

61. Coffey, *Imperial Tragedy*, 245.

62. Coffey alleges that Nishina also mentioned that the army had in its possession some 1,760 pounds (800 kilograms) of uranium oxide from South Africa in Shanghai, China, but that he could not speak to its availability. Coffey, *Imperial Tragedy*, 245. *SSNT*, 180–81.

63. *SSNT*, 180–81.

64. Kawamura and Yamazaki, "Butsuri Kondankai," 164–65. Based on minutes of the Physics Committee, 8 August 1942, *Tōshin Shiryō*, 12:A12.

65. PWRS, *The Day Man Lost*, 29–30.

66. Accounts of Iso Megumu and Chitō Michizō, *SSNT*, 182–83.

67. The exact date of their meeting with Arakatsu is uncertain. U.S. intelligence documents state that the meeting took place in June 1942, whereas Iso gives the date as October 1942, which seems unlikely given the chronology of events that followed. Dates also vary according to the recollections of the scientists interviewed in *SSNT*. See the accounts of Iso Megumu and Chitō Michizō in *SSNT*, 182–83. See also Major

Russell A. Fisher, "Interview with Tetsugo [*sic* Tetsuzō] Kitagawa," 8 March 1946, U.S. National Archives, College Park, MD, RG 331, Entry 224, Box 2, Folder 15: "Import: Presurrender Uranium, Thorium, Monazite, Amang."

68. "Brief Description on the Policy to Find out the Possibility of Utilizing Atomic Energy Adopted by the then Japanese Military Authorities in War Time: Report No. 3 On the Part of the Then Japanese Navy," U.S. National Archives, College Park, MD, RG 331, Box 7416, File: "Research, Wartime."

69. Mitsui stayed on as Arakatsu's liaison to the Navy Department of Ships, while Iso was transferred to the Kure Naval Arsenal in early in 1943. Commander Kitagawa Tetsuzō replaced Iso later in the year. Account of Iso Megumu, *SSNT*, 183. Second Lt. C. H. Nagano, "Interview with R. Adm. Sasagawa (Tech.)," 12 March 1946, U.S. National Archives, College Park, MD, RG 331, Entry 224, Box 2, Folder 15: "Import: Presurrender Uranium, Thorium, Monazite, Amang." See also Major Russell A. Fisher, "Inspection of Activities at Kyoto Imperial University," 28 February 1946, U.S. National Archives, College Park, MD, RG 331, Entry 224, Box 1, Folder: "Research, Nuclear, Japan."

70. PWRS, *The Day Man Lost*, 35.

71. *NKGT*, 471–74.

72. Fukui et al., *Kimitsu heiki no zembō*, 308. *SSNT*, 177–80.

73. *SSNT*, 180–81. Dower, "'NI' and 'F,'" 75.

74. On the Heisenberg controversy, see Walker, *Nazi Science*, passim; Paul Lawrence Rose, *Heisenberg and the Nazi Atomic Bomb Project*; and David Cassidy, *Uncertainty*.

75. The "F" probably stood for "fission," although there are also references to "fluoride," as in uranium hexafluoride. "Gō" is an ordinal suffix. See Arakatsu, *SSNT*, 221.

76. The officer is not identified. Account of Kimura Kiichi, *SSNT*, 190.

77. The navy supplied pure iron for the core of the Kyoto cyclotron sometime in 1943. See Second Lt. George Yamashiro, "Interview with Commander T. Kitagawa," 16 March 1946, U.S. National Archives, College Park, MD, RG 331, Entry 224, Box 2, Folder 15: "Import: Presurrender Uranium, Thorium, Monazite, Amang." See also "Brief Description on the Policy to find out Possibility of Utilizing Atomic Energy adopted by the then Japanese Military Authorities in the War Time: Report No 4—Descriptions made by the concerned, ex-officer," U.S. National Archives, College Park, MD, RG 331, Box 7416, File: "Research, Wartime."

78. Arakatsu, *SSNT*, 219.

79. *NKGT*, 468.

80. *NKGT*, 468. Kimura, *SSNT*, 191.

81. Arakatsu does not recall the date, and he does not elaborate on the extent of the information that was shared during this meeting. Arakatsu, *SSNT*, 219.

82. Kimura, *SSNT*, 193.

83. The Pacific War Research Society erroneously gives the number as 100,000 revolutions "a second." See PWRS, *The Day Man Lost*, 183. See also Second Lt. George Yamashiro, "Interview with Commander T. Kitagawa," 16 March 1946, U.S. National Archives, College Park, MD, RG 331, Entry 224, Box 2, Folder 15: "Import: Presurrender Uranium, Thorium, Monazite, Amang."

84. Kimura, *SSNT*, 195.

85. Spencer Weart, "Secrecy, Simultaneous Discovery." For a technical discussion

of Arakatsu's research on criticality, see Fukai Yūzo, "Kyū-Kaigun itaku 'F-kenkyū' ni okeru rinkai keisanhō no kaihatsu." See also Yamazaki Masakatsu, "Kyū-Nihon kaigun 'F-kenkyū' shiryō."

86. See "Interviews with Professors H. Yukawa and B. Arakatsu," 15 September 1945, in Major Robert R. Furman, "Field Progress Report No. 4—Group 1," 28 September 1945, from *Atomic Bomb Mission, Japan: Final Report, Scientific and Mineralogical Investigation*, U.S. National Archives, College Park, MD, RG 77, Entry 22, Box 172. [Hereafter cited as Furman Report.]

87. S. Nomura, "Brief Description of Policy to Find Out Possibility of Utilizing Atomic Energy," U.S. National Archives, College Park, MD, RG 331, Box 7416, File: "Research, Wartime."

88. No date is given. *NKGT*, 469.

89. *SSNT*, 196–200. Dower, "'NI' and 'F,'" 81.

90. Among those present at the meeting were the scientists, Arakatsu, Yukawa, Kobayashi, and Sasaki, from Kyoto Imperial University. Representatives from the Navy Department of Ships included Rear-Admiral Nitta Shigeharu, Captain Mitsui Matao, and Lieutenant Commander Kitagawa Tetsuzō. Account of Nitta Shigeharu, *SSNT*, 204–5.

91. "Brief Description of the Policy to Find Out Possibility of Utilizing Atomic Energy Adopted by the then Japanese Military Authorities in the War Time: Report No. 4—Descriptions made by the concerned, ex-officer," U.S. National Archives, College Park, MD, RG 331, Box 7416, File: "Research, Wartime."

92. Nishina's research at the Riken was to proceed in coordination with the Eighth Army Technical Institute. Yamashita, "Ma ni awanakatta Nihon no genbaku," 164. See also Nihon heiki kōgyōkai, *Rikusen heiki sōkan*, 693–98. For a concise overview of the army project and Nishina's role in it, see the series of articles by Tomari Jiro, "Genbaku kaihatsu" [Atomic Bomb Development], parts 1–6, *Asahi Shimbun*, 21 August 1995 through 2 October 1995. I am indebted to the author for sharing these articles.

93. "Brief Description of the Policy to Find out Possibility of Utilizing Atomic Energy Adopted by the then Japanese Military Authorities in the War Time: Report No. 4—Descriptions made by the concerned, ex-officer," U.S. National Archives, College Park, MD, RG 331, Box 7416, File: "Research, Wartime." See also Account of Koyama Kenji, *SSNT*, 85–86.

94. Tsuneishi, "Riken ni okeru uran bunri no kokoromi," 821–22. Account of Kigoshi Kunihiko, *SSNT*, 102.

95. Takeuchi had also worked with Yukawa Hideki and was the first to photograph his meson particle by using a Wilson cloud chamber. *SSNT*, 87.

96. Memoir of Takeuchi Masa, *NKGT*, 444–45. Account of Takeuchi Masa, *SSNT*, 87, 92–93. See also his recollections in Takeuchi Masa, "Uran bakudan kenkyū mukashibanashi."

97. Takeuchi, *NKGT*, 444.

98. Takeuchi, *NKGT*, 444. Takeuchi, *SSNT*, 93.

99. The Furman Report refers to an "Amaki Toshio," but this is likely a mistaken rendering of Tamaki Hidehiko. See Philip Morrison interview with Nishina Yoshio, "Riken Conversations," 10 September 1945, Furman Report. Like Arakatsu, Tamaki's work on the subject of critical mass was based on the work of Francis Perrin. For a technical analysis of Tamaki's calculations, see Yamazaki Masakatsu, "Riken no 'Uranium bakudan' kōsō."

100. Philip Morrison interview with Nishina Yoshio, "Riken Conversations," 10 September 1945, Furman Report.

101. Yamazaki, "Riken no 'Uranium bakudan' kōsō," 91–94.

102. For a technical discussion of Takeuchi's work on criticality during wartime, see Fukai Yūzo, "Kyū-gun itaku 'Ni-Go kenkyū' ni okeru rinkai keisan."

103. Takeuchi, *SSNT*, 94–97. The Pacific War Research Society mistakenly refers to the Clusius tube as an atomic reactor, stating, "Japan still did not possess an atomic reactor, but plans for the reactor were by now at least on paper." This is a seriously misleading error, as Nishina only briefly considered constructing a nuclear reactor and eventually abandoned the idea. For the source of the error, see PWRS, *The Day Man Lost*, 33.

104. Takeuchi, *NKGT*, 444.

105. Takeuchi, *SSNT*, 94–95.

106. Tsuneishi, "Riken ni okeru uran bunri no kokoromi," 823. *NKGT*, 447. Dower, "'NI' and 'F,'" 86.

107. Account of Kawashima Toranosuke, *SSNT*, 84–85, 145.

108. Accounts of Suzuki and Kawashima, *SSNT*, 83–85, 145.

109. Kawashima, *SSNT*, 84–85, 142.

110. "NI" was taken from the first syllable of Nishina's surname. Account of Koyama Kenji, *SSNT*, 85. PWRS, *The Day Man Lost*, 36–37.

111. *NKGT*, 444. Account of Yokoyama Sumi, *SSNT*, 88–89.

112. Kawashima, *SSNT*, 84–85, 141–42.

113. PWRS, *The Day Man Lost*, 36–37.

114. "Letter Received by ONI: from Japanese Radio Broadcast," U.S. National Archives, College Park, MD, RG 77, Entry 22, Box 173, Folder 44.70: "Japan, Misc."

115. Takeuchi provides details of the layout and floor plan of Building 49 in, Takeuchi, "Uran bakudan kenkyū mukashibanashi," 6–9. Tsuneishi, "Riken ni okeru uran bunri no kokoromi," 821–25. Dower, "'NI' and 'F'" 78.

116. Tsuneishi, "Riken ni okeru uran bunri no kokoromi," 823–24. Several diagrams, together with Takeuchi's research notes, are also provided in Takeuchi Masa, "NI-gō kenkyū nōto" [Ni-gō Research Notes], *NKGT*, 448–67. See also Takeuchi, "Uran bakudan kenkyū mukashibanashi," 20–35.

117. Tsuneishi, "Riken ni okeru uran bunri no kokoromi," 823–24. Takeuchi, *NKGT*, 448–449.

118. Nobuuji's first name is not given. Details of the meeting are recorded in the document, "Nishina kenkyūshitsu ni okeru U-kenkyū uchiawase jikō, Shōwa 18/7/6" [Memorandum on the Meeting concerning U-Research at the Nishina Laboratory, 6 July 1943], Rikagaku kenkyūjo toshoshitsu, Wako-shi, Saitama-ken, Japan. [Hereafter cited as Tōnizō Report.] This valuable document, which includes some of Nishina's research notes, was only recently repatriated back to the Riken after having been kept by the late Kuroda Kazuo, former professor at the University of Tokyo, who died in Las Vegas in 2001. Kuroda had taken the document out of Japan when he left for the United States shortly after the war. For background on the document, see Kenji Hall, "Rare Documents Returned Home after Half Century Sway Debate over Japan's WW II Research," Associated Press World Stream, Lexis-Nexis, 4 March 2003. See also Kenji Hall, "Wartime Documents Set Record Straight: Japan's A-bomb Goal Still Long Way Off in '45," *Japan Times*, 7 March 2003. A reprint of the report with commen-

tary can be found in Japanese in Yamazaki Masakatsu and Fukai Yūzo, "Dai-niji taisenki ni okeru Nihon no kakukenkyū shiryō." For further examination and additional technical commentary, see also Yamazaki Masakatsu, Fukai Yūzo, and Satomi Muneaki, "Tōkyō Dai-ni rikugun zōheisho ni tai suru Nishina Yoshio no hōkoku."

119. Tōnizō Report. For a technical discussion of aspects of Nishina's report concerning U-235 concentration and criticality, see Yamazaki Masakatsu, "Riken no 'Genshi bakudan' hitotsu no gensō."

120. Kigoshi's team consisted of Takeuchi, Ishiwatari Takehiko, and two unidentified women assistants. PWRS, *The Day Man Lost*, 37–40.

121. Account of Kigoshi Kunihiko, *SSNT*, 109–12.

122. Tsuneishi, "Riken ni okeru uran bunri no kokoromi," 822–23.

123. Kigoshi, *SSNT*, 104–5. Tsuneishi, "Riken ni okeru uran bunri no kokoromi," 823–25.

124. *SSNT*, 113–16, 201. Dower, " 'NI' and 'F,' " 78.

125. For the original text, see Tōnizō Report. The quote is from Rhodes, *Making of the Atomic Bomb*, 580–81. See also Yomiuri Shimbun, "Genbaku kaihatsu no uchimaku namanamashiku" [New Revelations of Atomic Bomb Research], *Yomiuri Shimbun* (13 August 1983), 1. Tsuneishi, "Riken ni okeru uran bunri no kokoromi," 824. *SSNT*, 121–36.

126. *SSNT*, 129–32.

127. Another rendering may be "That's no good." See Tōnizō Report, and Rhodes, *Making of the Atomic Bomb*, 581–82.

128. PWRS, *The Day Man Lost*, 44–45.

129. Account of Nakane Ryōhei, *SSNT*, 133–37.

130. PWRS, *The Day Man Lost*, 126–27. D. L. Mastick and B. J. O'Keefe interview with Sagane, "Report on Daily Activities of Ens. O'Keefe and Ens. Mastick," 11 September 1945, Furman Report. *SSNT*, 137–40.

131. Kawashima, *SSNT*, 142.

132. Hewlett and Anderson, *New World*, 67–68.

133. Walker, *German National Socialism*, 28. On the history of heavy water, see especially Per F. Dahl, *Heavy Water*.

134. This development came only two years after Harold C. Urey discovered the hydrogen isotope in 1932. Arakatsu, *SSNT*, 223.

135. Barbara Molony, *Technology and Investment*, 247, 355–56.

136. "Abstract of Attached Report Submitted by Mr. Saburo Tashiro, Director of Noguchi Kenkyūjo," 29 June 1949, U.S. National Archives, College Park, MD, RG 331, Entry 224, Box 2, Folder 14: "Heavy Water."

137. Ibid.

138. Masao Kubota to Director Tashiro, Noguchi Research Lab, 13 July 1949, translation, U.S. National Archives, College Park, MD, RG 331, Entry 224, Box 2, Folder 14: "Heavy Water."

139. "Abstract of Attached Report Submitted by Mr. Saburo Tashiro, Director of Noguchi Kenkyujo," 29 June 1949, U.S. National Archives, College Park, MD, RG 331, Entry 224, Box 2, Folder 14: "Heavy Water."

140. Masao Kubota to Director Tashiro, Noguchi Research Lab, 13 July 1949, translation, U.S. National Archives, College Park, MD, RG 331, Entry 224, Box 2, Folder 14: "Heavy Water."

141. Yoshio Toyoda, Researcher, "Preparation of Heavy Water," U.S. National Archives, College Park, MD, RG 331, Entry 224, Box 2, Folder 14: "Heavy Water."

142. After the war, U.S. intelligence investigators found approximately 100 grams of heavy water at Nishina's laboratory at the Riken. Curiously, Nishina claimed that it had been obtained from Norway before the war. See Philip Morrison interview with Nishina Yoshio, "Riken Conversations," 10 September 1945, Furman Report. On the production of heavy water, see Masao Kubota to Director Tashiro, Noguchi Research Lab, 13 July 1949, translation, U.S. National Archives, College Park, MD, RG 331, Entry 224, Box 2, Folder 14: "Heavy Water."

143. "Abstract of Attached Report Submitted by Mr. Saburo Tashiro, Director of Noguchi Kenkyujo," 29 June 1949, U.S. National Archives, College Park, MD, RG 331, Entry 224, Box 2, Folder 14: "Heavy Water."

144. "Abstract of Attached Report Submitted by Mr. Saburō Tashiro, Director of Noguchi Kenkyūjo," 29 June 1949, U.S. National Archives, College Park, MD, RG 331, Entry 224, Box 2, Folder 14: "Heavy Water." See also Masao Kubota to Director Tashiro, Noguchi Research Lab, 13 July 1949, translation, U.S. National Archives, College Park, MD, RG 331, Entry 224, Box 2, Folder 14: "Heavy Water." Philip Morrison interview with Nishina Yoshio, 10 September 1945, Furman Report.

145. The German nuclear research program itself suffered a major setback when, on 27 February 1943, Norwegian commandos under the supervision of British Intelligence destroyed the holding tanks of the Norwegian Hydroelectric Company in Vemork, thus eliminating the majority of Germany's stored heavy water supply. Because of the German program's dependence on heavy water, their research slowed to a crawl. On the Allied efforts to sabotage German nuclear research, see Dan Kurzman, *Blood and Water*.

146. "Abstract of Attached Report Submitted by Mr. Saburō Tashiro, Director of Noguchi Kenkyūjo," 29 June 1949, U.S. National Archives, College Park, MD, RG 331, Entry 224, Box 2, Folder 14: "Heavy Water."

147. "Interviews with Professors H. Yukawa and B. Arakatsu," 15 September 1945, Furman Report. See also George Yamashiro, ESS/STD Special Projects Branch, Visit Report to Zaidan-hojin Noguchi Kenkyujo, 23 June 1949, U.S. National Archives, College Park, MD, RG 331, Entry 224, Box 2, Folder 14: "Heavy Water."

148. Among these are Robert Wilcox, *Japan's Secret War*, passim, and Philip Henshall, *Nuclear Axis*, 131–203, which is largely derivative of the Wilcox book.

149. For a more detailed examination of this controversy, see Walter E. Grunden, "Hungnam and the Japanese Atomic Bomb."

150. Second Lt. C. H. Nagano, ESS/SPU, "Interview with Comdr. Masayoshi Kiyama on the reported 1,000 kg. of uranium nitrate in Yamaguchi-ken," 22 March 1946, RG 331, Entry 224, Box 2, Folder 15: "Import: Presurrender Uranium, Thorium, Monazite, Amang."

151. Masao Kubota to Director Tashiro, Noguchi Research Lab, 13 July 1949, translation, U.S. National Archives, College Park, MD, RG 331, Entry 224, Box 2, Folder 14: "Heavy Water." See also Yoshio Toyoda, Researcher, "Preparation of Heavy Water," U.S. National Archives, College Park, MD, RG 331, Entry 224, Box 2, Folder 14: "Heavy Water."

152. According to Shin Hata, a Japanese chemist, the uranium oxide was likely obtained from the Merke Corporation in England before the war, or it may have been acquired from the German company Kahlbaum. See R. D. Nininger, "Interview with Dr. Shin Hata, geo-chemist, Riken," 29 September 1945, Furman Report.

153. "Disposition of Uranium Oxide Impounded by SCAP," 3 May 1946, RG 331, Entry 224, Box 1, Folder 7: "Research, Nuclear, Policy." Dower, "'NI' and 'F,'" 76.

154. "Iimori Satoyasu," *Japan Biographical Encyclopedia*, 347. Dower, "'NI' and 'F,'" 79. Account of Iimori Satoyasu, *SSNT*, 149–50.

155. According to one account, some 150 middle school students were mobilized to help explore the mine. See Yamamoto Yōichi, "Nihon genbaku no shinsō." See also Kawashima, *SSNT*, 143. Dower, "'NI' and 'F,'" 79. "Radioactive Minerals in Korea, 20 June 1949," U.S. National Archives, U.S. National Archives, College Park, MD, RG 331, Box 2, Folder 20: "Radioactive Mines, Korea."

156. "Brief History of Research During the War," 7 January 1948, U.S. National Archives, College Park, MD, RG 331, Box 7416, File: "Research, Wartime."

157. Kawashima, *SSNT*, 143–44. Nihon Heiki Kōgyōkai, *Rikusen heiki sōkan*, 699–713.

158. "Radioactive Minerals in Korea, 20 June 1949," U.S. National Archives, College Park, MD, RG 331, Box 2, Folder 20: "Radioactive Mines, Korea."

159. Major Robert R. Furman to Brigadier-General J. B. Newman, 28 September 1945, Furman Report. Nagaoka suggested they search in Burma, because uranium was a heavy substance and it was likely to be concentrated where there were "wrinkles" in the earth. *SSNT*, 180–81. PWRS, *The Day Man Lost*, 38.

160. Kawashima, *SSNT*, 148. Iimori, *SSNT*, 153. Dower, "'NI' and 'F,'" 79.

161. *SSNT*, 173–74. Major Russell A. Fisher, "Notes on Japanese Navy Atomic Energy Project and Uranium Sources," 3 May 1946, U.S. National Archives, College Park, MD, RG 77, Entry 22, Box 163, Folder: "Japan."

162. Major Russell A. Fisher, "Inspection of Activities at Kyoto Imperial University," 28 February 1946, U.S. National Archives, College Park, MD, RG 331, Entry 224, Box 1, Folder: "Research, Nuclear, Japan." Major Russell A. Fisher, "Interview with Tetsugo [*sic* Tetsuzō] Kitagawa," 8 March 1946, U.S. National Archives, College Park, MD, RG 331, Entry 224, Box 2, Folder 15: "Import: Presurrender Uranium, Thorium, Monazite, Amang." Concerning the Shanghai connection, see Economic and Scientific Section, Industrial Division, Special Projects Unit, "Report of Activities of Special Projects Unit for March 1946," 3 April 1946, U.S. National Archives, College Park, MD, RG 331, Entry 224, Box 1, Folder 10: "Activity Report."

163. Among these were the Hongō, Arakawa, and Adachi works established under the aegis of Riken Rare Elements Ltd. See "Special Report on Scientific Activities in Japan," May 1946, U.S. National Archives, College Park, MD, RG 331, Entry 224, Box 1, Folder 10: "Activity Report." Japanese interviewed after the war insisted that as late as April 1945, only one plant existed in all of Japan that specifically processed uranium ore on even a small scale, and that, they claimed, was solely for commercial use in the manufacture of ceramics. See Memo for Record, H. von K. [presumably Henry von Kolnitz], 22 May 1946, U.S. National Archives, College Park, MD, RG 331, Entry 224, Box 1, Folder 4: Personnel.

164. A postwar survey of the plants and laboratories using stockpiles of rare ores showed them to be so disorganized at the end of the war that most people could not accurately account for the amount of materials on hand. "Activities Report for Period Nov 1946—Feb 1947," U.S. National Archives, College Park, MD, RG 331, Entry 224, Box 1, Folder 10: "Activity Report."

165. Memo for Record, H. von K. [presumably Henry von Kolnitz], 22 May 1946,

U.S. National Archives, College Park, MD, RG 331, Entry 224, Box 1, Folder 4: Personnel.

166. The total amount of uranium-bearing compounds in Japan located by SCAP officials as of July 1946 was 3,400 pounds. Additional stockpiles of uranium- and thorium-bearing ores totaled 5,113 tons, 80 tons of which was carnotite, 3,993 tons of which was black sand from Korea and Japan, 735 tons zircon, and 305 tons monazite. See "Special Report on Scientific Activities in Japan," July 1946, U.S. National Archives, College Park, MD, RG 331, Entry 224, Box 1, Folder 10: "Activity Report." Of these, the amounts imported from Korea and Southeast Asia from 1942 to 1945 are as follows: black sand, 3,025 tons; monazite concentrate, 553 tons; zircon, 742 tons; Korean monazite concentrate, 127 tons; columbite, 1.7 tons; lepidolite, 35.5 tons; Korean beryl, 9.5 tons; totaling 4,493.7 tons. See "Answer Regarding the Rare Element Ore," 28 April 1948, U.S. National Archives, College Park, MD, RG 331, Entry 224, Box 2, Folder 15: "Import, Presurrender Uranium, Thorium, Monazite, Amang."

167. Bernd Martin, *Japan and Germany in the Modern World*, 279.

168. See "Manifest of Cargo for Tokio [*sic*] on Board U-234," U.S. National Archives, Washington, DC, Records of the Office of the Chief of Naval Operations, ONI Files, OP23F2, Box 4, File: "Manifest of U-234." On the voyage of the German U-boat, see Joseph M. Scalia, *Germany's Last Mission to Japan*.

169. Arakatsu and Suzuki, *SSNT*, 184–85, 219.

170. S. Nomura, "Brief Description of Policy to Find Out Possibility of Utilizing Atomic Energy," U.S. National Archives, College Park, MD, RG 331, Box 7416, File: "Research, Wartime."

171. Yokoyama, *SSNT*, 88–89.

172. Major Russell A. Fisher, "Inspection of Activities at Kyoto Imperial University," 28 February 1946, U.S. National Archives, College Park, MD, RG 331, Entry 224, Box 1, Folder: "Research, Nuclear, Japan."

173. Major Richard R. Enthwhistle, "Inspection of Osaka Imperial University," 10 May 1946, RG 331, Entry 224, Box 1, Folder: "Research, Nuclear, Japan."

174. Charles Weiner, "Cyclotrons and Internationalism." See also Hinokawa Shizue, "Cyclotron Development."

175. Hewlett and Anderson, *New World*, 34–35.

176. "Brief Description on the Policy to find out Possibility of Utilizing Atom Energy adopted by the then Japanese Military Authorities in the War Time: Report No 4—Descriptions made by the concerned, ex-officer," U.S. National Archives, College Park, MD, RG 331, Box 7416, File: "Research, Wartime."

177. According to Suzuki Tatsusaburō, the Japanese army spent as much as ¥10 million (about $2.5 million), half of which may have been spent on the allocation of uranium-bearing ores. Dower, "'NI' and 'F,'" 99.

178. The Japanese navy subsidized early research with as much as ¥5,000 ($1,250) per year. By one account, the navy paid as much as $25 million for ore in Shanghai, but this amount seems preposterously high when considering the total allotment. See "Brief Description on the Policy to find out Possibility of Utilizing Atom Energy adopted by the then Japanese Military Authorities in the War Time: Report No 4—Descriptions made by the concerned, ex-officer," U.S. National Archives, College Park, MD, RG 331, Box 7416, File: "Research, Wartime." See also the discussion of expenditures in Dower, "'NI' and 'F,'" 83, 99.

179. Rhodes, for example, gives very high numbers for navy research funding ($1.5

million). This is probably an erroneous sum taken from the account of the PWRS, which gives an approximate 2-to-1 exchange ratio of the yen to the dollar. Dower gives the rate as roughly 4 to 1. U.S. military intelligence documents also give conflicting yen/dollar amounts. See Rhodes, *Making of the Atomic Bomb*, 459; PWRS, *The Day Man Lost*, 28; and Dower, " 'NI' and 'F,' " 99.

CHAPTER 3. ELECTRIC WEAPONS: RADAR AND THE "DEATH RAY"

1. Alan Beyerchen, "From Radio to Radar."
2. For an accessible technical account of radar fundamentals and history, see especially Sean S. Swords, *Technical History*, passim. For additional technical essays on the history of radar development in various nations, see Russell Burns, ed., *Radar Development to 1945*.
3. Hartcup erroneously credits *Gustav* Herz (1887–1975) as the discoverer of electromagnetic waves. See Guy Hartcup, *Effect of Science*, 18. James P. Baxter, *Scientists Against Time*, 139. Louis Brown, *Radar History of World War II*, 6–11.
4. Beyerchen, "From Radio to Radar," 267. David E. Fisher, *Race on the Edge of Time*, 43.
5. In its formative years, this new technology was known by many names, such as "radio direction finding" (RDF) in Britain, or "Radio Position Finding" (RPF) in the U.S. Army Signal Corps, or "derax," as it was commonly called by the U.S. Army Air Corps. The Australians called it by the curious name of "doover." It was not until November 1940 that an American naval officer, S. M. Tucker, coined the appellation that we know today: *radar*, an acronym for "radio detection and ranging." For simplicity, the various types of apparatuses utilizing radio detection, location, and ranging, and later using microwaves, will be referred to here simply as radar. See Swords, *Technical History*, 1–4, 42–81. Brown, *Radar History of World War II*, 40–42, 46, 83.
6. Fisher, *Race on the Edge of Time*, 10. Beyerchen, "From Radio to Radar," 277.
7. R. V. Jones, *Most Secret War*, 39–40. Ronald W. Clark, *Rise of the Boffins*, 30–32. Swords, *Technical History*, 82–91. On the life and career of Tizard, see also Ronald W. Clark, *Tizard*.
8. Jones, *Most Secret War*, 42. Clark, *Rise of the Boffins*, 32–35. Swords, *Technical History*, 174–88.
9. Fisher's account credits Wilkins with originating the idea for what was to become radar far more than previous versions, which generally tend to favor Watson Watt. Swords is perhaps more balanced toward both. See Fisher, *Race on the Edge of Time*, 57–59. Swords, *Technical History*, 174–88. Jones, *Most Secret War*, 42. Clark, *Rise of the Boffins*, 32–35.
10. Brown, *Radar History of World War II*, 52. Swords, *Technical History*, 180–86. Fisher, *Race on the Edge of Time*, 59–63, 116.
11. Beyerchen, "From Radio to Radar," 283. Fisher gives the figure as £60,000. Fisher, *Race on the Edge of Time*, 118.
12. Swords, *Technical History*, 236–42. Brown, *Radar History of World War II*, 58–60. Fisher, *Race on the Edge of Time*, 125, 138, 142.
13. Fisher, *Race on the Edge of Time*, 118. Brown, *Radar History of World War II*, 53–59. Regarding the impact of social interaction among scientists, engineers, and

administrators on the development of the resonant cavity magnetron at Bawdsey and the subsequent operation of facilities under the British Air Ministry Research Establishment, see especially Stephen N. Travis, " 'Seeing' is Believing."

14. Henry E. Guerlac, *Radar in World War II: Sections A–C,* 153–59.

15. For a more complete discussion of the various types of radar produced by the British during the war, see especially Guerlac, *Radar in World War II: Sections A–C,* 122–74. For technical discussions, see Swords, *Technical History,* 188–253.

16. On the invention of the resonant cavity magnetron, see Guerlac, *Radar in World War II: Sections A–C,* 561–77. Brown, *Radar History of World War II,* 145–59. Robert Buderi, *Invention that Changed the World,* 82–89.

17. Beyerchen identifies three stages of radar development. In stage one, 1904 through the 1920s, detection of large objects using continuous radio waves of any given length is understood and rudimentary radar sets are constructed. In the second stage, beginning in the mid-1930s, focused "floodlight" and "searchlight" types of radar using pulsed and increasingly shorter radio waves are produced. The third stage begins in 1940 with the introduction of centimetric (microwave) radar, bringing vast improvements in precision location and reduction in antenna and equipment size. This stage was reached only by the successful development of a sufficiently strong vacuum tube capable of generating great amounts of power, the cavity magnetron. See Beyerchen, "From Radio to Radar," 291.

18. Beyerchen, "From Radio to Radar," 282–84. Fisher, *Race on the Edge of Time,* 135–36. Swords (*Technical History,* 253–54) argues that the science of "Operational Research" had its origin in the study of the operations of Chain Home.

19. On the Lindemann-Tizard conflict, see Jones, *Most Secret War,* 42–43. Brown, *Radar History of World War II,* 55–56. Fisher, *Race on the Edge of Time,* 78–83, 99–102. Clark, *Rise of the Boffins,* 43–49.

20. Baxter, *Scientists Against Time,* 139.

21. Ibid. Swords, *Technical History,* 101–12. Brown, *Radar History of World War II,* 42–43.

22. Baxter, *Scientists Against Time,* 139–40. Swords, *Technical History,* 57. Brown, *Radar History of World War II,* 64–69.

23. Baxter, *Scientists Against Time,* 139–40. Swords, *Technical History,* 112–18. Brown, *Radar History of World War II,* 69–73.

24. Several notable figures from the world of science and industry were recruited for the committee, including Professor Ernest O. Lawrence of the University of California at Berkeley, who also served as an integral member of the Manhattan Project. Baxter, *Scientists Against Time,* 141. Swords, *Technical History,* 118–20.

25. The quote is from Baxter, *Scientists Against Time,* 142.

26. For Bowen's account of his involvement, see E. G. Bowen, *Radar Days.* For a Canadian perspective on Allied cooperation in radar, see Donald H. Avery, *Science of War,* 68–95. On the Tizard Mission and the formation of the Radiation Laboratory, see Buderi, *Invention that Changed the World,* 27–37 and 38–51, respectively. See also Baxter, *Scientists Against Time,* 142–45, 154.

27. Baxter, *Scientists Against Time,* 142–45, 154.

28. Beyerchen, "From Radio to Radar," 270–71. Swords, *Technical History,* 91–101. Brown, *Radar History of World War II,* 46–47, 73. For the most comprehensive analysis of radar development history in Germany, see David Pritchard, *Radar War.*

29. Beyerchen, "From Radio to Radar," 271–72. Brown, *Radar History of World War II*, 75–76.

30. Brown, *Radar History of World War II*, 76.

31. Ibid., 76.

32. Beyerchen, "From Radio to Radar," 272–73. Brown, *Radar History of World War II*, 77–78. Pritchard, *Radar War*, 37–38.

33. Brown, *Radar History of World War II*, 80.

34. On the various types of radar produced by Germany during the war, see Henry E. Guerlac, *Radar in World War II: Sections D–E*, 1073–75. See also Pritchard, *Radar War*, passim.

35. Swords, *Technical History*, 98.

36. Beyerchen, "From Radio to Radar," 273–75. Brown, *Radar History of World War II*, 73. Hartcup, *Effect of Science*, 37. Jones, *Most Secret War*, 261–62.

37. John Erickson, "Radio-location and the Air Defense Problem."

38. Ibid., 245–47.

39. Brown, *Radar History of World War II*, 86–87. Erickson, "Radio-location and the Air Defense Problem," 252–57.

40. Brown, *Radar History of World War II*, 85–89. Swords, *Technical History*, 135–42.

41. Baxter, *Scientists Against Time*, 139. On radar development elsewhere in Europe, see Swords, *Technical History*, passim.

42. Swords, *Technical History*, 126–30. Brown, *Radar History of World War II*, 91. For more on the history of radar-related research in Italy, see especially M. Calamia and R. Palandri, "The History of the Italian Radio Detector Telemetro."

43. Yagi codeveloped the antenna with Professor Uda Shintarō, and thus it is also known as the "Yagi-Uda antenna." See Sato Gentei, "Secret Story."

44. Sato, "Secret Story," 7–8. Guerlac, *Radar in World War II: Sections D–E*, 917.

45. Okabe graduated from Tōhoku Imperial University in 1922 with a degree in electrical engineering, was promoted to associate professor in 1925, and accepted a professor of engineering position at Osaka Imperial University in 1935. In 1937, he received an award for special recognition of his work in microwave research from the Asahi Shimbun. Okabe received the Medal of Culture in 1944. See the Japan Biographical Research Department, *Japan Biographical Encyclopedia*, 1145. Much of the information presented in the following section is based on Nakajima Shigeru, "Reedaa kaihatsu no rekishi." In English, see Nakajima Shigeru, "The History of Japanese Radar Development to 1945." This article was later published with few alterations as Nakajima Shigeru, "Japanese Radar Development in World War II." An expanded version was also published as Nakajima Shigeru, "General Outline of Japanese Radar Development up to 1945."

46. The optical Doppler system as developed by Okabe entailed sending a continuous radio frequency signal (with superposed audio modulation focused in as narrow a beam as possible) from a fixed transmitting station at one point to a distant receiving station at another, and detecting a passing object when it entered or disturbed the transmission path. The interference disturbed the transmitted signal and produced an auditory beat at the receiving station. This work was not unlike the experiments conducted by Taylor and Young in the United States in 1922. For a more detailed explanation of the Okabe system, see Roger I. Wilkinson, "Short Survey of Japanese Radar—I."

47. Bōeichō Bōei Kenshūjo Senshibu, *Hondo bōkū sakusen,* 149.
48. Swords, *Technical History,* 130–32.
49. U.S. Naval Technical Mission to Japan, December 1945, "Electronics Targets: Japanese Submarine and Shipborne Radar," Report No. E-01, 7, microfilm. [Hereafter cited as USNTM.]
50. Nakagawa Yasuzō, *Japanese Radar,* 7. This book is largely derived from his previous publication in Japanese, Nakagawa Yasuzō, *Kaigun gijutsu kenkyūjo.* See also Nakajima, "Reedaa kaihatsu no rekishi," 19.
51. Nakagawa, *Japanese Radar,* 10.
52. Historian Miwao Matsumoto credits Itō with performing a "nodal function on behalf of the military" as facilitator of what was to become an extensive, but largely informal, network of contacts among the military, industrial, and academic sectors, which was eventually to result in the formation of the Second Navy Technology Research Institute. See Miwao Matsumoto, "Military Research and Its Conversion."
53. Nakagawa, *Japanese Radar,* 10.
54. Swords, *Technical History,* 133.
55. Nakagawa, *Japanese Radar,* 10–11.
56. Ibid., 13–14.
57. Nakajima, "Japanese Radar Development Prior to 1945," 17.
58. Morris F. Low, "Useful War." Nippon Kagakushi Gakkai, *Nippon kagaku gijutsusi taikei,* vol. 19, *Denki gijutsu,* 357. [Hereafter cited as *NKGT.*]
59. Bōeichō, *Hondo bōkū sakusen,* 150. See also Nihon Heiki Kōgyōkai, *Rikusen heiki sōkan,* 572–74.
60. According to U.S. sources, research began in 1933 at a branch of the AISR in Toyama city. See "Japanese Wartime Military Electronics and Communications," Section VI, *Japanese Army Radar,* 1 April 1946, Prepared by Technical Liaison and Investigation Division, Office of the Chief Signal Officer, General Headquarters, United States Army Forces, Pacific, U.S. National Archives, College Park, MD, RG 331, Box 7428, Folder 15. [Hereafter cited as GHQ, "Japanese Army Radar."] According to records of the Nippon Electric Corporation (NEC), however, work on the Kō type detector was undertaken beginning in 1937. See Nihon Denki Kabushiki Kaisha [Japan Electric Corporation], "Denpa heiki kenkyū kiroku" [Record of Research on Electric-Wave Weapons], Bōeichō kenkyūjo toshokan, Meguro-ku, Tokyo, Japan, Rikugun: Chūo, Heiki Seisan 21. Nakajima also states army research began in 1937. Nakajima, "Japanese Radar Development Prior to 1945," 22.
61. Nakagawa, *Japanese Radar,* 15–16.
62. Wilkinson, "Short Survey of Japanese Radar—I," 370. GHQ, "Japanese Army Radar."
63. The official army history gives the date and location of the tests as having taken place 20 February 1939 at Kanamarugahama, an army air base in Tochigi prefecture. Bōeichō, *Hondo bōkū sakusen,* 150. The U.S. intelligence report on radar states the tests occurred in February 1938. See GHQ, "Japanese Army Radar." For a brief account of these tests, see also Andrew J. Robertson, "Mobilizing for War," 68–76.
64. For locations of Japanese army and navy radar installations, see the maps in U.S. Army Air Force Headquarters, "A Short Survey of Japanese Radar," vol. 4, 20 November 1945, Second and Third Operations Analysis Section, FEAF, and Air Intelligence Group, FEAF, ATIG Report No. 115, United States Air Force, Maxwell Air Force Base Library, Huntsville, AL, microfilm, No. A7277, File No. 720.310. [Here-

after cited as USAAF, "Short Survey of Japanese Radar."] See also Denpa Kanri Iinkai, *Nihon Musenshi*, 422–30. See also Robertson, "Mobilizing for War."

65. Bōeichō, *Hondo bōkū sakusen*, 150. GHQ, "Japanese Army Radar." Wilkinson, "Short Survey of Japanese Radar—I," 370.

66. Bōeichō, *Hondo bōkū sakusen*, 151. The U.S. intelligence report on radar erroneously states the mission returned in 1940. GHQ, "Japanese Army Radar." See also Nakagawa, *Japanese Radar*, 21–22.

67. GHQ, "Japanese Army Radar." Nihon Heiki Kōgyōkai, *Rikusen heiki sōkan*, 585–86.

68. Wilkinson, "Short Survey of Japanese Radar—I," 372–73. See also GHQ, "Japanese Army Radar."

69. For Itō, the trip was to last from January to October 1941, whereupon he returned to Japan. Some details of the report on the German mission can be found in an article written by Itō upon his return. See Itō Yōji, "Senjika dōitsu ni okeru kagaku gijutsu no sokushin ni tsuite." For background on the navy mission to Germany, see Nakagawa, *Japanese Radar*, 19–23; and Nakagawa, *Kaigun gijutsu kenkyūjo*, 80–84.

70. Nakajima, "General Outline of Japanese Radar," 280–81. Nakajima, "Reedaa kaihatsu no rekishi," 22–23.

71. Nakajima, "General Outline of Japanese Radar," 285.

72. By far the most comprehensive study of mobilization and research on radar under the Imperial Japanese Navy is Kawamura Yutaka, "Kyū-Nihon kaigun no dempa heiki kaihatsu katei o jirei toshita dai-niji taisenki Nihon no kagaku gijutsu dōin ni kan suru bunseki." On the administrative organization of the Japanese navy's research infrastructure in electronics, see especially 13–34. On radar research under the navy, see also Fukui Shizuo et al., *Kimitsu heiki no zembō*, 105–59.

73. Sources do not entirely agree on the organizational hierarchy. To resolve discrepancies, I have relied more on a synthesis of postwar Japanese and English secondary sources than on any single U.S. intelligence report, some of which are confused and not entirely accurate. See Kawamura Yutaka, "Kyū-Nihon kaigun no dempa heiki kaihatsu katei," 14, 20, 24. Nakagawa, *Kaigun gijutsu kenkyūjo*, 32–33. Mark R. Peattie, *Sunburst*, 26. USNTM, "Electronics Targets: Japanese Electronics—General," Report No. E-28, 7.

74. The USNTM refers to an "Aeronautical Research Institute," which is most likely the Navy Aeronautical Technology Arsenal (Kaigun Kōkū Gijutsushō) or one of its affiliated Navy Aeronautics Research Departments (Kaigun Kōkū Kenkyūbu). See USNTM, "Electronics Targets: Japanese Electronics—General," Report No. E-28, 10–11.

75. Ibid.

76. General Headquarters, United States Army Forces, Pacific, Scientific and Technical Advisory Section, "Report on Scientific Intelligence Survey in Japan: September and October 1945," 1 November 1945, vols. 1–5, U.S. National Archives, College Park, MD, RG 165, Box 2056, 1:20. [Hereafter cited as GHQ, "Scientific Intelligence Survey."]

77. USNTM, "Electronics Targets: Japanese Electronics—General," Report No. E-28, 10.

78. Ibid.

79. Wilkinson, "Short Survey of Japanese Radar—I," 372.

80. Nakajima Shigeru, "General Outline of Japanese Radar," 283.

81. Swords, *Technical History,* 133.

82. Whether it is historically factual that radar and electrical communications played a very significant role in the outcome of these engagements or not, that navy brass believed that they did is a claim often repeated in the Japanese secondary literature. See, for example, Fukui et al., *Kimitsu heiki no zembō,* 135–36. *NKGT,* 358. Hiroshige Tetsu, *Kagaku no shakai shi: (ue),* 50. See also Nakajima, "General Outline of Japanese Radar," 285. It is now known that U.S. superiority in decryption and military intelligence provided greater strategic advantage at Midway than did radar. On this point, see especially Edward J. Drea, *MacArthur's ULTRA,* 33, 43.

83. The switch was made from the superregeneration-type receiver, used initially, to the self-heterodyne system from 1943, and to the superheterodyne system in September 1944. Nakajima, "Japanese Radar Development in World War II," 34.

84. Roger I. Wilkinson, "Short Survey of Japanese Radar—II." Kawamura, "Kyū-Nihon kaigun no dempa heiki kaihatsu," 123–24.

85. USNTM, "Electronics Targets: Japanese Electronics—General," Report No. E-28, 7–11. Nakajima Shigeru, "General Outline of Japanese Radar," 272. Although the army and navy both had schools for training technicians in the operation and maintenance of radar sets, educating engineers exclusively for research and development in these fields was another matter. On Japanese radar training programs, see USAAF, "Short Survey of Japanese Radar."

86. Guerlac, *Radar in World War II: Sections D–E,* 918.

87. GHQ, "Japanese Army Radar."

88. GHQ, "Japanese Army Radar." See also General Headquarters, Technical Intelligence Detachment, Far East Command, 24 June 1949, "Japanese Research on High-Frequency Electric Wave Weapons," RG 319, Entry 82, U.S. National Archives, College Park, Md. [Hereafter cited as GHQ, "Electric Wave Weapons."] On the history of the Noborito Laboratory and weapons related research conducted there, see Ban Shigeo, *Rikugun Noborito kenkyūjo no shinjitsu.*

89. GHQ, "Electric Wave Weapons," 3.

90. Wilkinson, "Short Survey of Japanese Radar—II," 455.

91. Japan Radio, an affiliate of Telefunken, operated under the direction of Nakajima Shigeru. Its headquarters in Mitaka, Tokyo, employed 155 workers including 55 engineers on staff. Sumitomo Tsushin, with its headquarters in Ikuta, employed 400 engineers with 800 workers on staff. But only a fraction of these facilities' resources were available for the army's radar research program at any given time. GHQ, "Scientific Intelligence Survey," 1:20. Denpa Kanri Iinkai, *Nihon Musenshi,* 422. Nihon Heiki Kōgyōkai, *Rikusen heiki sōkan,* 586.

92. GHQ, "Japanese Army Radar." Bōeichō, *Hondo bōkū sakusen,* 156–58. See also Bōeichō bōei kenshūjo senshibu, *Rikugun kōkū heiki,* 411–13.

93. According to the Scientific Intelligence Survey, the Tama facility "did not have the specialized personnel required to do research on the radar sets." GHQ, "Scientific Intelligence Survey," vol. 2, appendix 1-A-b-1.

94. GHQ, "Scientific Intelligence Survey," vol. 2, appendix 1-A-a-3, 1-A-b-1. According to Wilkinson, who gives different numbers, the Tama staff was composed of 88 officers, 96 trained assistants, and an additional 600 personnel. Budget appropriations equaled ¥12 million (1943), ¥16 million (1944), and ¥16 million (1945), of which only ¥7.5 million was used by the end of the war. See Wilkinson, "Short Survey of Japanese Radar—I," 373.

95. On the organizational divisions at Tama, see Bōeichō Bōei Kenshūjo Senshibu, *Rikugun kōkū heiki*, 411–13. See also GHQ, "Scientific Intelligence Survey," vol. 2, appendix 1-A-b-2.
96. GHQ, "Japanese Army Radar."
97. GHQ, "Scientific Intelligence Survey," vol. 2, appendix 1-A-b-1. Wilkinson, "Short Survey of Japanese Radar—I," 373.
98. Yagi stated this model may have been deployed experimentally at Leyte. GHQ, "Scientific Intelligence Survey," vol. 3, appendix 3-b-1.
99. The antiaircraft artillery shell remained in the design stage at the end of the war. It was designed to use a 50-kilowatt, CW 10-centimeter transmitter in a 10-meter parabolic reflector to generate a narrow beam of high-intensity radiation to explode an antiaircraft shell by means of a high induced current when it passed through the beam, thus resulting in an explosion at the desired location. Research focused on the development of the magnetron without great attention to systems application. See GHQ, "Scientific Intelligence Survey," 1:21.
100. GHQ, "Scientific Intelligence Survey," 1:44, vol. 2, appendix 1-A-b-5, appendix 1-D-3.
101. GHQ, "Scientific Intelligence Survey," vol. 3, 3-A-4.
102. Brown, *Radar History of World War II*, 60.
103. Of the 600 to 700 personnel employed in the Tokyo district Information Center, about 350 were young civilian women. USAAF, "Short Survey of Japanese Radar," 44.
104. Swords, *Technical History*, 134–35.
105. Guerlac, *Radar in World War II: Sections D–E*, 919.
106. USAAF, "Short Survey of Japanese Radar," 46. See also Wilkinson, "Short Survey of Japanese Radar—II," 460–62.
107. USAAF, "Short Survey of Japanese Radar." Wilkinson, "Short Survey of Japanese Radar—II," 460–62.
108. GHQ, "Japanese Army Radar."
109. GHQ, "Scientific Intelligence Survey," 1:6.
110. GHQ, "Scientific Intelligence Survey," vol. 2, appendix 1-E-1.
111. GHQ, "Electric Wave Weapons," 3.
112. Ibid. Nihon Heiki Kōgyōkai, *Rikusen heiki sōkan*, 594–95.
113. Guerlac, *Radar in World War II: Sections A–C*, 190. R. W. Burns, "Background to the Development of the Cavity Magnetron."
114. GHQ, "Scientific Intelligence Survey," vol. 2, appendix 1-E-1.
115. GHQ, "Electric Wave Weapons," 3–4.
116. GHQ, "Scientific Intelligence Survey," vol. 2, appendix 1-E-1.
117. Figure is determined using the 4-to-1 yen-to-dollar ratio valid throughout most of the war. GHQ, "Scientific Intelligence Survey," 1:42, vol. 2, appendix 1-E-1. Nihon Heiki Kōgyōkai, *Rikusen heiki sōkan*, 595–96.
118. Kusaba Hideki is also identified as Kusaba Sueki. Kusaba attended the Army Science Academy from 1921 to 1926 while simultaneously studying physics at Tokyo Imperial University between 1923 and 1926. He had been a resident student in Germany from 1935 to 1937 and assumed the position of chief of the Noborito laboratory from December 1937 to March 1939. He was promoted to the rank of general before the end of the war. In August 1938, Sasada Sukesaburō, a medical doctor from Hokkaidō Imperial University, was assigned to the Noborito Laboratory, and from April 1939 to July 1942, he assumed the supervisory role for research on microwaves

while Kusaba took another assignment. Kusaba returned to the Noborito Laboratory in August 1942, again as director, but at this time he became responsible for supervising development and production of balloon bombs (Fu-gō) for the "strategic bombing" of the United States until around November 1944. At this time, Kusaba again resumed oversight of microwave research. See GHQ, "Scientific Intelligence Survey," vol. 2, appendix 1-E-1. GHQ, "Electric Wave Weapons," 3–4.

119. GHQ, "Scientific Intelligence Survey," vol. 2, appendix 1-E-1. GHQ, "Electric Wave Weapons," 3–4.

120. Japan Biographical Research Department, *Japan Biographical Encyclopedia*, 917. GHQ, "Electric Wave Weapons," 3–4.

121. Ikebe worked on the magnetron for high-frequency weapons from May to August 1945. Other civilian scientists serving as consultants for the death ray project included Nishimaki Masao, assistant professor at the Tokyo Institute of Technology, and principal designer of the 80-centimeter magnetron; Asami Yoshihiro, doctor and professor of physics and engineering at Hokkaidō University; Hayashi Kiyoshi, an engineer with the Kawanishi Corporation, Kobe; and Kawai Sutezo, former assistant professor of physics at Nippon University, who first theoretically proved the feasibility of the death ray, to name a few. See GHQ, "Electric Wave Weapons," 4–9. GHQ, "Scientific Intelligence Survey," vol. 2, appendix 1-E-1.

122. Minoshima's specific areas of interest included electrophysiology, physiology of ultrashort waves, and physiological oxidation and reduction with relation to aviation medicine. GHQ, "Electric Wave Weapons," 9–11.

123. Ibid.

124. GHQ, "Scientific Intelligence Survey," vol. 2, appendix 1-E-2.

125. Ibid., appendix 1-D-3.

126. GHQ, "Electric Wave Weapons," 4.

127. GHQ, "Scientific Intelligence Survey," 1:6, 42.

128. For a firsthand account of the development of the magnetron in Japan, see Nakajima Shigeru, "General Outline of Japanese Radar," 273–75. For a technical account based on recently discovered sources, see Kawamura Yutaka, "1930 Nendai no magunetoron kenkyū to kaigun gijutsu kenkyūjo."

129. Aspray, interview with Nakajima, 2–4.

130. Nakajima, "General Outline of Japanese Radar," 279–80.

131. Nakajima, "Japanese Radar Development in World War II," 33. For more on the history of magnetron development in wartime Japan, see the account by Itō Yōji in *NKGT*, 371–73.

132. Wilkinson, "Short Survey of Japanese Radar—II," 455.

133. By mid-1944, every ship in the Japanese navy was equipped with microwave radar sets. Nakajima, "General Outline of Japanese Radar," 285.

134. GHQ, "Scientific Intelligence Survey," vol. 2, appendix, 2-C-a-1.

135. Nakagawa, *Japanese Radar*, 14–15.

136. Nakajima, "Japanese Radar Development in World War II," 36. According to a U.S. intelligence report, there were two schools of magnetron design in wartime Japan. The first, the navy's model, designed by engineers at the Shimada Laboratory and at Japan Radio, utilized an anode with "alternating large and small cavities to provide de-coupling between adjacent resonant cavities for stability." This model used either no strapping or a three-phase strapping (coupling every third cavity) approach.

The second was the army's model, designed chiefly by Professor Morita Kiyoshi with engineers from Sumitomo, which utilized a 12-cavity strapped magnetron as the most common approach. The Japanese army apparently developed magnetrons quite similar to U.S. types in design, although these lines of development almost certainly occurred independently of one another. See GHQ, "Scientific Intelligence Survey," 1:23.

137. The tubes remained inferior to U.S. types in output, efficiency, and life span, which the Americans attributed to low-emission and short-life cathodes as well as a lack of precision construction. See GHQ, "Scientific Intelligence Survey," 1:23.

138. Wilkinson, "Short Survey of Japanese Radar—II," 455.

139. Low uses the term "Project Power" for Sei-gō, which could also be translated as "Project Energy" or "Project Force." For consistency, "Project Power" is also used here. See Low, "Useful War," 294. On the Physics Committee and Itō's role in death ray research, see Kawamura Yutaka and Yamazaki Masakatsu, "Butsuri kondankai." See also the materials presented in Nippon Kagakushi Gakkai, "Butsurigaku to senji kenkyū," 471.

140. Seisan gijutsu kyōkai [Production Technology Committee], *Kyū-kaigun gijutsu shiryō, Dai 1-hen,* (3) *Dai 5-shō,* Bōeichō kenkyūjo toshokan, Meguro-ku, Tokyo, Japan, Kaigun 6, Zenpan 5, 212–13, 308–9.

141. GHQ, "Scientific Intelligence Survey," 1:42–43.

142. GHQ, "Scientific Intelligence Survey," vol. 2, appendix 1-E-3.

143. GHQ, "Electric Wave Weapons," 21.

144. GHQ, "Scientific Intelligence Survey," 1:3–4, 18.

145. Ibid., 4.

146. Performance of their "best pulsed magnetrons," however, was still considered inferior to U.S. designs. See ibid.

147. Ibid., 23.

148. Nakajima was also credited for the successful design of the magnetron types in most common use by both the army and navy. See Wilkinson, "Short Survey of Japanese Radar—II," 459.

149. USNTM, "Electronics Targets: Japanese Submarine and Shipborne Radar," Report No. E-01, 20.

150. Radar on board Japanese ships was described as being of "conventional design and mediocre construction." See USNTM, "Electronics Targets: Japanese Submarine and Shipborne Radar," Report No. E-01, 1. In another report it was stated that "the ignorance of the Japanese as to potentialities and scope of American radar is striking." See GHQ, "Scientific Intelligence Survey," 1:25.

151. GHQ, "Scientific Intelligence Survey," 1:4, 25.

152. USNTM, "Electronics Targets: Japanese Centimeter Wave Techniques," Report No. E-04, 7. Investigators also noted "the absence of creative imagination" among Japanese researchers as another factor. See USNTM, "Electronics Targets: Japanese Land-Based Radar," Report No. E-03, 8. The former part of the U.S. navy report further states, "Even in the later months of the war, when captured or recovered microwave equipment was available to the [Japanese] navy, they were unable to appreciate and make use of some of its obvious advantages."

153. GHQ, "Scientific Intelligence Survey," 1:19.

154. Ibid., 25.

155. Guerlac, *Radar in World War II: Sections D–E,* 917–18.

156. GHQ, "Scientific Intelligence Survey," 1:25–26.
157. Ibid., 4.
158. Nakajima, "General Outline of Japanese Radar," n. 21, 289–90.
159. GHQ, "Scientific Intelligence Survey," 1:4. Guerlac also argues that the absence of proper organization was "the biggest handicap." Guerlac, *Radar in World War II: Sections D–E*, 917–18.
160. GHQ, "Scientific Intelligence Survey," vol. 2, appendix 1-A-b-2.
161. Bōeichō Bōei Kenshūjo Senshibu, *Rikugun kōkū heiki*, 427–29.
162. GHQ, "Japanese Army Radar."
163. GHQ, "Scientific Intelligence Survey," vol. 2, appendix 1-A-b-2.
164. GHQ, "Japanese Army Radar." GHQ, "Scientific Intelligence Survey," vol. 2, appendix 1-A-b-2.
165. GHQ, "Scientific Intelligence Survey," 1:1, 53.
166. GHQ, "Japanese Army Radar."
167. Ibid.
168. GHQ, "Scientific Intelligence Survey," 1:19, 25, appendix 1-A, 2-B-a, 2-C-a, 2-C-b.
169. USNTM, "Electronics Targets: Japanese Submarine and Shipborne Radar," Report No. E-01, 7.
170. Ibid.
171. Guerlac, *Radar in World War II: Sections D–E*, 917–18.
172. Wilkinson, "Short Survey of Japanese Radar—I," 372. One report states, "For example, although Nippon Musen built the D.F. equipment for submarines, all of the installation work was done by the navy and no Nippon Musen engineers were ever allowed aboard a submarine. Similarly, in spite of vigorous pressure by the Nippon Musen Company, very few of their engineers were ever allowed in airplanes in connection with radar equipment built by the company for aerial use." Interview with Nippon Musen Representatives, 19 September 1945, GHQ, "Scientific Intelligence Survey," vol. 3, appendix 7-3.
173. GHQ, "Scientific Intelligence Survey," vol. 3, appendix 7-3.
174. USNTM, "Electronics Targets: Japanese Land-Based Radar," Report No. E-03, 8.
175. Ibid.
176. Guerlac estimates that these tubes likely could not withstand more than two to four weeks of service. Guerlac, *Radar in World War II: Sections D–E*, 918.
177. USNTM, "Electronics Targets: Japanese Centimeter Wave Techniques," Report No. E-04, 1. See also GHQ, "Scientific Intelligence Survey," 1:26.
178. Nakajima Shigeru, "General Outline of Japanese Radar," 269.
179. Historian Bernd Martin notes that the German government issued an official warning on 11 February 1941 establishing a clear policy toward the Japanese military-technical missions that arrived in Germany early in that year, stating that "All Japanese wishes which come close to industrial espionage or look like technological transfer should be declined at once." Furthermore, he argues there were other, more fundamental reasons for Germany's attitude, stating, "Mistrust, envy, and even treachery, together with an outspoken feeling of racial superiority, were characteristic of German-Japanese trade relations, especially for the period of combined warfare." See Martin, *Japan and Germany*, 272 and 276, respectively.
180. GHQ, "Japanese Army Radar."

181. According to the U.S. Scientific Intelligence survey, "the most important exception" to the restrictive German policy toward technology transfer was in the field of underwater sound, where the Germans were more generous. Specifications, blueprints, and models of underwater supersonic detection equipment were sent to Japan along with the two technical experts. GHQ, "Scientific Intelligence Survey," 1:25.

182. Although officially on the payroll of the Japanese navy, Foders was also permitted to assist the army in radar production as well. Also on the mission from Germany were technicians, including Kurt Schiffner, who conducted research on sound and sound locators, and Willi Steckert, who was to supervise the installation of the equipment aboard ships. See GHQ, "Scientific Intelligence Survey," vol. 2, appendix 1-A-b-2. See also GHQ, "Japanese Army Radar."

183. GHQ, "Scientific Intelligence Survey," 1:4, 48–49.

184. Some undisclosed number of additional German technicians were also sent to Japan in the later years of the war, but they appear to have been "mostly specialists in mechanical design, plant construction, or production, rather than in research and development." See GHQ, "Scientific Intelligence Survey," 1:4, 48–49. GHQ, "Japanese Army Radar."

185. Wilkinson, "Short Survey of Japanese Radar—II," 455.

186. GHQ, "Scientific Intelligence Survey," 1:25, 49. The Germans also claimed to have shared information concerning modifications to various models, such as the Würzlaus, Nurnberg, Taunus, and Michael Oscillator for Wismar equipment in early 1944. The Japanese appear not to have made use of such information, and those interviewed at Sumitomo Tsushin denied having any knowledge of it. See GHQ, "Japanese Army Radar."

187. GHQ, "Japanese Army Radar."

188. Ibid.

189. Wilkinson, "Short Survey of Japanese Radar—II," 462.

190. Wilkinson, "Short Survey of Japanese Radar—I," 377.

191. Baxter, *Scientists Against Time*, 149. The British experience was admittedly less ideal. The Admiralty refused to join the AMRE research team at Bawdsey and initiated work at its own laboratory in Portsmouth at the HM Signal School. Secrecy between the services resulted in slower progress for the navy. With the involvement of the United States after the Tizard Mission in 1940, and with the establishment of the MIT Rad Lab, given the close cooperation between the U.S. and Britain, this problem was largely resolved. See Brown, *Radar History of World War II*, 62.

192. Baxter, *Scientists Against Time*, 155.

CHAPTER 4. AERONAUTICAL WEAPONS: ROCKETS, GUIDED MISSILES, AND JET AIRCRAFT

1. The Model 97, also known as the Kamikaze-gō "long-flight plane," was designed at Tokyo Imperial University's Aeronautical Research Institute and built by Mitsubishi. In 1938, it set a world distance record after flying more than 15,000 kilometers for ninety-four hours. Originally designed as a commercial aircraft, it was adapted by the army as the Model 97 reconnaissance plane. See René Francillon, *Japanese Aircraft*, 2–3. Richard J. Samuels, *Rich Nation, Strong Army*, 109–12, 364, n. 21. For more on the formative years of Japan's military aviation industry, see also David C.

Evans and Mark R. Peattie, *Kaigun*, 300–301. Mark R. Peattie, *Sunburst*. Alvin D. Coox, "The Rise and Fall of the Imperial Japanese Air Forces."

2. Economic historian Alan S. Milward states, "Japanese aircraft matched up to United States aircraft until 1942 only because the designers had been trained before 1939 in the United States, because the designs had for the most part been purchased from the United States, and because the planes were made on United States machines." See Alan S. Milward, *War, Economy and Society*, 172. On the integral role Germany played in the development of Japan's aircraft industry in the 1920s–1940s, see Sigrun Caspari, "Riku-kaigun kōkūshi to Doitsu-Ni gijutsu kōshō."

3. Martin van Creveld, *Technology and War*, 82–83. Frank H. Winter, "Genesis of the Rocket in China."

4. Jean-Paul Escalettes and Philippe Jung, "William Congreve and the City of Toulouse."

5. Oberth was the first to demonstrate mathematically the superiority of liquid propellants over solid fuels for rocket propulsion. Frank H. Winter, *Prelude to the Space Age*, 21–23.

6. Michael Stoiko, *Soviet Rocketry*, 17–33. G. A. Tokaty, "Soviet Rocket Technology." Asif Siddiqi, "Rockets' Red Glare." The GIRD is also known as the "Jet Propulsion Research Group," which is a less literal translation than that of Siddiqi. See Mark Harrison, "New Postwar Branches."

7. Harrison refers to the RNII as the "Jet Propulsion Research Institute." See Harrison, "New Postwar Branches," 119–21. Winter, *Prelude to the Space Age*, 55–61. Stoiko, *Soviet Rocketry*, 42–45.

8. Esther C. Goddard and G. Edward Pendray, *Papers of Robert H. Goddard*, passim. G. Edward Pendray, "Pioneer Rocket Development."

9. Winter, *Prelude to the Space Age*, 87–93.

10. Guy Hartcup, *Challenge of War*, 233–34.

11. Wernher von Braun and Frederick I. Ordway III, *History of Rocketry and Space Travel*, 36, 56–59. Winter, *Prelude to the Space Age*, 35–40.

12. Michael J. Neufeld, *The Rocket and the Reich*, 11–18.

13. Ibid., 5–6, 19–28.

14. Dr. H. K. Stephenson interview with Maj. Gen. M. Nomura, 13 October 1945, in General Headquarters, United States Army Forces, Pacific, Scientific and Technical Advisory Section, "Report on Scientific Intelligence Survey in Japan: September and October 1945," 1 November 1945, vols. 1–5, U.S. National Archives, College Park, MD, RG 165, Box 2056, vol. 2, appendix 1-F-1. [Hereafter cited as GHQ, "Scientific Intelligence Survey."] See also Leon M. S. Slawecki, "Notes on Modern Japanese Rocket Research."

15. The army's first rockets measured about 5 to 6.5 feet in length (1.5 to 2 meters) and were designed to have a range of some 547 yards (500 meters), but none reached this distance. The rocket-propelled artillery shell that measured 2.9 inches (75 millimeters) in diameter and had an estimated range of about 4.35 miles (7,000 meters). The fin-stabilized rocket measured just over 3 inches (8 centimeters) in diameter and had a range of 1,640 yards (1,500 meters). Slawecki, "Notes on Modern Japanese Rocket Research," 9–10. See also Nihon Heiki Kōgyōkai, *Rikusen heiki sōkan*, 126–33.

16. These first liquid-fuel rockets measured about 58.5 inches (150 centimeters) in length, 9.75 inches (25 centimeters) in diameter, and weighed 121 pounds (55 kilo-

grams). An automobile spark plug mounted in the combustion chamber was used to ignite the propellants. Slawecki, "Notes on Modern Japanese Rocket Research," 9–10.

17. Winter, *Prelude to the Space Age*, 111.

18. Harrison mistakenly gives the year as 1938, but the battle of Nomonhan began in May 1939. Harrison, "New Postwar Branches," 119. On this subject, see also David Holloway, "Innovation in the Defense Sector," 368–414.

19. Holloway, "Innovation in the Defense Sector," 388.

20. Among other rocket types used by the Soviet army were the RBS-132 aircraft-launched rocket bomb, the Type-M8 3.2-inch (82 millimeter) army rocket, and the Type-M13 5.1-inch (130 millimeter) river gunboat rocket. See John Campbell, *Naval Weapons of World War Two*, 373. James Phinney Baxter, *Scientists Against Time*, 201. Stoiko, *Soviet Rocketry*, 67. Tokaty, "Soviet Rocket Technology," 276–78.

21. Harrison, "New Postwar Branches," 127–30.

22. On top of this may be added a type of "technological conservatism," where scientists and engineers failed to promote more innovative designs for fear of the consequences of failure or otherwise being branded a traitor to the state for diverting much needed resources. Siddiqi, "Rockets' Red Glare," 478–87. Harrison, "New Postwar Branches," 128–30.

23. Stoiko, *Soviet Rocketry*, 67.

24. Baxter, *Scientists Against Time*, 201–2.

25. John E. Burchard, *Rockets, Guns and Targets*, 17–19.

26. Burchard, *Rockets, Guns and Targets*, 19. Baxter, *Scientists Against Time*, 119–20, 202.

27. Frank J. Malina, "Origins and First Decade of the Jet Propulsion Laboratory."

28. Lauritson served as director until September 1943, when he was replaced by Frederick L. Hovde. Baxter, *Scientists Against Time*, 204–8. Burchard, *Rockets, Guns and Targets*, 31–49. Irvin Stewart, *Organizing Scientific Research for War*, 85–86.

29. Among these were the Mousetrap antisubmarine warfare (ASW) rocket launcher, which was derived from the design of the British Hedgehog, the 5-inch (127 millimeter) high-velocity aircraft rocket (HVAR), or Holy Moses, and the 11.75-inch (298.5 millimeter) Tiny Tim antishipping rocket (ASR), which was produced in 1944. For a detailed history of the development of these, see Burchard, *Rockets, Guns and Targets*, 95–103, 153–64; Baxter, *Scientists Against Time*, 205–10; and Campbell, *Naval Weapons of World War Two*, 169–71.

30. These ranged in size from 4.5 inches (114.3 millimeters) to 7.2 inches (183 millimeters). A 5-inch spin-stabilized rocket (SSR) type was developed in the summer of 1944 and used with great efficacy during landing attacks in the Philippines. Burchard, *Rockets, Guns and Targets*, 196–97. Campbell, *Naval Weapons of World War Two*, 169–71.

31. Baxter, *Scientists Against Time*, 211.

32. Hartcup, *Challenge of War*, 234–38. M. M. Postan, D. Hay, J. D. Scott, *Design and Development of Weapons*, 286–87.

33. Among the rockets developed by the Admiralty in World War II were the 7-inch (177.8 millimeter) UP Mk I aerial mine and the 3-inch (76.2 millimeter) UP Mk I antiaircraft rocket, both of which saw only limited use in combat. The Admiralty produced two types of aircraft-launched rockets, one 3.5-inch (88.9 millimeter) and a 5-inch (127-millimeter), and a 5-inch (127-centimeter) barrage rocket was produced for ship-to-shore bombardment. The British Admiralty developed two guided missiles,

the Breakmine and Stooge, which were designed late in the war as countermeasures for kamikaze attacks in the Pacific. Neither of these was used in combat. See Campbell, *Naval Weapons of World War Two*, 100–101. Hartcup, *Challenge of War*, 237–47.

34. Baxter, *Scientists Against Time*, 194–95.

35. Ibid., 194–95.

36. Ibid., 195.

37. The navy also began development of the Little Joe and Lark radio-guided missiles. The Little Joe project was abandoned as a result of the long production schedule required, and the Lark was still under development when the war came to an end. Development of the Bat continued after the war, but the project was completely abandoned by 1948. The NDRC also cooperated with the army in the development of remotely controlled bombs. The most successful of these was the AZON, designed in the summer of 1942 and used successfully in Europe throughout the rest of the war. The army also attempted to produce a television-guided missile, designated Roc, and a heat-homing bomb, known as Felix. Both were still under development at the end of the war. Other missiles of note that remained uncompleted at the end of the war included the navy's air-to-air jet-propelled Gorgon series, the Gargoyle rocket-propelled glide bomb, the army's Private series, which was codeveloped with Caltech, and the Wac Corporal. See Baxter, *Scientists Against Time*, 196–200. Campbell, *Naval Weapons of World War Two*, 171.

38. Walter Dornberger, *V-2*, 39–54. Norman Longmate, *Hitler's Rockets*, 81–91. Neufeld, *The Rocket and the Reich*, 35–55.

39. Neufeld, *The Rocket and the Reich*, 54–57, 62–63.

40. Walter Dornberger, "German V-2," 80, 94, 108.

41. A more advanced type of guided missile, similar to the V-1 but resembling the Me 163, was the Enzian series rail-launched surface-to-air missile. It progressed from concept to flight test within twelve months during 1944. The many versions of the Enzian incorporated the most advanced homing devices developed by Germany during the war, including acoustic and infrared systems. But the Enzian never entered combat because production was halted to divert resources to other missiles. See Rudolf Lusar, *German Secret Weapons*, 131–33, 180–81. For more on the numerous German missile types, see Rowland F. Pocock, *German Guided Missiles*, 21–28, 69–70; Ian V. Hogg, *German Secret Weapons*, passim; and Anthony L. Kay and J. R. Smith, *German Aircraft*, 312–46.

42. The V-2 was a long-range, fin-stabilized ballistic missile measuring about 46 feet (14 meters) in length and approximately 5.4 feet (1.65 meters) in diameter. Fully loaded, it weighed nearly 13 tons, with the warhead alone weighing some 2,150 pounds (975 kilograms). The V-2 was powered by a liquid-fuel engine utilizing a mixture of 75 percent ethyl alcohol and 25 percent water with liquid oxygen fed under pressure as an oxidizer. The engine was capable of 68,000 pounds (31,000 kilograms) of thrust, propelling the rocket at a maximum speed of 3,399 mph (5,470 kph) to an altitude of about 56 miles (90 kilometers). The maximum range of the V-2 proved to be approximately 250 miles (400 kilometers), well within striking distance of London when launched from sites on the northwest coasts of the Netherlands and Belgium. See Lusar, *German Secret Weapons*, 134–37. Pocock, *German Guided Missiles*, 12–20. Neufeld, *The Rocket and the Reich*, passim.

43. On the whole, the ten types of guided missiles under development in the Aggregat series absorbed a disproportionate amount of resources relative to their actual

use and effectiveness in combat. The A-5 through A-9 rockets were essentially variations of the A-4 (V-2), with changes in fin design and the rocket motors. The A-10 was to be a two-stage transatlantic missile intended to strike the United States, but it did not advance beyond the design stage. A submersible version of the V-2 rocket towed by a U-boat was also developed and tested, but it was not used in actual combat. The Wasserfall infrared self-homing antiaircraft rocket, which resembled the V-2 in design, was used experimentally against enemy bomber formations at the end of 1944. Delays caused by protracted testing prevented the Wasserfall from being mass-produced before the end of the war. See Longmate, *Hitler's Rockets,* 272–83. Dornberger, "German V-2," 29–45. Lusar, *German Secret Weapons,* 135–42, 178–79. Pocock, *German Guided Missiles,* 56–58. Neufeld, *The Rocket and the Reich,* passim. Concerning V-2 attacks on England and Belgium, see also Bejnamin King and Timothy J. Kutta, *Impact.* David Johnson, *V-1, V-2.*

44. The German navy produced only two basic types of rockets during the war, including the 2.8 inch (7.3 centimeters) Föhn barrage rocket and a 3.38-inch (8.6 centimeter) SSR, of which five models were developed for antiaircraft defense. An anti-submarine rocket and a rocket-propelled skip bomb were also under development, but these were introduced only late in the war and proved largely ineffective. Campbell, *Naval Weapons of World War Two,* 276.

45. A later version, the Hs-293 D, was to be equipped with a television for remote-control. Lusar, *German Secret Weapons,* 147–48. Kay and Smith, *German Aircraft,* 327–30. Campbell, *Naval Weapons of World War Two,* 277.

46. Neufeld, *The Rocket and the Reich,* 108, 135–36, 146–48, 176–89, 197–213.

47. GHQ, "Scientific Intelligence Survey," vol. 2, appendix 1-F-1, appendix 1-D-2.

48. The barrage rocket was an SSR measuring 5.8 feet (1.73 meters) in length, 17.9 inches (46 centimeters) in diameter, and weighing approximately 2,000 pounds (4,400 kilograms). See "Technical Intelligence Notes from the Pacific: World's Largest Barrage Rocket," *ONI Weekly* 4 (14 March 1945): 881–83; NASM, File: "Japan, Missiles (WW II)."

49. Air Technical Intelligence Group, "Aircraft Rockets," Report No. 307, 15 December 1945, appendix A, NASM, File: "Japan, Missiles (WW II)."

50. U.S. Naval Technical Mission to Japan, December 1945, "Japanese Naval Rockets," Report No. 0-09, 5–6, U.S. Navy Archive, Washington, DC, microfilm. [Hereafter cited as USNTM.] Fukui Shizuo et al., *Kimitsu heiki no zembō,* 298–99. Naitō Hatsuho, *Kimitsu heiki Funryū,* 42.

51. Nihon kaigun kōkūshi hensan iinkai, *Nihon kaigun kōkūshi,* 3:667. [Hereafter cited as *NKKS.*] Air Technical Intelligence Group, "Aircraft Rockets," Report No. 307, 15 December 1945, appendix A, NASM. File: "Japan, Missiles (WW II)."

52. Kaigun Suiraishi Kankōkai, *Kaigun suiraishi,* 657–61.

53. USSBS, *Japanese Naval Ordnance,* 16–17.

54. Military Intelligence Division, War Department, "Japanese Development of Rocket Weapons," *Intelligence Bulletin* 3 (April 1945): 29–30; NASM, File: "Japan, Missiles (WW II). USSBS, *Japanese Naval Ordnance,* 16–17. GHQ, "Scientific Intelligence Survey," 1:37. USNTM, "Japanese Naval Rockets," Report No. 0-09, 5–6.

55. GHQ, "Scientific Intelligence Survey," vol. 2, appendix 1-c.

56. Ibid., appendix 2-C-e-2; see also accompanying Enclosure 2.

57. *NKKS,* 3:775–78.

58. The Japanese military services developed various types of basic radio-guided, remote-controlled aircraft and bombs using technologies common to all the principal belligerents by the late 1930s. These will not be discussed here because they mostly did not attempt to incorporate significant advances in electronics or propulsion technologies. For that reason, only the I-gō series, which represented the apex of this technological trend, and other guided bomb and missile types that arguably attempted to push the technological envelope to a greater degree will be discussed in detail below. A general discussion of Japanese R&D efforts in radio-guided, remote-control technology can be found in Andrew J. Robertson, "Mobilizing for War," 77–84. See also Nihon Heiki Kōgyōkai, *Rikusen heiki sōkan*, 599–611. Specifications and general descriptions of various Japanese missile types can be found in Martin Caidin, "Japanese Guided Missiles."

59. Robertson suggests the impetus for development of this missile came originally from engineer Kobayashi Masatsugu of Nippon Electric, who, in his desire to "influence the war situation positively," contacted the army in January 1944 to discuss his idea for a remote-control antiship rocket. See Robertson, "Mobilizing for War," 81–84. For more details on this project, see Bōeichō bōei kenshūjo senshibu, *Rikugun kōkū heiki*, 458–59. Air Technical Intelligence Group, "Japanese Radio Controlled Flying Bomb 'I-gō,'" Report No. 114, 20 November 1945, appendix B, NASM, File: "Japan, Missiles (WW II)." [Hereafter cited as ATIG, "I-gō."] See also Caidin, "Japanese Guided Missiles," 691–92. Francillon, *Japanese Aircraft*, 532–33.

60. Bōeichō Bōei Kenshūjo Senshibu, *Rikugun kōkū heiki*, 458. Caidin identifies him as "Engineer Major *Takeo* Omori." Caidin, "Japanese Guided Missiles," 691.

61. Bōeichō Bōei Kenshūjo Senshibu, *Rikugun kōkū heiki*, 458. Caidin, "Japanese Guided Missiles," 691–92.

62. ATIG, "I-gō."

63. Ibid.

64. ATIG, "I-gō." United States Strategic Bombing Survey, Aircraft Division, *Japanese Aircraft Industry*, 87. Bōeichō Bōei Kenshūjo Senshibu, *Rikugun kōkū heiki*, 458–59.

65. ATIG, "I-gō." USNTM, "Japanese Guided Missiles," Report No. 0-02, 21–22.

66. ATIG, "I-gō."

67. Francillon states 180 as the number of I-gō-1B missiles built, whereas Caidin gives "approximately 150" as the total. Francillon, *Japanese Aircraft*, 532. Caidin, "Japanese Guided Missiles," 692.

68. ATIG, "Supplementary Photographs and Blueprints for ATIG Report No. 114, Japanese Radio Controlled Flying Bomb, I-gō," Report No. 313, 21 December 1945, NASM, File: "Japan, Missiles (WW II)."

69. Caidin, "Japanese Guided Missiles," 692. Bōeichō Bōei Kenshūjo Senshibu, *Rikugun kōkū heiki*, 459.

70. USSBS, *Japanese Aircraft Industry*, 87. Caidin, "Japanese Guided Missiles," 694, 696. Francillon, *Japanese Aircraft*, 532–33.

71. He was mistaken on the time required. The I-gō-C alone had been in development and production for over a year. The quote is from ATIG, "I-gō."

72. USNTM, "Japanese Guided Missiles," Report No. 0-02, 11.

73. GHQ, "Scientific Intelligence Survey," vol. 3, 3-b-2.

74. Bōeichō Bōei Kenshūjo Senshibu, *Rikugun kōkū heiki,* 460–61. Nihon Heiki Kōgyōkai, *Rikusen heiki sōkan,* 549–65.

75. GHQ, "Scientific Intelligence Survey," 1:38. Air Technical Intelligence Group, "Japanese Heat Homing Bombs," Report No. 146, 20 November 1945, NASM, File: "Japan, Missiles (WW II)." [Hereafter cited as ATIG, "Japanese Heat Homing Bombs."]

76. GHQ, "Scientific Intelligence Survey," vol. 2, appendix 1-H-3. ATIG, "Japanese Heat Homing Bombs."

77. GHQ, "Scientific Intelligence Survey," vol. 2, appendix 1-H-1. ATIG, "Japanese Heat Homing Bombs." Caidin, "Japanese Guided Missiles," 693. For a more comprehensive list of the many private firms and universities that participated, see the personnel charts provided in Nihon Heiki Kōgyōkai, *Rikusen heiki sōkan,* 550, 552–54.

78. ATIG, "Japanese Heat Homing Bombs."

79. ATIG, "Japanese Heat Homing Bombs." GHQ, "Scientific Intelligence Survey," 1:38. Caidin, "Japanese Guided Missiles," 693.

80. GHQ, "Scientific Intelligence Survey," vol. 2, appendix 1-H-2. ATIG, "Japanese Heat Homing Bombs." Caidin, "Japanese Guided Missiles," 693. Bōeichō Bōei Kenshūjo Senshibu, *Rikugun kōkū heiki,* 460.

81. GHQ, "Scientific Intelligence Survey," vol. 2, appendix 1-H-2. ATIG, "Japanese Heat Homing Bombs."

82. Compton interview with Yagi, 11 September 1945, GHQ, "Scientific Intelligence Survey," vol. 3, appendix 3-A-4.

83. Naitō, *Kimitsu heiki Funryū,* 23–28. Caidin, "Japanese Guided Missiles," 693.

84. Naitō, *Kimitsu heiki Funryū,* 27–28, 77–79.

85. Naitō, *Kimitsu heiki Funryū,* 77–79, 97–102. Caidin, "Japanese Guided Missiles," 693.

86. Caidin, "Japanese Guided Missiles," 693.

87. Naitō, *Kimitsu heiki Funryū,* 181–83.

88. Naitō, *Kimitsu heiki Funryū,* 166–71. Caidin, "Japanese Guided Missiles," 693–94. Francillon, *Japanese Aircraft,* 533–34.

89. Naitō, *Kimitsu heiki Funryū,* 166–69. Caidin, "Japanese Guided Missiles," 693–94. Francillon, *Japanese Aircraft,* 534.

90. Naitō, *Kimitsu heiki Funryū,* 137–43. Caidin, "Japanese Guided Missiles," 693–94. Francillon, *Japanese Aircraft,* 534.

91. Naitō, *Kimitsu heiki Funryū,* 171. Caidin, "Japanese Guided Missiles," 693–94.

92. As translated from Naitō, *Kimitsu heiki Funryū,* 176.

93. Naitō, *Kimitsu heiki Funryū,* 184–85. Francillon, *Japanese Aircraft,* 533–34.

94. Michael Neufeld, "Rocket Aircraft and the 'Turbojet Revolution.'" Kay and Smith, *German Aircraft,* 247–53.

95. Another type of rocket-propelled intercept aircraft was the Bachem Natter, which remained under development at the end of the war. Kay and Smith, *German Aircraft,* 37–40. See also Jeffrey Ethell and Alfred Price, *Word War II Fighting Jets.*

96. Jean Alexander, *Russian Aircraft Since 1940,* 7. The Soviet Union's first true rocket aircraft, the RP-318-1, actually flew in 1940, but it was an experimental model, unarmed, and not produced for combat. See Harrison, "New Postwar Branches," 119–20.

97. Wayne Biddle, *Barons of the Sky,* 311.

98. Constant considers this a veritable "paradigm shift" in aeronautics. See Edward W. Constant, *Origins of the Turbojet Revolution.*

99. The Campini-Caproni CC.2 is sometimes erroneously given this distinction, having completed its maiden flight a year later on 27 August 1940, but it was not even powered by a true turbojet engine. Designed by the Italian engineer Secondo Campini, the "ducted fan" type power plant of the CC.2 was actually a piston engine that powered a compressor to force air into a combustion chamber where the fuel was ignited, thus providing motive force through the expulsion of the exhaust. Campini called this engine a "thermojet," which differed significantly from true turbojets as they are known today. According to Constant, the Campini system was "simply too big, heavy, and inefficient for the thrust it produced." The project was canceled as a result of poor performance. Constant, *Origins of the Turbojet Revolution,* 227–28.

100. Ibid., 194–200, 208–13.

101. The Me 262 was but one of several jet aircraft, including bombers, that were under development in Germany during the war. On the several types, see especially Kay and Smith, *German Aircraft,* passim.

102. Hugh Morgan, *Me 262,* 29. Kay and Smith, *German Aircraft,* 257–65.

103. James O. Young, "Riding England's Coattails."

104. Ibid.

105. Alexander, *Russian Aircraft Since 1940,* 1–21.

106. *Kamikaze,* meaning "divine wind," is an alternate reading of the Chinese characters for *Shinpū.* The use of the term was meant to evoke a well-known historical event of 1281 in which a typhoon devastated the invading Mongol fleet on the coast of Japan. The timely arrival of the typhoon was seen as nothing less than divine intervention. It was hoped that the modern kamikaze would achieve the same result. Ienaga Saburō, *Pacific War,* 182–83. Ivan Morris, *Nobility of Failure,* 288–89. For an in-depth study of the kamikaze phenomenon, see Emiko Ohnuki-Tierney, *Kamikaze, Cherry Blossoms, and Nationalisms.*

107. He is also referred to as Ota Shōichi in other sources. Nihon kaigun kōkūshi hensan iinkai, *Nihon kaigun kōkūshi,* 1:484. [Hereafter cited as *NKKS.*] Naito states he was with the 1081st Flying Corps. See Naitō Hatsuho, *Thunder Gods,* 9, 23.

108. Naitō, *Thunder Gods,* 40–41. Francillon, *Japanese Aircraft,* 476. The official army history presents a different version of the origin of this project, stating that a special research group was established at the Third Army Aeronautical Technology Research Institute and research began around May 1944. According to the army's version, the project was inspired by knowledge of German missiles that had been successful in sinking Allied ships. Germany provided some blueprints of these to the Japanese, which were transferred via submarine, but no additional explanations or data were given. Army development followed German designs. Collaborative experiments in ballistics were apparently conducted with the navy at the Kure Arsenal from around October 1944. See Bōeichō Bōei Kenshūjo Senshibu, *Rikugun kōkū heiki,* 459.

109. *NKKS,* 1:484. Naitō, *Thunder Gods,* 41.

110. Naitō, *Thunder Gods,* 31–42.

111. Some original sketches and specifications for the *Marudai* project (Yokusuka MXY7) can be found in "Roketto kankei nōto setsu" [File of Notes Concerning Rockets], Bōeichō kenkyūjo toshokan [National Defense Agency Research Institute, Military History Library], Meguro-ku, Tokyo, Japan, Kaigun Shiryō 6, Hikōki 82.

112. *NKKS*, 2:230–31. Morris, *Nobility of Failure*, 276–77. Ohnuki-Tierney, *Kamikaze, Cherry Blossoms, and Nationalisms*, 102–24.

113. Naitō, *Thunder Gods*, 42.

114. *NKKS*, 3:542–43. Ozaki, "Memory of the Design of the Ohka 43B," *Kōkūfan*, photocopy of translation by Hideya Ando, Wright-Patterson United States Air Force Museum Library, Dayton, OH. [Wright-Patterson collection hereafter abbreviated as "WPAFM."] Royal Aircraft Establishment, Farnborough, "F.A. Technical Note No. 272/1," May 1946, WPAFM. Headquarters, Freeman Field, "Description of the Japanese Baka Bomb," 1 April 1946, WPAFM. Francillon, *Japanese Aircraft*, 477.

115. *NKKS*, 3:543–44. Ozaki, "Memory of the Design of the Ohka 43B," *Kōkūfan*, WPAFM. Naitō, *Thunder Gods*, 69.

116. United States Technical Air Intelligence Center, Confidential Brief No. 5, "Baka," 12 April 1945, WPAFM. Headquarters, Freeman Field, "Description of the Japanese Baka Bomb," 1 April 1946, WPAFM. USSBS, *Japanese Aircraft Industry*, 81. Naitō, *Thunder Gods*, 69–70.

117. Ozaki, "Memory of the Design of the Ohka 43B," *Kōkūfan*, WPAFM. For a more detailed account of this event, see Naitō, *Thunder Gods*, 112–18; and Inoguchi Rikihei, Nakajima Tadashi, and Roger Pineau, *Divine Wind*, 141–46.

118. *NKKS*, 1:504–5. Headquarters, Freeman Field, "Description of the Japanese Baka Bomb," 1 April 1946, WPAFM. USSBS, *Japanese Aircraft Industry*, 81.

119. *NKKS*, 3:545–47, 602, 678. Ozaki, "Memory of the Design of the Ohka 43B," *Kōkūfan*, WPAFM. USSBS, *Japanese Aircraft Industry*, 81.

120. *NKKS*, 3:602. Ozaki, "Memory of the Design of the Ohka 43B," *Kōkūfan*, WPAFM. USSBS, *Japanese Aircraft Industry*, 81.

121. *NKKS*, 3:545–48, 602–3. Ozaki, "Memory of the Design of the Ohka 43B," *Kōkūfan*, WPAFM. Francillon, *Japanese Aircraft*, 481.

122. Specifications for the Baika vary among these sources, but all are within an approximate range. See *NKKS*, 3:553–54. Technical Air Intelligence Center, "Possible Japanese Jet and Rocket Development," 1 July 1945, NASM, File: "Japan, Missiles (WW II)." Francillon, *Japanese Aircraft*, 490.

123. The officer is identified as Lieutenant General Endo, Chief of the Japanese Aircraft Ordnance Administration of the Munitions Ministry. See Technical Air Intelligence Center, "Possible Japanese Jet and Rocket Development," 1 July 1945, NASM, File: "Japan, Missiles (WW II)." For an interesting discussion of the body-technology metaphor used during wartime, see Robertson, "Mobilizing for War," passim.

124. *NKKS*, 3:553.

125. Francillon, *Japanese Aircraft*, 388–96, 404–7.

126. A list of the cargo carried from Germany to Japan aboard the *I-29* throughout the war can be found in "Ni-Doitsu gijutsu kōkan ni kan suru kiroku" [Record of Japanese-German Technology Transfers], Bōeichō kenkyūjo toshokan, Meguro-ku, Tokyo, Japan, Kaigun 6, Zenpan 32, 11.

127. Sources differ concerning which materials survived the trip. Iwatani is reported to have had only a written description of the engine with performance data, the formula for the fuel, schematics of the plane showing three views, part of an operator's manual, principal wing cross sections, and notes on propellant-resistant materials. The most recently updated and perhaps most accurate account of this episode is T. Yokoyama,

K. Yuyama, I. Akojima, and S. Moriya, "Rocket Fighter Shusui." Iwatani's own account is given in Fukui et al., *Kimitsu heiki no zembō*, 3–46. See also *NKKS*, 3:549–50, 603–4. USSBS, *Japanese Aircraft Industry*, 73. Hans-Joachim Braun, "Technology Transfer." Iwatani is referred to as "Iwaya" in Francillon, *Japanese Aircraft*, 404–5.

128. Bōeichō Bōei Kenshūjo Senshibu, *Rikugun kōkū heiki*, 427, 432–33.

129. *NKKS*, 3:549–50, 603–4. Bōeichō Bōei Kenshūjo Senshibu, *Rikugun kōkū heiki*, 432. USSBS, *Japanese Aircraft Industry*, 73.

130. *NKKS*, 3:603–4. USSBS, *Japanese Aircraft Industry*, 144–45. Yokoyama et al., "Rocket Fighter Shusui," 259–61.

131. A record of fuselage tests conducted between 8 December 1944 and 24 March 1945 can be found in "Kenkyū jikken seiseki hōkoku: Shisei Shūsui keika kūki kitai kyōdo shaken" [Report on Research Test Results: Results of the Testing of the Shūsui Light Glider Fuselage Strength], 17 May 1945, Bōeichō kenkyūjo toshokan, Meguro-ku, Tokyo, Japan, Kaigun Shiryō 6, Kenkyū Shiryō 137.

132. Bōeichō Bōei Kenshūjo Senshibu, *Rikugun kōkū heiki*, 432. Yokoyama et al., "Rocket Fighter Shusui," 263–65. Francillon, *Japanese Aircraft*, 406–7.

133. *NKKS*, 3:538–39, 549–52. USSBS, *Japanese Aircraft Industry*, 144–45. Francillon, *Japanese Aircraft*, 406–7. For a more extensive discussion of the Shūsui, see Fukui et al., *Kimitsu heiki no zembō*, 78–102.

134. Caidin, "Japanese Guided Missiles," 693.

135. Yokoyama et al., "Rocket Fighter Shusui," 266–71.

136. Ishizawa Kazuhiko, *Kikka*, 69–72.

137. On 23 December 1943, the Ne-0 was loaded into the bomb-bay of a Kawasaki Ki-48 twin-engine light bomber and tested in midflight, technically making it Japan's first jet engine to fly. Ishizawa, *Kikka*, 72–73. Francillon, *Japanese Aircraft*, 106.

138. Ishizawa, *Kikka*, 72–73. Bōeichō Bōei Kenshūjo Senshibu, *Rikugun kōkū heiki*, 433.

139. There were fourteen different types of jet engines developed in Japan between 1943 and 1945. For a listing with specifications, see Ishizawa, *Kikka*, 82–83. For another account of the development of the jet engines for the Kikka, see also Fukui et al., *Kimitsu heiki no zembō*, 46–77.

140. There was also a plan for development of a catapult-assisted launch version. Original documents giving specifications of the Kikka and the Ki 201 Karyū with engineers' notes can be found in "Nakajima hikōki oboegaki: Nakamura, Fukuda-shi nōto yori bassui" [Notes of Nakajima Aircraft: Excerpts from the Notes of Nakamura and Fukuda], Bōeichō kenkyūjo toshokan, Meguro-ku, Tokyo, Japan, Kaigun 6, Hikōki 85, 13–132.

141. Bōeichō Bōei Kenshūjo Senshibu, *Rikugun kōkū heiki*, 433. USSBS, *Japanese Aircraft Industry*, 86. Francillon, *Japanese Aircraft*, 443–45.

142. USSBS, *Japanese Aircraft Industry*, 86. Francillon, *Japanese Aircraft*, 443–45, 488. For a more detailed history of the Kikka, see Ishizawa, *Kikka*, passim.

143. Bōeichō Bōei Kenshūjo Senshibu, *Rikugun kōkū heiki*, 433.

144. Air Technical Intelligence Group, "Comprehensive Report on Solid Rocket Propellants in the Japanese Navy," Report No. 314, 22 January 1946, NASM, File: "Japan, Missiles (WW II)." For biographical information on Hino, see entry "Hino Kumao," *Gendai jinbutsu jiten*, 849.

145. Air Technical Intelligence Group, "Aircraft Rockets," Report No. 307, 15 De-

cember 1945, appendix A, NASM, File: "Japan, Missiles (WW II)." USNTM, "Japanese Propellants, Article 2: Rocket and Gun Propellants—General," Report No. 0-10-2, 5–6. Naitō, *Kimitsu heiki Funryū*, 42–45.

146. Naitō, *Kimitsu heiki Funryū*, 42–45. Caidin, "Japanese Guided Missiles," 693.

147. USNTM, "Japanese Fuels and Lubricants," Report No. X-38 (N)-5.

148. Bōeichō Bōei Kenshūjo Senshibu, *Rikugun kōkū heiki*, 432.

149. A more comprehensive account of Japanese efforts to develop alternative fuels is beyond the scope of this study. On this subject, see Anthony N. Stranges, "Synthetic Fuel Production."

150. *NKKS*, 3:604–5, 884–86. One type of rocket fuel developed was the Ko liquid propellant produced by the Chemical Department of the NTRI. The Ko type was prepared for use in rockets and torpedoes. It contained an 80 percent H_2O_2 solution with a stabilizer. GHQ, "Scientific Intelligence Survey," vol. 2, 2-B-b-5.

151. Nenryō konwakai-hen, eds., *Nihon kaigun nenryōshi—shita*, 1067–68.

152. See Oshio Takeshi, *Nitchitsu kontsuerun no kenkyū*, 244–45. Kan Jeon et al., *Chōsen ni okeru Nitchitsu kontsuerun*, 265–66. Barbara Molony, *Technology and Investment*, 230. For a detailed description of the Hungnam industrial complex under Noguchi, see Walter E. Grunden, "Hungnam and the Japanese Atomic Bomb."

153. Account of Kusama Jun, "Kōnan jidai no kaisō," 17.

154. Kamata Shōji, *Hokusen no Nihonjin kunanki*, 259. Nenryō konwakai-hen, *Nihon kaigun nenryōshi—shita*, 1080–84.

155. Kan et al., *Chōsen ni okeru Nitchitsu kontsuerun*, 266.

156. Chief among these was ceramic production. Kan et al., *Chōsen ni okeru Nitchitsu kontsuerun*, 266–67. USNTM, "Japanese Fuels and Lubricants: Article 5, Research on Rocket Fuels of the Hydrogen Peroxide-Hydrazine Type," No. X-38 (N)-5.

157. The Yamagita plant could produce 100 tons per month. USNTM, "Japanese Fuels and Lubricants," No. X-38 (N)-5. Nenryō konwakai-hen, *Nihon kaigun nenryōshi—shita*, 1067–68.

158. GHQ, "Scientific Intelligence Survey," 1:37.

159. Neufeld, "Rocket Aircraft and the 'Turbojet Revolution,'" 229.

160. USSBS, *Japanese Aircraft Industry*, 24–27. In the prevailing ideology of the day, employment outside the home, especially of married women, was considered contrary to the national interest because it could destabilize the traditional family structure by tainting the "virtue" of women and interfering with a woman's proper role as mother. For fascinating explorations of this topic, see especially Regine Mathias, "Women and the War Economy in Japan"; and Thomas R. Havens, "Women and War in Japan."

161. GHQ, "Scientific Intelligence Survey," 1:48–50.

162. Air Technical Intelligence Group, "Possible Japanese Jet and Rocket Development," 1 July 1945, NASM, File: "Japan, Missiles (WW II)."

163. "Ni-Doitsu gijutsu kōkan ni kan suru kiroku" [Record of Japanese-German Technology Transfers], Bōeichō kenkyūjo toshokan, Meguro-ku, Tokyo, Japan, Kaigun 6, Zenpan 32, 11.

164. Stephenson interview with Kurt Schmidt, GHQ, "Scientific Intelligence Survey," vol. 3, appendix 26-2.

165. Stephenson interview with Franz Pohl, 16 October 1945, and Stephenson interview with Kurt Schiffner, 17 October 1945, GHQ, "Scientific Intelligence Survey," vol. 3, appendix 26-2.

166. Longacre interview with Heinrich Foders, 12 October 1945, GHQ, "Scientific Intelligence Survey," vol. 3, appendix 26.
167. Information on various rocket types was transported aboard the *I-8* in 1943, and data on the V-1 and various missiles was shared in 1944. See listing in "Ni-Doitsu gijutsu kōkan ni kan suru kiroku" [Record of Japanese-German Technology Transfers], Bōeichō kenkyūjo toshokan, Meguro-ku, Tokyo, Japan, Kaigun 6, Zenpan 32, 10–13.
168. John W. M. Chapman, " 'Have-Nots' Go to War." See also Bernd Martin, *Japan and Germany in the Modern World*, 272–81.
169. USNTM, "Japanese Naval Rockets," Report No. 0-09, 1.

CHAPTER 5. CHEMICAL AND BIOLOGICAL WARFARE

1. On the history of CBW in general, see Julian Perry Robinson, *Rise of CB Weapons;* Erhard Geissler and John Ellis van Courtland Moon, *Biological and Toxin Weapons;* Robert Harris and Jeremy Paxman, *Higher Form of Killing;* Edward M. Spiers, *Chemical Warfare;* Victor A. Utgoff, *Challenge of Chemical Weapons;* and Frederic J. Brown, *Chemical Warfare*.
2. Spiers, *Chemical Warfare*, 13–14.
3. Spiers, *Chemical Warfare*, 18–19. Robinson, *Rise of CB Weapons*, 26–31, 127–34.
4. Spiers, *Chemical Warfare*, 24–25. Robinson, *Rise of CB Weapons*, 38. Harris and Paxman, *Higher Form of Killing*, 10–38, 39.
5. Leo P. Brophy, Wyndham D. Miles, and Rexmond C. Cochrane, *Chemical Warfare Service: From Laboratory to Field*, 2–8.
6. Leo Brophy and George J. B. Fisher, *Chemical Warfare Service: Organizing for War*, 3–5.
7. On the formative years of CW research in Japan, see Tanaka Hiroaki, "Kagaku heiki kenkyū." See also Bu Ping, *Nihon no Chūgoku shinryaku to doku gasu heiki*, 43–50. For a more complete history of Japan's wartime CW program, see Obara Hiroto et al., *Nihongun no dokugasusen;* and Murata Tadayoshi et al., *Nihongun no kagakusen*.
8. Tsuneishi Keiichi, "C. Koizumi." For a more complete biographical account of Koizumi, see Tsuneishi Keiichi and Asano Tomizō, *Saikinsen butai*, 15–30.
9. Rikugun Gun'i Gakkō, *Rikugun gun'i gakkō gojūnenshi*, 89. See also Tsuneishi and Asano, *Saikinsen butai*, 51.
10. According to *Rikugun gun'i gakkō gojūnenshi*, Koizumi was involved in "secret research" for the Army Technology Review Board as early 1911, but the details and nature of this research are not given (89).
11. Tanaka, "Kagaku heiki kenkyū," 66.
12. Rikugun gun'i gakkō, *Rikugun gun'i gakkō gojūnenshi*, 90. Tanaka, "Kagaku heiki kenkyū," 66–67. Tsuneishi and Asano, *Saikinsen butai*, 51–56.
13. Spiers, *Chemical Warfare*, 26–27.
14. Brophy et al., *Chemical Warfare Service: From Laboratory to Field*, 18.
15. Office of Naval Intelligence, Technical Intelligence Center, "Naval Aspects of Biological Warfare," 5 August 1947, U.S. National Archives, Washington, DC, General Records of the Department of the Navy, RG 80, Box 55, appendix 7, 60. [Hereafter cited as ONI, "Naval Aspects of Biological Warfare."]

16. ONI, "Naval Aspects of Biological Warfare," 60. For a more complete account of German biological sabotage during this period, see especially Mark Wheelis, "Biological Sabotage in World War I."

17. Robinson, *Rise of CB Weapons*, 17, 216–17.

18. Spiers, *Chemical Warfare*, 46–47. Harris and Paxman, *Higher Form of Killing*, 46–48. Robinson, *Rise of CB Weapons*, 246–47. Utgoff, *Challenge of Chemical Weapons*, 16–18. Brown, *Chemical Warfare*, 97–125.

19. Japan's reasons for abstention are not entirely clear, but it may be that, like the United States, it felt it "had very little to gain and a great deal to lose" by signing the chemical weapons ban. See Brown, *Chemical Warfare*, 119. Loss of potential military advantage in CBW was the most likely factor for Japan. See Military Intelligence Service, Intelligence Research Project No. 2263, "Japanese Biological Warfare," 26 July 1945, U.S. National Archives, College Park, MD, RG 226, Folder No. 3, Section 4, 2. See also Murata Tadayoshi et al., *Nihongun no kagakusen*, 7–9.

20. Before World War II, the CWS mostly assisted civilian organizations in the development of pesticides and chemical agents for rodent control. Brophy et al., *Chemical Warfare Service: From Laboratory to Field*, 4, 24–25, 32–34.

21. Military cooperation between Germany and the USSR lasted for about ten years until terminated by Hitler, along with the Tomka Project, in 1933. See Valentin Bojtzov and Erhard Geissler, "Military Biology in the USSR, 1920–45," 154. Harris and Paxman, *Higher Form of Killing*, 45–49.

22. ONI, "Naval Aspects of Biological Warfare," 46–59. Edward M. Spiers, *Chemical Weaponry*, 83–84. Bojtzov and Geissler, "Military Biology in the USSR," 156. Robinson, *Rise of CB Weapons*, 141–42, 231–41, 284–87.

23. Harris and Paxman, *Higher Form of Killing*, 53.

24. Robinson, *Rise of CB Weapons*, 142–44. Harris and Paxman, *Higher Form of Killing*, 51–52.

25. Bob Tadashi Wakabayashi, "Documents on Japanese Poison Gas Warfare in China." Harris and Paxman, *Higher Form of Killing*, 70–108. Robinson, *Rise of CB Weapons*, 271–86.

26. In the United Kingdom, Gruinard Island in Gruinard Bay on the northwest coast of Scotland was used as a major testing ground. For more on the British BW program, see Gradon B. Carter and Graham S. Pearson, "British Biological Warfare and Biological Defense." Robinson, *Rise of CB Weapons*, 117–19. Harris and Paxman, *Higher Form of Killing*, 70–108. On testing in Australia, see Bridget Goodwin, "Australia's Mustard Gas Guinea Pigs."

27. Robinson, *Rise of CB Weapons*, 278.

28. Brophy et al., *Chemical Warfare Service: From Laboratory to Field*, 36, 42–44. See also James Phinney Baxter, *Scientists Against Time*, 271, 278–79.

29. See especially, Donald H. Avery, *Science of War*, 122–50.

30. Brophy et al., *Chemical Warfare Service: From Laboratory to Field*, 32–46. Baxter, *Scientists Against Time*, 272–78. Robinson, *Rise of CB Weapons*, 276, n. 9.

31. ONI, "Naval Aspects of Biological Warfare," 38. Brophy et al., *Chemical Warfare Service: From Laboratory to Field*, 102–4. Robinson, *Rise of CB Weapons*, 120, n. 44. Harris and Paxman, *Higher Form of Killing*, 97–98.

32. The U.S. navy collaborated with the army at Camp Detrick, Frederick, Maryland. The navy also conducted BW research at its Naval Medical Research Unit Number One at the University of California. See ONI, "Naval Aspects of Biological Warfare,"

38. See also Brophy et al., *Chemical Warfare Service: From Laboratory to Field*, 107–10. Robinson, *Rise of CB Weapons*, 121 (fn. 45).

33. Brophy et al., *Chemical Warfare Service: From Laboratory to Field*, 106–8.

34. Ibid., 109–11. Robinson, *Rise of CW Weapons*, 120.

35. Robinson, *Rise of CW Weapons*, 119–20. For more on the U.S. BW program, see also John Ellis Van Courtland Moon, "U.S. Biological Warfare Planning and Preparedness."

36. Military Intelligence Division, War Department, Washington, DC, "Biological Warfare: Activities & Capabilities of Foreign Nations," 30 March 1946, U.S. National Archives, College Park, MD, RG 319, 1946–1948, P&O Files, P&O 381, "Biological Warfare," TS, Case 67/3, Annex H, 4–5. ONI, "Naval Aspects of Biological Warfare," 46–59. Bojtzov and Geissler, "Military Biology in the USSR," 157–60.

37. According to German documents captured by the U.S. Naval Intelligence Office, the Soviets may also have conducted BW research on "political prisoners" in Mongolia. ONI, "Naval Aspects of Biological Warfare," 46–59. Robinson, *Rise of CB Weapons*, 309, n. 5. Harris and Paxman, *Higher Form of Killing*, 144–51.

38. Bojtzov and Geissler, "Military Biology in the USSR," 160–62.

39. U.S. intelligence estimates for Italy's chemical weapons production were much lower. See United States Military Intelligence Service, *Enemy Capabilities for Chemical Warfare*, 54. Compare to figures given in Harris and Paxman, *Higher Form of Killing*, 51–52.

40. The quote is from Spiers, *Chemical Warfare*, 73.

41. ONI, "Naval Aspects of Biological Warfare," 12.

42. The U.S. Military Intelligence Service (MIS) had also identified twelve German-run poison gas manufacturing plants in France, eleven in Poland, seven in Czechoslovakia, three each in Austria and Belgium, and one each in Hungary, Romania, and Holland. Fifty-one additional plants were known to have been producing chlorine, but it was not known whether these were to be used for poison gas production. See MIS, *Enemy Capabilities for Chemical Warfare*, 6.

43. Harris and Paxman, *Higher Form of Killing*, 55–60.

44. Robinson, *Rise of CB Weapons*, 155–56. Harris and Paxman, *Higher Form of Killing*, 62–68. See also Robert J. Lifton, *Nazi Doctors*, 160–62.

45. Among these were the Kliewe Laboratory, the Sachsenburg Institute for Microbiology, the Central Institute for Cancer Research, the Insel Riems State Research Institute, and the Kaiser Wilhelm Institute for Horticultural Research, to name a few. The Army Proving Ground at Raubkammer was the primary facility for testing. See Erhard Geissler, "Biological Warfare Activities in Germany."

46. ONI, "Naval Aspects of Biological Warfare," 61–63, 67.

47. ONI, "Naval Aspects of Biological Warfare," 61–63. Geissler, "Biological Warfare Activities in Germany," 102–4. Robinson, *The Rise of CB Weapons*, 116–17.

48. ONI, "Naval Aspects of Biological Warfare," 73.

49. The majority of human experimentation in BW research appears to have been conducted at sites at or near concentration/work/death camps. See "SS Medical Research," 4 September 1945, Field Information Agency, Technical Control Commission for Germany, Scientific and Technological Branch, U.S. National Archives, College Park, MD, RG 112, Entry 295A, Box 8, Folder: "German Info on CBW." ONI, "Naval Aspects of Biological Warfare," 69–70. Robert Proctor, *Racial Hygiene*, 217–22. Harris and Paxman, *Higher Form of Killing*, 62–67.

50. Proctor, *Racial Hygiene,* 221. On these subjects, see also Götz Aly, Peter Chroust, and Christian Pross, *Cleansing the Fatherland,* passim. Michael Burleigh, *Death and Deliverance,* passim.

51. Tanaka Yuki, "Poison Gas." Brown, *Chemical Warfare,* 246–47. Robinson, *Rise of CB Weapons,* 287.

52. Tsuneishi, "C. Koizumi," 102–5. Tsuneishi and Asano, *Saikinsen butai,* 57–62, 97–98.

53. Quotations are from Tanaka, "Poison Gas," 10–11. Robinson, *Rise of CB Weapons,* 287.

54. Tsuneishi Keiichi, "Research Guarded by Military Secrecy."

55. Tanaka, "Poison Gas," 11.

56. General Headquarters, United States Army Forces, Pacific, Science and Technical Advisory Section, "Report on Scientific Intelligence Survey in Japan: September and October 1945," 1 November 1945, vol. 4, *Chemical Warfare,* U.S. National Archives, College Park, MD, RG 165, Box 2056, 18, and appendix CW-2-3. [Hereafter cited as GHQ, "Scientific Intelligence Survey," vol. 4.] See also Tanaka, "Poison Gas," 11.

57. GHQ, "Scientific Intelligence Survey," 4:18.

58. Tanaka, "Poison Gas," 11.

59. "Kagaku heiki kyōiku kōgi sōmokujihei tannin kubun" [Section with Responsibility for the Complete Contents of the Chemical Weapons Education Lectures], Bōeichō kenkyūjo toshokan, Meguro-ku, Tokyo, Japan, Rikugun, Chūō 48, Tenpan 595.

60. Two Japanese, identified only as Major K. Iida and a Mr. S. Uyeno, an engineer with an army arsenal, were granted permission to visit a federal laboratory in Pittsburgh, Pennsylvania, on 3 December 1934 with approval of the U.S. Chemical Warfare Service. See K. Matsumoto, Colonel, I.J.A., Military Attaché, Japanese Embassy to Colonel C. Burnett, General Staff, Foreign Liaison Officer, War Department, November 14, 1934, U.S. National Archives, College Park, MD, MID File: 2016-919.

61. GHQ, "Scientific Intelligence Survey," 4:2–3, 39, 46–47, appendix CW-3-1.

62. Major H. E. Skipper interview of Major General Kinsei Akiyama, 2 October 1945, GHQ, "Scientific Intelligence Survey," vol. 4, appendix CW-8-1. The subject interviewed here, Major General Akiyama Kinsei, was a prominent figure in Japan's CW program and provided U.S. scientific intelligence investigators a great deal of information after the war. From 1933 to 1935, Akiyama studied CW and chemical weapons under the French army in Paris. After returning to Japan in 1935, he became director of the CW training school in Narashino, and in 1940, was named director of the Chemical Department branch laboratory in Tsitsihar, Manchuria. He was director of the Sixth Army Technical Institute at the end of the war.

63. GHQ, "Scientific Intelligence Survey," 4:3, 19, 22, Appendices CW-3-1, CW-4-1, and CW-8-5.

64. GHQ, "Scientific Intelligence Survey," 4:4, appendix CW-2-2. Robinson, *Rise of CB Weapons,* 289.

65. Tanaka, "Poison Gas," 12–14. For a more complete history of the Okunoshima factory, see Takeda Eiko, *Chizu kara kiesareta jima.*

66. U.S. Naval Technical Mission to Japan, "Reports of the U.S. Naval Technical Mission to Japan, 1945–1946: Japanese Chemical Warfare," December 1945, U.S.

National Archives, Washington, DC, U.S. Naval History Division, Operational Archives, microfilm. See also GHQ, "Scientific Intelligence Survey," 4:42, appendix CW-2-2, CW-6-1, and CW-6-2.

67. MIS, *Enemy Capabilities for Chemical Warfare*, 89–90.

68. GHQ, AFPAC, Office of the Chief Chemical Officer, "Intelligence Report on Japanese Chemical Warfare, Volume I, General Organization Policies and Intentions, Tactics," 15 May 1946, U.S. National Archives, College Park, MD, RG 319, Box 2097, Assistant Chief of Staff for Intelligence, Document Library Branch, Publications File, 19.

69. Ibid.

70. MIS, *Enemy Capabilities for Chemical Warfare*, 87–88.

71. Wakabayashi, "Documents on Japanese Poison Gas Warfare in China," 3–33.

72. Bob Tadashi Wakabayashi, "Research Notes on Japanese Poison Gas Warfare in China."

73. The figures given for incidents of poison gas attacks range from 886 to 2,091 separate occasions. See "Condensed Statement of Information Available Concerning Japanese Use of War Gas," U.S. National Archives, College Park, MD, RG 319, Assistant Chief of Staff for Intelligence, Document Library Branch, Publications File. See also Awaya Kentarō, "Japanese Mustard Gas in China," 3–6. Robinson, *Rise of CB Weapons*, 217–19. Harris and Paxman, *Higher Form of Killing*, 50–51. For a more complete account of Japanese CW and related activities in China, in Japanese, see Bu Ping, *Nihon no Chūgoku shinryaku to doku gasu heiki*, passim; Obara et al., *Nihongun no dokugasusen*, passim; and Murata Tadayoshi et al., *Nihongun no kagakusen*, passim.

74. Spiers, *Chemical Warfare*, 73–75, 83.

75. "Interrogation of General Hideki Tojo," 2 April 1946, General Headquarters, United States Army Forces, Pacific, Office of the Chief Chemical Office, "Japanese Chemical Warfare Policies and Intentions," U.S. National Archives, College Park, MD, RG 38, Records of the Chief of Naval Operations, ONI Monograph Files, Box 69, File: "Japan: Chemical Warfare," Microfilm: MIS: 261223. Other Japanese army officers interviewed after the war echoed Tōjō's statements. See GHQ, AFPAC, Office of the Chief Chemical Officer, "Intelligence Report on Japanese Chemical Warfare, Volume I, General Organization Policies and Intentions, Tactics," 15 May 1946, U.S. National Archives, College Park, MD, RG 319, Box 2097, Assistant Chief of Staff for Intelligence, Document Library Branch, Publications File, 7.

76. Major H. Skipper interview with Major General K. Akiyama, 16 October 1945, GHQ, "Scientific Intelligence Survey," vol. 4, appendix CW-13-3.

77. Arvo T. Thompson, "Report on Japanese Biological Warfare (BW) Activities," 31 May 1946, Army Service Forces, Camp Detrick, Frederick, Maryland, U.S. National Archives, College Park, MD, RG 319, Box 2097, File: "Japanese Biological Warfare Activities, Army Defense Forces," 2. [Hereafter cited as Thompson, "Report on Japanese Biological Warfare."] General Headquarters, United States Army Forces, Pacific, Science and Technical Advisory Section, "Report on Scientific Intelligence Survey in Japan: September and October 1945," 1 November 1945, vol. 5, *Biological Warfare*, U.S. National Archives, College Park, MD, RG 165, Box 2056, 1. [Hereafter cited as GHQ, "Scientific Intelligence Survey," vol. 5.] See also testimony of Kajitsuka Ryūji, in *Materials on the Trial of Former Servicemen*, 105–6. For more complete background on Ishii and Japan's BW program in general, see Sheldon H. Harris, *Factories of Death*; and Peter Williams and David Wallace, *Unit 731*. In Japanese, see especially the several works by Tsuneishi Keiichi.

78. One former member of the General Staff, Endō Saburō, recalls Ishii making the rounds at General Staff Headquarters trying to interest army brass in BW research. See Endō Saburō, *Nitchū jyūgonen sensō to watakushi*, 162–63.

79. Ishii initially paid for the trip himself, but is reported to have subsequently received government funding under "quasi-official status." GHQ, "Scientific Intelligence Survey," 5:2. Thompson, "Report on Japanese Biological Warfare," 2. Tsuneishi and Asano, *Saikinsen butai*, 80–81.

80. Testimony of Kajitsuka, *Materials on the Trial of Former Servicemen*, 295.

81. Testimony of Kawashima Kiyoshi, *Materials on the Trial of Former Servicemen*, 113–14. GHQ, "Scientific Intelligence Survey," 5:2, appendix 29-E-a-1.

82. Perhaps one reason Ishii initially had such difficulty gaining the support of top army brass was because he hailed from the wrong school faction (*gakubatsu*). Graduates of Japan's elite Tokyo Imperial University dominated among high-ranking officers, particularly in the Department of the Army Surgeon General, and as a graduate of Kyoto Imperial University, Ishii would have been seen as something of an outsider. It is otherwise difficult to explain the sudden change of opinion among army brass concerning BW research once Ishii gained Koizumi's support. See Tsuneishi Keiichi, *Kieta saikinsen butai*, 24–25. Tsuneishi and Asano, *Saikinsen butai*, 79–81. Tsuneishi, "C. Koizumi," 104.

83. Ishii allegedly demonstrated the efficiency of the filtration unit to superior officers by urinating into it and then drinking the processed output. Author Edward Behr states that on one occasion, during an imperial inspection where the purifier became the focus of attention, Ishii even offered the "end product" to the emperor to drink. This alleged act seems very unlikely if Ishii were indeed the nationalist he is portrayed to be by Behr and Harris. Such behavior would have been far beyond the bounds of protocol concerning conduct before the emperor. The account given in Williams and Wallace, where filtered water, but not from urine, was offered to the emperor, seems more likely. The account given by Behr is undocumented. See Edward Behr, *Hirohito*, 164. Harris, *Factories of Death*, 41. Williams and Wallace, *Unit 731*, 10–11. The imperial inspection of the Ishii water purifier is mentioned in Tsuneishi, *Kieta saikinsen butai*, 46.

84. Tsuneishi, "Research Guarded by Military Secrecy," 79–92. Testimony of Kawashima, *Materials on the Trial of Former Servicemen*, 114. Harris, *Factories of Death*, 27–34.

85. I am indebted to Morris F. Low for the discussion of Manchuria as a "moral space" for Ishii's research. In this capacity, it might be compared to the Allies' use of the Australian outback for chemical weapons testing in World War II. On the latter subject, see Bridget Goodwin, "Australia's Mustard Gas Guinea Pigs," and Donald Avery, "Canadian Scientists," 139–71 and 229–51, respectively.

86. Testimony of Kawashima, *Materials on the Trial of Former Servicemen*, 118–19.

87. On the history of Harbin, see Søren Clausen and Stig Thøgersen, *Making of a Chinese City*, passim.

88. *Materials on the Trial of Former Servicemen*, 165–67.

89. There are conflicting descriptions of the Beiyinhe site. Harris, on the basis of an article by Chinese scholar Han Xiao, describes Beiyinhe and the adjoining Zhong Ma prison camp as a veritable fortress, whereas Endō Saburō in his account of visiting the site in 1932 describes it as a former large soy sauce factory surrounded by high mud

walls that had been commandeered by the Japanese. See Harris, *Factories of Death*, 27–38; and Endō, *Nitchū jyūgonen sensō to watakushi*, 162.

90. Harris, *Factories of Death*, 27–38. Williams and Wallace, *Unit 731*, 32–36. Testimony of Kawashima, *Materials on the Trial of Former Servicemen*, 114. Endō, *Nitchū jyūgonen sensō to watakushi*, 162.

91. Tōjō Hideki, who served concurrently as chief of the Police Affairs Department of the Kwantung Province Bureau and Commander of the Kwantung Army Military Police from September 1935 to March 1937, was allegedly among the first to see these graphic films by Ishii. The source of this claim remains uncertain. Both Williams and Wallace, *Unit 731*, 32–33, and Harris, *Factories of Death*, 185, cite Tsuneishi, who discusses how Ishii also allegedly used such films for "training" new personnel later in the BW program. See Tsuneishi, *Kieta saikinsen butai*, 105–11.

92. Endō, *Nitchū jyūgonen sensō to watakushi*, 162.

93. Kajitsuka, *Materials on the Trial of Former Servicemen*, 295.

94. Testimony of Kawashima, *Materials on the Trial of Former Servicemen*, 10–11, 106, 114, 313–14. For details on the formation and operation of the Epidemic Prevention and Water Supply Unit, see Thompson, "Report on Japanese Biological Warfare," 4–8. For additional background, see Harris, *Factories of Death*, 39–43; Tsuneishi, *Kieta saikinsen butai*, 53–56; and Tsuneishi and Asano, *Saikinsen butai*, 86–87.

95. Unit 100 employed between 600 and 800 military and civilian personnel and also allegedly engaged in research using human beings. *Materials on the Trial of Former Servicemen*, 10–11.

96. Harris, *Factories of Death*, 42–50.

97. It became standard in the early historiography of Unit 731 to romanize this place name as *Pingfan*, on the basis of the spelling in U.S. intelligence reports and the Khabarovsk trials. The correct romanization is *Pingfang*.

98. GHQ, "Scientific Intelligence Survey," 5:1–4, appendix 29-F-b.

99. Interview with Colonel Tomosada Masuda and Lieutenant Colonel Seiichi Niizuma, GHQ, "Scientific Intelligence Survey," vol. 5, appendix 29-F-b. Harris, *Factories of Death*, 45–48.

100. For a description of Pingfang based on interviews with relevant Japanese personnel, see Thompson, "Report on Japanese Biological Warfare," 8–9. GHQ, "Scientific Intelligence Survey," vol. 5, map of Pingfang site in supplement 2-a. Tsuneishi, *Kieta saikinsen butai*, 70–84.

101. One number given for the production rate of microbes in a single cycle is 30,000,000 billion. See *Materials on the Trial of Former Servicemen*, 13. See also Lt. Col. Murray Sanders interview of Doctor Ryōichi Naitō, 6 October 1945, GHQ, "Scientific Intelligence Survey," vol. 5, appendix 29-E-a-2.

102. Organization Table of the KW-Water Purification Department, GHQ, "Scientific Intelligence Survey," vol. 5, supplement 1-d.

103. Tsuneishi and Asano, *Saikinsen butai*, 224–25. A Japanese medical officer, under interrogation as a POW, also alleged that some aspects of BW research were being conducted at the Kitasato Institute of Infectious Diseases in Tokyo. Details on the connections to Ishii, however, are not given. See Military Intelligence Service, Intelligence Research Project No. 2263, "Japanese Biological Warfare," 26 July 1945, U.S. National Archives, College Park, MD, RG 226, Folder No. 3, Section 4, 3.

104. Lt. Col. Murray Sanders interview of Col. Tomosada Masuda; Lt. Col. Seiichi

Niizuma, 11 October 1945, GHQ, "Scientific Intelligence Survey," vol. 5, appendix 29-F-a-7. ONI, "Naval Aspects of Biological Warfare," 85.

105. On the Nomonhan Incident, see Alvin D. Coox, *Nomonhan*.

106. Ironically, Japanese wartime propaganda accused the Soviets of conducting BW as early as 1935, and Japanese army officers used this as a pretext to justify BW research to U.S. intelligence officers after the war. See Military Intelligence Service, Intelligence Research Project No. 2263, "Japanese Biological Warfare," 26 July 1945, U.S. National Archives, College Park, MD, RG 226, Folder No. 3, Section 4, 3–6. See also Thompson, "Report on Japanese Biological Warfare," 3–4. Testimony of Nishi Toshihide, *Materials on the Trial of Former Servicemen*, 288.

107. *Materials on the Trial of Former Servicemen*, 22–25. Military Intelligence Service, Intelligence Research Project, No. 2263, "Japanese Biological Warfare," 26 July 1945, U.S. National Archives, College Park, MD, RG 226, Folder No. 3, Section 4, 30, lists ten possible occasions of Japanese BW use in China.

108. Interviews of Dr. Shirō Ishii, 22 November 1947, and Dr. Toyohiro Hamada, 28 November 1947, in "Summary Report on B.W. Investigations," Edwin V. Hill to General Alden C. Waitt, 12 December 1947, U.S. National Archives, College Park, MD, collection file "Biological Warfare in WW II (Japan)."

109. Robert P. McQuail to Assistant Chief of Staff, G-2, Far East Command, 17 January 1947, U.S. National Archives, College Park, MD, collection file "Biological Warfare in WW II (Japan)." A compilation of research notes from Unit 731 has been published in Tanaka Akira and Matsumura Takao, *731-Butai sakusei shiryō*. The range of Unit 731 human experimentation in China during the war has become a popular topic of discussion in Japan. There are now numerous publications on this difficult subject. The more scholarly treatments (not previously cited) include: Tsuneishi Keiichi, *731-Butai*; and Tsuneishi Keiichi, *Igakushatachi no sōshiki hanzai*. Books written for a more popular audience include Morimura Seiichi, *Akuma no hōshoku*; Morimura Seiichi, *Sabakareta 731 butai*; and Han Xiao, *Nanasanichi-butai no hanzai*, to name only a few. Published testimonials of Unit 731 members have also become popular.

110. Han Xiao, "Compilation of the Fascist Atrocities," 145.

111. Han, "Compilation of the Fascist Atrocities," 146–47. Tanaka and Matsumura, *731-Butai sakusei shiryō*, 225–38. Tsuneishi, *731-Butai*, 122–27. Testimony of Nishi and Furuichi, *Materials on the Trial of Former Servicemen*, 289, 357–58.

112. Although there are indeed parallels to Nazi "research" in eugenics, one might argue there was a significant difference between the agendas of Ishii and, for example, Josef Mengele. Nazi activities were genocidal in nature and, as previously noted, targeted specifically Jews and other so-called *untermenschen* as designated under the policies of the Final Solution. For the most part, their research served no real medical purpose. Although Ishii allegedly was interested in studying the variation in responses to diseases among the races, he appears not to have harbored any such grand scheme as genocide or ethnic cleansing against any particular group. In general, his research was ostensibly to serve some medical purpose, such as finding treatments for frostbite, malnutrition, and the like. But his actions were of course no less immoral or criminal than his Nazi counterparts. On Japanese wartime atrocities in general, see especially Tanaka Yuki, *Hidden Horrors*.

113. Tsuneishi, *Kieta saikinsen butai*, 102–5. Williams and Wallace, *Unit 731*, 36. Tanaka, *Hidden Horrors*, 163.

114. Sources give conflicting production numbers and years. See Thompson, "Report on Japanese Biological Warfare," 11; and Military Intelligence Division, U.S. War Department, "Biological Warfare: Activities and Capabilities of Foreign Nations," 30 March 1946, U.S. National Archives, College Park, MD, RG 319, 1946–1948, P&O Files, 381, "Biological Warfare," TS, Case 67/3.

115. ONI, "Naval Aspects of Biological Warfare," 88–89. For line drawings and specifications of the various bombs, see Thompson, "Report on Japanese Biological Warfare," 12–13, supplements 4A–4G. See also Military Intelligence Division, War Department, Washington, DC, "Biological Warfare: Activities & Capabilities of Foreign Nations," 30 March 1946, U.S. National Archives, College Park, MD, RG 319, 1946–1948, P&O Files, 381, "Biological Warfare," TS, Case 67/3.

116. ONI, "Naval Aspects of Biological Warfare," 88. Lt. Col. Murray Sanders interview of Dr. Ryōichi Naitō, 6 October 1945, GHQ, "Scientific Intelligence Survey," vol. 5, appendix 29-E-a-5.

117. Edwin V. Hill to General Alden C. Waitt, "Summary Report on BW Investigations," 12 December 1947, U.S. National Archives, College Park, MD, collection file, "Biological Warfare in WW II (Japan)."

118. On the plans to use balloons for BW against the United States, see Williams and Wallace, *Unit 731*, 58, 86–87, 145. For more on the Japanese balloon bomb project, see Robert C. Mikesh, *Japan's World War II Balloon Bomb Attacks*. In Japanese, see Yoshino Koichi, *Fūsen bakudan*.

119. GHQ, AFPAC, Office of the Chief Chemical Officer, "Intelligence Report on Japanese Chemical Warfare, Volume I, General Organization Policies and Intentions, Tactics," 15 May 1946, U.S. National Archives, College Park, MD, RG 319, Box 2097, Assistant Chief of Staff for Intelligence, Document Library Branch, Publications File, 21.

120. Ibid. A similar statement can be found in GHQ, "Scientific Intelligence Survey," 4:2–3.

121. GHQ, "Scientific Intelligence Survey," 4:2–3.

122. Ibid., 2.

123. Ibid., 2–4.

124. Ibid., appendix CW-3-12.

125. Ibid., 2–4.

126. GHQ, "Scientific Intelligence Survey," vol. 4, appendix CW-15-2. See also GHQ, AFPAC, Office of the Chief Chemical Officer, "Intelligence Report on Japanese Chemical Warfare, Volume I, General Organization Policies and Intentions, Tactics," 15 May 1946, U.S. National Archives, College Park, MD, RG 319, Box 2097, Assistant Chief of Staff for Intelligence, Document Library Branch, Publications File, 5.

127. GHQ, "Scientific Intelligence Survey," 4:5–6, appendix CW-2-3.

128. Ibid., 5–6.

129. Ibid., appendix CW-2-3, appendix CW-15-2.

130. Ibid., 21–22, 44, 47.

131. Ibid., 44.

132. Major H. Skipper interview with Major General K. Akiyama, 16 October 1945, GHQ, "Scientific Intelligence Survey," vol. 4, appendix CW-13-1.

133. GHQ, "Scientific Intelligence Survey," vol. 4, appendix CW-22-1.

134. Ishii was promoted to lieutenant general on 1 March 1945. See Thompson, "Report on Japanese Biological Warfare," 3.

135. From 1937 to 1940, the majority of the funding went to construction of the

Pingfang compound. Thereafter, nearly all of the budget allotment went to research. Lt. Col. Murray Sanders interview of Col. Tomosada Masuda; Lt. Col. Seiichi Niizuma, 11 and 16 October 1945, GHQ, "Scientific Intelligence Survey," vol. 5, appendix 29-F-a-6, 29-F-b-1.

136. General Umezu Yoshijirō served as Commander of the Kwantung Army until his promotion to Army Chief of Staff in July 1944. He was succeeded by Yamada Otozō who served in that post until August 1945. Testimony of Yamada Otozō, *Materials on the Trial of Former Servicemen*, 273–74.

137. Interrogation report, Major General Kawashima Kiyoshi, at Khabarovsk, 12–16 September 1946, U.S. National Archives, College Park, MD, collection file "Biological Warfare in WW II (Japan)." GHQ, "Scientific Intelligence Survey," 5:3 and appendix 29-C-a-2.

138. GHQ, "Scientific Intelligence Survey," vol. 5, Lt. Col. Murray Sanders interview of Lt. Col. Saichi Niizuma (Army) and Col. Tomosada Masuda, appendix 29-E-d-2.

139. GHQ, "Scientific Intelligence Survey," 5:6–7.

140. Lt. Col. Murray Sanders interview of Lt. Col. Saichi Niizuma (Army); Col. Tomosada Masuda, GHQ, "Scientific Intelligence Survey," vol. 5, appendix 29-E-d-2.

141. ONI, "Naval Aspects of Biological Warfare," 97–99.

142. See U.S. Naval Technical Mission to Japan, "Japanese Bacteriological Warfare," November 1945, U.S. National Archives, College Park, MD, RG 112, Entry 295A, Box 6, Folder: "WBC—General," Summary, 3.

143. Record of Interrogation of Witness Matsumura Tomokatsu, *Materials on the Trial of Former Servicemen*, 124. Harris, *Factories of Death*, 190–91.

144. Robert Whymant, "Hirohito 'Personally Approved Germ Warfare Unit,'" *The Guardian*, 17 September 1982, 16.

145. State-War-Navy Coordinating Subcommittee for the Far East, SFE 188/3, September 1947, appendix A, U.S. National Archives, College Park, MD, War Department General and Special Staffs, RG 165, Folder: SWNCC 351.

EPILOGUE. THE IMPACT OF WORLD WAR II ON SCIENCE IN JAPAN

1. Science historian Nakayama Shigeru writes, "For scientists and technical experts, however, this was a happy period, since the significance of their work was recognized by the national authorities." Nakayama, "The Role Played by Universities."

2. John W. Dower, "Useful War," 16.

3. Hiroshige, "Role of the Government," 332.

4. John W. Dower, *Embracing Defeat*, 494–95.

5. Hiroshige, "Role of the Government," 335.

6. Hiroshige, *Kagaku no shakai shi: (shita)*, 147–51.

7. The Ministry of Munitions, for example, was transformed into the Ministry of International Trade and Industry (MITI), which with its practice of "administrative guidance" was to lead in the development of critical industries such as semiconductors and biotechnology from the 1980s and into the twenty-first century. Other examples include the managerial practices of subcontracting and the "just-in-time" system, which were introduced during the war and were widely adopted in the postwar period.

Chalmers Johnson, *MITI and the Japanese Miracle*. Tessa Morris-Suzuki, *Technological Transformation of Japan*, 153–55.

8. On science and technology in the period of U.S. occupation, see especially Bowen C. Dees, *Allied Occupation*.

9. As far as is known, all scientists and institutions complied with the directive. General Headquarters Supreme Commander for the Allied Powers, "SCAPINS: Supreme Commander for the Allied Powers' Instructions to the Japanese Government, From 4 September 1945 to 8 March 1952," GHQ/SCAP 20 March 1952, SCAPIN 154, 24. [Hereafter cited as SCAPINS.] See also Hideomi Tuge, ed., *Historical Development of Science and Technology*, 140–45.

10. General Headquarters, United States Army Forces, Pacific, Scientific and Technical Advisory Section, "Report on Scientific Intelligence Survey in Japan: September and October 1945," 1 November 1945, National Archives, College Park, MD, RG 165, Box 2065, vol. 3, appendix 8-B-1.

11. SCAPINS, SCAPIN 196, 33.

12. SCAPINS, SCAPIN 307, 46.

13. On the destruction of the cyclotrons, see Nishina Yoshio, "A Japanese Scientist Describes the Destruction of His Cyclotrons." See also Yoshikawa Hideo and Joanne Kauffman, *Science Has No National Borders*, 5–12. Alice Kimball Smith, *A Peril and a Hope*, 303–5. Shigeru Nakayama, "Destruction of Cyclotrons."

14. Smith, *A Peril and a Hope*, 303–5.

15. Charles Weiner, "Retroactive Saber Rattling?"

16. Leslie M. Groves, *Now It Can Be Told*, 367–72.

17. Weiner, "Retroactive Saber Rattling?" 11.

18. Samuel K. Coleman, "Riken from 1945 to 1948."

19. Indeed, the paranoia harbored by a few U.S. scientific intelligence officers about the wartime activities of Japanese physicists may have fueled the belief by some western journalists after the war that Japan actually did produce and successfully test a nuclear weapon. This subject was taken up by journalists long after the war and continues to be somewhat controversial even to this day. See Deborah Shapley, "Nuclear Weapons History," which was picked up by wire services and repeated extensively throughout the U.S. media; and Robert K. Wilcox, *Japan's Secret War*. For an early historiographical discussion on the subject, see Phillip S. Hughes, "Wartime Fission Research in Japan." For responses to Wilcox et al., see Dower, "'NI' and 'F': Japan's Wartime Atomic Bomb Research." Low, "Japan's Secret War." Grunden, "Hungnam and the Japanese Atomic Bomb."

20. Laurie M. Brown and Yoichiro Nambu, "Physicists in Wartime Japan."

21. As quoted in Brown and Nambu, "Physicists in Wartime Japan," 102.

22. Ibid., 102. See also Konuma Michiji, Chieko Masuzawa, and Yoshio Takada, "Resumption of International Relationship of Japanese Particle Physicists." On Japanese Nobel Prize candidates and winners, see James R. Bartholomew, "Japanese Nobel Candidates."

23. U.S. Department of State, *Confidential U.S. State Department Central Files*. "Kikuchi Seishi," *Kodansha Encyclopedia of Japan*, 207.

24. "Nishina Yoshio," *Kodansha Encyclopedia of Japan*, 18. The Japan Biographical Research Department, *Japan Biographical Encyclopedia*, 1063. On the life and career of Nishina, see R. Kubo et al., *Evolutionary Trends in the Physical Sciences*. In Japanese, see Tamaki Hidehiko and Ezawa Hiroshi, *Nishina Yoshio*.

25. Morris F. Low and Yoshioka Hitoshi, "Buying the 'Peaceful Atom.'"
26. *Gendai Nihon jinbutsu jiten*, 121. *Gendai Nihon jinmeiroku*, 1:533. *Nihon shinshiroku*, 253. "Itokawa Hideo," *Kodansha Encyclopedia of Japan*, 354. Nippon denki kabushiki gaisha, *Uchū kaihatsu jigyobu 30-nen no ayumi*, 2–5.
27. Air Technical Intelligence Group, Report No. 314, 22 January 1946, "Comprehensive Report on Solid Rocket Propellants in the Japanese Navy," NASM, File: "Japan, Missiles (WW II)." M. Sanuki, *Proceedings of the Second International Symposium on Rockets and Astronautics*.
28. "Biographical Files of Japanese Scientists," U.S. National Archives, College Park, MD, RG 331, Box 7439. Japan Biographical Research Department, *Japan Biographical Encyclopedia*, 1654.
29. "Biographical Files of Japanese Scientists," U.S. National Archives, College Park, MD, RG 331, Box 7439. Japan Biographical Research Department, *Japan Biographical Encyclopedia*, 1552. Itokawa Hideo et al., *Survey of Japanese Space Program*, 44, 179, 205, 216.
30. On this interesting but little known case, see Hal Drake, "The Bomb with the Human Brain." See also Miki Tadanao, "Design of the Ohka Airplane," *Kōkūfan*, photocopy of translation by Hideya Ando, WPAFM.
31. It has also been noted that many aeronautical engineers found employment in the automobile industry and made important contributions there after the war as well. See Nishiyama Takashi, "Cross-Disciplinary Technology Transfer." The Central Aeronautical Research Institute was established under the Ministry of Communications in 1939 in conjunction with the navy. The army later asserted influence over this institution through the Technology Agency. For more on this subject, see Mizusawa Hikari, "Rikugun ni okeru 'Kōkū kenkyūjo.'"
32. Dower, "Useful War," 9–10.
33. See especially selected essays in Nakayama, *Social History of Science and Technology*, passim. Samuels, *Rich Nation, Strong Army*, 106. Nishiyama, "Cross-Disciplinary Technology Transfer," is an excellent example of more recent scholarship on this important subject. See also his broader study in Nishiyama Takashi, "Swords into Plowshares."
34. In addition to Yukawa and Tomonaga was Fukui Kenichi, professor of petroleum chemistry at Kyoto University, who shared the Nobel Prize for chemistry with Roald Hoffmann of Cornell University in 1981 for their research on the theory of chemical reactions. Fukui's wartime experience had a "major impact" on his subsequent career. See James R. Bartholomew, "Perspectives on Technology in Japan."
35. Yukuo Sasamoto, "Demilitarization and the Peaceful Remobilization of Manpower." Miwao Matsumoto, "Military Research and Its Conversion." Nakagawa Yasuzō, *Japanese Radar*, 8.
36. John W. Powell was among the first journalists in the West to break the story of Unit 731 and U.S. complicity in protecting Ishii and his collaborators. See John W. Powell, "Japan's Germ Warfare"; and John W. Powell, "A Hidden Chapter in History."
37. William Lanouette, "Biotech Lab Recalls Biowar."
38. Tsuneishi Keiichi, "The Ishii Unit."
39. References are to Dower, "Useful War," 9–32; and Morris F. Low, "Useful War."

BIBLIOGRAPHY

ARCHIVAL COLLECTIONS AND UNPUBLISHED
PRIMARY DOCUMENTS

United States

General Headquarters Supreme Commander for the Allied Powers, "SCAPINS: Supreme Commander for the Allied Powers' Instructions to the Japanese Government, From 4 September 1945 to 8 March 1952," GHQ/SCAP 20 March 1952. Microfilm.
North Carolina State University. Harry C. Kelly Collection. Raleigh, North Carolina.
Smithsonian Institution, National Air and Space Museum Library, Washington, DC.
United States Air Force, Maxwell Air Force Base Library, Huntsville, Alabama.
United States Air Force, Wright-Patterson Air Force Museum Library, Dayton, Ohio.
United States Department of State. *Confidential U.S. State Department Central Files: Japan Internal Affairs, 1950–1954.* Frederick, MD: University Publications of America, Inc., 1984. Microfilm.
United States National Archives. College Park, MD. Office of the Chief of Naval Operations, RG 38; Office of the Chief of Engineers, RG 77; General Records of the Department of the Navy, Office of Naval Intelligence, RG 80; Office of the Surgeon General (Army), RG 112; U.S. Army, Scientific and Technical Advisory Section, RG 165; Records of the Office of Strategic Services, RG 226; United States Strategic Bombing Survey, RG 243; Army Staff, Military Intelligence Division, RG 319; Allied Operational and Occupation Headquarters, World War II, RG 331; Manhattan Project Section, RG 374.

Japan

Bōeichō kenkyūjo toshokan [National Defense Agency Research Institute, Military History Library]. Meguro-ku, Tokyo, Japan.
Kokugakuin daigaku toshokan [Kokugakuin University Library], ed. *Inoue Tadashirō Monjo* [The Inoue Tadashirō Files]. Tokyo: Yūshōdō Co., 1994. Microfilm.
Kyū-Nihon kaigun gijutsu kenkyūjo denki kenkyūbu: Tōshin Shiryō [Former Japanese Navy Technical Research Institute Electronics Research Division: Progress Report]. Tokyo: Yūshōdō Co., 2000. Microfilm.

Minobe Yōji Monjo [Minobe Yōji Files]. Tokyo daigaku sōgō toshokan shozō, Kokusaku kenkyū kyuzō: Senji keizai seisaku shiryō [Former Collection of the National Policy Association: Wartime Economic Policy Documents, Collection of the Tokyo University Libraries]. Tokyo: Yūshōdō Co., 1991. Microfilm.

Rikagaku kenkyūjo toshoshitsu [Reading Room of the Institute for Physical and Chemical Research]. Wako-shi, Saitama-ken, Japan.

Tokyo Institute of Technology. Library and Microfilm Collection of the Graduate School of Decision Science and Technology. Meguro, Tokyo, Japan.

Tokyo University. Library and Microfilm Collection. Tokyo, Japan.

Newspapers

Asahi Shimbun
Guardian
Japan Times
Los Angeles Times
New York Times
Yomiuri Shimbun

ARTICLES, BOOKS, AND MONOGRAPHS

Alexander, Jean. *Russian Aircraft Since 1940*. London: Putnam, 1975.

Aly, Götz, Peter Chroust, and Christian Pross. *Cleansing the Fatherland: Nazi Medicine and Racial Hygiene*. Baltimore: Johns Hopkins University Press, 1994.

Avery, Donald H. "Canadian Scientists, CBW Weapons and Japan, 1939–1945." In MacLeod, *Science and the Pacific War*, 229–51.

———. *The Science of War: Canadian Scientists and Allied Military Technology During the Second World War*. Toronto: University of Toronto Press, 1998.

Awaya Kentarō. "Japanese Mustard Gas in China: Then and Now." *Sino-Japanese Studies* 4 (April 1992): 3–6.

Badash, Lawrence, Elizabeth Hodes, and Adolph Tiddens. "Nuclear Fission: Reaction to the Discovery in 1939." *Proceedings of the American Philosophical Society* 130 (June 1986): 196–231.

Ban Shigeo. *Rikugun Noborito kenkyūjo no shinjitsu* [The Truth about the Noborito Laboratory]. Tokyo: Fuyū Shobō Shuppan, 2001.

Baracca, Angelo. "'Big Science' vs. 'Little Science': Laboratories and Leading Ideas in Conflict; Nuclear Physics in the Thirties and Forties in USA, Europe, and Japan." *Organon* 25 (1989/1993): 39–54.

Barber, John, and Mark Harrison, eds. *The Soviet Defence-Industry Complex from Stalin to Khrushchev*. London: Macmillan, 2000.

Barnhart, Michael A. *Japan Prepares for Total War: The Search for Economic Security, 1919–1941*. Ithaca: Cornell University Press, 1987.

Bartholomew, James R. "The 'Feudalistic' Legacy of Japanese Science." *Knowledge: Creation, Diffusion, Utilization* 6 (June 1985): 350–76.

———. *The Formation of Science in Japan: Building a Research Tradition*. New Haven: Yale University Press, 1989.

———. "Japanese Culture and the Problem of Modern Science." In *Science and Values: Patterns of Tradition and Change,* edited by Arnold Thackray and Everett Mendelsohn, 109–55. Atlantic Highlands, NJ: Humanities Press, 1974.

———. "Japanese Nobel Candidates in the First Half of the Twentieth Century." In *Beyond Joseph Needham: Science, Technology, and Medicine in East and Southeast Asia,* edited by Morris F. Low, 238–84. *Osiris,* vol. 13. Chicago: University of Chicago Press, 1998.

———. "Perspectives on Science and Technology in Japan: The Career of Fukui Ken'ichi." *Historia Scientiarum* 4 (1994): 47–54.

———. "Science in Twentieth Century Japan." In *Science in the Twentieth Century,* edited by John Krige and Dominique Pestre, 879–96. Amsterdam: Harwood Academic, 1997.

Baxter, James Phinney. *Scientists Against Time.* Cambridge, MA: MIT Press, 1968.

Behr, Edward. *Hirohito: Behind the Myth.* New York: Villard Books, 1989.

Berger, Gordon Mark. *Parties out of Power in Japan, 1931–1941.* Princeton: Princeton University Press, 1977.

Beyerchen, Alan. "From Radio to Radar: Interwar Military Adaptation to Technological Change in German, the United Kingdom, and the United States." In *Military Innovation in the Interwar Period,* edited by Williamson Murray and Allan R. Millett, 265–99. Cambridge: Cambridge University Press, 1996.

———. *Scientists Under Hitler: Politics and the Physics Community in the Third Reich.* New Haven: Yale University Press, 1977.

Biddle, Wayne. *Barons of the Sky: From Early Flight to Strategic Warfare—The Story of the American Aerospace Industry.* New York: Simon & Schuster, 1991.

Bisson, Thomas A. *Japan's War Economy.* New York: Macmillan, 1945.

Bōeichō Bōei Kenshūjo Senshibu [National Defense Agency, National Institute for Defense Studies, Military History Department]. *Hondo bōkū sakusen* [Strategies for the Air Defense of the Mainland]. Tokyo: Asagumo Shinbunsha, 1968.

———. *Rikugun kōkū heiki no kaihatsu, seisan, hokyū* [Development, Production, and Supply of Army Aeronautical Weapons]. Senshi Sōshi series. Tokyo: Asagumo Shimbunsha, 1975.

Bojtzov, Valentin, and Erhard Geissler. "Military Biology in the USSR, 1920–45." In Geissler and Moon, *Biological and Toxin Weapons,* 153–67.

Bowen, E. G. *Radar Days.* Bristol: Adam Hilger, 1987.

Braun, Hans-Joachim. "Technology Transfer Under Conditions of War: German Aero-Technology in Japan during the Second World War." In *History of Technology,* edited by Norman Smith, 11:1–23. London: Mansell, 1986.

Brophy, Leo, and George J. B. Fisher. *The Chemical Warfare Service: Organizing for War. United States Army in World War II: The Technical Services.* Washington, DC: Department of the Army, 1959.

Brophy, Leo P., Wyndham D. Miles, and Rexmond C. Cochrane. *The Chemical Warfare Service: From Laboratory to Field. United States Army in World War II: The Technical Services.* Washington, DC: Office of the Chief of Military History, Department of the Army, 1959.

Brown, Frederic J. *Chemical Warfare: A Study in Restraints.* Princeton: Princeton University Press, 1968.

Brown, Laurie M., and Yoichiro Nambu. "Physicists in Wartime Japan." *Scientific American* (December 1998): 96–103.

Brown, Louis. *A Radar History of World War II: Technical and Military Imperatives.* Bristol: Institute of Physics Publishing, 1999.

Bu Ping. *Nihon no Chūgoku shinryaku to doku gasu heiki* [Japan's Invasion of China and Poison Gas Weapons]. Tokyo: Meiishi shoten, 1995.

Buderi, Robert. *The Invention that Changed the World: How a Small Group of Radar Pioneers Won the Second World War and Launched a Technological Revolution.* New York: Simon & Schuster, 1996.

Burchard, John E. *Rockets, Guns, and Targets: Rockets, Target Information, Erosion Information, and Hypervelocity Guns Developed During World War II by the Office of Scientific Research and Development.* Boston: Little, Brown, 1948.

Burleigh, Michael. *Death and Deliverance: "Euthanasia" in Germany c. 1900–1945.* Cambridge: Cambridge University Press, 1994.

Burns, Russell, ed. *Radar Development to 1945.* Peter Peregrinus, 1988.

Burns, R. W. "The Background to the Development of the Cavity Magnetron." In *Radar Development to 1945,* edited by Russell Burns. Peter Peregrinus, 1988.

Caidin, Martin. "Japanese Guided Missiles in World War II." *Jet Propulsion* 26 (August 1956): 691–96.

Calamia, M., and R. Palandri, "The History of the Italian Radio Detector Telemetro." In *Radar Development to 1945,* edited by Russell Burns, 97–105. Peter Peregrinus, 1988.

Campbell, John. *Naval Weapons of World War Two.* London: Conway Maritime Press, 1985.

Capshew, James H., and Karen A. Rader. "Big Science: Price to the Present." In *Science After '40,* edited by Arnold Thackray, 3–25. *Osiris,* vol. 7. Chicago: University of Chicago Press, 1992.

Carter, Gradon B., and Graham S. Pearson, "British Biological Warfare and Biological Defense, 1925–45." In Geissler and Moon, *Biological and Toxin Weapons,* 168–89.

Caspari, Sigrun. "Riku-kaigun kōkūshi to Doitsu-Ni gijutsu kōshō." *Gunji shigaku* 31 (1996): 37–51.

Cassidy, David. *Uncertainty: The Life and Science of Werner Heisenberg.* San Francisco: Freeman, 1992.

Chapman, John W. M. "The 'Have-Nots' Go to War: The Economic and Technological Basis of the German Alliance with Japan." In *The Tripartite Pact of 1940: Japan, Germany, and Italy,* edited by Ian Nish, 25–73. London: London School of Economics, 1984.

Clark, Ronald W. *The Rise of the Boffins.* London: Phoenix House, 1962.

———. *Tizard.* Cambridge, MA: MIT Press, 1965.

Clausen, Søren, and Stig Thøgersen, eds. *The Making of a Chinese City: History and Historiography in Harbin.* Armonk, NY: M. E. Sharpe, 1995.

Coffey, Thomas M. *Imperial Tragedy.* New York: Pinnacle Books, 1970.

Cohen, Jerome B. *Japan's Economy in War and Reconstruction.* Westport, CT: Greenwood Press, 1973.

Coleman, Samuel K. "Riken from 1945 to 1948: The Reorganization of Japan's Physical and Chemical Research Institute Under the American Occupation." *Technology and Culture* 31 (April 1990): 228–50.

Constant, Edward W. *The Origins of the Turbojet Revolution.* Baltimore: Johns Hopkins University Press, 1980.

Coox, Alvin D. "The Kwantung Army Dimension." In *The Japanese Informal Empire in China, 1895–1937,* edited by Peter Duus, Ramon H. Myers, and Mark R. Peattie, 395–428. Princeton: Princeton University Press, 1989.

———. *Nomonhan: Japan Against Russia, 1939.* 2 vols. Stanford: Stanford University Press, 1985.

———. "The Rise and Fall of the Imperial Japanese Air Forces." In *Air Power and Warfare: The Proceedings of the Eighth Military History Symposium, United States Air Force Academy, 18–20 October 1978,* edited by Alfred F. Hurley and Robert C. Ehrhart, 84–97. Washington, DC: U.S. GPO, 1979.

Creveld, Martin van. *Technology and War: From 2000 B.C. to the Present.* New York: Free Press, 1989.

Crowley, James B. "Japanese Army Factionalism in the Early 1930s." *Journal of Asian Studies* 21 (May 1962): 309–26.

———. *Japan's Quest for Autonomy: National Security and Foreign Policy, 1930–1938.* Princeton: Princeton University Press, 1966.

Cusumano, Michael A. "'Scientific Industry': Strategy, Technology, and Entrepreneurship in Prewar Japan." In *Managing Industrial Enterprise: Cases from Japan's Prewar Experience,* edited by William D. Wray, 269–315. Cambridge, MA: Harvard University Press, 1989.

Dahl, Per F. Heavy *Water and the Wartime Race for Nuclear Energy.* Bristol: Institute of Physics, 1999.

Dees, Bowen C. *The Allied Occupation and Japan's Economic Miracle: Building the Foundations of Japanese Science and Technology 1945–1952.* Surrey: Japan Library, 1997.

Denpa Kanri Iinkai, ed. *Nihon Musenshi: Dai Kyū-kan.* Tokyo: Denpa Kanri Iinkai, 1950.

Dornberger, Walter. "The German V-2." In Emme, *History of Rocket Technology,* 29–45.

———. *V-2.* New York: Viking, 1958.

Dower, John. *Embracing Defeat: Japan in the Wake of World War II.* New York: Norton/New Press, 1999.

———. "'NI' and 'F': Japan's Wartime Atomic Bomb Research." In *Japan in War and Peace: Selected Essays,* 55–100. New York: New Press, 1993.

———. "The Useful War." In *Japan in War and Peace: Selected Essays,* 9–32. New York: New Press, 1993.

Drake, Hal. "The Bomb with the Human Brain." *Mankind: The Magazine of Popular History* 3 (February 1973): 52–58.

Drea, Edward J. *MacArthur's ULTRA: Codebreaking and the War Against Japan, 1942–1945.* Lawrence: University Press of Kansas, 1992.

Duus, Peter, Ramon H. Myers, and Mark R. Peattie, eds. *The Japanese Informal Empire in China, 1895–1937.* Princeton: Princeton University Press, 1989.

Emme, Eugene M., ed. *The History of Rocket Technology: Essays on Research, Development, and Utility.* Detroit: Wayne State University Press, 1964.

Endō Saburō. *Nitchū jyūgonen sensō to watakushi* [The Fifteen-Year Sino-Japanese War and Me]. Tokyo: Nichō Shōrin, 1974.

Erickson, John. "Radio-location and the Air Defense Problem: The Design and Development of Soviet Radar, 1934–40." *Science Studies* 2 (1972): 241–68.

Escalettes, Jean-Paul, and Philippe Jung. "William Congreve and the City of Toulouse." In *History of Rocketry and Astronautics: Proceedings of the Twenty-Second and Twenty-Third History Symposia of the International Academy of Astronautics,* edited by John Becklake, 13–32. AAS History Series, vol. 17. San Diego, CA: American Astronautical Society, 1995.

Ethell, Jeffrey, and Alfred Price. *Word War II Fighting Jets.* Shrewsbury, UK: Airlife Publishing, 1994.

Evans, David C., and Mark R. Peattie. *Kaigun: Strategy, Tactics, and Technology in the Imperial Japanese Navy, 1887–1941.* Annapolis, MD: Naval Institute Press, 1997.

Fermi, Laura. *Atoms in the Family: My Life with Enrico Fermi.* Chicago: University of Chicago Press, 1954.

Fisher, David E. *A Race on the Edge of Time: Radar—The Decisive Weapon of World War II.* New York: Paragon House, 1989.

Francillon, René. *Japanese Aircraft of the Pacific War.* 4th ed. Annapolis, MD: Naval Institute Press, 1994.

Fukai Yūzo. "Kyū-gun itaku 'Ni-Go kenkyū' ni okeru rinkai keisan" [Calculations of Criticality in the 'Ni-Project Research' Under the Japanese Army]. *Gijutsu bunka ronsō* 3 (May 2000): 1–24.

———. "Kyū-Kaigun itaku 'F-kenkyū' ni okeru rinkai keisanhō no kaihatsu" [Development of the Method for Calculating Criticality in the Japanese Navy's 'F-Project']. *Gijutsu bunka ronsō* 2 (February 1999): 27–44.

Fukui Shizuo, et al., eds. *Kimitsu heiki no zembō: Waga gunji kagaku gijutsu no shinsō to hansei* [The Full Story of Secret Weapons: Reflections and Truth Concerning Japan's Military Science and Technology]. Tokyo: Koyosha, 1953.

Galison, Peter, and Bruce Hevly, eds. *Big Science: The Growth of Large-Scale Research.* Stanford: Stanford University Press, 1992.

Geissler, Erhard. "Biological Warfare Activities in Germany, 1923–45." In Geissler and Moon, *Biological and Toxin Weapons,* 91–126.

Geissler, Erhard, and John Ellis van Courtland Moon, eds. *Biological and Toxin Weapons: Research, Development and Use from the Middle Ages to 1945.* Oxford: Oxford University Press, 1999.

Gendai jinbutsu jiten [Contemporary Who's Who]. Tokyo: Sun Data Systems, 1982.

Gendai Nihon jinbutsu jiten: 20-seiki Who's Who [Contemporary Biographical Dictionary of Japan]. Tokyo: Obunshahen, 1986.

Gendai Nihon jinmeiroku [Contemporary Who's Who in Japan]. Vol. 1. Tokyo: Nichigai Associates, 1987.

Gijutsuin kōetsu, Kagakudōin kyōkai hensan [Technology Agency Editorial Board, Science Mobilization Association, eds.]. *Kagaku gijutsu nenkan: Shōwa 17 Nenpan* [Science and Technology Yearbook: 1942]. Tokyo: Kagaku dōin kyōkai, 1942.

Goddard, Esther C., and G. Edward Pendray, eds. *The Papers of Robert H. Goddard.* New York: McGraw-Hill, 1970.

Gold, Hal. *Unit 731 Testimony: Japan's Wartime Human Experimentation Program.* Tokyo: Yen Books, 1996.

Goldberg, Stanley. "Inventing a Climate of Opinion: Vannevar Bush and the Decision to Build the Bomb." *Isis* 83 (1992): 429–52.

Goodwin, Bridget. "Australia's Mustard Gas Guinea Pigs." In MacLeod, *Science and the Pacific War,* 139–71.

Gowing, Margaret. *Britain and Atomic Energy, 1939–1945*. London: St. Martin's, 1964.
Graham, Loren R. *Science in Russia and the Soviet Union: A Short History*. Cambridge: Cambridge University Press, 1993.
Groves, Leslie R. *Now It Can Be Told: The Story of the Manhattan Project*. New York: Da Capo, 1962.
Grunden, Walter E. "Hungnam and the Japanese Atomic Bomb: Recent Historiography of a Postwar Myth." *Intelligence and National Security* 13 (summer 1998): 32–60.
Grunden, Walter E., Kawamura Yutaka, Eduard Kolchinsky, Helmut Maier, and Yamazaki Masakatsu. "Laying the Foundation for Wartime Research: A Comparative Overview of Science Mobilization in Nazi Germany, Japan, and the Soviet Union." In *Politics and Science in Wartime: Comparative International Perspectives on Kaiser Wilhelm Institutes*, edited by Carola Sachse and Mark Walker. *Osiris*, vol. 20. Chicago: University of Chicago Press, forthcoming.
Grunden, Walter E., Mark Walker, and Yamazaki Masakatsu. "Nuclear Weapons and Nuclear Energy in Wartime Germany and Japan." In *Politics and Science in Wartime: Comparative International Perspectives on Kaiser Wilhelm Institutes*, edited by Carola Sachse and Mark Walker. *Osiris*, vol. 20. Chicago: University of Chicago Press, forthcoming.
Guerlac, Henry E. *Radar in World War II: Sections A–C*. The History of Modern Physics, 1800–1950. Vol. 8. New York: Tomash/American Institute of Physics, 1987.
———. *Radar in World War II: Sections D–E*. The History of Modern Physics, 1800–1950. Vol. 8. New York: Tomash/American Institute of Physics, 1987.
Han Xiao. "A Compilation of the Fascist Atrocities Committed by Unit 731 of the Japanese Army (Excerpts)." In *The Making of a Chinese City: History and Historiography in Harbin*, edited by Søren Clausen and Stig Thøgersen, 142–48. Armonk, NY: M. E. Sharpe, 1995.
Han Xiao. *Nanasanichi-butai no hanzai: Chūgokujinmin wa kokuhatsu suru* [The Crimes of Unit 731: The People of China Accuse]. Tokyo: Sanichi shobō, 1995.
Harris, Robert, and Jeremy Paxman. *A Higher Form of Killing: The Secret History of Chemical and Biological Warfare*. New York: Random House, 2002.
Harris, Sheldon H. *Factories of Death: Japanese Biological Warfare, 1932–1945 and the American Cover-Up*. Rev. ed. London: Routledge, 2002.
Harrison, Mark, ed. *The Economics of World War II: Six Great Powers in International Comparison*. Cambridge: Cambridge University Press, 1998.
———. "New Postwar Branches (1): Rocketry." In *The Soviet Defence-Industry Complex from Stalin to Khrushchev*, edited by John Barber and Mark Harrison, 118–49. London: Macmillan, 2000.
Hartcup, Guy. *The Challenge of War: Britain's Scientific and Engineering Contributions to World War Two*. New York: Taplinger, 1970.
———. *The Effect of Science on the Second World War*. New York: St. Martin's Press, 2000.
Havens, Thomas R. "Women and War in Japan, 1937–1945." *American Historical Review* 80 (October 1975): 913–34.
Hayakawa Satio. "The Development of Meson Physics in Japan." In *The Birth of Particle Physics*, edited by Laurie M. Brown and Lillian Hoddeson, 82–107. Cambridge: Cambridge University Press, 1983.

Heilbron, J. L., and Robert W. Seidel. *Lawrence and His Laboratory: A History of the Lawrence Berkeley Laboratory, Volume 1*. Berkeley: University of California Press, 1989.

Henshall, Philip. *The Nuclear Axis: Germany, Japan and the Atom Bomb Race 1939–1945*. Stroud, UK: Sutton, 2000.

Hevly, Bruce. "Reflections on Big Science and Big History." In *Big Science: The Growth of Large-Scale Research*, edited by Peter Galison and Bruce Hevly, 355–63. Stanford: Stanford University Press, 1992.

Hewlett, Richard G., and Oscar E. Anderson Jr. *The New World: A History of the United States Atomic Energy Commission*, vol. 1, *1939–1946*. Berkeley: University of California Press, 1990.

Hinokawa Shizue. "Cyclotron Development at the Institute of Physical and Chemical Research in the 1930s." *Gijutsu bunka ronsō* [Tokyo Institute of Technology Studies in Science, Technology, and Culture] 4 (2001): 14–37.

Hiroshige Tetsu. *Kagaku no shakai shi: (shita) Keizai seichō to kagaku* [A Social History of Science: Part II: Economic Development and Science]. Tokyo: Iwanami Shoten, 2003.

———. *Kagaku no shakai shi: (ue) Sensō to kagaku* [A Social History of Science: Part I: War and Science]. Tokyo: Iwanami Shoten, 2002.

———. *Kagaku no shakai shi: Kindai Nihon no kagaku taisei* [Social History of Science: The Scientific Structure of Modern Japan]. Tokyo: Chūō Kōronsha, 1973.

———. "The Role of the Government in the Development of Science." *Journal of World History* 9 (1965): 320–39.

———. "Social Conditions for Prewar Japanese Research in Nuclear Physics." In *Science and Society in Modern Japan: Selected Historical Sources*, edited by Nakayama Shigeru, David L. Swain, and Eri Yagi, 208–10. Tokyo: University of Tokyo Press, 1973.

Hogg, I. V. *German Secret Weapons of the Second World War: The Missiles, Rockets, Weapons and New Technology of the Third Reich*. London: Greenhill Books, 1999.

Holloway, David. "Innovation in the Defense Sector: Battle Tanks and ICBMs." In *Industrial Innovation in the Soviet Union*, edited by Ronald Amann and Julian Cooper, 368–414. New Haven: Yale University Press, 1982.

———. "The Soviet Style of Military R&D." In *The Genesis of New Weapons: Decision Making for Military R&D*, edited by Franklin Long and Judith Reppy, 137–57. New York: Pergamon Press, 1980.

———. *Stalin and the Bomb: The Soviet Union and Atomic Energy 1939–1956*. New Haven: Yale University Press, 1994.

Home, R. W., and Morris F. Low. "Postwar Scientific Intelligence Missions to Japan." *Isis* 84 (September 1993): 527–37.

Hughes, Phillip S. "Wartime Fission Research in Japan." *Social Studies of Science* 10 (August 1980): 345–49.

Humphreys, Leonard. *The Way of the Heavenly Sword: The Japanese Army in the 1920s*. Stanford: Stanford University Press, 1995.

Ichikawa Hiroshi. "An Empirical Study of the Realities of the Wartime Research in Japan During World War II—With a Case Study on the Atomic Bomb Development Project." *Shakai bunka kenkyū* [Studies in Social Science] 25 (December 1999): 109–92.

Ienaga Saburō. *The Pacific War, 1931–1945: A Critical Perspective on Japan's Role in World War II*. New York: Pantheon Books, 1978.
Inoguchi Rikihei, Nakajima Tadashi, and Roger Pineau. *The Divine Wind: Japan's Kamikaze Force in World War II*. Annapolis, MD: Naval Institute Press, 1958.
Irving, David. *The Virus House: Germany's Atomic Research and Allied Counter-Measures*. London: William Kimber, 1967.
Ishizawa Kazuhiko. *Kikka: Nihon hajime no jietto enjin, Ne 20 gijutsu kenshō* [Kikka: Japan's First Jet Engine, A Technical Examination of the Ne 20]. Tokyo: Miki Press, 2001.
Itakura Kiyonobu, and Eri Yagi. "The Japanese Research System and the Establishment of the Institute of Physical and Chemical Research." In *Science and Society in Modern Japan: Selected Historical Sources*, edited by Nakayama Shigeru, David L. Swain, and Eri Yagi. Tokyo: University of Tokyo Press, 1973.
Itō Yōji. "Senjika dōitsu ni okeru kagaku gijutsu no sokushin ni tsuite" [The Promotion of Science and Technology in Wartime Germany]. *Denki Gakkai Zasshi* (September 1942): 517–26.
Itokawa Hideo, et al., eds. *Survey of Japanese Space Program with Emphasis on Kappa and Lambda Type Observation Rockets*. Washington, DC: NASA, 1965.
Japan Biographical Research Department. *The Japan Biographical Encyclopedia and Who's Who*. Tokyo: Rengo Press, 1958.
Japan Statistical Association, Statistics Bureau, Management and Coordination Agency, ed. *Historical Statistics of Japan, 1868–1985* [electronic resource/CD-ROM]. Tokyo: Japan Statistical Association, 1999.
Johnson, Chalmers. *MITI and the Japanese Miracle*. Stanford: Stanford University Press, 1982.
Johnson, David. *V-1, V-2: Hitler's Vengeance on London*. Chelsea, MI: Scarborough House, 1981.
Jones, R. V. *Most Secret War: British Scientific Intelligence 1939–1945*. London: H. Hamilton, 1978. Also published in the United States as *The Wizard War*. New York: Coward, McCann & Geoghegan, 1978.
Jones, Vincent C. *Manhattan: The Army and the Atomic Bomb. United States Army in World War II: Special Studies*. Washington, DC: U.S. Army, 1985.
Josephson, Paul R. "Early Years of Soviet Nuclear Physics." *Bulletin of the Atomic Scientists* (December 1987): 36–39.
———. *Totalitarian Science and Technology*. Atlantic Highlands, NJ: Humanities Press, 1996.
Kagaku gijutsu seisakushi kenkyūkai [Science and Technology Policy History Research Society]. *Nihon no kagaku gijutsu seisakushi* [History of Japanese Science and Technology Policy]. Tokyo: Mitō Kagaku Gijutsu Kyōkai, 1990.
Kaigun Suiraishi Kankōkai [Navy Torpedo History Publishing Committee]. *Kaigun suiraishi* [A History of the Torpedoes of the Japanese Navy]. Tokyo: Shinkōsha, 1979.
Kamata Shōji. *Hokusen no Nihonjin kunanki: Nitchitsu Kōnan kōjō no saigo* [Record of the Hardship of the Japanese in North Korea: The Last Days of the Nitchitsu Kōnan Factory]. Tokyo: Jiji Tsushinsha, 1970.
Kamata Shōji, ed. *Nihon Chisso shi e no shōgen*. Vol. 14. Tokyo: Nihon Chisso shi e no Shōgen Henshu Iinkai, 1981.

Kamatani Chikayoshi. "The History of Research Organization in Japan." *Japanese Studies in the History of Science* 2 (1963): 1–79.

Kan Jeon, et al. *Chōsen ni okeru Nitchitsu kontsuerun* [The Nitchitsu Konzern in Korea]. Tokyo: Fuji Shuppan, 1985.

Kawamura Yutaka. "1930 Nendai no magunetoron kenkyū to kaigun gijutsu kenkyūjo: Itō Yōji no tasō kōshūha kenkyū kōsō to jitsuyō magunetoron kaihatsu" [The Development of the Cavity Magnetron at the Japanese Naval Technical Research Institute in the 1930s]. *Kagakushi Kenkyū* 38 (1999): 71–82.

———. "Kyū-Nihon kaigun no dempa heiki kaihatsu katei o jirei toshita dai-niji taisenki Nihon no kagaku gijutsu dōin ni kan suru bunseki" [A Case Study of Electric Wave Weapons Development Process in the Former Japanese Navy: An Analysis of Japanese Science and Technology Mobilization in World War II]. PhD diss., Tokyo Institute of Technology, Japan, 2002.

———. "Tairiku kagakuin setsuritsu ni kan suru oboegaki: Nihon no kagaku gijutsu seisaku no kigen o kangaeru" [Notes on the Establishment of the Continental Science Academy; Thoughts on the Origin of Japan's Science and Technology Policy]. *Il Saggiatore* 30 (2001): 132–39.

Kawamura Yutaka and Yamazaki Masakatsu. "Butsuri kondankai to kyū-Nihon kaigun ni okeru kaku oyobi kyōryoku magunetoron kaihatsu" [The Physics Committee and the Japanese Navy's Project for Development of Atomic Energy and a Powerful Magnetron during the Second World War]. *Kagakushi Kenkyū* 37 (1998): 163–71.

Kay, Anthony L., and J. R. Smith. *German Aircraft of the Second World War: Including Helicopters and Missiles.* Annapolis, MD: Naval Institute Press, 2002.

Kevles, Daniel J. *The Physicists: The History of a Scientific Community in Modern America.* New York: Knopf, 1987.

Kim Dong-Won. "The Emergence of Theoretical Physics in Japan: Japanese Physics Community Between the Two World Wars." *Annals of Science* 52 (1995): 383–402.

Kim Yung Sik, and Francesca Bray, eds. *Current Perspectives in the History of Science in East Asia.* Seoul: Seoul National University Press, 1999.

King, Benjamin, and Timothy J. Kutta. *Impact: The History of Germany's V-Weapons in World War II.* Cambridge, MA: Da Capo Press, 1998.

Kodansha Encyclopedia of Japan. Tokyo: Kodansha, 1983.

Koizumi Kenkichirō. "The Emergence of Japan's First Physicists: 1868–1900." *Historical Studies in the Physical Sciences* 6 (1975): 3–108.

Kojevnikov, Alexei. "The Great War, the Russian Civil War, and the Invention of Big Science." *Science in Context* 15 (2002): 239–75.

Konuma Michiji, Chieko Masuzawa, and Yoshio Takada. "Resumption of International Relationship of Japanese Particle Physicists after World War II." *Historia Scientiarum* (1989): 23–41.

Kramish, Arnold. *Atomic Energy in the Soviet Union.* Stanford: Stanford University Press, 1959.

Kristy, Benjamin H. "Science, Technology, and Weapons Development." In *World War II in Asia and the Pacific and the War's Aftermath, with General Themes: A Handbook of Literature and Research,* edited by Loyd E. Lee. Westport, CT: Greenwood Press, 1998.

Kubo, R., et al. *Evolutionary Trends in the Physical Sciences: Proceedings of the Yoshio Nishina Centennial Symposium.* Tokyo: Springer-Verlag, 1990.

Kurzman, Dan. *Blood and Water: Sabotaging Hitler's Bomb.* New York: Holt, 1997.

Lanouette, William. "Biotech Lab Recalls Biowar." *Bulletin of the Atomic Scientists* (January–February 1990): 6.

Lanouette, William, with Bela Szilard. *Genius in the Shadows: A Biography of Leo Szilard—The Man Behind the Bomb.* New York: Charles Scribner's Sons, 1992.

Lee, Loyd E., ed. *World War II in Asia and the Pacific and the War's Aftermath, with General Themes: A Handbook of Literature and Research.* Westport, CT: Greenwood Press, 1998.

Lewis, Robert A. "Some Aspects of the Research and Development Effort of the Soviet Union, 1924–35." *Science Studies* 2 (1972): 153–79.

Li, Lincoln. *The Japanese Army in North China, 1937–1941: Problems of Political and Economic Control.* London: Oxford University Press, 1975.

Lifton, Robert J. *The Nazi Doctors: Medical Killing and the Psychology of Genocide.* New York: Basic Books, 1986.

Longmate, Norman. *Hitler's Rockets: The Story of the V-2s.* London: Hutchinson Press, 1985.

Low, Morris F. "The Architecture of Japanese Colonial Science: The Establishment of the Shanghai Science Institute." In *Current Perspectives in the History of Science in East Asia,* edited by Yung Sik Kim and Francesca Bray, 226–37. Seoul: Seoul National University Press, 1999.

———. "Japan's Secret War? 'Instant' Scientific Manpower and Japan's World War II Atomic Bomb Project." *Annals of Science* 47 (1990): 347–60.

———. "The Useful War: Radar and the Mobilization of Science and Industry in Japan." In MacLeod, *Science and the Pacific War,* 291–301.

Low, Morris F., and Yoshioka Hitoshi. "Buying the 'Peaceful Atom': The Development of Nuclear Power in Japan." *Historia Scientiarum* (1989): 29–44.

Lusar, Rudolf. *German Secret Weapons of the Second World War.* New York: Philosophical Library, 1959.

Lyons, Michael J. *World War II: A Short History.* 4th ed. Saddle River, NJ: Pearson/Prentice Hall, 2004.

MacLeod, Roy, ed. *Science and the Pacific War: Science and Survival in the Pacific, 1939–1945.* Dordrecht: Kluwer Academic, 2000.

Macrakis, Kristie. *Surviving the Swastika: Scientific Research in Nazi Germany.* New York: Oxford University Press, 1993.

Malina, Frank J. "Origins and First Decade of the Jet Propulsion Laboratory." In Emme, *History of Rocket Technology,* 46–50.

Martin, Bernd. *Japan and Germany in the Modern World.* Providence: Berghahn Books, 1995.

Materials on the Trial of Former Servicemen of the Japanese Army Charged with Manufacturing and Employing Bacteriological Weapons. Moscow: Foreign Languages Publishing House, 1950.

Mathias, Regine. "Women and the War Economy in Japan." In *Japan's War Economy,* edited by Erich Pauer, 65–84. London: Routledge, 1999.

Matsumoto Miwao. "Military Research and Its Conversion: Naval Radar Development." In Nakayama, *Social History of Science and Technology,* 1:133–45.

Medvedev, Zhores A. *Soviet Science.* New York: Norton, 1978.
Mendelsohn, Everett. "Science, Scientists, and the Military." In *Science in the Twentieth Century,* edited by John Krige and Dominique Pestre, 175–98. Amsterdam: Harwood Academic, 1997.
Menzel, Johanna M. "German-Japanese Relations During the Second World War." PhD diss., University of Chicago, 1957.
Mikesh, Robert C. *Japan's World War II Balloon Bomb Attacks on North America.* Smithsonian Annals of Flight Series. Washington, DC: Smithsonian Institution Press, 1973.
Milward, Alan S. *War, Economy and Society: 1939–1945.* Berkeley: University of California Press, 1979.
Mizuno Hiromi. "Science, Ideology, Empire: A History of the 'Scientific' in Japan from the 1920s to the 1940s." PhD diss., University of California, Los Angeles, 2001.
Mizusawa Hikari, "Rikugun ni okeru 'Kōkū kenkyūjo' setsuritsu kōsō to Gijutsuin kōkū jyūtenka" [The Army's Plan to Build the 'Central Aeronautical Institute' and the Technology Board's Prioritizing the Aviation Industry]. *Kagakushi Kenkyū* 42 (spring 2003): 31–39.
Molony, Barbara. *Technology and Investment: The Prewar Japanese Chemical Industry.* Cambridge, MA: Harvard University Press, 1990.
Moon, John Ellis Van Courtland. "U.S. Biological Warfare Planning and Preparedness: The Dilemmas of Policy." In Geissler and Moon, *Biological and Toxin Weapons,* 215–54.
Morgan, Hugh. *Me 262: Stormbird Rising.* London: Osprey, 1994.
Morimura Seiichi. *Akuma no hōshoku* [The Devil's Gluttony]. Tokyo: Kadokawa Shoten, 1985.
———. *Sabakareta 731 butai* [Unit 731 Judged]. Tokyo: Banshōsha, 2000.
Morris, Ivan. *The Nobility of Failure: Tragic Heroes in the History of Japan.* New York: Meridian, 1975.
Morris-Suzuki, Tessa. *The Technological Transformation of Japan: From the Seventeenth to the Twenty-First Century.* Cambridge: Cambridge University Press, 1994.
Morton, Louis. "War, Science, and Social Change." In *The Social Reality of Scientific Myth,* edited by Kalman H. Silvert, 22–57. New York: American Universities, 1969.
Murata Tadayoshi, et al. *Nihongun no kagakusen* [The Japanese Army's Chemical War]. Tokyo: Otsuki Shoten, 1996.
Myers, Ramon H. "Japanese Imperialism in Manchuria: The South Manchuria Railway Company, 1906–1933." In *The Japanese Informal Empire in China, 1895–1937,* edited by Peter Duus, Ramon H. Myers, and Mark R. Peattie, 101–32. Princeton: Princeton University Press, 1989.
Naitō Hatsuho. *Kaigun gijutsu senki* [War Commentary on Navy Technology]. Tokyo: Tosho Shuppansha, 1976.
———. *Kimitsu heiki Funryū* [Secret Weapon "Raging Dragon"]. Tokyo: Tosho Shuppansha, 1979.
———. *Thunder Gods: The Kamikaze Pilots Tell Their Story.* Translated by Ichikawa Mayumi. Tokyo: Kodansha International, 1989.
Nakagawa Yasuzō. *Japanese Radar and Related Weapons of World War II.* English edi-

tion edited by Louis Brown, John H. Bryant, and Naohiko Koizumi. Laguna Hills, CA: Aegean Park Press, 1997.

———. *Kaigun gijutsu kenkyūjo* [The Navy Technical Research Institute]. Tokyo: Nihon Keizai Shimbunsha, 1987.

Nakajima Hideto. "A Categorization of Technology and the History of Japanese Modern Technology." In *Japanese Civilization in the Modern World, X: Technology*, edited by Umesao Tadao, James R. Bartholomew, and Shigeharu Sugita, 29–44. Senri Ethnological Studies, vol. 46. Osaka, 1998.

Nakajima Shigeru. "Japanese Radar Development in World War II." *Radioscientist* 3 (June 1992): 33–37.

———. "Japanese Radar Development Prior to 1945." *IEEE Antennas and Propagation Magazine* 34 (December 1992): 17–22.

———. "Reedaa kaihatsu no rekishi" [A History of Radar Development]. *Koden Technical Journal* 4 (1988): 19–34.

———. "General Outline of Japanese Radar Development up to 1945." In *Papers on the History of Industry and Technology of Japan*, vol. 2, *From the Meiji-Period to Postwar Japan*, edited by Erich Pauer, 269–94. Marburg: Förderverein, 1995.

———. "The History of Japanese Radar Development to 1945." In *Radar Development to 1945*, edited by Russell Burns, 243–58. Peter Peregrinus, 1988.

Nakayama Shigeru. "Destruction of Cyclotrons." In Nakayama, *Social History of Science and Technology*, 108–18.

———. "History of East Asian Science: Needs and Opportunities." In *Constructing Knowledge in the History of Science*, edited by Arnold Thackray, 80–94. *Osiris*, vol. 10. Chicago: University of Chicago Press, 1995.

———. "The Role Played by Universities in the Scientific and Technological Development in Japan." *Journal of World History* 9 (1965): 340–62.

Nakayama Shigeru, ed. *A Social History of Science and Technology in Contemporary Japan. Volume I: The Occupation Period, 1945–1952*. Melbourne: Trans Pacific Press, 2001.

Nakayama Shigeru, David L. Swain, and Yagi Eri, eds. *Science and Society in Modern Japan: Selected Historical Sources*. Tokyo: University of Tokyo Press, 1973.

Nenryō konwakai-hen [Fuel Roundtable], eds. *Nihon kaigun nenryōshi—shita* [A History of Japanese Naval Fuel]. Tokyo: Genshobō, 1971.

Neufeld, Michael J. "Rocket Aircraft and the 'Turbojet Revolution': The Luftwaffe's Quest for High-Speed Flight, 1935–39." In *Innovation and the Development of Flight*, edited by Roger D. Launius, 207–34. College Station: Texas A&M University Press, 1999.

———. *The Rocket and the Reich: Peenemünde and the Coming of the Ballistic Missile Era*. New York: Free Press, 1995.

Neushul, Peter. "Science, Technology and the Arsenal of Democracy: Production Research and Development During World War II." PhD diss., University of California, Santa Barbara, 1993.

Nihon heiki kōgyōkai. *Rikusen heiki sōkan*.Tokyo: Shuppansha, 1977.

Nihon kaigun kōkūshi hensan iinkai [Japanese Naval Aeronautics History Editorial Committee]. *Nihon kaigun kōkūshi* [A History of Japanese Naval Aviation]. Vols. 1–4. Tokyo: Jiji Tsūshinsha, 1969.

Nihon shinshiroku [Japan Who's Who]. Tokyo: Gyoseisha Shuppankyoku, 1977.

Nippon denki kabushiki gaisha [Nippon Electric Corporation]. *Uchū kaihatsu jigyobu*

30-nen no ayumi [Outline of the Thirty Year History of the Space Development Industry]. Tokyo: Nippon denki, 1987.

Nippon Kagakushi Gakkai [Japan History of Science Society], ed. *Nippon kagaku gijutsusi taikei* [Outline of the History of Japanese Science and Technology]. Vol. 4, *Tsūshi* [General History]. Tokyo: Daiichi Hōgen Shuppan, 1970.

———. *Nippon kagaku gijutsusi taikei* [Outline of the History of Japanese Science and Technology]. Vol. 13, *Butsuri kagaku* [The Physical Sciences]. Tokyo: Daiichi Hōgen Shuppan, 1970.

———. *Nippon kagaku gijutsusi taikei* [Outline of the History of Japanese Science and Technology]. Vol. 19, *Denki gijutsu* [Electrical Technology]. Tokyo: Daiichi Hōgen Shuppan, 1970.

Nishina Yoshio. "A Japanese Scientist Describes the Destruction of His Cyclotrons." *Bulletin of the Atomic Scientists* 3 (June 1947): 145, 167.

Nishiyama Takashi. "Cross-Disciplinary Technology Transfer in Trans-World War II Japan: The Japanese High-Speed Bullet Train as a Case Study." *Comparative Technology Transfer and Society* 1 (December 2003): 305–27.

———. "Swords into Plowshares: Civilian Application of Wartime Military Technology in Modern Japan, 1945–1964." PhD diss., Ohio State University, 2004.

O'Neil, William D. "Interwar U.S. and Japanese National Product and Defense Expenditure." *CNA Corporation Publication* (June 2003): 1–57.

Ohnuki-Tierney, Emiko. *Kamikaze, Cherry Blossoms, and Nationalisms: The Militarization of Aesthetics in Japanese History*. Chicago: University of Chicago Press, 2002.

Oshio Takeshi. *Nitchitsu kontsueren no kenkyū* [Studies on the Nitchitsu Konzern]. Tokyo: Nihon Keizai Hyoronsha, 1989.

Overy, Richard. *Why the Allies Won*. New York: Norton, 1995.

Oyodo Shōichi. *Miyamoto Takenosuke to kagaku gijutsu gyōsei* [Miyamoto Takenosuke and the Administration of Science and Technology]. Tokyo: Tōkai daigaku shuppankai, 1989.

Pacific War Research Society [PWRS]. *The Day Man Lost: Hiroshima, 6 August 1945*. Tokyo: Kodansha International, 1972.

Pauer, Erich. "Japan's Technical Mobilization in the Second World War." In *Japan's War Economy*, edited by Erich Pauer, 39–64. London: Routledge, 1999.

Pauer, Erich, ed. *Papers on the History of Industry and Technology of Japan*, vol. 2: *From the Meiji-Period to Postwar Japan*. Marburg, Germany: Förderverein Marburger Japan-Reihe, 1995.

Peattie, Mark R. *Sunburst: The Rise of Japanese Naval Air Power, 1909–1941*. Annapolis, MD: Naval Institute Press, 2001.

Pendray, Edward. "Pioneer Rocket Development in the United States." In Emme, *History of Rocket Technology*, 19–24.

Pocock, Rowland F. *German Guided Missiles of the Second World War*. New York: Arco, 1971.

Postan, M. M., D. Hay, and J. D. Scott. *Design and Development of Weapons: Studies in Government and Industrial Organization*. London: Longmans, Green, 1964.

Powell, John W. "A Hidden Chapter in History." *Bulletin of the Atomic Scientists* (October 1981): 43–53.

———. "Japan's Germ Warfare: The U.S. Cover-Up of a War Crime." *Bulletin of Concerned Asian Scholars* 12 (1980): 2–17.

Price, Derek J. De Solla. *Little Science, Big Science*. New York: Columbia University Press, 1963.
Pritchard, David. *The Radar War: Germany's Pioneering Achievement 1904–45*. Wellingborough, UK: Patrick Stephens, 1989.
Proctor, Robert N. *Racial Hygiene: Medicine Under the Nazis*. Cambridge, MA: Harvard University Press, 1988.
Pursell, Carroll. "Science Agencies in World War II: The OSRD and Its Challengers." In *The Sciences in the American Context: New Perspectives*, edited by Nathan Reingold, 359–78. Washington, DC: Smithsonian Institution Press, 1979.
Rhodes, Richard. *The Making of the Atomic Bomb*. New York: Simon and Schuster, 1986.
Rikugun gun'i gakkō [The Army Military Academy]. *Rikugun gun'i gakkō gojūnenshi* [The Fifty-Year History of the Army Military Academy]. Tokyo: Rikugun gun'i gakkō, 1936.
Robertson, Andrew J. "Mobilizing for War, Engineering the Peace: The State, the Shop Floor, and the Engineer in Japan, 1935–1960." PhD diss., Harvard University, 2000.
Robinson, Julian Perry. *The Rise of CB Weapons*. Stockholm International Institute for Peace and Conflict Research, series editor. *The Problem of Chemical and Biological Warfare: A Study of the Historical, Technical, Military, Legal, and Political Aspects of CBW, and Possible Disarmament Measures*, vol. 1. Atlantic Highlands, NJ: Humanities Press, 1971.
Roland, Alex. "Science and War." In *Historical Writing on American Science*, edited by Sally Gregory Kohlstedt and Margaret W. Rossiter, 247–72. *Osiris*, vol. 1. Chicago: University of Chicago Press, 1985.
———. "Science, Technology, and War." *Technology and Culture* 36, supplement (April 1995): S83–S99.
Rose, Paul Lawrence. *Heisenberg and the Nazi Atomic Bomb Project: A Study in German Culture*. Berkeley: University of California Press, 1998.
Sakata Shōichi. "Kenkyū to sōshiki" [Research and Organization]. *Shizen* 2 (1947): 10–13.
Samuels, Richard J. *"Rich Nation, Strong Army": National Security and the Technological Transformation of Japan*. Ithaca: Cornell University Press, 1994.
Samuelson, Lennart. *Plans for Stalin's War Machine: Tukhachevskii and Military-Economic Planning, 1925–1941*. London: Macmillan, 2000.
Sanuki, M. ed. *Proceedings of the Second International Symposium on Rockets and Astronautics, Tokyo, 1960*. Tokyo: Yokendo, 1961.
Sasamoto Yukuo. "Demilitarization and the Peaceful Remobilization of Manpower." In Nakayama, *Social History of Science and Technology*, 119–32.
———. "The Scientific Intelligence Survey: The Compton Survey." In Nakayama, *Social History of Science and Technology*, 59–72.
Sato Gentei. "A Secret Story About the Yagi Antenna." *IEEE Antennas and Propagation Magazine* 33 (June 1991): 7–18.
Sawai Minoru. "Kagaku gijutsu shintaisei kōzō no tenkai to Gijutsuin no tanjō" [The Formation and Development of the New Order of Science and Technology and the Birth of the Technology Agency]. *Osaka daigaku keizaigaku* 41 (December 1991): 367–95.

Scalia, Joseph Mark. *Germany's Last Mission to Japan: The Failed Voyage of U-234.* Annapolis, MD: Naval Institute Press, 2000.
Shapley, Deborah. "Nuclear Weapons History: Japan's Wartime Bomb Projects Revealed." *Science* 199 (13 January 1978): 152–57.
Shimao Eikoh. "Some Aspects of Japanese Science, 1868–1945." *Annals of Science* 46 (1989): 69–91.
Siddiqi, Asif. "The Rockets' Red Glare: Technology, Conflict, and Terror in the Soviet Union." *Technology and Culture* 44 (July 2003): 470–501.
Simon, Leslie E. *German Research in World War II: An Analysis of the Conduct of Research.* New York: Wiley, 1947.
Slawecki, Leon M. S. "Notes on Modern Japanese Rocket Research: Prewar and Early War Years." *Journal of Space Flight* 9 (1957): 9–10.
Smith, Alice Kimball. *A Peril and a Hope: The Scientists' Movement in America, 1945–1947.* Cambridge, MA: MIT Press, 1970.
Speer, Albert. *Inside the Third Reich: Memoirs by Albert Speer.* New York: Macmillan, 1970.
Spiers, Edward M. *Chemical Warfare.* Urbana: University of Illinois Press, 1986.
———. *Chemical Weaponry: A Continuing Challenge.* New York: St. Martin's Press, 1989.
Stewart, Irvin. *Organizing Scientific Research for War: The Administrative History of the Office of Scientific Research and Development.* Boston: Little, Brown, 1948.
Stoiko, Michael. *Soviet Rocketry: Past, Present, and Future.* New York: Holt, Rinehart, and Winston, 1970.
Stranges, Anthony N. "Synthetic Fuel Production in Prewar and World War II Japan: A Case Study in Technological Failure." *Annals of Science* 50 (1993): 229–65.
Swords, Sean S. *Technical History of the Beginnings of RADAR.* IEE History of Technology Series, vol. 6. London: Peter Peregrinus, 1986.
Szöllösi-Janze, Margit, ed. *Science in the Third Reich.* Oxford: Berg, 2001.
Takeda Eiko. *Chizu kara kiesareta jima—Okunoshima dokugasu kōjō* [The Island Erased from the Map: The Okunoshima Poison Gas Factory]. Tokyo: Domesu Shuppan, 1987.
Taketani Mitsuo. "Methodological Approaches in the Development of the Meson Theory of Yukawa in Japan." In *Science and Society in Modern Japan: Selected Historical Sources,* edited by Nakayama Shigeru, David L. Swain, and Eri Yagi, 24–38. Tokyo: University of Tokyo Press, 1973.
Takeuchi Masa. "Uran bakudan kenkyū mukashibanashi" [Reminiscences of Uranium-bomb Research]. *Gijutsushi* 3 (May 2002): 1–53.
Tamaki Hidehiko and Ezawa Hiroshi. *Nishina Yoshio: Nihon no genshi kagaku no sho* [Nishina Yoshio: The Dawn of Nuclear Science in Japan]. Tokyo: Misuzu Shobo, 1991.
Tanaka Akira and Matsumura Takao, eds. *731-Butai sakusei shiryō* [Report Materials on Unit 731]. Tokyo: Fuji Press, 1991.
Tanaka Hiroaki. "Kagaku heiki kenkyū taiseishi no kōsō (ue)" [The Story of the History of the Chemical Weapons Research System, Part I]. *Il Saggiatore* 30 (2001): 64–75.
Tanaka Yuki. *Hidden Horrors: Japanese War Crimes in World War II.* Boulder, CO: Westview Press, 1996.

———. "Poison Gas: The Story Japan Would Like to Forget." *Bulletin of the Atomic Scientists* (October 1988): 10–19.
Tarter, Donald E. "Peenemünde and Los Alamos: Two Studies." In *History of Technology*, edited by Graham Hollister-Short and Frank A. J. L. James, 14:150–70. London: Mansell, 1996.
Theismeyer, Lincoln R., and John E. Burchard, eds. *Combat Scientists*. Boston: Little, Brown, 1947.
Tokaty, G. A. "Soviet Rocket Technology." In Emme, *History of Rocket Technology*, 272–74.
Tokuda Hachirōe. *Ma ni awanakatta heiki* [The Weapons that Came too Late]. Tokyo: Kōjinsha, 2001.
Tomari Jiro. "Genbaku kaihatsu" [Atomic Bomb Development]. Parts 1–6. *Asahi Shimbun*, 21 August 1995–2 October 1995.
Travis, Stephen N. "'Seeing' is Believing: The Development of Microwave Radar in Britain, Summer 1940." In *History of Technology*, edited by Graham Hollister-Short and Frank A. J. L. James, 18:113–37. London: Mansell, 1996.
Trischler, Helmuth. "Aeronautical Research Under National Socialism: Big Science or Small Science?" In *Science in the Third Reich*, edited by Margit Szöllösi-Janze, 79–110. Oxford: Berg, 2001.
Tsuneishi Keiichi. *731-Butai: Seibutsu heiki hanzai no shinjitsu* [Unit 731: The Truth of Biological Warfare Crimes]. Tokyo: Kōdansha, 1995.
———. "C. Koizumi: As a Promoter of the Ministry of Health and Welfare and an Originator of the BCW Research Program." *Historia Scientiarum* 26 (1984): 95–113.
———. *Igakushatachi no sōshiki hanzai: Kantōgun dai-731 butai* [The Systematic Crimes of the Physicians: Kwantung Army Unit 731]. Tokyo: Asahi Shimbunsha, 1994.
———. "The Ishii Unit." In Nakayama, *Social History of Science and Technology*, 146–58.
———. *Kieta saikinsen butai: Kantōgun dai-731 butai* [The Bacteriological Warfare Unit that Disappeared: Kwantung Army Unit 731]. Tokyo: Kaimeisha, 1981.
———. "The Research Guarded by Military Secrecy: The Isolation of the EHF Virus in Japanese Biological Warfare Unit." *Historia Scientiarum* 30 (1986): 79–92.
———. "Riken ni okeru uran bunri no kokoromi" [Uranium Separation Experiments at the Riken]. *Nihon butsurigaku kaishi* 45 (1990): 820–25.
Tsuneishi Keiichi and Asano Tomizō. *Saikinsen butai to jiketsu shita futari no igakusha* [The Bacteriological Warfare Unit and the Suicide of Two Physicians]. Tokyo: Shinchōsha, 1982.
Tuge Hideomi, ed. *Historical Development of Science and Technology in Japan*. Tokyo: Kokusai Bunka Shinkōkai, 1968.
United States Military Intelligence Service. *Enemy Capabilities for Chemical Warfare*. Washington, DC: U.S. War Department, 1943.
United States Strategic Bombing Survey. Aircraft Division. *The Japanese Aircraft Industry*. Washington, DC: GPO, 1947.
———. Military Supplies Division. *Japanese Naval Ordnance*. Washington, DC: GPO, 1946.
Utgoff, Victor A. *The Challenge of Chemical Weapons: An American Perspective*. London: Macmillan, 1990.

Van Creveld, Martin. *Technology and War: From 2000 B.C. to the Present.* New York: Free Press, 1989.
Von Braun, Wernher, and Frederick I. Ordway III. *History of Rocketry and Space Travel.* New York: Thomas Y. Crowell, 1966.
Wakabayashi, Bob Tadashi. "Documents on Japanese Poison Gas Warfare in China." *Sino-Japanese Studies* 7 (October 1994): 3–33.
———. "Research Notes on Japanese Poison Gas Warfare in China." *Sino-Japanese Studies* 5 (October 1992): 4–10.
Walker, Mark. "A Comparative History of Nuclear Weapons." In *Geschichte der Kaiser-Wilhelm-Gesellschaft im Nationalsozialismus,* edited by Doris Kaufmann, 309–27. Göttingen: Wallstein Verlag, 2000.
———. *German National Socialism and the Quest for Nuclear Power, 1939–1949.* Cambridge: Cambridge University Press, 1989.
———. *Nazi Science: Myth, Truth, and the German Atomic Bomb.* New York: Plenum Press, 1995.
Walker, Mark, ed. *Science and Ideology: A Comparative History.* London: Routledge, 2003.
Weart, Spencer. "Secrecy, Simultaneous Discovery, and the Theory of Nuclear Reactors." *American Journal of Physics* 45 (November 1977): 1049–60.
———. *Scientists in Power.* Cambridge, MA: Harvard University Press, 1979.
Weiner, Charles. "Cyclotrons and Internationalism: Japan, Denmark, and the United States, 1935–1945." In *Proceedings No. 2: XIVth International Congress of the History of Science,* 2:353–65. Tokyo: Science Council of Japan, 1975.
———. "Retroactive Saber Rattling?" *Bulletin of Atomic Scientists* 34 (April 1978): 10–12.
Wheelis, Mark. "Biological Sabotage in World War I." In Geissler and Moon, *Biological and Toxin Weapons,* 35–62.
Wilcox, Robert K. *Japan's Secret War: Japan's Race Against Time to Build Its Own Atomic Bomb.* 2nd ed. New York: Marlowe, 1995.
Wilkinson, Roger. "Short Survey of Japanese Radar—I." *Electrical Engineering* (August–September 1946): 370–77.
———. "Short Survey of Japanese Radar—II." *Electrical Engineering* (October 1946): 455–63.
Williams, Peter, and David Wallace. *Unit 731: Japan's Secret Biological Warfare in World War II.* New York: Free Press, 1989.
Winter, Frank H. "The Genesis of the Rocket in China and Its Spread to the East and West." In *History of Rocketry and Astronautics: Proceedings of the Twelfth, Thirteenth, and Fourteenth History Symposia of the International Academy of Astronautics,* edited by Å. Ingemar Skoog, 3–23. AAS History Series, vol. 10. San Diego, CA: American Astronautical Society, 1990.
———. *Prelude to the Space Age: The Rocket Societies, 1924–1940.* Washington, DC: Smithsonian Institution Press, 1983.
Wray, William D., ed. *Managing Industrial Enterprise: Cases from Japan's Prewar Experience.* Cambridge, MA: Harvard University Press, 1989.
Yamamoto Yōichi. "Nihon genbaku no shinsō" [The Truth About Japan's Atomic Bomb]. *Daihōrin* 20 (August 1953): 6–40.
———. *Nihonsei genbaku no shinsō* [The True Story of the Japanese Atomic Bomb]. Tokyo: Yūjusha, 1976.

Yamashita Nobuo. "Ma ni awanakatta Nihon no genbaku" [The Japanese Atomic Bomb that Was Too Late]. *Kaizō,* special edition (15 November 1952): 162–65.

Yamazaki Masakatsu. "Dainiji sekai taisenji no Nihon no genbaku kaihatsu" [Japan's Atomic Bomb Development in World War II]. *Nihon butsurigaku kaishi* 56 (2001): 584–90.

———. "Kyū-Nihon kaigun 'F-kenkyū' shiryō" [Technical Reports of the Japanese Navy's "F" Project]. *Gijutsu bunka ronsō* 5 (April 2002): 28–73.

———. "Riken no 'Genshi bakudan' hitotsu no gensō—'Kanzen nenshō' kōsō" [One Illusion of the Riken's 'Atomic Bomb'—The 'Perfect Combustion' Design]. *Gijutsu bunka ronsō* 3 (May 2000): 25–32.

———. "Riken no 'Uranium bakudan' kōsō: Dai-niji sekai taisenki no Nihon no kakuheiki kenkyū" [*Riken's Uraniumu Bakudan:* Japanese Nuclear Weapons Research during the Second World War]. *Kagakushi Kenkyū* 40 (2001): 87–96.

———. "The Mobilization of Science and Technology During the Second World War in Japan—A Historical Study of the Activities of the Technology Board Based upon the Files of Tadashiro Inoue." *Historia Scientiarum* 5 (1995): 167–81.

Yamazaki Masakatsu and Fukai Yūzo. "Dai-niji taisenki ni okeru Nihon no kakukenkyū shiryō (1), Rikugun Tōkyō Dai-ni zōheisho ni tai suru Nishina Yoshio no hōkoku kiroku: 1943-nen 7-gatsu kara 1944-nen 11-gatsu" [*Nishina Yoshio's* Research Report to the Japanese Army during the Second World War]. *Gijutsu bunka ronsō* 2 (February 1999): 45–54.

Yamazaki Masakatsu, Fukai Yūzo, and Satomi Muneaki. "Tōkyō Dai-ni rikugun zōheisho ni tai suru Nishina Yoshio no hōkoku: 1943-nen 7-gatsu kara 1944-nen 11-gatsu" [Nishina Yoshio's Report to the Tokyo Second Army Arsenal: July 1943 to November 1944]. *Gijutsu bunka ronsō* 3 (May 2000): 53–70.

Yasuda Takeo. "Nihon ni okeru genshibakudan seizō ni kansuru kenkyū no kaiko" [Recollection of Research Concerning the Production of an Atomic Bomb in Japan]. *Genshiryoku kōgyō* 10 (July 1955): 44–47.

Yokoyama, T., K. Yuyama, I. Akojima, and S. Moriya. "The Rocket Fighter Shusui—As Re-developed from Incomplete and Vague Me163B Data." *Transactions of the Newcomen Society for the Study of the History of Engineering and Technology* 70 (1998–1999): 257–76.

Yomiuri Shimbunsha [Yomiuri News], ed. "Nihon no genbaku" [Japan's Atomic Bomb]. In *Shōwa shi no Tennō,* 4:78–228. Tokyo: Yomiuri Shimbunsha, 1968.

———. *Shōwashi no Tennō* [The Emperor in the Shōwa Period]. Vol. 4. Tokyo: Yomiuri Shimbun, 1968.

Yoshikawa Hideo and Joanne Kauffman. *Science Has No National Borders: Harry C. Kelly and the Reconstruction of Science and Technology in Postwar Japan.* Cambridge, MA: MIT Press, 1994.

Yoshino Koichi. *Fūsen bakudan: Junkokusan heiki "Fu-gō" no kiroku* [Balloon Bomb: Record of the Purely Japanese Made Weapon Fu-gō]. Tokyo: Asahi Shimbunsha, 2000.

Young, James O. "Riding England's Coattails: The U.S. Army Air Forces and the Turbojet Revolution." In *Innovation and the Development of Flight,* edited by Roger D. Launius, 262–98. College Station: Texas A&M University Press, 1999.

Young, Louise. *Japan's Total Empire: Manchuria and the Culture of Wartime Imperialism.* Berkeley: University of California Press, 1998.

Zamagni, Vera. "Italy: How to Lose the War and Win the Peace." In *The Economics of World War II: Six Great Powers in International Comparison,* edited by Mark Harrison, 177–223. Cambridge: Cambridge University Press, 1998.

Zimmerman, David. *The Great Naval Battle of Ottawa.* Toronto: University of Toronto Press, 1989.

———. *Top Secret Exchange: The Tizard Mission and the Scientific War.* Montreal: McGill–Queen's University Press, 1996.

INDEX

A-1 (Aggregat-1) missile, 134
A-2 (Aggregat-2) missile, 134
A-Research (Radar and Electric-Wave Weapons), 61, 64, 255n54
Abyssinia, 172
Aerial Mines, 89
Aeronautical Research Institute, Tokyo Imperial University. *See* Tokyo Imperial University: Aeronautical Research Institute
Aeronautics Department Army Aeronautics Arsenal, 205
Afghanistan, 172
Aggregat-1 missile (A-1), 134
Aggregat-2 missile (A-2), 134
Aichi Aircraft Company, 152
Aircraft Manufacturing Law (1938), 246n39
AISR. *See* Army Institute of Scientific Research (Japan)
Aizawa Saburō, 30, 31
Akiyama Kinsei, 287n62
Aleutian Campaign, 104
Allied Committee on the Enforcement of the Versailles Treaty, 179
Allied International Military Tribunal, 204
All Japan Federation of Scientists and Technicians Association (Zen-Nihon Kagaku Gijutsu Dantai Rengō), 34, 43, 211
All-Union Electro-Technical Institute (Vsesoy-uzny Elektro-teknicheskii Institut, VEI), 95–96
Amaldi, Edoardo, 50
American Rocket Society, 129
AMRE research team, 273n191
Anderson, Laurie, 6
Andō Koji, 238

Arakatsu Bunsaku, 56, 57, 63–66, 74–76, 78, 80, 81, 212, 214, 232, 253nn31,32, 257n86
Araki Sadao, 27, 34
Arimori Mitsuo, 139
Army Aeronautical Technology Department (Rikugun Kōkū Gijutsu Honbu), 205
Army Aeronautical Technology Research Institutes (Rikugun Kōkū Gijutsu Kenkyūjo), First through Eighth, 56, 67, 137, 139, 140, 157, 180, 181, 202, 205, 209
Army Aeronautical Testing Division (Rikugun Hikō Jikkenbu), 206
Army Aeronautics Arsenal (Rikugun Kōkū Kōshō), 205
Army Aeronautics Department (Rikugun Kōkū Honbu), 56, 61, 67, 69, 71, 77, 139, 141, 153, 205, 209, 253
Army Aeronautics Division (Rikugun Kōkūbu), 205
Army Arsenal Bureau, Tadanoumi, 181
Army Fuels Arsenal (Rikugun Nenryōshō), 205
Army Fuels Institute (Rikugun Nenryō Kenkyūjo), 206, 208
Army Institute of Scientific Research (Rikugun Kagaku Kenkyūjo, AISR), 23, 40, 101, 106, 107, 110–111, 112, 142, 169, 178–181, 205
Army Medical College (Rikugun Gun'i Gakkō), 168, 179, 182, 184, 185
  Epidemic Prevention Laboratory, 185
Army Meteorological Department, 209
Army Ministry (Ministry of War), 25–27, 31, 40, 69, 106–107, 110, 112, 116, 169, 178, 184, 187, 194, 211
  Equipment Bureau (Seibikyoku), 26

317

Army Ministry (Ministry of War), (continued)
  General Military Affairs Bureau (Gunmu-kyoku), 106
  Military Affairs Bureau, 30
  Military Affairs Section (Gunkika), 106
  Munitions Bureau (Gunjukyoku), 26
  Provisional Committee on Poison Gas Research, 169, 178
Army-Navy Aeronautical Technology Committee (Riku-Kaigun Kōkū Gijutsu Iinkai), 39, 154, 156, 157, 162
Army-Navy Aeronautics Committee (Riku-Kaigun Kōkū Iinkai), 39
Army-Navy Aeronautics Cooperation Committee (Riku-Kaigun Kōkū Kyōtei Iinkai), 250n98
Army-Navy Fuel Technology Committee (Riku-Kaigun Nenryō Gijutsi Iinkai), 39
Army-Navy Radio Wave Technology Committee (Riku-Kaigun Denpa Gijutsu IInkai), 39, 109, 119
Army-Navy Technology Application Committee, 250n98
Army-Navy Technology Committee (Riku-Kaigun Gijutsu Iinkai), 38, 161
Army-Navy Technology Enforcement Committee (Riku-Kaigun Gijutsu Unyō Iinkai), 40, 42, 46, 66, 104, 139, 142, 144, 156–157, 160, 162
Army Technical Department (Rikugun Gijutsu Honbu), 23, 102, 129, 137–138, 169, 179, 205
Army Technical Institutes (Rikugun Gijutsu Kenkyūjo), First through Tenth, 107, 112, 129, 137, 142, 161, 169, 180, 181, 192, 207–208, 257n92
Army Technology Review Board, 168, 169
Army Weapons Administrative Department (Rikugun Heiki Gyōsei Honbu), 42, 142, 205, 208
Artificial radioactivity, 49
Asada Tsunesaburō, 60–63, 108, 213, 235
Asahi Glass, 23
Asahina Masajirō, 238
Asami Yoshihirō, 235, 270
Asian Development Board (Kō-A-in), 35, 38
Association for the Advancement and Investigation of Science (Kagaku Shinkō Chōsakai), 34, 43, 211
Atelier de Pyrotechnie du Bouchet, Paris, 172
Athos radar intercept receiver, 121
Atomic Nucleus Research Project, 57, 254n37

Auer Company, 52
Auschwitz, 176, 189
Australia, 173
Austro-American Magnesium Company, 74
Automobile Manufacturing Industry Law (1936), 246n39
AZON remote bomb, 276n37

BI rocket fighter, 148
B-29 Superfortress, 108, 116, 122–123, 141, 144, 154, 156, 198
B-29 H2X radar, 117
B-Research, 9, 61, 64
Baby series rocket, 202
Bachem Natter rocket aircraft, 279n95
Bagge, Erich, 55
Baika piloted missile, 153, 154, 281n122
Baldwin, Stanley, 89, 90
Balikpapan, Borneo, 134
Balloon bombs, 191, 269n118
Barkhausen, Heinrich, 60, 98, 100
Battle of Britain, 87, 117
Battle of Cape Matapan, 97, 105
Battle of Midway, 38, 61, 104–105
Bawdsey Manor, 87, 88, 94, 263n13, 273n191
Baxter, James P., 123
Bazooka, 127, 133, 137
Becker, Karl, 21, 128–129, 161
Belgian Congo, 53–54
Bell Telephone Laboratories, 18, 91, 132
Bentley Priory, 88, 95, 110
Bethe, Hans, 6
Berkeley. *See* University of California at Berkeley
Big Engineering, 203
Big Science, 5–6, 11, 15, 197, 199, 201
Biological warfare (BW), 165, 166, 170, 173, 231
  Germany (National Socialist), 170, 173, 177–178, 286nn37,45–49
  Great Britain, 173, 175
  Japan, 5, 7, 10, 183–191, 193–196, 231
  United States, 11, 166, 173, 174–175
  Soviet Union (USSR), 175–176
  World War I, 170
Blackett, P. M. S., 85
Blome, Kurt, 177
BMW 003A jet engine, 157
Board of Technology. *See* Technology Agency (Japan)
Boer War (South Africa), 166
Bohr, Niels, 50, 51, 54

Boot, Henry, 88, 112
Bowen, E. G., 92
Bow Wow Type Interference Detector, 102
Brandt, Walter, 93
Breit, Gregory, 90
Briggs, Lyman J., 54
Briggs Committee, 54–55
Brinker, Emil, 121–122
Britain, Battle of, 87, 117
Brown, Louis, 93
Buchenwald, 177
Buck Rogers, 1
Building 49, 70, 71, 73
Bullet train, 203
Bundy, Harvey H., 174
Burma, 77
Bush, Vannevar, 14, 18, 19, 59
BW. *See* Biological warfare

Cabinet, Japanese Government, 35–37, 39, 43, 69, 145
  Investigative Bureau, 247n61
  Planning Agency, (Kikaku-in), 32–37, 38, 42–43, 211, 248nn72,83, 249nn88,89
  Planning Agency Science Division (Kikaku-in Kagakubu), 38
  Planning Board Incident, 37
  Planning Office (Kikaku-chō), 21, 30–32
  Policy Council (Naikaku Shingikai), 30
  Research Bureau (Naikaku Chōsakyoku), 30–31, 247n61
  Resources Bureau (Shigenkyoku), 24, 26, 32
  Science Council (Kagaku Shingikai), 33, 43, 211
  Science Deliberative Society, 37
  Science Division (Kagakubu), 43
  Science Mobilization Association (Kagaku Dōin Kyokai), 33, 43, 211, 248n74
  Science Mobilization Council (Kagaku Dōin Kyōgikai), 33, 43, 202, 211
  Science Mobilization Council, Aeronautical Research Group, 202
  Science Section (Kikaku-in Kagakubu), 33
California Institute of Technology (Caltech), 132–133, 276n37
Cambridge University, 49, 77
Camp Detrick (Frederick, Maryland), 174, 177
Campini-Caproni CC.2 jet aircraft, 280n99
Campini jet engine, 152
Cape Matapan, Battle of, 97, 105
Carnegie Institution, 18, 54, 90, 252n12
Cavendish Laboratory, 49, 50, 53

CEA, 6
Central Aero and Hydrodynamics Institute (Tsentralyni Aero-Gidrodinamichescky Institut, TsAGI), 126
Central Aeronautical Research Institute (Chūō Kōkū Kenkyūjo), 203, 205, 246n40, 249n93, 295n31
Central Powers, 167
Central Radio Laboratory (Tsentral'naya Radiolaboratoriya, TsRL), 96
Central Chemical Laboratory (Chūō Shikensho), 30
Chadwick, James, 49, 55
Chain Home, 10, 14, 87, 88, 109, 110, 135
Chain Home Low, 87
Chang Hsueh-Liang, 29
Charkov Scientific Research Institute of Microbiology, Vaccine, and Serum Studies, 175
Chemical warfare (CW), 165, 166–170, 171
  France, 166, 167, 169, 171, 172
  Germany (National Socialist), 20, 166–167, 169, 172, 176–177, 193
  Great Britain, 166–167, 169, 171–172, 174
  Italy, 167–170, 176, 178–183, 191–193
  Japan, 7, 10, 28, 167–170, 178–183, 191–193
  Soviet Union (USSR), 172, 175–176
  United States, 167, 169, 171–175
  World War I, 2, 165, 166–170, 178, 180
Cherwell, Lord, 89, 90
Chiang Kai-Shek, 29
Chichihara (Tsitsihar) Laboratory, 181
China, 26, 29, 31, 33–35, 77, 101–102, 109, 125, 129, 159, 165, 168, 182–183, 185–186, 188–189, 193, 197
  Beiyinhe (Hainga), 185–187
  Changchun, 30
  Hangzhou, 102
  Mukden (Shenyang), 29, 194
  Shanghai, 78, 182
China Army garrison, 31
Chinese Nationalist Army, 29
Chitani Toshizō, 75, 193, 212
Chlorine gas, 166–167
Chlorine trifluoride gas, 176
Churchill, Winston, 89–90, 176
Civil War, Soviet Union, 172
Civil War, United States, 166
Clarendon Laboratory, 89
Clark University, 127

Cleator, Phil, 127
Clusius, Klaus, 57, 254n40
Clusius tube, 55, 57, 59, 68, 70–73, 80–81
Cockroft, John, 49, 55
Cockroft-Walton particle accelerator, 49, 56, 80
Columbia University, 44, 51, 54, 174, 252n12
Commissariat a l'Energie Atomique (CEA), 6
Committee for Research on the Application of Nuclear Physics, 9, 61, 64
Communications Research Laboratory (Nachrictenmittel-Versuchs-Anstalt, NVA), 92–93
Comprehensive Policy for the Mobilization of Science and Technology, 39
Compton, Karl T., 18–19, 46, 91
Conant, James B., 18–19, 173
Congo, Belgian, 53–54
Congreve, William, 126
Continental Science Academy, 30
Continental Science Institute (Tairiki Kagakuin), 30
Continuous wave (CW), 90, 93
Control faction (Tōseiha), 28, 187
Cooperative Committee of the Army-Navy Aeronautics Department (Riku-Kaigun Kōkū Honbu Kyōchō Iinkai), 38–39
Cornell University, 201, 295n34
Cosmic Ray Group, 67
Cunliffe-Lister, Philip (Lord Swinton), 89–90
Curie, Iréne, 49–50
CW. *See* Chemical warfare; Continuous wave
CW oscillator, 113
CW Doppler-type radar system, 101–102
CWS. *See* U.S. Army: Chemical Warfare Service
Cyclotrons, 6, 72–75, 80, 199–200

Dachau, 177, 190
Dahlgren, Virginia, 132
Dairen (Port), 28, 30
Death ray
  Great Britain, 86
  Japan, 9, 64, 100, 110–116, 197
Department of Scientific and Industrial Research (DSIR), 14–15, 20, 86
DéTe-I radar, 93
DéTe-II radar, 93–94
Deuterium oxide. *See* Heavy water
Dickel, Gerhard, 254n40

Diebner, Kurt, 52
Divine Wind Special Attack Forces (Shinpū Tokubetsu Kōgekitai), 149
Dneipropetrovak University, 175
Doihara Kenji, 29
Dominik, Hans, 84, 92
Dornberger, Walter, 135–136, 161
Dowding, Sir Hugh, 87–88, 109
Dragon aerial torpedo, 134
Dresden Technical University, 60
DSIR, 14–15, 20, 86
DuBridge, Lee, 92
Dugway Valley, Utah (CW Proving Ground), 174
Duisberg, Carl, 167
Dundee University, 88
Du Pont Corporation, 79
Dunning, John R., 54
Duplexer, 91
Dyson, Freeman, 201

EC-2 radar set, 97
Edgewood (Maryland) Arsenal, 167, 171–172, 180
Einstein, Albert, 53–55
Electric-wave weapons. *See* A-Research
Electromagnetic separation, 58, 68, 81
Enzian series missile, 276n41
Erbslöh, Paul-Günther, 92–93
Esau, Abraham, 52
Ethiopia, 172
Eugenics, 178, 291n112
Explosives Act of 1875, 127

Fax machine, 99
February 26 Incident, 30–31, 34
Felix homing bomb, 276n37
Fermi, Enrico, 22, 49, 50–51, 54, 58, 67, 73
Feynman, Richard, 201
F-gō project, 9, 64–66, 75, 78, 80, 193
Fildes, Paul, 173
Final Solution, 178
Fire-control radar, 83
Fishman, Jacov, 175, 176
Flanders, Belgium, 168
Flash Gordon, 1, 241n4
Flerov, Goergii, 53
Flügge, Siegfried, 65
FM CW radar, 99
Foders, Heinrich, 121, 122
Föhn Rocket, 277n44

Formosa (Taiwan), 26
France
   chemical warfare (*see* Chemical warfare: France)
   radar, 97
Frau im Mond, 128
Frederick, Maryland (Camp Detrick), 174, 177
French Atomic Energy Commission (Commissariat á l'Energie Atomique), 6
Freya radar set, 94–95, 121
Fries, Amos A., 171
Frisch, Otto, 50–51, 53–55
Fu-gō (balloon bombs), 191, 269n118
Fuji Aircraft Company, 151, 152
Fuji Electric Company, 100
Fuji Precision Company, 202
Fujioka Yoshio, 201, 232
Fukuda Nobuyuki, 213
Fukui Kenichi, 295n34
Funryū (Raging Dragon) guided missile, 9, 144–147, 162, 229
Furukawa Company, 23
Futagi Hideo, 238

G-2, 48
Gamov, Georgi, 53
Gargoyle glide bomb, 276n37
Gaseous barrier diffusion, 57, 68
Gas masks, 168
GAU, 95–96
GDL, 126–127
Geiger, Hans, 52
Geiger-Müller counter, 52
GEMA (Gesellschaft für Electroakustische und Mechanische Apparate), 92–93, 121
General Order for the Mobilization of Experiments and Research, 35
Geneva Conference of 1925, 184
Geneva Convention of 1864, 166
Geneva Protocols of 1925, 165, 172–173, 176, 185
George Washington University, 132
German Army
   Gas Defense School, 173
   General Staff, 172
   Medical Department, 170
   Medical Inspectorate Surgeon General's Office, 177
   Ordnance Office, 52, 172, 176–177
   Sanitary Corps, 170
   Weapons Office (Heereswaffenamt), 21

German-Japanese Technical Exchange Agreement, 78
German Research Association (Deutsche Forschungsgemeinschaft), 21
German-Soviet Nonaggression Pact, 247n71
Germany (and National Socialist Germany)
   Biological warfare (*see* Biological warfare: Germany)
   Blitzableiter Committee on Biological Warfare, 177
   Central Institute for Cancer Research, 286n45
   Chemical Troops and Gas Defense Inspectorate, 172–173
   Chemical warfare (*see* Chemical warfare: Germany)
   Chemical Warfare Defense Section, 176–177
   Civil Service Law, 20
   Four Year Plan, 20
   Guided missiles (*see* Guided missiles: Germany)
   Imperial Navy, 84
   Industrial Toxins Research Committee, 168–169
   Inspectorate of Smoke Screen Forces and Gas Defense, 176
   Jet aircraft (Jet engines) (*see* Jet aircraft: Germany)
   Kriegsmarine, 93–94
   Luftwaffe Signals Research Institute, 94
   Ministry of Armaments and War Production, 21
   Nuclear weapons (atomic bombs) (*see* Nuclear weapons: Germany)
   Radar, 92–94
   Rockets (*see* Rockets: Germany)
   Science policy, 13, 19–22
   Veterinary Inspectorate, 177
   War Department, 170, 172
   War Office, 52, 128
   War Research Association, 21
GIRD, 127
GIRD-09 rocket, 127
Gloster E.28/39 jet aircraft, 148
Gloster Meteor jet aircraft, 148
Goddard, Robert H., 126, 127, 130, 131
Goebbles, Josef, 128
Gorgon missile, 276n37
Göring, Hermann, 94, 128, 177

Gorodomlia Island, Lake Seliger, 175
Gotha bombers, 85
Göttingen University, 52
Granite Peak Proving Ground, 174
Great Britain
   Admiralty Research Laboratory, 15
   Aeronautical Research Committee, 86
   Air Defense Research Committee, 87
   Air Ministry, 87
   Air Ministry Director of Scientific Research, 85
   Biological warfare, 173, 175
   British Admiralty, 51, 133
   British Air Ministry, 148
   British Air Ministry Research Establishment, 88
   British Association for the Advancement of Science, 49
   British Interplanetary Society, 127
   Chemical warfare (see Chemical warfare: Great Britain)
   Committee for the Scientific Survey of Air Defense, 55, 85
   Committee on Air Defense Research, 89
   Death ray, 86
   Guided missiles, 134, 275n33
   Imperial Defense Committee, 89, 173
   Imperial Defense Committee's Subcommittee on Air Defense Research, 128
   Jet aircraft, 148–149
   London Interservice Subcommittee on Biological Warfare, 175
   Microbiological Warfare Committee, 173
   Ministry of Aircraft Production, 133
   Nuclear weapons, 54
   Public Health Laboratory, 173
   Radar (see Radar: Great Britain)
   Rockets (see Rockets: Great Britain)
   Royal Air Force (RAF), 88, 133, 148, 171
   Royal Flying Corps, 85, 86
   Royal Garrison Artillery, 86
   Royal Navy, 86
   Science policy, 14, 15, 16
   Swinton Committee, 89–90
   War Office, 109
Great Depression, 24–25
Great Kantō Earthquake, 24, 27, 179
"Great Terror" (Stalinist purges, 1936–1938), 17, 96, 131, 161, 176
Greater East Asian Co-Prosperity Sphere, 35
Groth, Wilhelm, 52
Group for the Study of Reactive Motion (Gruppa Izucheniia Reaktivnogo Dvizheniia, GIRD), 127
Groves, Leslie, 48, 59, 79–80, 200
Gruinard Island, 285n26
Guadalcanal, 105
Guggenheim Aeronautical Research Laboratory, 132
Guided missiles, 124
   Germany (National Socialist), 2, 21, 40, 124–125, 134–136, 146, 153, 159, 160–163, 284
   Great Britain, 134, 275n33
   Japan, 7, 9, 124, 137–147, 161–164, 229
   United States, 134, 276n37

Habann, Erich, 111
Haber, Fritz, 20, 166–167
Ha bomb, 190
Hagiwara Tokutarō, 56–57, 212
Hague Convention of 1864, 166
Hahn, Otto, 50–51, 56
Hainga, 185–187
Hale, William, 126
Hanford, Washington, 59, 79
Hanle, Wilhelm, 52
Hankey, Maurice, 89–90, 173
Hansgrig, Fritz, 74
Hara Rienzaburō, 192
Harbin Laboratory, 185–186, 187
Harbin Military Hospital, 187
Harteck, Paul, 52, 55, 59
Harvard University, 18, 201
Hata Shin, 213
Hattori Rokurō, 150, 234
Hayakawa Kiyoshi, 235
Hayashi Ichirō, 238
Hayashi Kiyoshi, 238, 270n121
Hayashi Teruo, 141
Heavy water (Deuterium oxide), 55, 59, 66, 73–76, 193
Hedgehog rocket (Holy Moses), 275n29
Heinkel Aircraft, 163
Heinkel, Ernst, 148
Heinkel He 176 jet aircraft, 147
Heinkel He 178 jet aircraft, 148
Heinrich-Herz Institute, 93
Heisenberg, Werner, 55, 59, 64
Henschel Hs-293 monoplane, 136
Hertz, Gustav, 263n3
Hertz, Heinrich, 84
Hickman, Clarence, 131–132

Higashikuni Naruhiko, Prince, 198
High-speed centrifuge, 57
Hikari express bullet train, 203
Hill, A. V., 85
Hino Juichi, 60–61
Hino Kumao, 158, 202, 234
Hippocratic Oath, 191
Hirohito, Emperor, 195
Hiroshima, 79, 198
Hisamura Taneki, 179, 180, 181
Hitachi Corporation, 142
Hitler, Adolf, 48, 59, 89, 94, 128, 135, 161, 163, 177
Hodogaya Chemical Company, 159, 182
Hoffman, Roald, 295n34
Hokkaidō Imperial University, 113, 192
Hokushin Electric Works, 141
Hollman, Hans, 93
Holy Moses, 275n29
Honda Kotarō, 33
Horiba Shinkichi, 212
Horiuchi Jirō, 192
Horn Island Proving Ground, Mississippi, 174
Hoshino Naoki, 36
Hovde, Frederick L., 275n28
Hülsmeyer, Christian, 84, 85, 92
Hungnam (Kōnan), Korea, 74–76, 159–160
Hs-117 rocket, 163
Hs-293 missile, 163, 277n45
Hs-294 missile, 163
Hs-298 missile, 163
Hyland, Lawrence, 90
Hyuga (battleship), 104

I-8 (submarine), 284n167
I-29 (submarine), 154, 163, 281n126
Ibuka Masaru, 204, 235
IG Farben, 167
I-gō series missile, 139, 140, 229
Iimori Satoyasu, 77, 213
Ikebe Tsuneto, 113, 235
Imperial Institute for Physics (Physicalisch-Technische Reichsanstalt, PTR), 19, 20
Imperial Japanese Army, 26–28, 34, 118, 144, 183, 192
  Air Service, 137, 139
  Air Service Headquarters, 106, 108
  Air Service Research Institutes (*see* Army Aeronautical Technology Research Institutes: First through Eighth)
  Aircraft-Launched Rocket Ordnance, 227
  Chemical Weapons Laboratory, 169
  General Staff, 107, 110, 111, 184, 192, 194, 211
  Ordnance Department, 71
  Research Laboratories, 211
  Rocket Ordnance, 227
  Second Army Arsenal, 71, 137
  Technical Institutes (*see* Army Technical Institutes: First through Tenth)
  Technical mission to Germany, 102
Imperial Japanese Navy, 28, 34, 38, 61, 105, 118, 144, 192
  Aircraft-Launched Rocket Ordnance, 228
  Chemical Research Division, 181
  Department of Naval Affairs, 103
  Department of Radio, 103
  General Staff, 103, 116, 150, 211
  Research Laboratories, 211
  Rocket Ordnance, 228
  Technical Mission to Germany, 102–103, 106
Imperial Rule Assistance Association (Taisei Yokusankai), 249n87
Imperial Way Faction (Kōdōha), 28, 30, 31
Inaba Ryōtaro, 178
India, 173
Indian Head, Maryland, 132
Indonesia, 188
Industrial Control Law, 25
Industry Management Committee (Kōseikai), 38
Infrared, 7, 89, 91, 95, 96, 142, 143
Inoue Tadashirō, 37, 40, 249n95
Insel Reims State Research Institute, 286n45
Institute for Advanced Study, 51, 201
Institute for General and Military Hygiene, Berlin, 177
Institute for Physical and Chemical Research (Rikagaku Kenkyūjo). *See* Riken
Institute of Bacteriological Warfare, Manchuria (Rikugun Saikinsen Kenkyūjo), 205
Institute of Chemical Physics, Moscow, 17
Institute of Theoretical Physics, Denmark, 50
Interessen Gemeinschaft Cartel (IG Farben), 167
International Consultative Committee in Radio Communications, 100
International Science Council, 23
Ioffe, Abram F., 53, 95
Ise (battleship), 104
Ishiguro Masao, 212
Ishii Shirō, 184–191, 204
Ishikawa Mine, 77

Ishikawa Tachiomaru, 188, 238
Ishikawajima Aircraft Corporation, 157
Ishikawajima Shibaura Turbine Corporation, 157
Ishitate Morizō, 193
Ishiwara Kanji, 29, 31
Iso Megumu, 63–64
Isoroku Yamamoto, 45
Itagaki Seishirō, 29
Italy
  Chemical warfare (*see* Chemical warfare: Italy)
  Jet aircraft (Jet engines), 152, 280n99
  Military Chemical Service (Servizio Chemico Militare), 172, 176
  Radar, 85, 97
  Science policy, 22
Itō Tsuneo, 115
Itō Yōji, 45, 60–64, 80, 98–102, 114–115, 122
Itokawa Hideo, 142, 202, 234
Iwatani Eiichi, 154–155, 157
Iwo Jima, 138

Japan
  Air Defense System, 109–110
  Biological warfare (*see* Biological warfare: Japan)
  Communist Party, 195
  Death ray (*see* Death ray: Japan)
  Diet (Parliament), 26, 30–31, 40, 70
  Emperor, 211
  General Staff Headquarters, 106
  Government (*see* Cabinet, Japanese Government; Japan: Diet [Parliament])
  Government ministries (*see* names of ministries)
  Guided missiles (*see* Guided missiles: Japan)
  Imperial Headquarters, 211
  Jet aircraft (Jet engines) (*see* Jet aircraft: Japan)
  Nuclear weapons (atomic bombs) (*see* Nuclear weapons: Japan)
  Patent Office, 37
  Radar (*see* Radar: Japan)
  Rockets (*see* Rockets: Japan)
  Science policy, 22 *passim*
  Science Research Bureau, 31
  State Shinto, 45
Japan Atomic Energy Commission, 201
Japan Broadcasting Corporation (Nippon Hōsō Kōkai, NHK), 100
Japan Economic Federation, 36
Japan National Aeronautics and Space Development Agency (NASDA), 203
Japan National Institute of Health, 204
Japan National Railways, 203
Japan National Research Council (Nippon Gakujutsu Kenkyū Kaigi), 23–24, 33, 43–44, 99, 211, 245n36, 251n122
  Radio Propagation Research Committee, 99
Japan Nitrogenous Fertilizer Company (Nitchitsu), 74-76
Japan Radio Corporation (Nippon Musen), 101, 107, 114–15, 117, 120–121, 268n91
Japan Railway Technical Reserve Institute (RTRI), 203
Japan Science Council (Nihon Gakujutsu Kaigi), 245n36
Japan Scientific Research Council, 245n36
Japan Society for the Promotion of Science (Nihon Gakujutsu Shinkōkai, JSPS), 24–25, 33, 43–44, 101, 211, 254n37
Japan Synthetic Chemical Research Instutite, 246n40
Japan Victor Company (JVC), 204
Jet aircraft (Jet engines), 124
  Germany (National Socialist), 9, 147–148, 279nn94,95, 280n101
  Great Britain, 148–149
  Italy, 152, 280n99
  Japan, 9, 47, 124, 149, 152, 153, 156–158
  United States, 148
  Soviet Union (USSR), 148, 279n96
Jet-Assisted Takeoff Rockets (JATO), 127
Jet Propulsion Laboratory (JPL), 132
Jewett, Frank B., 18, 19, 174
Jiguro Aircraft Company, 152
Joachimsthal, 52
Joliot, Frédéric, 49, 51, 53
Joos, Georg, 52
JPL, 132
JSPS. *See* Japan Society for the Promotion of Science
Jumo 004B jet engine, 157
Jungk, Robert, 6
Junkers Aircraft Company, 148
JVC, 204

Kaiser Wilhelm Foundation for Military
    Technical Science (Kaiser Wilhelm
    Stiftung für kreigstechnische
    Wissenschaft), 20
Kaiser Wilhelm Institutes, 30, 166
  Biology and Virus Research, 55
  Center for Cancer Research, 177
  Chemistry, 50
  Horticultural Research, 286
  Physical Chemistry, 20
  Physics, 55
Kaiser Wilhelm Society for the Advancement
    of the Sciences (Kaiser Wilhelm
    Gesellschaft zur Förderung der
    Wissenschaften, KWG), 19–20
Kaiten minisubmarine, 159
Kanazawa Kenichi, 238
Kanda Eizō, 212
Kapitsa, Piotr S., 53
Kappa series rocket, 202
Karlsruhe, Germany, 84
Karyū Ki-201 (Fire Dragon), 157–158
Karyū twin jet-engine fighter, 156–157
Katiusha rockets, 130–131
Kato Nobuyoshi, 98, 235
Kawai Sutezo, 270n121
Kawanishi Aircraft Corporation, 153, 202
Kawanishi Machine Manufacturing
    Company, 100
Kawasaki Aircraft Corporation, 140–141,
    145, 147, 157, 202
Kawasaki Corporation, 108, 124
Kawasaki Ki-48-II bomber, 140
Kawasaki Ki-67 bomber, 140
Kawasaki Ki-102b bomber, 140
Kawashima Toranosuke, 69, 70, 76, 77,
    255n55
Ke-gō missile, 142–144, 202
Kempeitai Police Force, 186
Kennelly-Heaviside layer, 99, 114
Khabarovsk, 195
Khalkin-Gol, 130, 188, 275
Khalkin-Gol River, 189
Ki-200 aircraft, 155
Kiel, Germany, 92
Kigoshi Kunihiko, 67, 70, 71, 72, 76
Kikka twin jet-engine fighter (Orange
    Blossom), 9, 156–158, 160, 162, 164
Kikuchi Seishi, 61–62, 68–69, 201, 214,
    232, 235
Kikune mine, 77

Kimura Hidemasa, 150, 234
Kimura Kenjirō, 232
Kimura Kiichi, 65, 69, 74, 212, 232
Kimura Motoharu, 232
Kiska (Aleutian Campaign), 104
Kitagawa Tetsuzō, 256n83, 257n90
Kitano Jun, 141
Kitano Masaji, 238
Kleimenov, I. T., 131
Kliewe, Heinrich, 177
Kō-A-in. *See* Asian Development Board
Kobayashi Ichizō, 37
Kobayashi Masatsugu, 101, 212, 278n59
Kobayashi Minoru, 65–66, 212, 275
Koizumi Chikahiko, 168–169, 178, 185
Ko liquid propellant, 283n150
Komet. *See* Messerschmitt Me 163
Kōnan, Korea. *See* Hungnam
Konoe Fumimaru, Prime Minister, 36
Korea, 26, 29, 35, 74–77, 159–160, 204
Kō radar, 101
Korea Synthetic Petroleum Company Ltd.
    (Chosen Jinseki Kabushiki Kaisha), 76
Korovin, Y. K., 95
Kotani Masao, 235
Kowarski, Lew, 6, 51
Koyama Kenji, 70, 213
Kubota Masao, 74
Kühnhold, Rudolph, 92–93
Kujirai Tsunetarō, 98
Kumezawa Ikurō, 203
Kummersdorf Weapons Range, 128–129,
    135
Kuomintang Army (Chinese Nationalist
    Army), 29
Kurchatov, Igor, 53, 58
Kure Naval Arsenal, 138, 256n69
Kusaba Sueki (a.k.a. Hideki), 112, 113, 235,
    269n118
Kusaka Ryunosuke, 99
Kwantung Army, 29, 130, 185–188,
    193–195, 197
  Epidemic Prevention and Water Supply
    Unit (Bōeki Kyūsuibu) (*see* Unit 731)
  Hippo-Epizootic Administration, 187
KWG, 19–20
Kyoto Imperial University, 56–57, 63–65, 74,
    80, 100, 184, 188, 214, 257n90,
    289n82
Kyoto Medical School, 188
Kyūshū Imperial University, 214

L-IV uranium pile, 59
Lambda series rocket, 202
Landau, Lev D., 17
Lang, Fritz, 1, 128
Langemak, Georgii, 131
Lark guided missile, 276n37
Lauritsen, Charles C., 132–133
Law for Iron and Steel Manufacturing Industries (1937), 246n39
Lawrence, Ernest O., 6, 57, 81, 251n1, 264n24
League of Nations, 172, 182
League of Nations Disarmament Conference (1925), 171
Leary (battleship), 91
Leeb, Walter, 177
LEFI, 96
Lend-Lease Program, 97
Leningrad Bacteriological Institute, 175
Leningrad Electro-Physics Institute (Leningradskii Elektrofizicheskii Institut, LEFI), 96
Leningrad Gas Dynamics Laboratory (Gazodinamicheskaia Laboratoriia, GDL), 126–127
Leningrad Physical-Technical Institute, 17, 53
Liaotung Peninsula, 28, 29
Lindemann, Frederick, Lord Cherwell, 89, 90
Lindemann-Tizard conflict, 89
Lippisch, Alexander, 147
Lippisch (Delta-Wing) aircraft, 155
Little Joe guided missile, 276n37
London Naval Treaty (1930), 28
Loomis, Alfred L., 91
Lorenz Company, 94
Los Alamos, New Mexico, 59, 79
Luftwaffe, 94, 135, 136, 148
Lukouchiao, 31

M3 cavity magnetron, 115
MacArthur, Douglas, 149, 195, 199
MacDonald, Ramsay, 89
Machine Tool Industry Law (1938), 246n39
Magnetrons, 9
Malaya, 77–78
Malaysia, 154
Manchuria, 28–29, 31, 35, 77, 159, 180, 185–186, 188–189, 194, 204
Manchurian Incident, 29, 31, 185
Manchukuo, 29
Manhattan Engineering District, 59
Manhattan Project, 6, 8, 42, 48, 53, 59, 79–81
Mannert L. Abele (destroyer), 152

Marco Polo Bridge (Lukouchiao), 31
Marco Polo Bridge Incident, 31, 182
Marconi, Guglielmo, 85, 100
Mark I, Models 1–4 series radar, 105–106
Mark II, Models 1–2 series radar, 106
Mark III, Models 1–3 series radar, 106
Mark IV series radar, 106
Mark V series radar, 106
Mark VI series radar, 106
Mark 22 series radar, 119
Marshall Islands, 102
Martini, Wolfgang, 94
Marudai Project, 150
Masao Kusami, 238
Maslokovitch, Professor, 175
Mass spectrometer, 68, 81
Massachusetts Institute of Technology (MIT), 18, 44, 92, 94, 174
Masuda Tomosada, 194, 238
Matsudaira Tadashi, 203
Matsumura Kenichi, 157
Matsuoka Shigeru, 113, 235
Matsuura Yokei, 151
MAUD Committee, 55
Maxwell, James Clerk, 84
MCA, 172, 175
Medical Society of Tokyo, 168
Meitner, Lise, 50, 51
Mengele, Josef, 291n112
Mentzel, Rudolf, 21
Merck, George W., 174
Merke Corporation, 260n152
Meson particle theory, 201
Messerschmitt Me 163 (Komet), 9, 135, 147, 148, 154, 163
Messerschmitt Me 262, 9, 135, 148, 155, 157, 163, 280n101
"Mezner, Dr.," 180
Midway, Battle of, 38, 61, 104–105
Miki Tadanao, 150, 203, 234
Military Secrets Act of 1927, 181
Ministry of Agriculture and Forestry, 34
Ministry of Commerce and Industry, 25, 32, 34, 36, 44
  Provisional Bureau of Industrial Rationalization (Rinji Sangyō Gōrikyoku), 25
Ministry of Communications, 34, 205, 246n40, 249n93
Ministry of Education, 25, 32–34, 36–38, 42–43, 46, 114, 202, 211, 251n122
  Aeronautical Deliberative Society, 37

Invention Promotion Committee, 37
Science Division (Kagakubu), 34, 37, 38, 43, 211
Ministry of Finance, 34
Ministry of Foreign Affairs, 179
Ministry of Industry and Commerce, 38
Ministry of International Trade and Industry (MITI), 293n7
Ministry of Munitions, 38, 149, 151, 159, 293n7
Ministry of the Navy. *See* Navy Ministry
Ministry of War. *See* Army Ministry
Minoshima Takashi, 113, 235
MIT. *See* Massachusetts Institute of Technology
MIT Rad Lab. *See* Radiation Laboratory (Rad Lab), MIT
MITI, 293n7
Mittelwerk factory, Nordhausen, 162
Mitsubishi, 23, 108, 124, 140–141, 155, 161
Mitsubishi A6M5 (Aircraft). *See* Zero
Mitsubishi Engine Works, 157
Mitsubishi G4M2e (Betty) Aircraft, 151, 152
Mitsubishi Heavy Industries, 145, 147
Mitsubishi Ki-48 bomber, 140
Mitsubishi Ki-67 (Peggy) bomber, 140, 141
Mitsubishi Nagoya Engine Research Division, 140
Mitsubishi Shipbuilding Company, 24
Mitsubishi Synthetic, 159
Mitsui Chemical, 159
Mitsui Matao, 63–64, 66, 80, 257n90
Miyamoto Takenosuke, 35, 38, 43
Miyata Tsuneyoshi, 195
Miyazaki Kiyoshi, 212
Mizushima Sanichirō, 61
Model 2 Type 1 radar set, 104
Model 97 reconnaissance plane, 124
Mongolia, 77
Moon, Philip B., 55
Morimoto Shigetaki, 236
Morita Akio, 204, 236
Morita Kiyoshi, 112, 236
Moscow Institute of Epidemiology and Microbiology, 175
Mousetrap rocket launcher, 275n29
Muller, Max Adolph, 148
Munitions Mobilization Law, 26
Murakami Aircraft Company, 152
Murata Tsutomu, 63
Mu series rocket, 202
Mussolini, Benito, 22

Mustard gas, 167
Muto Institute of Physical and Chemical Research, 246
MXY8 Akigusa (Autumn Grass) glider, 155

N-Stoff, 176
NACA, 18, 149
Nagai Kenzo, 99
Nagamori Kyūzo, 141
Nagaoka Hantarō, 44, 61, 100, 116
Nagasaki, 198
Nagasaki Ordnance Works, 140, 145, 147
Nagata Tetsuzan, 26, 27, 30–31, 187
Nagoya Arsenal, 142
Nagoya Imperial University, 80
Naitō Ryōichi, 188, 238
Nakahara Juichirō, 203
Nakajima Aircraft Company, 124, 157, 202
Nakajima Otokichi, 213
Nakajima Shigeru, 114, 117, 236, 268nn82,83
Nakanishi Fujio, 157
Narashino Training School, 182, 192, 287n62
Narimoto Takahiro, 213
National Advisory Committee for Aeronautics (NACA), 18, 149
NASD, 203
National Defense Research Committee (NDRC), 14, 19, 37, 44, 55, 57, 79, 91–92, 132–134, 149, 173, 174
Division of Armor and Ordnance, 132
Division Three, 133
Division Fourteen (Microwave Committee), 91–92
Section D-1, 91
Section H, 132, 133
Section L, 132, 133
Special Committee on Jet Propulsion, 149
Technical Committee, 173
National Defense Technology Committee (Kokuho Gijutsu I-in), 35
National General Mobilization Law, 32, 35
Natzwieler (Concentration Camp), 177
Naval Air Arsenal. *See* Navy Aeronautical Technology Arsenal (Japan)
Naval Research Laboratory (NRL), 51, 90, 91
Navy Aeronautical Technology Arsenal (Kaigun Kōkū Gijutsushō); abbreviated as Kūgishō (Naval Air Arsenal), with affiliated departments, 150–153, 155, 159, 205, 267n74

Navy Aeronautics Department (Kaigun Kōkū Honbu), 103, 105, 144, 147, 205
Navy Aeronautics Laboratory (Kaigun Kōkūki Shikensho), 50, 205
Navy Aeronautics Research Departments (Kaigun Kōkū Kenkyūbu), 103, 105, 150, 205, 276n74
Navy Communications School, Yokosuka, 110
Navy Department of Ships (Kaigun Kansei Honbu), 42, 63–66, 78, 99, 103, 144, 145, 157–158, 205, 210, 256n69, 257n90
  Special Materials Division, 78
Navy Fuel Arsenal, 159, 160
  Division of Experiments and Research (Kaigun Nenryōshō Jikkenbu), 205
  Special Fuels Division, 159
Navy Ministry, 40, 66, 103, 104, 211
Navy Powder Arsenal and numbered divisions, 138, 181
Navy Technical Arsenal and numbered divisions (Kaigun Gijutsushō), 105, 138, 139, 157, 206, 210
Navy Technical Department (Kaigun Gijutsu Honbu), 105, 205
Navy Technical Research Institute (Kaigun Gijutsu Kenkyūjo, NTRI), 23, 42, 50, 60–62, 64, 98–99, 101, 103, 105, 114, 123, 145, 156, 158–159, 181, 202, 204–205, 210
Navy Technical Research Institute Short-Wave Laboratory (Tanpa Kenkyūshitsu), 205
  Propulsion Research Department, 145–147
Ne-series ramjet engine (0-4), 157
Ne-20 turbojet engine, 153, 157
Ne-201 turboprop engine, 157
Nebel, Rudolf, 128, 129
Neighborhood Research Associations, 248n74
Netherlands, 97
New Guinea, 109
New Order of Science and Technology, 8, 9, 22, 32, 35, 36
New York (battleship), 91
NDRC. *See* National Defense Research Committee (United States)
NHK, 100
NHK Broadcasting Technology Research Institute, 204
NI-Gō Project, 9, 66, 67–73, 77, 80–81
Nihon Chissō, 159
NII-3 Division, 131
Nippon Aircraft Company, 151, 156

Nippon Broadcasting Company, 145, 147
Nippon Electric Corporation (NEC), 101, 107, 202, 204, 278n59
Nippon Rocket Society, 129
Nishikawa Seiji, 56, 61
Nishimaki Masao, 270n121
Nishina Tamotsu, 61
Nishina Yoshio, 57, 61–62, 65–69, 80, 100, 199–201, 213, 214, 232, 253n33
Nissan Corporation, 202
Nitchitsu Fuel Industries, 160
Nitchitsu Konzern, 159
Nitta Shigeharu, 212, 257n90
Niwa Yasujiro, 212
Nobeoka Laboratory, 74–76
Noborito Laboratory, 106–107, 111–113, 123
Nobuuji, Major General, 71–72
Noguchi Enterprises, 74
Noguchi Jun, 74, 159–160
Nomonhan, 130, 188, 275
Nomonhan Incident, 247n71, 291n105
Nomura Yasuo, 142
Normandie (ocean liner), 98
Northrup Corporation, 148
Norwegian Hydroelectric Company (Norsk Hydro), 55, 73, 75, 76, 260n145
NRC, 18, 167
NRL, 51, 90, 91
NTRI. *See* Navy Technical Research Institute (Japan)
Nuclear energy, 48
Nuclear fission, 48–54, 83
Nuclear weapons (atomic bombs)
  Germany (National Socialist), 48, 52, 55, 59
  Great Britain, 54
  Japan, 7, 9, 49, 56–57, 59–79, 197
  United States, 5, 6, 48, 51, 53–55, 58–59
  Soviet Union (USSR), 58
NVA, 92–93

Oak Ridge, Tennessee, 59, 79
Oak Ridge National Laboratory, Tennessee, 6
Obara Tsunendo, 129
Oberth, Hermann, 126, 128, 130
Office of Scientific Research and Development (OSRD), 14, 19, 37, 44, 48, 58, 59, 79, 120, 134, 161, 174
Ogata Kenji, 204, 236
Ogata Tadaichi, 213
Ogata Tomio, 238
Ogawa Taichirō, 150, 153, 234
Ogawa Tōru, 238

Ogoshi Kunihiko, 213
Ohka Model 11 rocket plane, 203
Ohka rocket plane, 150–152, 203
Ohno Kazuo, 157
Ohta Mitsuo, 150
Okabe Kinjirō, 97–98, 101, 102–103, 111–112, 114
Okada Shinzō, 65, 66, 212
Okamoto Kōzō, 188, 238
Okamoto Masahiko, 156
Okamura Sōgo, 236
Okinawa, 152
Ōkōchi Masatoshi [Seibin], 30, 33, 57
Okunoshima, 181–182
Oliphant, Mark, 53–54, 88
Olympic Games, Tokyo (1940), 101
Omori Masuo, 140
Onishi Takajirō, 149
Oppama Rocket Test Site, 155
Oppenheimer, J. Robert, 79, 80, 200–201
Orfordness Research Facility, 87
ORM-1 rocket motor, 127
Osaka Arsenal, 137
Osaka Imperial University, 50, 61, 68, 70, 75, 80–81, 97, 101–102, 108, 142, 201, 214, 265n45
Osaka Imperial University Industrial Science Research Laboratory, 246n40
Oschchepkov, Pavel, 95, 96
Osenberg, Werner, 21
Oshima Hiroshi, 78
OSRD. *See* Office of Scientific Research and Development (United States)
Ota Takeshi, 212, 213
Ouchi Atsuyoshi, 204, 236
Outer Mongolia, 188
Outline for the Establishment of a New Order of Science and Technology, 36–37
Outline of Urgent Measures for Scientific Research, 39
Oxford University, 77, 86
Oyagi Shizuo, 146
Ozaki Seinosuke, 213
Ozawa Hisanojo, 140
Ozawa Yasutomo, 236

Page, Robert, 90
Panama, 174
Patterson, Robert P., 200
Pearl Harbor, 83, 91, 156
Peenemünde, 125, 134–137, 148, 162
Peenemünde-East, 135, 147

Peenemünde-West, 135
Pegram, George, 252n12
Peierls, Rudolf, 53, 54, 55
Pelican radar-guided missile, 134
Pencil rocket, 202
Perrin, Francis, 65
Petroleum Industry Law (1934), 246n39
Philippines, 109, 116
Physics Committee, 61–62, 64, 68, 98, 116, 254n53
Pingfang, 187–190, 193–195
Plant, Jimmy, 90
Plum Blossom missile, 153
Plutonium, 58
Political purges. *See* "Great Terror" (USSR)
Pontecorvo, Bruno, 22
Porton Down Experimental Station, 167, 171, 173
Posen Military Medical Academy, 177
Price, Derek J. de Solla, 6
Princeton Institute for Advanced Study, 51, 201
Project Energy, 271n139
Project Force, 271n139
Project Power, 271n139
Prospectus on Fundamental National Policy, 36
Proximity fuse, 64, 108, 109
PTR, 19, 20
Pu Yi, "Henry," 29
PVO, 96

Rabaul airlift, 150
Rad Lab. *See* Radiation Laboratory (Rad Lab), MIT
Radar
 France, 97
 Germany (National Socialist), 92–94
 Great Britain, 5, 10, 14, 85–90, 109
 Italy, 85, 97
 Japan, 5, 7, 9, 61, 64, 97–110, 117 *passim*, 197
 Netherlands, 97
 United States, 83, 90–92
 Soviet Union (USSR), 95–97
Radar and Electric-Wave Weapons Research, Japan, 61, 64, 255n54
Radiation Laboratory (Rad Lab), MIT, 92, 94, 123, 134, 273n191
Radio Educational Research Institute, Tokyo, 202
Radio Research Station, Slough, 86
Radium, 52, 60, 62, 77

330　Secret Weapons and World War II

Radium Institute, Leningrad, 17
Raeder, Erich, 93
RAF. *See* Great Britain: Royal Air Force
Raging Dragon. *See* Funryū guided missile
Raiden aircraft, 154
Rakete zu den Planetenräumen, Die, 128
Raketenflugplatz Testing Ground, 128
Randall, John, 88, 112
Rascher, Sigmund, 190
RATO wing rockets, 158
Raubkammer Research Facility, 176
Ray gun, 86
Reactive Scientific Research Institute (Reaktivnyi Naucho-Issledovatel'skii Institut, RNII), 127, 131
Red Army. *See* Soviet Union, Red Army of the
Red Cross, 170
Reich Air Ministry (Reichsluftfahrtministerium, RLM), 147, 148
Reich Bureau of Standards, 52
Reich Ministry of Culture, 52
Reich Ministry of Education (Reichserziehungsministerium, REM), 20, 52
Reich Research Council (Reichsforschungsrat, RRC), 13, 20–21, 52, 59, 177
REM, 20, 52
Research Mobilization Committee (Kenkyū Dōin Kaigi), 39, 43, 211
Resonant cavity magnetron, 5, 88, 91, 95, 112, 197
RIEC, 97
Riehl, Nikolaus, 52
Riese radar set, 121
Riken (Institute for Physical and Chemical Research, Tokyo), 23–24, 30, 33, 57, 61–63, 65 *passim*, 73–74, 76–77, 81, 100, 193, 199–201, 214, 255n55
Riken Rare Elements Ltd., 261n163
RKKA, NIIIS KA, 96
RLM, 147, 148
RNII, 127, 131
Ro-3 Type I rocket, 137
Roc guided missile, 276n37
Rocket into Planetary Space, The, 128
Rockets, 124–130 *passim*
　Germany (National Socialist), 128, 129, 134–136, 277n44
　Great Britain, 127–128, 133–134, 275n33
　Japan, 124, 129, 130, 137–139, 202, 227, 228
　United States, 127, 131–133
　Soviet Union (USSR), 126, 127, 130–131
Ro-Gō Z-Stoff Committee (Ro-gō Z-yaku Iinkai), 159, 161
Roosevelt, Franklin D., 18, 19, 53-54, 174, 176, 182, 183
Rowe, Albert P., 85, 87–88
Royal Institute for Electro-Technics and Communication (Regio Instituto Elettrotecnico e della Communicazioni della Marina, RIEC), 97
RP-318 rocket aircraft, 279n96
RRC. *See* Reich Research Council
RTRI, 203
Runge, Wilhelm, 92
RUS-1 Rhubarb radar set, 97
RUS-2 Redoubt radar set, 97
Rusinov, Lev, 53
Russo-Japanese War (1904–1905), 26–27, 30
Rust, Bernhard, 20
Rutherford, Ernest, 49–51, 55, 77
Ryūkyū Islands, 109

S-1, 58
Sa-gō project, 139
Saba Jirō, 151
Sachs, Alexander, 53, 54
Sagami Naval Research Department, 180, 181
Sagane Ryōkichi, 56, 60–62, 214, 251n1
St. Athan, South Wales, 88
St. Sophia Cathedral, 186
Sakata Shōichi, 212, 232
Sakata Tamio, 213
Sakhalin Islands, 26
Samejima Taesaburō, 193
Sänger, Eugen, 148
San Francisco Peace Treaty (1952), 201
San José Island, 174
Sarin gas, 176
Sasada Sukesaburō, 236, 269n118
Sasaki Kiyoyasu, 60, 257n90
Sasaki Shinji, 65, 66, 212
Sasebo Naval Arsenal, 138
Satake Kinji, 101, 121, 122
Savitch, Paul, 50
SCAP, 149, 195, 199–201
Schiffner, Kurt, 273n182
Schmidt, Kurt, 163
Schultes, Theodor, 93
Schumann, Erich, 21
Schwinger, Julian S., 201

Science and Technology Council (Kagaku Gijutsu Shingikai), 37, 43, 211
Science policy
  Germany (National Socialist), 13, 19–22
  Great Britain, 14, 15, 16
  Italy, 22
  Japan, 22 *passim*
  United States, 14, 18, 19
  Soviet Union (USSR), 16–18
  World War I, 13, 15–16
SCR-270, 91
SCR-271, 91
Second Navy Technical Arsenal (Dai-Ni Kaigun Gijutsushō), 105, 122, 195
Seetakt series radar, 93
Segré, Emilio, 22, 50
Sei-Gō Research (Project Power), 116, 271n139
Selassie, Haile, 172
Shanghai Science Institute, 30
Shenyang, 29, 194
Shibata Zenichi, 192
Shibusawa Genji, 33
Shimada Navy Technical Research Institute (Shimada Kaigun Gijutsu Kenkyūjo), 115, 206, 270n136
Shimizu Sakae, 65, 212
Shinji Ichirō, 204, 236
Shinkansen (bullet train), 203
Shinma Keizō, 213
Shinohara Kenichi, 214
Shinryū piloted missile, 153, 154
Shinto, 45
Shipbuilding Manufacturing Law, 246n39
Shūsui J8M1 (Sword Stroke) rocket-propelled intercept fighter, 9, 47, 154, 155, 156, 159, 160, 162, 164
Siemens Brothers Corporation, 113
Sinelnikov, Kirill, 53
Singapore, 98, 109, 116
SMR, 28–30
Society for Space Travel (Verein für Raumschiffahrt, VfR), 128–129, 135, 161
Soddy, Frederick, 77
Sommerfeld, Arnold, 169
Sonar, 105
Sony Corporation, 204
South Manchuria Railway (SMR), 28–30
South Manchuria Railway Company, 28
South Sea Islands, 77
Soviet Academy of Sciences, 16–18, 30, 96
  Division of Technical Sciences, 17
Soviet Union (USSR)
  Air Defense Command (PVO), 96
  Biological Warfare (*see* Biological warfare: Soviet Union)
  Chemical Warfare (*see* Chemical warfare: Soviet Union)
  Civil War, 172
  Communist Party, 17
  Council of Ministers, 17
  Defense Commission (Commissariat), 16, 96
  Defense Commission, Special Scientific-Technical Committee (Osobyi Nauchno-Teknicheskii Komitet pri Komissii Oborony), 16
  Five Year Plan, 16
  General Headquarters of the Supreme High Command (Stavka Verkhovnogo Glavnokomandovaniya), 18
  Jet aircraft (Jet engines), 148, 279n96
  Military-Chemical Agency (MCA), 172, 175
  Nuclear weapons (atomic bombs), 58
  People's Defense Committee, 17, 18
  Politburo, 17, 175
  Radar, 95–97
  Revolutionary Military Council, 127
  Rockets, 126, 127, 130–131
  Science policy, 16–18
  Scientific Research Institute of Health, 175
  Stalinist purges, 1936–1938. *See* "Great Terror"
  State Defense Committee (Gosudarstvennyi Komitet Oborony, GKO), 17–18
  State Defense Committee, Scientific-Technical Council, 18
  State Planning Commission, 17
Soviet Union, Red Army of the, 16, 95, 172, 178, 186, 188–189
  Biochemical Institute, 175
  General Headquarters of the Supreme High Command (USSR), 18
  Higher Military School for Chemistry, 172
  Main Artillery Administration (Glavnoe Artilkeriiskoe Upravlenie, GAU), 95–96
  Scientific Research Institute, 175
  Signal Corps, 96
  Signal Corps, Scientific-Research Experimental Institute (Nauchnoissledovatel'skii Ispytatel'nyi Institut Svyazi, RKKA, NIIIS KA), 96
Spandau Research Facility, 176

Sparta, 166
Special propulsion missile. *See* Funryū guided missile
Speer, Albert, 21, 59
Sperry Gyro Company, 113
Split-anode magnetron, 111
SS, 21, 136
Stalin, Josef, 17, 18
Stavka, 18
Strassmann, Fritz, 50–51, 56
Stimson, Henry L., 174
Sugimoto Asao, 213, 232
Sugimoto Masao, 138, 145, 234
Sumitomo, 23, 142
Sumitomo Chemical Company, 159, 182
Sumitomo Communication Machine Corporation, 141
Sumitomo Electric Department of Research, 246n40
Sumitomo Tsushin, 107, 268n91
Sunday Soviets, 88
Supreme Commander of Allied Powers in the Pacific (SCAP), 149, 195, 199–201
Suzuki Tatsusaburō, 56, 57, 60
Suzuki Teiichi, 249n88
Swinton, Lord, 89–90
SWOD Mk 9 guided missile (Mk 57 Bomb, Bat), 134, 276n37
Synthetic Petroleum Manufacturing Law (1937), 246n29
Szilard, Leo, 51, 53–55, 252n9

Tabei Kazu, 238
Tabun gas, 176
Tachi series radar, 108
Tachibane (Mandarin Orange Blossom) microwave oscillator, 114
Tada Reikichi, 40, 77, 101
Tadanoumi, 181
Taiwan, 154
Tajima Eizō, 213
Takagi Noboru, 202
Takahashi Isao, 212
Takahashi Kanjiro, 115
Takahashi Mijiro, 155
Takano Shizuo, 204, 236
Takao Tetsuya, 78
Takayanagi Kenjiro, 204, 236
Takeda Eiichi, 68–69, 232
Takeda Tsuneyoshi, 195
Takeuchi Masa, 67–73, 81, 213
Taketani Mitsuo, 45

Taki series radar, 108
Tama Army Technical Institute (Tama Rikugun Gijutsu Kenkyūjo), 41–42, 107–108, 123, 206, 208
Tamaki Hidehiko, 68, 73, 213, 257n99
Tamiya Takeo, 238
Tanaka Hideo, 239
Tanaka Masamichi, 61
Tanakadate Aikitsu, 70
Tanegashima Tokiyasu, 156
Taniguchi Hatsuzō, 69, 70
Tani Ichirō, 147, 150, 153, 162, 202, 234
Tase series radar, 108, 119
Tase 6 radar, 108, 119
Taylor, A. Hoyt, 90
Technische Hochschule, Berlin, 21
Technische Hochschule, Hannover, 21
Technology Agency (Gijutsu-in), 8, 22–23, 36–38, 40–44, 46–47, 77, 79, 108, 119, 125, 144, 198, 211, 245n33, 249nn87,93,95, 251n122
Technology Agency Science and Technology Council, 39
Technology Board. *See* Technology Agency (Japan)
Telefunken, 92, 94, 121, 268n91
Television, 7, 134
Teller, Edward, 54
Tesla, Nikola, 84
Texas (battleship), 91
Thermal diffusion, 55, 58, 68, 71
Thomson, George, 55
Thorium, 62, 77
Tiberio, Ugo, 97
Tiny Tim rocket, 275n29
Tizard, Sir Henry, 15, 54–55, 85, 87–90
Tizard Committee, 85–86, 89–90 (Great Britain)
Tizard Mission, 55, 91–92, 115, 132–133, 273n191
Tōgō Unit, 185, 186
Tōhoku Imperial University, 33, 61, 80, 97, 99–100, 111, 113, 192, 215, 265n45
Tōjō Hideki, 39, 43, 183, 290n91
Toko Ro-2 rocket engine, 146, 155
Tokyo Aircraft Instrument Company, 140, 145
Tokyo Army Arsenal, 168
Tokyo Electric Company Research Laboratory, 246n40
Tokyo Imperial University, 56, 60–61, 67, 70, 98, 100–101, 158, 193, 214, 289n82

Aeronautical Research Institute, 33, 141–142, 147, 150, 153, 157, 162, 273n1
   Faculty of Medicine, 113
   Medical College, 60, 168
Tokyo Institute of Technology, 112, 113, 246n40
Tokyo Shibaura Electric Company. *See* Toshiba
Tokyo University, 201–202
   Institute for Nuclear Studies, 201
   Institute of Industrial Science, 202
Tomka Project, 172, 175, 285n21
Tomonaga Shinichirō, 201, 233
Tonographie, 92
Torpedo Research Institute (Torpedoversuchsanstalt), German Navy, 93–94
Toshiba, 23, 61–62, 100, 101, 107
Totsuko Corporation (Tokyo Communications Industry), 204
Toyoda Teijirō, 249n88
Toyota Motor Research Laboratory, 246n40
TR-10 jet turbo engine, 157
TsAGI, 126
Tsiolkovsky, Konstantin, 126, 127, 130
Tsitsihar Laboratory, 181
Tso-lin, Chang, 29
TsRL, 96
Tsunesaburō, Asada, 50, 255n54
Tukhachevskii, Mikhail, 16–17, 127, 131
Tupolev, Andrei N., 17
Tuve, Merle A., 90
Type A bistatic CW radar, 109
Type A Bistatic Doppler Interference Detector, 102
Type A (Kō) radar, 101
Type B pulse radar, 102, 109
Type RS-82 rocket, 130
Typhoon fighter, 133

U-234 (submarine), 78, 79
U-512 Satsuki (submarine), 154
Uda Shintaro, 111
Ugaki Kazunari (a.k.a. Kazushige), 26–27
Uji Type 50 bomb, 190
Ukranian Physical-Technical Institute, 53
Ultracentrifuge, 65, 66, 68
Umezu Yoshijirō, 194, 293n136
Union Carbide, 79
Unit 100, 187
Unit 731, 10, 187, 189–190, 193–196, 204, 238–239
United States

Biological warfare, (*see* Biological warfare: United States)
Biological Warfare Committee, 175
BW Research and Development Center, Camp Detrick, 174, 177
Bureau of Mines, 167
Chemical warfare, (*see* Chemical warfare: United States)
Chemical Warfare Committee (USCWC), 174
Civil War, 166
Committee on Medical Research, 19
Department of the Navy, 51, 90
Department of War, 167
Federal Security Agency, 174
Guided missiles, 134, 276n37
House of Representatives' Committee on Naval Appropriations, 91
Jet aircraft (jet engines) (*see* Jet aircraft: United States)
Military Policy Committee, 59
National Academy of Sciences (NAS), 18
National Bureau of Standards, 54, 134, 149
National Defense Act (1920), 171
National Research Council (NRC), 18, 167
National Research Council Chemistry Committee, 167
National Research Council Subcommittee on Noxious Gases, 167, 171
Nuclear weapons (atomic bombs) (*see* Nuclear weapons: United States)
President's Advisory Committee on Uranium, 54
Radar, 83, 90–92
Rockets, 127, 131–133
Science policy, 14, 18, 19
War Bureau of Consultants (WBC), 174
War Research Service (WRS), 174
United States Army
   Air Corps, 149
   Chemical Warfare Board, 171
   Chemical Warfare Branch Committee, 171, 192
   Chemical Warfare Service (CWS), 167, 171, 173–174
   Chemical Warfare Service Special Projects Division, 174–175
   Chemical Warfare Service Technical Committee, 173
   Chemical Warfare Technical Committee, 171
   Corps of Engineers, 59
   Intelligence (G-2), 48

United States Army (continued)
  Ordnance Department, 167
  Signal Corps, 91
United States Navy
  Bureau of Aeronautics, 133
  Bureau of Engineering, 90
  Bureau of Ordnance, 132–134
  Naval Ordnance Test Station (Inyokern, California), 133
  Naval Powder Factory (Indian Head, Maryland), 132
  Naval Proving Ground (Dahlgren, Virginia), 132
  Naval Research Laboratory, 51, 90, 91
United States–Canadian Advisory Committee, 174
University of Birmingham, 88, 112
University of California, 44
University of California at Berkeley, 6, 48, 57, 81, 201, 264n24
University of Chicago, 67, 174
University of Rochester, 92
Uranium, 49, 50, 52 *passim*, 59, 62–65, 72, 76–77, 79, 262n166
Uranium-235 (U-235), 54–55, 57, 59, 62, 66, 68, 71–73, 78, 80–81
Uranium-238 (U-238), 54, 57, 68
Uranium hexafluoride, 57, 66–73, 76
Uranium oxide, 65–66, 76, 78–79
Uranium Section (S-1), 58
Urey, Harold C., 54, 259n134
Usedom Island, 135
USS *Wichita* (battleship), 91

V-1 (Vergeltundswaffe-Eins) missile (FZG-76), 21, 40, 135, 153, 159, 161, 276n41, 284n167
V-2 (Vergeltungswaffe-Zwei) missile (Aggregat-4), 2, 21, 40, 125, 128, 135–136, 160–163, 276nn38,40,42
Van de Graaff generator, 81, 214
VEI. *See* All-Union Electro-Technical Institute (USSR)
Verne, Jules, 1, 241n1
Versailles Treaty (1919), 13, 20, 128, 161, 172, 176, 179
VfR, 128–129, 135, 161l
Vigo Ordnance Plant, Indiana, 174
Virus House, 55
Von Braun, Wernher, 128–129, 134, 161
Von Halban, Hans, 51
Von Ohain, Hans, 148

Von Richtofen, Manfred, 148
Von Richtofen, Wolfram Freiherr, 148, 161
Von Willisen, Hans-Karl Freiherr, 92–93
Vozrozhdeniya Island, 175

Wada Koroku, 33
Wagner, Herbert, 148
Wakamatsu Yujirō, 187
Walther, Helmut, 147
Walther HWK 109-509 rocket engine, 146, 154
Walton, Ernest T. S., 49
Washington Conference on Arms Limitations 1922, 171
Washington Conference on Theoretical Physics, 51
Washizu Kyūichiro, 150
Wasserfall rocket, 277n43
Wasserman radar set, 121
Watanabe Satoshi, 41, 46, 61
Watanabe Yasushi, 98, 99, 236
Watson Watt, Robert, 86, 87, 88
WBC, 174
Wehrmacht, 94
Weimar Republic, 20, 126
Weinberg, Alvin, 6
Wells, H. G., 1, 241n2
Westinghouse, 91
West Virginia (battleship), 152
Whittle, Frank, 148
Wigner, Eugene, 53–54
Wilkins, Arnold F. "Skip," 86–88, 110
Wimperis, H. E., 85–87
Wismar radar set, 121
Woman in the Moon, 128
Woolwich Royal Arsenal, 126–127 (Great Britain)
World War I, 2, 7–8, 13, 15-16, 22–23, 84–86, 91, 110, 127, 171–172
  Aeronautic weapons, 124, 127–128, 131, 161
  Biological warfare, 170
  Chemical warfare, 2, 7, 165, 166–170, 178, 180
  Radar, 84–85
  Science policy, 15, 18
Wright Field, Dayton, Ohio, 133
Würzburg radar set, 94–95, 119, 121

Yagi Antenna, 98
Yagi Hidetsugu, 40–41, 45, 97–98, 100–102, 108, 111, 113, 144, 236

Yamada Otozō, 293n136
Yamada Toshikazu, 239
Yamamoto Isoroku, 61
Yamamura Tatsuo, 203
Yamana Masao, 150
Yamanaka Taboku, 239
Yamato (superbattleship), 116
Yamazaki Fumio, 213
Yasaki Tameichi, 251n1
Yasuda Takeo, 56–57, 67, 69, 80
Yokoi Aircraft, 155
Yokosuka MXY7 aircraft, 150
Yokosuka P1Y1 Ginga (Frances) bomber, 152, 202
Ypres, Belgium, 167
Yoshida Ryū, 144, 145, 146
Yoshihiro Asami, 237
Yoshimura Hisato, 188, 239
Young, Leo C., 90
Yukawa Hideki, 3, 65, 66, 201, 212, 233, 257n90
Yukawa Institute for Theoretical Physics, 201

Z-Research, 115–116
Z-Stoff rocket fuel, 160
Zenith radar set, 97
Zeppelins, 85
Zero (Mitsubishi A6M5), 124, 154, 203
Zlatogrov-Maslokovich Laboratory of the Leningrad Veterinary and Zoological Technical Institute, 175
Zyklon B pesticide, 176